Eastern Europe and European Security

William R. Kintner
Wolfgang Klaiber

Eastern Europe and European Security

A Foreign Policy Research Institute Book

Foreword
William E. Griffith

DUNELLEN

New York

© 1971 by the Dunellen Publishing Company, Inc.
145 East 52nd Street
New York, New York 10022

International Standard Book Number 0-8424-0012-5.

Library of Congress Catalogue Card Number 79-136248.

Printed in the United States of America.

Eastern Europe and European Security

Contents

List of Tables

Appendix A

Foreword

This book is, in my view, an important contribution to the study of the contemporary political scene in Eastern Europe. This is so for three reasons. First, it provides a comparative analysis, based on a theory of political development, of economic reforms and their political consequences in three East European states. Second, it offers empirically-tested hypotheses concerning the changing relations between the East European states and the Soviet Union. Third, it concludes with a discussion of the issues of West German *Ostpolitik* and European security within the East European context.

East European political development is a complex and rapidly changing process. In recent years scholars have increasingly attempted to apply theories of political development to its study, with varying results.[1] The rising interest in comparative Communist studies has stimulated this effort.[2]

Within contemporary Eastern Europe, the high visibility of recent Czechoslovak developments has unfortunately tended to obscure the perhaps more lasting significance of the economic reforms, and their effect on political development, in other East European countries. This book offers a careful, systematic, and illuminating comparison of these developments in Bulgaria, Hungary, and East Germany, joining developmental theory to historical and cultural analysis of each country – a rare combination.

The second major section of this book does not, fortunately, retrace the detailed story of Soviet-East European relations, available in the books of Professor Brzezinski[3] and others. Rather, it gives an extensive empirical, statistical analysis of several hypotheses concerning it, a pioneer attempt in this field for which scholars will be grateful.

Finally, this book concludes with a section on two developments, West German *Ostpolitik* and European security, which are of increasing importance for Eastern Europe and concerning which scholars in the East European field normally write little. In spite of the Soviet invasion of Czechoslovakia and current East-West tension in the Middle East, detente seems likely to continue in Europe. In particular, the Soviet-West German treaty will probably be a forerunner of similar treaties between Bonn and the other East European states, following upon the earlier ones with Bucharest and Belgrade. For Eastern Europe these treaties will mean primarily West German economic and technological inputs into their economies.[4] As to European security, the authors point out all the dangers of the still overwhelming Soviet ground military superiority in Europe, but rightly add that the European security rubric will be an increasingly important one in the years to come, for East as well as West Europe.

In the largest sense, this book confirms, documents, refines, and extends the overall insight of Richard Lowenthal that in much of Eastern Europe

> ... the basic relation between the political system and the development of society has been reversed. Formerly the political system was in command, subjecting an underdeveloped society both to forced development and to a series of revolutions from above. Now the political system has to respond to the pressures generated by an increasingly advanced society ...[5]

The book will be of great value to all students of the East European scene.

William E. Griffith

Massachusetts Institute of Technology
Cambridge, Massachusetts

---

1. In my view the outstanding attempt has been by Andrew Janos, "The One-Party State and Social Mobilization: East Europe Between the Wars," in Samuel P. Huntington and Clement H. Moore, *Authoritarian Politics in Modern Society* (New York and London: Basic Books, 1970), pp. 204-238.

2. See especially Chalmers Johnson, ed., *Change in Communist Systems* (Stanford, Calif.: Stanford University Press, 1970).

3. Zbigniew K. Brzezinski, *The Soviet Bloc,* 3rd. revsd. ed. (Cambridge, Mass.: Harvard University Press, 1968).

4. See Richard V. Burks, "Technology and Political Change in Eastern Europe," in Johnson, ed., *op. cit.,* pp. 265-312.

5. In Johnson, *op. cit.,* pp. 112.

Acknowledgments

Of the many people who intermittently participated in the Foreign Policy Research Institute's study of Eastern Europe, only those who directly contributed to the present volume can be mentioned.

Wayne Ferris, a Ph.D. candidate in Political Science at the University of Pennsylvania, participated in this project from the beginning. He drafted the chapter on East European countries' conformity to Soviet policy, based on his own computations of data he collected for the project. He also researched and wrote the first draft of the post-Novotny era in the chapter on the Czechoslovak crisis, using Radio Free Europe reports as his principal source.

Special mention is due to Marie Burke and Marcia Rose for their skill and patience in typing successive drafts of the manuscript.

The substance of the second part of this book was submitted by Wolfgang Klaiber as a Ph.D. dissertation to, and accepted by, the Graduate Group in International Relations of the University of Pennsylvania in July 1968.

1 Introduction

The dramatic confrontation in 1968 between Czechoslovakia and the Soviet Union was the latest and most striking manifestation of important change throughout Eastern Europe.[1] Political relationships within and between the states of the Soviet bloc have changed rapidly in recent years, thereby altering the political contours of Europe. Ever since the popular upheavals of 1956, the political patterns of the countries that were formerly called "satellites" have become increasingly diversified, departing in varying degrees from the Soviet blueprint which once served as their model. Granted that in the social sciences the concept of "trends" is still a somewhat fuzzy one, this concept is nevertheless useful in identifying changes in Eastern Europe. Most analysts would now agree that the direction of movement in Eastern Europe has been away from a Stalinist rule based on terror toward a looser framework within which the interests of special economic and social groups could be asserted against incumbent doctrinaire leaderships.

The rate and dimension of the evolutionary trends have been by no means uniform. One can still speak of Stalinist rule in East Germany and Rumania—and to a lesser extent in Bulgaria—although the rulers of these three countries are searching for more effective ways to achieve the dual purpose of maintaining control and mobilizing the population

This Introduction has been adapted from William R. Kintner and Wolfgang Klaiber, "Eastern Europe in Flux," *ORBIS,* Summer 1968, pp. 391-414.

1

to greater efforts in the pursuit of their chosen goals. The Polish regime, though steadily retrogressing from the liberal political atmosphere that characterized the "Polish October" of 1956, has never been able to regain the degree of totalitarian control it once had over the population. Gomulka's leadership must continually face the challenge of the Church, the intellectuals, and the students, as well as factions among his own entourage. In Hungary, the once subservient trade union leadership now claims to defend the interests of the workers as opposed to those of the state; and the Hungarian legislature (though it still lacks political power) can suggest minor modifications for legislative proposals made by the regime.

The Soviet bloc's component countries (including the Soviet Union) have been susceptible to a variety of influences beyond the control of their party-governments. Stalin's demise paved the way for leadership changes not only in the Soviet Union but also in several East European countries. The subsequent desacralization of Stalin's cult undermined rule by terror and forced Communist leaders to find less oppressive methods of control. The 1956 popular upheavals in Hungary and Poland forced the Soviet leadership to grant the satellite leaderships greater domestic autonomy. The Sino-Soviet dispute undermined the leading position of the Soviet Union in the world Communist movement. Because the Soviets were now forced to seek rather than command support from their allies, East European leaders gained more influence over the Soviet Union and thus increased their autonomy. The rising prosperity and technological advance in Western Europe also influenced the political development of the East European countries.

Domestic developments are carrying each of the East European countries on its individual path, and the result is a growing diversity of political patterns in an area which, under Stalin, pursued a single path to Communism. Diversity among the countries makes it difficult to speak about Eastern Europe in general terms: as in all efforts to generalize about geographic regions, what is true of one country seldom holds completely true for another.

The same principle applies to the evolving relationships of the East European Communist parties and governments to the Soviet Union. Since Albania broke away from the Soviet bloc in 1961 and the Rumanian party-government established its right to dissent on issues affecting its national interests (between 1963 and 1964), Western reporters and analysts have, perhaps prematurely, proclaimed the demise of the "monolithic" bloc system and the emergence of inde-

2

pendent states. Generalizations such as these are, to say the least, inaccurate, inasmuch as they leave out of consideration the united front maintained by the Soviet Union with Bulgaria, East Germany, Hungary, Poland, and (excepting its short-lived flirtation with independence) Czechoslovakia.

Meaningful generalizations about trends in Eastern Europe today must be based upon systematic analysis of the political evolution of these countries and of their changing relationships to the Soviet Union. In 1965 the authors embarked upon a two-year research effort, seeking to identify continuity and change in the relationships of these countries to the Soviet Union since the end of the Stalin era. Aided by the research staff of the Foreign Policy Research Institute, we endeavored to gather and analyze data on a large number of indicators—subcomponents, causal factors, or demonstrative phenomena—of continuity and change in the political systems of (a) the East European countries (domestic) and (b) the Soviet bloc (international). These indicators were arrived at through the progressive breakdown of large topics ("trends"—such as "the relationships of state to people" or "relationships of East European states to the Soviet Union") into their component units.

By way of example, the topic pertaining to the role of the party in the management of society was first broken down into four subtopics (which we called "vectors"):

1. Division of authority between party and government
2. Party control over the economy
3. Party control over social life
4. Party control over cultural activities.

The trend associated with one of the components of the first of these vectors, "the legislative power of the legislature," was then determined by the following indicators:

a. Control by the party of the nominations to elective posts
b. Length and frequency of Parliament sessions
c. Existence and frequency of question time (interpellations)
d. Cabinet responsibility to Parliament: extent to which government decisions are submitted for ratification
e. Nature of Parliament debates: whether critical of the government or of its domestic and foreign policies or of the legislation proposed

3

f. Extent of newspaper space devoted to meetings of the National Assembly: number of columns relative to the total number of columns in the major newspaper of the capital city

g. Extent of legislative initiative in drafting of laws.

Some 500 indicators were developed to examine all of the trends and component vectors included in the study. Each indicator was formulated in such a way that it could be expressed unidimensionally, giving the magnitude of a particular change as an increase or decrease in the relevant variable. The resulting research design was subsequently refined and the number of indicators reduced to what we considered to be the critical minimum number. This study resulted in the three-volume report "Changing Trends in East Central Europe and Implications for US Security."[2]

The present volume is based in part on data collected for this initial study. Additional data relating to some of the questions in this book were gathered until 1970. Since the writing of the 1967 report, further thought and analysis have led to new insights and theses, as well as new analytical techniques for testing the theses.

What this book attempts to present is a partial explanation of the domestic and international politics of the countries in Eastern Europe through the testing of hypotheses in a historical context. The qualifier "partial" applies to both the explanation and the historical treatment of the subject. As for the empirical testing of hypotheses that explain the politics of the Soviet bloc countries, this will, of course, be a never-ending preoccupation of students of the social sciences, particularly of political science and international relations in this ever more rapidly changing world. If the reader desires a more complete treatment of the history of the Soviet bloc, he should look into the sources listed in the bibliography at the end of this book. The present treatment endeavors to trace the historical thread of continuity and change, focusing on major events that underpin the analysis, and will, we hope, provide a useful background for those readers who are not familiar with the evolutionary trends in East Europe.

Since this is an exercise in comparative politics, every thesis and hypothesis will be analyzed on the basis of data for at least three countries of Eastern Europe. Within this frame we have thought it useful to lay bare our analytical approach—from the initial hypotheses, through the testing process, to the empirical findings. The occasional finding that the hypotheses are not borne out by the data in the process of the analysis should, therefore, occasion no more surprise to the reader than it did to us—for us, this led to further questioning and attempts to answer why they were not borne out. It is our hope that this exposition of the analysis will add to its credibility.

We have tried to integrate historical and empirical-analytical approaches in our presentation. In the inquiry into continuity and change in the domestic politics of East European countries, consecutive or overlapping time spans highlight different theses. Thus, after a brief description of the Communist political system under Stalin, we focus on the period 1953-61 and the inability of this system to withstand wavering, vacillation, or change in methods of rule or ideological doctrine. Factionalism within the leaderships of East European countries or changing signals from the Soviet Union are shown to be detrimental to totalitarian control over the subjected peoples. The Communist systems are, thus, shown to be in a precarious state of equilibrium held together primarily by the power of the regimes to deny basic political rights to their respective citizenries—and this only with the back-up of Soviet military force. At the same time, just as it is unnatural for people (given a choice) to be willingly subject to the whims of their self-appointed rulers, so it is unnatural for the rulers of Eastern Europe to be subject to the whims of the Soviet leadership—both tend to assert their own interests when the opportunity presents itself.

Part 2 of this study, dealing with the economic reform period of 1962-68 on a more selective data basis of three countries (Bulgaria, Hungary, and East Germany), examines the proposition that political development tends to vary with socioeconomic development—i.e., that once the Communist systems of Eastern Europe were susceptible to the necessity of change in their economic structures and processes, there should also be change in their political structures and processes. This proposition is simply a variant of the more normative adage that meaningful economic reform is impossible without political reform—although the former is more susceptible to empirical testing than the latter. The latter is more amenable to subjective interpretation according to one's political values than is the former. In this investigation we were interested in the empirical test of this proposition and in finding reasonable explanations for the deviant cases.

Part 3 examines the changing relationships between the Soviet Union and East European bloc countries in an effort to bring into focus the factors that tend to enable some "satellites" to act more independently

5

of Soviet directives than others. After a brief historical-descriptive presentation of the major events that have helped to widen the autonomy of Eastern Europe vis-à-vis the Soviet union, the analysis centers on correlations based on ordinal and interval scale data, with a large number of bivariate hypotheses in which conformity to Soviet policy serves as the dependent variable. The data cover eight East European countries (including Albania and Yugoslavia, which were once members of the Soviet bloc) over a 13-year time span (1955-68).

Part 4 comprises a case study of the crises and invasion of Czechoslovakia. Here we attempt to sum up and put into perspective the various theses examined previously, as a background against which lessons for U.S. and Western policy are to be drawn.

So much for the history of this endeavor and the structure of this book. In writing it, we had a wide audience in mind: we intended this book to be informative to the layman, instructive in theses and methods to the student of politics, heuristic for the researcher seeking to advance the frontiers of knowledge, and useful to those whose task it is to shape U.S. policy. Needless to say, in the process, some compromises had to be made in the selection of the topics and the presentation of the analysis. This book will appear at a time when Europe is in flux, when the role of the United States in Europe's affairs (particularly its security) appears to be undergoing a "searching reappraisal" on both sides of the Atlantic, and when the Soviet Union is embarked on an unprecedented diplomatic offensive to change the European security system and its foundation. If the present volume contributes to a better understanding of the changing trends in Eastern Europe and of the issues involved in the discussion on European security, we will consider the effort of its writing well rewarded.

Notes

1. In this study we use the term "Soviet bloc" as a geographical expression encompassing the countries active in the Warsaw Pact: Bulgaria, Czechoslovakia, East Germany, Hungary, Poland, and Rumania.

2. "Changing Trends in East Central Europe and Implications for US Security" (3 vols.; Philadelphia: The Foreign Policy Research Institute of the University of Pennsylvania, 1967). (Mimeographed).

Part 1: The Consolidation of Communist Control

2   The Stalin Period : Consolidation of Communist Control

During the first two or three years after World War II, Communist strategies in Eastern Europe aimed at the usurpation of political power differed greatly in the several countries. Although the general staff formulating these strategies was undoubtedly headquartered in Moscow, the East European Communists geared their tactics to national conditions and proceeded cautiously to establish the bases for their political control. Having for the most part spent the war years in the Soviet Union (if not in prison, concentration camps, or underground movements) and having had little if any actual experience in government, the new Communist elites displayed an understandable measure of uncertainty as they went about their task of organizing and staffing an effective control apparatus. Until 1947, moreover, there was some uncertainty in Moscow and East European capitals concerning the attitude of the major Western powers toward the Communist takeover. It was only in 1947 that the Western Allies (the United States, Great Britain, and France) formalized their acquiescence in the Soviet takeover of Eastern Europe by signing peace treaties and diplomatic recognition instruments with the several Communist-dominated regimes.* Thus, until the end of 1947, Communist rule followed no uniform pattern. Terror was mixed with attempts at cooperation with politically influential parties and groups.

---

*The United States had formally recognized the Communist-dominated regime of Poland in 1945.

9

The relations between the Communist parties of Eastern Europe, though ultimately controlled by Moscow, were marked by some diversity and occasional displays of independent ambitions. One has only to think of the plan envisaged by Tito and Dimitrov for a union of Yugoslavia and Bulgaria which Stalin ostentatiously and authoritatively scrapped before it could come to fruition.[1] There was also considerable diversity in Communist theory,[2] particularly as it was to be applied to the different national conditions in the countries then rapidly coming under the complete control of Moscow's agents. Undoubtedly, the "Moscovites" (Communist apparatchiks who had lived in the Soviet Union during the War and had helped prepare the Communist takeover of Eastern Europe within the Comintern) were as a group more disciplined and more closely attuned to Stalin's desires than were their home-grown counterparts. But there were also those among them who harbored hopes of building national models of Communism according to their own conceptual schemes—based, to be sure, on Marxism-Leninism, but calibrated to peculiar national problems.[3] This sentiment, of course, was shared by "home Communist" leaders (those who had spent the war years in their native countries)—men like Wladyslaw Gomulka, Imre Nagy, Josip Broz-Tito, and Gheorghe Gheorghiu-Dej—who, though they were dyed-in-the-wool Communists, were more sensitive to the problems in their respective countries.

In Stalin's scheme of things, however, diversity could be only a transitional state of affairs. In the long run it would deprive the Soviet Union of its control over Eastern Europe. The formation of the Communist Information Bureau (Cominform) in September, 1947, marked the beginning of the end of Communist diversity in Eastern Europe. Soon thereafter the relationships of the East European Communist party-governments to the Soviet Union became devoid of any visible autonomy. The Soviet leadership sought to establish and maintain its absolute and arbitrary domination over the East European satellite leaderships, regardless of how faithfully they might have been (or actually were) emulating the Soviet model of Communist dictatorship on their own accord. This attempt at domination was the most important single factor which brought friction into Soviet-Yugoslav relations and, in 1948, led to the expulsion of the Yugoslav Communist Party from the Cominform.

Nevertheless, as Brzezinski has plausibly suggested, the consolidation of unity in Eastern Europe under Moscow's domination was not altogether unwelcome to many of the new Communist ruling groups:

For the Moscow-trained *apparatchiki. . . .* there was a certain
security to be gained from conformity. Liberated from the
tensions and strains of diversity which frequently served to reveal
their own domestic weakness, the East European Communists
could now expect the transitional period of Soviet noninvolve-
ment to give way to more direct Soviet participation in the
"socialist construction."[4]

With highly disciplined Moscovite apparatchiks at the nucleus of
political power in the satellite countries, those Communists who might
have been inclined to steer their countries along more individualistic
paths to Communism were at a great disadvantage. There was no room
for political opposition in Stalin's scheme of things. Those who would
deviate from the Soviet-charted course of Communist construction
were purged from the satellite leaderships and either imprisoned or
executed. Titoism* became part of the Communist catalogue of
cardinal sins against which no penalty was too severe. It became a
convenient pretext for the removal of incumbents who were undesir-
able, for one reason or another, either to Stalin or to his closest satellite
lieutenants—particularly those dissidents who thought that the Communist creed was open to individual interpretation.

In Stalin's scheme there was only one way to Communism—the way
of the Soviet Union, which he had guided over almost a full generation.
With reliable, utterly subservient lieutenants at the helm of the satellite
political systems, the peoples of Eastern Europe were destined to relive
a condensed version of the Soviet historical experience. Coercive terror
was part of that experience. Control consolidation à la Stalin meant the
extension of Communist political authority over all but the most
intimate aspects of human life and the building of a control machine
that would assure obedience to this all-pervasive political authority.
Basic to this endeavor was the banning of those human rights which are
usually held sacred in Western societies—freedom of speech, movement,
and association, and the sanctity of the home. Furthermore, all of the
means of production and livelihood had to be in the hands of the state.

---

*"Titoism" is difficult to define accurately because it has evolved—
domestically—over time from "premature Stalinism" (Brzezinski, *The Soviet Bloc,*
p. 62) to an entirely separate and individualistic development of Communism.
One constant feature of Titoism, and undoubtedly the most fundamental one, has
been to reject Soviet claims to, and attempts at, political and economic domination over Yugoslavia. This, of course, is the underpinning of monolithic unity
which characterized Soviet-satellite relationships until Stalin died and, to a de-
creasing degree, for some time thereafter.

Needless to say, human loyalties to objects or beings other or higher than the Communist-ruled state could not be tolerated.

Within the span of a few years the Communist governments of Eastern Europe established state ownership and control of all the means of nonagricultural production. The process of nationalizing private industry was, for all practical purposes, completed by 1950 in all East European countries save East Germany. "Although some states claimed to have established means of compensating the former owners of the expropriated industrial facilities, usually no indemnity whatsoever was paid."[5] In fact, the Communist constitutional and legal framework which was imposed upon these countries was founded on the principle of class discrimination which relegated the "bourgeois" class (to which private entrepreneurs belonged) to the status of nonpersons.

Private artisans and craftsmen were regimented into cooperatives or state-owned factories as the Communist governments sought to eliminate from the societies they ruled all private endeavors pursued for profit.

The drive to collectivize agriculture was begun in the East European satellite countries toward the end of the 1940's, and thereafter proceeded at varying rates. There were those within the satellite leaderships who would have emulated the Soviet example of agricultural collectivization at a forced pace, but Moscow reportedly cautioned a slower approach in this sector. This caution may have been prompted by several important considerations. The Soviet experience showed that the peasant, attached to his private holdings, can find ways to resist expropriation that would damage the economy. Under the circumstances attending the immediate post-World War II period, when most of the Soviet bloc economies (the Soviet Union most of all) lay war-torn, it was probably more important to the Soviet Union that the agricultural sectors of the satellite countries produce the necessary foodstuffs. The satellite countries, isolated from the rest of the world, were almost totally dependent on their own agricultural resources. Should the peasant refuse to deliver the food, famine would ensue. In addition, the Communist regimes, having been in power for only a short period, may not have felt sufficiently strong to overcome the resistance of the peasant—among other things, they probably did not have enough reliable cadres to execute the collectivization plan and to manage the agricultural sector thereafter. Any or all of these considerations may have weighed heavily on the minds of the Communist leaders (including those in Moscow) as they pondered the doctrinal necessity of eliminating private enterprise in the countryside and creating an agricultural proletariat in its stead. Thus, the collectivization of agriculture proceeded at a slower pace than did the nationalization of private industry. By 1952, the governments of East Central Europe had brought into the socialist sector the following percentage of the total arable land in their respective countries:[6] Bulgaria, 50 percent; Czechoslovakia, 24 percent; East Germany, 27 percent; Hungary, 25 percent; Poland, 13 percent; Rumania, 19 percent; Yugoslavia (1953), 24 percent.

Having nationalized the industrial and craft enterprises, the Communist governments had to manage the productive process. The bureaucracy expanded tremendously in all of the East European states. Copying the Soviet model of state administration, the East European Communists established dual hierarchical structures, the party hierarchy standing parallel to—and overlapping—the government. At the top of the pyramid the functionaries usually held two offices—one in the party and one in the government. Until 1953, for instance, the highest posts of party and government were held by the same man in each country (except East Germany, where Walter Ulbricht maintained a facade of collective leadership with Wilhelm Pieck and Otto Grotewohl).* Lines of control lead both horizontally and vertically from the Politburo. Throughout the structure, down to the lowest administrative units in party and government, strict obedience and discipline became the measure of satisfactory performance in the Communist bureaucracy; it was also the foremost criterion for recruitment of personnel, particularly into positions of responsibility.

In all areas of politically relevant activity, the Communists eliminated or neutralized the existing opposition to their rule. Untold thousands of people from almost every walk of life were deported to labor camps or remote parts of the country. Many more were imprisoned or executed.

In order to maintain a facade of legitimacy, the Communists permitted some of the political parties, which had been popular for decades, to exist† but purged their ranks of leaders and members who

---

*From July, 1950, to July, 1953, Ulbricht served as Secretary General of the SED State and cochairman of the SED; Grotewohl, as Prime Minister and the other cochairman of the party.

†The retention of the "multiparty system" facade presents one of the few striking differences in structure between the Soviet and the East European governments. It is undoubtedly an outgrowth of the uncertain circumstances under which the Communists assumed power in Eastern Europe and is justified in the theory of the system of "people's democracies" (a label pinned on the East European political systems except East Germany, which was called a "democratic republic")

might offer opposition to Communist rule. These parties were confined within Communist-controlled front organizations and thus lost all powers and prerogatives of independent action—indeed, they ceased to be political parties in any real sense. The socialist parties, for their part, were incorporated outright into the Communist parties. The National legislatures, composed of representatives selected by the Communist party according to rigid criteria of political reliability, became rubber stamps of their respective party-governments. They performed no legislative function except to approve the annual state budget and such decrees as the party-government chose to submit. Their sessions were infrequent and of such short duration that debate, had it been permitted on the floor, would have been impossible in any case.* The delegates listened to speeches by party and government leaders; their primary function was to explain the policies of the rulers to their constituents.

The effort to consolidate Communist control was extended to society at large. All spontaneous—non-Communist-controlled—social activity was condemned as bourgeois behavior. Private life was confined to the home, and even there its sanctity was not vouchsafed by the state. Block wardens made sure that the citizens participated in mass events (street rallies, elections, and the like) scheduled by the leadership. Compulsory lectures and discussion meetings were designed to educate the population in socialist thought and action, and to promote the participation of the population in programs initiated by the Communist leadership.

Mass organizations encompassing major groups (workers, farmers, women, youth, etc.) were either created or remodeled under Communist leadership to facilitate control and promote popular participation. The trade unions, for instance, came under Communist leadership and were put exclusively at the service of the state. According to Communist ideology, the working class, having expropriated the bourgeoisie, was no longer being exploited. Led by the Communist

---

developed in the Soviet Union. This theory views the countries of Eastern Europe as being at a lower stage of socialist development, under which different classes temporarily continue to exist under the dictatorship of the proletariat. For an illuminating discussion of this theory, see Brzezinski, *The Soviet Bloc,* pp. 45-57 and 72-77.

*For instance, in 1952, the total number of days the legislature of each country met was East Germany, 7; Hungary, 10; Poland, 17; Rumania, 6; and Czechoslovakia, 10. In each country, these totals were accumulated in several sessions throughout the year.

party, it was now the ruling class in the country. By executing the instructions of the party leadership, the workers served their own interests. Therefore, the relationship of the trade unions to the workers could no longer be the same as it had been under capitalism. Communist trade unions had to mobilize the workers to greater efforts in their own ultimate behalf; they became little more than the transmission routes of the state's commands to the workers.

Religion came under severe attack in all Communist countries. The Roman Catholic Church, professing spiritual allegiance to the Pope, competing with the Communists for the minds of its subjects, and generally more uncompromising in its opposition to Communist methods of rule, was particularly loathsome to these regimes.* Under Stalin, wholesale arrests of priests decimated clerical ranks. Many churches and religious schools were closed or destroyed, and training for the priesthood was severely curtailed. Militant organizations of atheists made attendance at churches a hazardous undertaking. But in all East European countries, particularly in the predominantly Roman Catholic ones, large segments of the population were so firmly attached to their religious beliefs and institutions that the most that Communist terror tactics could accomplish was to eliminate political opposition from the clergy, to prohibit religious instruction of the youth, and to make it generally difficult for the Church to propagate the faith. Wherever possible, the Communists sought to install people loyal to the regime (peace priests) in religious offices.

All public media (radio, press, and publishing houses) came under the control of the state and its censorship organs. The creative intelligentsia was regimented into the service of the rulers. Unions under Communist Party leadership were established for the creative writers. Art was supposed to extol the virtues of socialist man in word and deed. Writers who conformed to this criterion were lucratively rewarded; those who did not, fared miserably in countries where Communists controlled the means of livelihood.

Thus, under Stalin the countries of Eastern Europe were an integral part of a highly centralized empire controlled from Moscow. Had the satellites been formally incorporated into the Soviet Union, they could

---

*Countries in Eastern Europe with a predominantly Roman Catholic population are Poland (95 percent), Hungary (75 percent), and Czechoslovakia (75 percent). Bulgaria is predominantly Eastern Orthodox, with a sizable minority of Bulgaro-Moslems, whereas 75 percent of the Rumanian population professes the Greek Orthodox faith. East Germany is predominantly Lutheran.

not have been any more tightly controlled. Their leaders served at Stalin's pleasure; and while they maintained the facade of indigenous rule, they could not make autonomous decisions.

The political system which had been developed under Stalin rested on fear rather than consensus. The people of Eastern Europe probably feared Stalin more than they did their indigenous rulers. Coercion backed by violent terror took the place of law. But there was a certain consistency in Stalin's political system. People at all levels knew what to expect from the political authority. Potential opponents of Communism or of the leaders appointed by Stalin had either been cowed into submission or removed from circulation. At all levels there was unity of action, according to Soviet command. There were no alternatives; hence, there was no choice.

Notes

1. For a detailed account of the Balkan Union scheme, see Fitzroy MacLean, *Tito* (New York: Ballatine Books, 1957). See also Milovan Djilas, *Conversations with Stalin,* translated by Michael B. Petrovila (New York: Harcourt, Brace and World, 1962).

2. Excellent in-depth discussion of this can be found in Zbigniew K. Brzezinski, *The Soviet Bloc: Unity and Conflict* (New York: Frederick A. Praeger, 1961).

3. Wolfgang Leonhard was one of these hopefuls. See his *Child of the Revolution* (Chicago: Henry Regnery Co., 1959).

4. Brzezinski, op. cit., p. 61.

5. Nicolas Spulber, *The Economies of Communist Eastern Europe* (Cambridge, Mass., and New York: The Technology Press of the Massachusetts Institute of Technology and John Wiley and Sons, Inc., 1957), p. 86.

6. See Brzezinski, op. cit., p. 99; Bundesministerium für Geramtdeutsche Fragen, *Die Zwangskollektivierung des Selbstandigen Bauernstandes in Mitteldeutschland* (Bonn and Berlin, 1960), pp. 23-25. Brzezinski's figure for East Germany is five percent. This figure comprises only the state-owned farms (comparable with sovkhozes in the USSR). It does not include the other types of collectivized farms (comparable with the Soviet kolkhozes).

3 After Stalin: The Challenge of Change

Until Josef Stalin's demise, the satellite Communist system was built upon his unchallengeable authority. His death, on March 5, 1953, was therefore as fundamental to political development in Eastern Europe as his life and rule had been. The satellite regimes, whose authority and legitimacy had rested on Stalin's shoulders, were suddenly vulnerable to external and internal forces which could interact in a variety of ways. The policies enacted on Stalin's orders, based on doctrinaire foundations that were claimed to be universally valid and everlasting, could be changed by his successors in the Kremlin without prior warning. Unexpected policy shifts tore at the fabric of infallibility that the Communist propaganda machines so consistently extolled. Change brought the choice of alternatives into the political process. Communists would soon look back with nostalgia upon the relative simplicity of ruling under Stalin's watchful eye, and lament the curse of diversity. As one American reporter was told by Polish Communists:

> Everything is such a problem now. In the worst times of Stalinism, at least you knew exactly what you could and could not do, what you should and should not think. It was all so simple then. Now my head aches with trying to figure things out.[1]

In the Soviet Union, Stalin's death gave rise to an immediate power struggle. The foremost contenders were Georgi M. Malenkov, Stalin's heir apparent; Lavrenti P. Beria, chief of the security apparatus which under Stalin had become a "state within a state"; and Nikita S. Khrushchev, then a relatively obscure Presidium member and Secretary of the Central Committee. Within ten days of Stalin's death, on March 14, Malenkov was relieved of his position as Senior Secretary of the Central Committee, which left his power base restricted to the government apparatus, where he remained Chairman of the Council of Ministers. Late in June, Beria was arrested (the official announcement came only on July 10); he had tried to use the secret police apparatus to serve his own power ambitions against his colleagues. Beria was executed in December, 1953. In September of the same year, Khrushchev was officially appointed First Secretary of the Communist Party.

Obviously, Stalin's successors wielded neither the power nor the authority sufficient to maintain Stalin's terror-based political system. Initially, then, the new triumvirate sought to base its claim to legitimacy on "collective leadership" of the Communist Party and to mitigate some of the more strident dissatisfaction within the country. The economy was to be channeled into a "new course" to provide more consumer goods at the expense of heavy industry. A cultural "thaw" melted some of the doctrinal ice that had frozen the creative activities of the Soviet intelligentsia under Stalin. People could move about and speak more freely, especially after Beria's arrest and the curbing of the powers of the secret police.

If the Kremlin's new leaders feared popular insurrection in the Soviet Union soon after Stalin's death, they also feared it in the East European satellites—and with good reason, as will be seen below. Furthermore, they regarded, as Stalin had before them, the domestic political developments in the Soviet Union as a guide to action in the satellites.

Satellite Reluctance to Conform to
Changing Soviet Policy: The New Course.

Most of the East European leaders viewed the winds of change from Moscow with considerable apprehension. Some probably felt that Stalin's death made it imperative to enforce the status quo even more vigorously, lest they betray their political weakness and encourage dissent among their oppressed populations. Some regimes also lacked the economic wherewithal to improve the lot of their peoples.

But with Stalin's death and the policy changes emanating from Moscow, the peoples of Eastern Europe lost some of their fear of Communist brutality, and the brittle nature of the satellites' political systems soon became apparent, to the dismay of both indigenous rulers and those in the Kremlin.

Czechoslovakia, for instance, enacted a currency reform on May 31, 1953. On the following day, the workers of the Skoda works in Pilsen went on the streets in a massive demonstration against the regime. They seized the administrative buildings of the city and occupied them for several hours before the regime could quell the uprising.

The East German regime, far from alleviating the economic plight of the people, decided to raise the work norms, so that the workers had to produce more in order to get the same wages. In view of the fact that the Soviets had been exploiting the East German economy to the bone, there was probably some justification for this belt-tightening decree. (Pankow had indeed pleaded with Moscow for economic aid but had been turned away.) Nevertheless, the Kremlin dispatched A. A. Semenov* (the Soviet High Commissioner for East Germany) to East Berlin with instructions to bring the East German leadership around to the "new course." Several days after Semenov's arrival, the East German leadership underwent public self-criticism for its mistakes, but this was too late to ward off the workers' uprising which began in East Berlin on June 16 and spread throughout most of East Germany. For two days, the Communist regime lost all control of East Germany. Soviet troops were deployed to restore order.

In the wake of the workers' uprising in Pilsen and East Berlin—and probably to forestall similar uprisings in Hungary—Hungary's party-government leader, Matyas Rakosi, and his closest associates were called to Moscow.† There Rakosi was confronted by the Soviet leadership with charges that he had brought Hungary to bankruptcy and the Hungarian people to the verge of revolt. Khrushchev is reported to have

---

*Semenov is sometimes found transliterated as Semyonov, which is more true to the Russian pronounciation of the name.

†The exact date of this summons is not known, but the meeting took place within a week after the East German uprising. After the Hungarian delegation returned from Moscow, the Hungarian Central Committee issued a resolution heralding the "new course." Of this resolution, which was never published, Imre Nagy wrote: "The chief purpose of the Central Committee's June resolution was to stave off the catastrophe and to counter-balance the effect of the disturbances in East Germany and Czechoslovakia, to ease the growing tension manifested in frequent mass demonstrations in the Great Plains, and in general to bring about a turn of the tide." See Imre Nagy, *On Communism: In Defense of the New Course* (New York: Frederick A. Praeger, 1957), p. 66. The book is a collection of essays which Nagy wrote in defense of the policies he had pursued as Premier from 1953 to 1955. He wrote these essays between 1955 and 1956, after he had been divested of the premiership and ousted from the Communist Party.

told Rakosi that if the situation were not immediately and radically improved, "they will chase you with pitchforks."[2] Already in May, 1953, the Soviet leadership had apparently advised Rakosi of the necessity of dividing party and state functions and when, in Moscow, Rakosi was still not prepared to name a "deputy," the Soviet leaders named one for him: Imre Nagy, a man whose temperament and sentiments were well-known to be attuned to the "new course."

Poland, on the whole, made very few concessions to the "new course." But its regime, too, saw cause for concern in the uprisings which had occurred in Pilsen and East Berlin. The leadership summoned a group of highly placed individuals, not all of them party members, to suggest measures the regime might take in order to forestall possible revolt. Among the suggestions received by the Politburo were that it should allow the press to print some of the news the people were already receiving from other sources, and that the Communist Party should try to gain the confidence of the people. But before the Politburo would heed this advice, more earth-shaking events (to be discussed below) were to wrack the Polish political scene.

Thus, within three months after Stalin's death, the vulnerability of the East European Communist regimes to popular insurrection had become as amply apparent as the reluctance of the leaders to depart from Stalin's ways. Economic concessions were regarded (if only after some severe prodding from Moscow) as unavoidable if Communism was to survive in Eastern Europe. In sum, the new course offered a temporary respite from the forced pace of industrialization and socialization. Incomes rose somewhat and taxes were lowered. The supply of food and consumer goods improved in most of the East European countries. Some of the severe restrictions on private enterprise in crafts and services were lifted in Poland, Hungary, Romania, and Bulgaria.* In some of the East European countries the collectivization of agriculture was brought to a temporary halt or was reversed. In Czechoslovakia, for

---

*In Poland, the number of private artisans rose from 123,865 in 1953 to 133,184 in 1954. In Hungary, there were 46,199 private artisans in 1953 and 103,922 in 1954. In 1955 their number declined again to 94,158, reflecting the ouster of Imre Nagy and a reversal to Stalinist policies under Rakosi. Similar data are not available for Bulgaria and Romania, but it is known that these two regimes tried in 1954 to revitalize the private artisan sector in order to increase consumer goods and repair services. For Poland, Hungary, and Bulgaria, see Nicolas Spulber, *The Economics of Eastern Europe* (Cambridge, Mass., and New York: The Technology Press of the Massachusetts Institute of Technology and John Wiley and Sons, Inc., 1957), pp. 65, 74, and 80-81. For Rumania, see "What is Left of Private Enterprise?," *East Europe* (February, 1959), p. 22. In East Germany the crafts sector had remained largely in private hands.

instance, the percentage of the total arable land in the collectivized sector fell from 48 to 44 percent between 1953 and 1954; in Hungary it dropped from 37 to 32; in East Germany from 26 to 24.5; and in Bulgaria from 62 to 60 during the same period. Poland and Romania had made slower progress in collectivizing their privately held farmland, and in these countries the percentage of the total arable land in the collective sector continued to increase.

The Soviet Union helped alleviate the economic stress in Eastern Europe by lowering its exploitative demands upon the satellite governments. In 1954, for instance, the USSR transferred its shares in the "joint stock companies" to Romania, Bulgaria, and Hungary, and returned its control of some 200 East German enterprises to the Pankow regime.*

Satellite Reluctance to Conform
to Changing Soviet Policy: Collective Leadership.

Stalin's immediate successors, Khrushchev and Malenkov, made "collective leadership" mandatory in Eastern Europe, splitting the powers and functions of party and state and thereby depriving the incumbents of their hitherto absolute control over their colleagues in the ruling organs.

The incumbents who held the top posts of both party and government combined were evidently and understandably reluctant to share their power even with men of their own choice. In Hungary, as has already been mentioned, the Soviet leadership dictated the choice of the Premier after Rakosi had shown himself unwilling or unable to decide upon a man with whom he would share his power. Considering the importance which the Soviets evidently placed upon Eastern Europe's emulation of their "collective leadership" example, it is surprising that in Bulgaria, Poland, and Romania the functions of party and government were divided only in March-April, 1954. In Czechoslovakia, the switch to collective leadership had already occurred in March, 1953, following the death of Klement Gottwald, who had held both the chairmanship of the party and the presidency of the Republic. Antonin Novotny succeeded Gottwald as party chief, while the erstwhile Premier, Antonin Zapotocky, assumed the presidency. In East Germany

*The "joint stock companies" had been established soon after World War II in the three countries mentioned. Each partner was to invest 50 percent of the capital and take 50 percent of the proceeds. The Soviet share of the investment, however, came from German assets seized in the three countries. (All three had been allied with the Axis powers during the war.) See Zbigniew Brzezinski, *The Soviet Bloc* (New York: Frederick A. Praeger, 1961), pp. 125, 158, and 164, note.

there had existed a formal division of powers and functions between Wilhelm Pieck, Otto Grotewohl, and Walter Ulbricht, a situation presumably satisfactory to the "collective leadership" in Moscow. Considering the delay in the shift to collective leadership in all those satellites still ruled by one man, one may be justified in making the assumption that the Soviets ordered the change to be made by a certain date, i.e., March or April, 1954.

This change to "collective leadership" introduced an element of fluidity into the power structure. Furthermore, factionalism, rampant in the Kremlin, came into public view when *Pravda* and *Izvestia* (official daily organs of the party and government, respectively) published contradictory statements on domestic and foreign policy.[3] Among the identifiable issues in dispute were (1) the organization and methods of agricultural production (this became Khrushchev's specialty); (2) priorities of capital goods versus consumer goods (this was to bring about Malenkov's downfall); and (3) foreign policy questions such as peaceful coexistence, the nature of nuclear war, the threat of imperialism, and the treatment to be accorded Yugoslavia. Conflict also emerged over organizational questions in party and government, concerning in particular the organization of economic planning and management at the center. The fortunes of contending factions in the Kremlin rode on the resolution of these issues. Rival groups in the Politburos and lower echelons of the satellite regimes learned to watch carefully "whose flag was up" in Moscow, and to bet their political futures on the most promising candidate in the Kremlin's succession struggle.

Divided Leaderships

Stalin's death and the resultant change of collective leadership left the satellite regimes vulnerable to factionalism within their own ranks.

Inasmuch as totalitarian rule is underpinned by the steadfast and enforceable claims that only the party leadership can—and invariably does—make "correct" decisions and that there are no alternatives to its policies, the leadership has to speak with one voice. Understandably, therefore, divisions within the ruling body of the party are kept from the public as much and as long as possible. As one of the leading scholars on Czechoslovakia has put it:

> . . . No secrets are more closely guarded than those pertaining to the personal ties and rivalries within the ruling oligarchy. Not until a close associate defects or a Politbureau member is purged does the curtain rise for a moment to allow a quick glimpse of what goes on behind it.[4]

In Communist countries virtually all aspects of national life come under the purview of the party's highest ruling body. It is difficult to conceive of a group of men in high leadership positions* who can agree with each other on all points of policy making. But while Stalin ruled the Soviet empire, his party chiefs in the various East European satellites had little difficulty in maintaining unanimity within their Politburos. From 1948 to 1952, "purges" cleansed these ruling bodies of people who would deviate from the rigid Moscow line or who could otherwise impede the absolute powers of Stalin's top lieutenant in each satellite. Outwardly, then, the satellite Politburos were homogeneous leadership groups oriented to Stalin's orders. If there were some Politburo members who harbored alternative views or desires, they were probably prudent enough to hold their tongues.

Depending on its scope and intensity, and also on the issues involved, factionalism can lead to indecision, vacillation, or change in policy, with consequences potentially disruptive of the status quo. The very existence of factionalism represents a net loss of decision-making power in the hands of the party chief, inasmuch as he has to take into account the will of the dissenters within the Politburo. Dissenting factions can, given time and opportunity, gather support not only within the Politburo but also at lower levels of the party and (as will be seen below) from segments of the general population. Therein lies the most compelling reason for the secrecy which surrounds the debates and activities of the Politburos of ruling Communist parties.

It goes without saying that the ruling party secretaries sought to maintain unity within their Politburos and, therefore, to remove any dissident elements from the group. During Stalin's time this kind of "surgical" operation was more easily performed than after his demise.

In East Germany, by 1953, a faction led by Wilhelm Zaisser, Minister of State Security, and R. Herrnstadt, editor of *Neues Deutschland* (the daily organ of the SED) counted heavily on Lavrenti Beria's support to oust Walter Ulbricht from the party leadership. Beria's arrest was announced July 10, 1953, and Ulbricht immediately removed Zaisser and Herrnstadt from their important posts.

In Bulgaria, a factional struggle developed between the political strongman, Vulko Chervenkov, and his erstwhile protégé, Todor Zhivkov. When the time for collective leadership arrived in Bulgaria,

---

*The size of the Politburo (or Presidium of the Central Committee, as some of the East European Communist parties have called their ruling bodies during the post-Stalin period) has varied from time to time and from country to country between nine and 15 members.

Chervenkov had given his leading post in the party to Zhivkov (whether by choice or design is not known) and retained the premiership. Confirming the general rule of Communist power struggles, the secretary-generalship of the party proved to be the more powerful post. Chervenkov entered a gradual political eclipse in 1956, when he was demoted to Deputy Premier, the victim of a factional struggle which had probably begun in 1954.

In Czechoslovakia, no evidence of factionalism came into public view during the immediate post-Stalin period. Clement Gottwald, the party-government leader of Czechoslovakia, died a few days after Stalin. Antonin Novotny, who succeeded him to the top post in the party, had been a Secretary of the Central Committee since 1951. Although he was perhaps among the most powerful men in the party leadership, his appointment to the top party post may be assumed to have been approved in Moscow. The departure of a dictator of a Communist country is usually followed by a succession crisis of factionalism within the top ruling body, and it would be surprising if Czechoslovakia were an exception to this rule. But if factionalism divided the ranks of Czechoslovakia's Politburo after Stalin's death, it was successfully kept secret.

Similarly, concerning the Rumanian Politburo, no factional activity came to public view. However, in April, 1954, a Rumanian military tribunal tried Lucretiu Patrascanu and Remus Koffler, two wartime leaders of the Rumanian Communist Party, and condemned them to death. Patrascanu had been purged from the Politburo in 1948 on charges of alleged nationalism, bourgeois leanings, and alliance with the peasantry, among other things.[5] It is not definitely known whether Patrascanu was imprisoned between 1948 and 1954; he was simply not seen in public.[6] He may, however, have retained a following at various levels of the party, perhaps even within the Politburo. Furthermore, from the little information available about Patrascanu, he seems to have shown some of the leadership qualities of Imre Nagy who, it will be remembered, had been installed as Premier of Hungary by the Soviets in June, 1953. From this one may surmise—as one of the more plausible explanations of Patrascanu's trial and execution—that he may have presented an alternative to Gheorghiu-Dej; indeed, there may have been a faction within the Rumanian Politburo seeking the return of the erstwhile leader. Two years later (in the wake of Khrushchev's secret denunciation of Stalin's personality cult) two Politburo members, Miron Constantinescu and Iosif Chisinevschi, denounced Gheorghiu-

Dej's Stalinist practices before an enlarged Central Committee plenum held March 23-25, 1956.[7] It may well be that these two men harbored misgivings about Gheorghiu-Dej's management of Rumania's party and state affairs as early as the beginning of 1954.

In Poland, an extraneous factor helped to promote divisions within the ranks of the Politburo. Toward the end of 1953 a highly placed agent of the Polish secret police, Lieutenant Colonel Joseph Swiatlo, defected to the West. In March, 1954, Swiatlo agreed to speak to the Polish people over the transmitters of Radio Free Europe. In a series of broadcasts he laid bare the moral depravity of a police system relying on a vast network of informants and torture of its victims. Swiatlo's revelations were reminiscent of Stalin's Great Purge in the Soviet Union. The impact of Swiatlo's broadcasts derived not from the fact that he was describing a situation not yet known to the man in the Polish streets; it lay, rather, in his bringing into the open what no one had dared to talk about for fear of falling victim to the secret police system. More importantly, Swiatlo revealed the names of many secret police informants as well as the allegations they had made. People learned that their best friends or closest relatives had succumbed to secret police pressure or blackmail and had furnished information about them. Through Swiatlo's exposés, the informer network was seriously weakened. Informants became afraid, if not ashamed; and many even confessed what they had done.

Swiatlo's reports brought tremors into the highest levels of the Polish Communist Party leadership. The most notorious of Poland's secret police chiefs were dismissed or transferred to other posts; one of them was arrested. The secret police system was revamped. Although its powers were not officially curbed, the secret police system lost much of its secrecy and many of its informants. Swiatlo's words had weakened the mainstay of Communist totalitarianism in Poland.

The tremors continued to rock the Polish party leadership throughout the rest of the year. When the Central Committee met in plenary session in January, 1955, not only the secret police apparatus but also the party leadership were severely and spontaneously attacked from the floor. Questions were raised about the fate of Wladyslaw Gomulka, the former party leader who had been purged in 1948 for "Titoism" and other nationalist deviations. Gomulka had been arrested in 1951 (by Swiatlo himself) and subjected to lengthy interrogations. Nevertheless, he was never charged with a specific crime, nor was he tried, mainly because the secret police could not obtain his confession to whatever charges they meant to bring against him. In January, 1955, Central Committee members wanted to know why Gomulka was still in jail. Party chief Boleslaw Bierut could not answer the question. Quietly Gomulka's confinement was changed from imprisonment in the secret police headquarters to a hospital and "limited" freedom.[8]

Swiatlo's disclosures and their debilitating consequences for Poland's terroristic police system coincided with a cultural relaxation in the Soviet Union, symbolized in Ilya Ehrenburg's novel *The Thaw*. Polish writers took heart. Novels, short stories, and poems gave expression to the disillusionment of the Polish intelligentsia with Communist practice; and between 1955 and 1956 criticism of the Communist leadership and its policies became increasingly articulate and widespread. Initially the leadership was inclined to crack down on the intellectuals, but in this changed political environment, the intelligentsia could resist the pressures and threats of the party. The secret police had been drastically weakened, and sentiments within the Polish leadership were sufficiently divided to forestall the adoption of repressive measures against dissent. As it turned out, instead of purging the writers' union, the party leadership purged itself.*

Polish youth was difficult to control after 1954. A catalyst of ferment among the young people of Poland was the World Youth Festival held in Warsaw in the summer of 1955, attended by youth groups from many countries of the West. Polish youth caught its first good glimpse of Western life in more than a decade and evidently found it much more appealing than the drudgery of Communist mobilization. Western jazz, dance, hair styles, and blue jeans rapidly replaced the colorless manifestations of Communist "culture." Communist authority could not stop this ferment; if youth was to be saved for Communism, the youth organizations themselves must change so as to become more

---

*One specific sequence of events may be cited here as an example. In August, 1955, the poet Adam Wazyk, formerly a eulogist of Stalinism, published a poem ("Poem for Adults") critical of economic and social ills in Poland and expressive of his own disillusionment with the Communist Party. (The chief censor of Warsaw happened to be on vacation when the poem was published in *Nowa Kultura,* the periodical of the Polish Writers' Union.) The entire editorial board of the journal was dismissed as a result. But when Jakub Berman, Poland's Minister of Interior, Politburo member, and Deputy Premier, called a special meeting of the Writers' Union to expel Wazyk, the poet was staunchly defended and his expulsion was refused. Berman was purged from the party leadership in May, 1956, after a "critical evaluation" of "the activities . . . in the fields over which he exercised control." See Richard Hiscocks, *Poland: Bridge for the Abyss?* (London: Oxford University Press, 1963), pp. 176-77, 187.

appealing to Polish youth.[9] Again the Polish Communist Party exercised self-criticism and decided that the Union of Polish Youth organizations should be revitalized. An expansion of democracy, freedom of discussion, and Western jazz and dance were to constitute part of the change. Under this impetus, the organ of the Union of Polish Youth, *Po Prostu,* soon became one of the liveliest and (for the party leadership) most challenging periodicals in the country.[10]

In Hungary, the Soviet-imposed Rakosi-Nagy condominium turned into a two-year-long factional feud. Although the practical affairs of government had been removed from Rakosi's sphere of competence and given to Imre Nagy, Rakosi continued to rule the Communist party— i.e., the functionaries entrusted with the execution of Nagy's government programs. With their help, Rakosi did his best to undermine Nagy's new course.

Imre Nagy, a convinced Communist of liberal-humanist persuasions, more interested in people's welfare than in power, did earnestly try to improve the lot of Hungarians. Under his administration the drive to collectivize agriculture was abandoned and peasants were allowed to leave collectives already established. Wages were raised and taxes lowered to increase personal income. Private enterprise in crafts was encouraged in order to increase consumer goods and services. Investment in heavy industry was curtailed and resources were shifted to the consumer goods sector. Secret police activity was curbed. Internment camps were closed down and a partial amnesty was decreed.

The direction of Hungary's new course did not fundamentally differ from that of other bloc countries, particularly the Soviet Union. But Hungary's new course was of greater scope and more rapidly enacted. More importantly, in Hungary the new course was identifiable with Imre Nagy, not with Rakosi—the break with the past occurred simultaneously with the change in leadership.

Thus, when, in April, 1955 (three months after Malenkov's resignation as Premier of the Soviet Union), Rakosi succeeded in ousting Nagy from office and returning to Stalinist methods of rule, the alternative of more liberal Communist government had been clearly established in the minds of Hungary's intellectuals and progressive party members. Furthermore, this alternative, embodied in the person of Imre Nagy, remained alive. Though stripped of his office and powers, Nagy remained free to move about and to write; and although he did not attempt to build a political power group of his own, the intellectual elite, party and nonparty, gravitated to him.

Human tolerance of oppression appears to end when the perception of alternatives raises hopes for a better life. Rakosi's reintroduction of Stalinist rule in Hungary, therefore, could not but arouse ferment among the Hungarian people, which after little more than a year brought about his downfall.

The foregoing pages have shown that the Communist system built by Stalin thrived best when it could perpetuate its own status quo, reinforced by coercive methods and devoid of social communication other than that endorsed by the party leadership. The Stalinist system was ill-equipped to cope with change inasmuch as it rested on the "monolithic" foundation of a doctrine that denied and suppressed all possible alternatives. Change is the realization of alternatives; hence it is likely to split groups within the leadership that, under the threat of coercion, have supported the status quo. Such a split, if it is prolonged, can lead to the association of leadership factions with lower-echelon party groups as well as with segments of the population at large.

Notes

1. Flora Lewis, *A Case History of Hope* (Garden City, N.Y.: Double-day & Company, 1958), p. 12.

2. Tibor Meray, *Thirteen Days That Shook the Kremlin*, translated by Howard L. Katzandor (New York: Frederick A. Praeger, 1959), p. 6.

3. See John S. Reshetar, Jr., *Concise History of the Communist Party of the Soviet Union* (New York: Frederick A. Praeger, 1964), pp. 263-64. See also Howard R. Swearer, *The Politics of Succession in the U.S.S.R.* (Boston: Little, Brown and Company, 1964), pp. 59-117; and Leonard Schapiro, *The Communist Party of the Soviet Union* (New York: Vintage Books, 1964), pp. 547-62.

4. Edward Taborsky, *Communism in Czechoslovakia, 1948-1960* (Princeton, N.J.: Princeton University Press, 1961), p. 116.

5. See Ghita Ionescu, *Communism in Rumania, 1944-1962* (London: Oxford University Press, 1964), pp. 152-55.

6. Another writer on Rumania, David Floyd, suggests that Patrascanu may have been imprisoned after having been purged from the Politburo. See David Floyd, *Rumania, Russia's Dissident Ally* (New York: Frederick A. Praeger, 1965), p. 54.

7. Ionescu, op. cit., pp. 260-61.

8. Flora Lewis, op. cit., p. 45. Miss Lewis does not reveal the date of

Gomulka's release from the custody of the secret police. Brzezinski, op cit., p. 238; and Richard Hiscocks, *Poland: Bridge for the Abyss?* (London: Oxford University Press, 1963), p. 183, maintain that Gomulka had been released in December, 1954, but that his release had been kept secret. It is interesting to note, therefore, that at the January, 1955, Central Committee plenum—one month after Gomulka's release—Bierut was not willing to reveal this information to the Central Committee. In the Polish Politburo the issue of Gomulka was evidently regarded as one which could arouse strong sentiments among large groups of the party membership at various levels.

9. On the World Youth Festival in Warsaw, see Flora Lewis, op. cit., Chapter 5. For good treatment of the Communist Party's reaction to the "Westernization" of Polish youth, see Hiscocks, op. cit., pp. 177-78.

10. Hiscocks, op. cit., pp. 178-79.

4   Hungary and Poland: The Politics of Popular Revolt and Communist Control

In the Soviet Union, Malenkov was ousted from his post as Premier in February, 1955, after he had lost his factional struggle, apparently over the issue of economic development priorities. In line with the new course, Malenkov had maintained that Soviet consumer goods industries should continue to receive large-scale investments at the expense of heavy industry. Khrushchev had argued the opposite view, and he prevailed.

The effect of Malenkov's ouster upon political developments in Eastern Europe (though Malenkov's name and political fortunes may, in themselves, have been purely symbolic) was almost a foregone conclusion. It meant the end of the new course and at least a partial return to orthodox Stalinism. Symbolic of this was the removal of Imre Nagy as Premier of Hungary and the return to full power of Matyas Rakosi. The temporary respite in the drive toward nationalized economies in the satellites was over. Collectivization of agriculture began with renewed vigor in all bloc countries. Private artisan activity was once again frowned upon, and central planning offices subverted the everyday needs of the people to the more important priorities of heavy industry.

The regimes of the Soviet bloc had weathered the storms created in the vacuum left by Stalin's demise; apparently they felt that now they could again secure their ships of state and continue to chart the Stalinist course. Only Poland continued to sail in the troubled waters of intellectual ferment. In Hungary, Rakosi succeeded in ousting Nagy and reversing his new course with relative ease, as yet untroubled by any public expression of discontent. But the Hungarian people, Communists and non-Communists alike, had learned that there were alternatives to the Stalinist way of life.

Into this relative calm Khrushchev exploded two political bombshells that were to rock Communism in Eastern Europe to its very foundations. First, in June, 1955, Khrushchev and the new Soviet Premier, Nikolai Bulganin, flew to Belgrade to recement Soviet-Yugoslav relations, which had been completely disrupted by Stalin in 1948. At the Belgrade airport Khrushchev apologized publicly to Tito for Soviet transgressions in its relations with Yugoslavia and pleaded for the reestablishment of fraternal ties. Although Khrushchev heaped all of the blame for these Soviet transgressions posthumously upon Stalin's former secret police chief, Lavrenti Beria, no one could fail to see that his "trip to Conossa" represented a reversal of one of Stalin's most consequential policies concerning the Communist world. "Titoism," for which a great many Communists (up to and including the leadership level) had been expelled from the party, imprisoned, and even executed during the purges of 1948-52, was no longer a crime—on the contrary, some of its most un-Stalinist manifestations received Khrushchev's stamp of respectability. Khrushchev conceded to Tito that although Yugoslavia's approach differed from that of the bloc countries in several important respects, it was equally valid for building "socialism." Thus, there was no single, exclusive way to Communism; rather, there were several roads.

Needless to say, this admission could only embarrass those East European leaders who had purged some of their colleagues during the Stalinist era on grounds of "Titoism" and associated revisionist deviations. Their discomfort, however, grew immeasurably when Khrushchev dropped his second bombshell—his secret speech to the Twentieth CPSU Congress in February, 1956, in which he denounced Stalin's personality cult and crimes against humanity. Khrushchev's secret speech was read and discussed in party meetings throughout Eastern Europe as well as in the Soviet Union. The rank and file was stunned; but in the minds of some party members shock soon gave way to outrage.

Intellectuals were particularly aroused. In all East European countries the secret speech denouncing Stalin touched off "writers' revolts" in meetings of the Writers' Unions. These revolts were quickly quelled in Czechoslovakia, East Germany, Bulgaria and Rumania,[1] where the censors managed to keep dissenting views out of public sight.

In Poland, however, Khrushchev's secret speech only added fuel to an already flaming fire; in Hungary the resentment of intellectuals had been stirred by the removal of Imre Nagy from office, to the point where, by February, 1956, the party leadership had considerable difficulty screening out the heresies that flowed from the intellectuals' pens. In both countries factionalism had introduced indecision, hesitation, if not paralysis into the leadership chambers, rendering the maintenance of totalitarian control over the activities of the people virtually impossible.

Had the opposition to existing Communist rule been confined to the masses outside the Communist Party, the leaderships of Poland and Hungary might have been able to quell the ferment without major difficulty. But in both of these countries large segments of the party membership, as well as sizable groups within the leadership at various levels, were "finding their conscience," particularly after Khrushchev's secret speech. They demanded discussion of public policy; and the leaders, perhaps hoping that such discussion might lessen the tension, allowed discussion clubs to be formed. Perhaps the leaders of Poland and Hungary hoped also that under the surveillance of reliable party members, these clubs could be kept in line. Instead, the discussion groups crystallized popular discontent.

The "Polish October" and the Hungarian Revolution

The specific events leading up to the popular upheavals of October, 1956, in Poland and Hungary cannot be treated here. They are eloquently described in a number of books published during the past 12 years.[2] Instead, we will suggest pertinent factors in each country which may help to explain why the ferment in Poland was contained within a nonviolent frame, while prevailing discontent in Hungary erupted in violence.

Leadership

In both Poland and Hungary there existed an alternative to the Stalinist incumbents. Wladyslaw Gomulka in Poland and Imre Nagy in Hungary were men around whom most of the dissident groups could rally. But here the parallel ends.

Poland's Wladyslaw Gomulka had been the Secretary General of his party until he was purged on charges of Titoism and other nationalist deviations in 1948 and replaced by Boleslaw Bierut. As already mentioned, he was imprisoned in 1951 and spent the following three years under detention and interrogation by the secret police. While Gomulka owed his release, in part, to the discredit heaped upon the Polish secret police by Swiatlo, it was Khrushchev's public apology to Tito in June, 1955, that, if only by implication, rendered the charges against Gomulka invalid.

More important, Boleslaw Bierut died in Moscow on March 12, 1956, little more than two weeks after Khrushchev's damaging exposés of Stalin's crimes. His demise deprived the party leadership of its head, and the rank and file of the principal focal point of guilt by association. Edward Ochab assumed the top party post, but the evidence suggests that he never had or gained the stature or power of his predecessor. He remained, in fact, equal to his colleagues in the Politburo. Under these circumstances it was probably less difficult to resolve factional conflicts by compromise, but much more difficult to act decisively to suppress popular discontent. The Polish leadership showed a much greater inclination to move toward conciliation with the discontented rank and file of the party, as well as with the population at large, than did those of the other East European countries. When it became clear (probably soon after the Poznan riots of June, 1956) that the present leadership represented in the Polish Politburo could no longer save Poland from violent revolt, Ochab relinquished his post to Gomulka, the only man in Poland who could muster enough appeal to act as the lightning rod of popular unrest.

The political evolution of Hungary during this brief time span stood in sharp contrast with the Polish one just described. Two pertinent differences can be pointed out here.

First, the time factor. In Poland, the intellectual and popular opposition ferment had begun in 1954, stirred by Swiatlo's revelations, while in Hungary at that time (one may assume) much of the potential unrest was mitigated by Imre Nagy's liberal leadership steering a new course. Thus, open discontent grew more gradually in Poland than it did in Hungary, where muted but deep resentment of Nagy's ouster (in February, 1955) was rather suddenly transformed into open opposition by Khrushchev's secret speech at the Twentieth CPSU Congress.

Second, the intransigence of leadership. At the time when Boleslaw Bierut, the Polish party chief, died, Hungary's party leader, Matyas Rakosi, was reentrenching himself, with the obvious intent of perpetuating his oppressive rule. Whereas in Poland, a collective leadership was inclined to compromise with the irrevocable demands of the citizenry, in Hungary the policies of the party leadership tended toward the opposite extreme of the wishes and views of liberal groups within the party, thus making an open tug of war inevitable.

Focus of Moral Grievance

Perhaps of major significance, psychologically, was the fact that in Poland the most prestigious purge victim, Gomulka, was still alive; his ascension to leadership could undo in the public mind some of the grave injustice symbolized by the purge of Titoists. In Hungary, on the other hand, the most prestigious purge victim, Laszlo Rajk, had been executed after a publicized "show trial." The fact that the Hungarian leadership felt it necessary to "rehabilitate" Rajk posthumously attests to the importance of the purge issue and to the moral recrimination suffered by the Communist party. Rajk was cleared of the charges of Titoism against him; and, in June, 1956, his remains were exhumed and ceremoniously reinterred. The leadership may have viewed this bizarre ritual as a gesture of appeasement to the discontented population; but for the people it had the effect of a provocation.

In short, in October, 1956, neither the Polish nor the Hungarian leadership had bridged the gulf between the rulers and the ruled; but in Poland that gulf was less wide and, at the crucial moment, was bridged by Gomulka's appeal. In Hungary, that gulf had grown beyond the elasticity of whatever political cohesion there remained. Thus, on October 23, 1956, Hungary's political rift erupted in violent revolution. No one planned it; apparently no one wanted it; but no one could divert the forces at work. Imre Nagy was hastily reinstated in the party leadership and called upon to lead the government, but not before the party's political power had disintegrated and the government had lost all authority and control. His return to power could no longer appease the fury of the population at large. Under these circumstances, Nagy was swept along by the tides of the Hungarian Revolution.

Responsive Government in
Times of Crisis

The popular upheavals in Poland and Hungary have been eloquently chronicled in numerous books and articles. Poland is most remembered for the rise of Wladyslaw Gomulka in defiance of the Soviet leadership and the ensuing (albeit short-lived) "Polish October," a period of relative popular freedom. The Hungarian Revolution still lives in memory as the heroic struggle of an unarmed people against Soviet tanks.

Less notice has been given to the spontaneous effort in both of these countries during the popular upheavals to curb the powers of the rulers and to make government responsive to the needs and demands of the people. If only for a brief period of a few weeks, the regimes of Poland and Hungary ruled by the consent of the governed. Interest groups formed spontaneously and issued demands to the government either directly or through the newly uncontrolled press.

In both Poland and Hungary religious institutions shook off the fetters of their respective Communist regimes. Hungary's Cardinal Mindszenty and Poland's Cardinal Wyszynski were freed. "Peace priests," who had acted as the ecclesiastical arm of the secret police, were ousted, as were bishops who had collaborated with the regime. Religious instruction was again introduced in public schools on a voluntary basis; within three months Hungarian schools registered enrollments of 80 to 100 percent of the student population. In December, 1956, the Polish regime concluded a new agreement, reflecting essentially the one of 1950 (so flagrantly violated by the regime), guaranteeing, among other things, freedom of worship, religious instructions, and pastoral service among the armed forces. Trade unions expelled their regime-appointed leaders and elected new ones by free and secret ballot. In both countries they demanded a voice in government and the right to strike. Workers' Councils were formed at the factories to participate in the managerial process. In Hungary, moreover, the Workers' Councils took over the functions of local government during the tumultuous days of the revolution, when the bureaucratic functionaries were utterly paralyzed and discredited. In both countries, Workers' Councils were finally (albeit briefly) recognized by the regimes as legitimate elements in the enterprise structure.*

Demands for genuine multiparty democracy were compelling in Poland and Hungary. In Hungary, Imre Nagy acceded to this demand in his radio speech of October 31, 1956. In Poland, the elevation of the Sejm (Parliament) from the status of a rubber stamp to that of a pseudolegislature was one of the lasting gains of the revolt.

Needless to say, the free functioning of political interest groups is

---

*Apparently the events in Poland and Hungary prompted the East German and Rumanian leaderships to allow a semblance of worker participation in the management of their enterprises. In East Germany, Workers' Committees were established experimentally in a number of industrial establishments, only to be abolished in 1958, after the threat of labor unrest had subsided. In Rumania, "production meetings" were instituted in order to mitigate discontent among the workers.

36

the very antithesis of Communist totalitarianism; dictatorship lapsed for the duration of their spontaneous activity. Their continuing existence presented a grave threat to the survival of the ruling groups. Therefore, as soon as these ruling groups had retrenched themselves (the Hungarian one with Soviet military help), they sought to regain control over these interest groups.

Re-Stalinization, 1957-62

Following the Polish and Hungarian upheavals, the period from 1957 to 1962 witnessed a general tightening of Communist control in Eastern Europe. The denunciation of Stalin's personality cult and crimes against humanity arising therefrom had done much damage to the cause of Communist totalitarianism in the Soviet bloc. Even Khrushchev had to admit this.* As a result, Stalin was partially rehabilitated—the atrocities he had perpetrated were played down and he was credited with some positive contributions to Communist development.

In Hungary and Poland, the trade unions were brought back into the totalitarian fold. Their freely elected leaders were dismissed and replaced with apparatchiks subservient to central command. Their primary role again became the mobilization of the workers for the fulfillment of the economic plan. Workers' Councils were dissolved altogether in Hungary in 1957 (and in East Germany in 1958); in Poland they were merged into "self-government conferences," together with trade union councils and party factory committees, under central control.

Control over the intelligentsia was more difficult to reestablish. In Hungary, some prominent writers who were directly implicated in the revolt were arrested and imprisoned. Others stopped writing altogether, rather than debase their talents to the mediocrity of the "socialist

---

*For instance, soon after the Hungarian Revolution, Khrushchev made the following remarks at a Chinese Embassy reception:

> The enemies of Communism tried to capitalize on our criticism of Stalin's shortcomings and errors and utilize this criticism for their own purposes. They wanted to direct the criticism of Stalin's cult of personality against the foundations of our system, against the basis of Marxism-Leninism. . . . Though Stalin did commit errors ("noticed first of all by Lenin"), he did this in the interests of . . . socialism. . . . In the fundamental and important things—the fundamental and important things to Marxist-Leninists are the protection of working-class interests, the work of socialism, the struggle with enemies of Marxism-Leninism—in these fundamental and important things, as they say, let God help every communist to fight as Stalin fought.[3]

realism" that the Kadar regime demanded of them. In Poland, on the other hand, the Gomulka regime's efforts to curb intellectual freedom encountered fierce resistance, and it had to manipulate its levers of power more cautiously. Using such "salami tactics" as the banning of an offensive literary journal, reshuffling editorial boards, and the piecemeal restriction of the rights of journalists' and writers' unions, as well as a few arrests of writers for "antistate activity," the regime succeeded in partially reimposing its control over the intellectual sector. But at the end of the decade Poland still remained a haven of relative intellectual freedom, compared with other countries of the Soviet bloc, despite constantly increasing efforts by the regime to reimpose its control over the intelligentsia.

Religious institutions, which had regained their freedom during the upheavals, also fell victim to the re-Stalinization drive. Fearing imminent arrest and imprisonment, Hungary's Cardinal Mindszenty sought refuge in the U.S. legation in Budapest. The Kadar regime removed the bishops of both Catholic and Protestant faiths who had been freely elected during the revolution and replaced them with men more pliable to political manipulation. The "peace priest" movement was relaunched, and security police agents were again assigned to supervise the activities of ecclesiastical offices. Recurrent waves of arrests of clergymen, even in the 1960's, however, betrayed the tenuousness of the Hungarian regime's control over the religious sector.

In Poland, the regime moved much more cautiously against the freedom of religious institutions, and with much less decisive effect. Until 1958 a state of uneasy coexistence characterized the relations between the Catholic Church and the Polish regime. Thereafter, however, the Polish regime launched a sustained offensive against the Church that grew in intensity into the 1960's. By 1960, religious instruction was again abolished from public schools, and privately conducted instruction by the Church was placed under government regulation. Taxes on Church property and income were increased from year to year. Fierce resistance by the Church to these and other repressive measures made the state move warily in the execution of its anti-Church laws, for in Poland the Church commands the loyalty of the people as nowhere else in Eastern Europe. As of 1970, the Polish Church continues to be hampered by state interference and threatened by repression, but it remains the freest and most powerful of any church in the Soviet bloc.

In Hungary, pressures for multiparty democracy, to which Imre

Nagy had acceeded during the revolution, were quickly squelched by the Kadar regime. Only the Communist Party was eligible for representation in Parliament. The legislature again reverted to the status of a rubber stamp for the enactments of the regime.

In Poland, on the other hand, the Sejm acquired a positive, albeit limited, role in the making of policy. Its 19 standing committees became lively forums for debate of the regime's bills. Although their numerous meetings (1,203 counted from 1957 to 1961) were closed to the public, it has been reported that the debates in these meetings were relatively free and sometimes very sharp.[4] Occasionally, government bills were rejected in toto, and more often than not (in 144 cases out of 174) the government had to modify its bills before the relevant committee would approve them.

In part, this unusual relationship between the regime and the Sejm may be explained by the relative "tolerance" of Gomulka's ruling group, which was unable to recapture complete control of the many politically relevant groups in the country and therefore felt it prudent to widen the parameters of popular representation and participation in the political process. In 1957, a new electoral law stipulated that the number of candidates for election to the Sejm could exceed the number of seats, but by no more than two-thirds (it did, in fact, by 55 percent). Aside from the Communist Party, the United Peasant Party, the Democratic Party, and a number of nonparty groups are eligible for representation in the Sejm, but the entire electoral process is governed by the Communist-dominated National Front. Needless to say, the Communist Party has consistently been able to assure itself an absolute majority in the Sejm. Nevertheless, after the upheavals of 1956, it could no longer be said that the Polish legislature was simply the legislative rubber stamp of the Gomulka regime.

In other countries of Eastern Europe that had not experienced popular upheavals in 1956, these indicators of re-Stalinization were, of course, less noticeable. But throughout the Soviet bloc the 1957-62 period witnessed at least a partial withdrawal of the concessions to consumer demands that were granted under the New Course. Industrial development once again became a top-priority objective, at the expense of consumer goods. The reprieve of restrictions on small-scale private enterprise that had helped to alleviate the consumer plight was revoked.

The peasants were the last segment of East Central European society to feel the heavy hand of the Communist state apparatus, as collectivization (begun while Stalin still ruled, but retarded during the mid-1950's) was rushed to completion toward the end of the decade. Only Poland had abandoned collectivization in the wake of its popular upheavals in 1956;* the rest of East Central Europe completed collectivization during, if not before, 1961.

Poland: The Weakest Link?

Poland, then, stands out in the Soviet bloc's re-Stalinization effort as a country that turned back the clock. It stands in particularly sharp contrast with Hungary, whose re-Stalinization drive began at about the same point but was swift and often brutal. The explanation for this contrast can only be speculative, but it can be based on concrete variable differences that distinguished Poland from the other bloc countries.

There is little doubt that Gomulka had no more sympathy with basic popular freedoms than did his ruling colleagues in other bloc countries. But his dislike for democracy was at least matched, if not surpassed, by his aversion to Soviet domination of his country's domestic affairs. This feeling was apparently shared by his colleagues in the Politburo and Central Committee, who not only elected him but also supported his stand in October, 1956, against the irate Soviet leader, Nikita S. Khrushchev, who sought to thwart Gomulka's rise to the party throne.

Having successfully resisted Soviet (political) intervention and re-stored stability in the country without Soviet help, the Polish leadership felt entitled (and perhaps also compelled by popular demand) to opt for a "Polish road to socialism," which might differ in some respect from the Soviet one. Throughout 1957, and with diminishing force thereafter, Gomulka openly defended the Polish road to socialism against Soviet efforts to regain supremacy.[5]

To pursue "national roads to socialism," broadly defined, meant to adapt the Marxist-Leninist creed and patterns of rule developed under Stalin and his successors to the peculiar national conditions facing each ruling Communist Party. Khrushchev had to concede this prerogative to the Yugoslav and Chinese Communists (and, by implication, to any other ruling party that dared to demand it openly) in order to keep the bloc together. There were several important national conditions compelling the Polish leadership to approach re-Stalinization with extreme caution.

One of these was a deep-seated resentment of Soviet domination,

---

*Yugoslavia, not treated in this study, abandoned collectivization in 1953.

widespread even within the ruling hierarchy, a resentment rooted in centuries of history. Gomulka's defiance of the Kremlin, and his insistence on Poland's autonomy, was very popular; but it also deprived his regime of its ability to impose its predilections on a still restive population. Unlike other regimes, Gomulka's did not wish to invoke the support of Soviet power—the *ultima ratio* of Communist control in Eastern Europe—for that would have spelled its own political demise. A rapid withdrawal of the concessions made in 1956 might provoke popular unrest; and the invocation of Soviet support would, under the circumstances then prevailing, certainly spell the political demise of Gomulka and perhaps that of his colleagues as well. In other words, initially Gomulka could ill afford to alienate the popular support that had catapulted him to the top of the ruling hierarchy.

Presumably the ruling group around Gomulka was agreed on this point; but it was divided on many other issues. Nowhere else in Eastern Europe was a Communist Party divided into so many factions as in Poland.* And while the politics of factionalism and the impact of each faction on policy making have remained obscure, it seems accurate to say that Gomulka has sought to emasculate the liberal factions in his entourage and that, in order to achieve this aim, he has had to strike some political bargains with hard-line groups. The end effect of the re-Stalinization drive, which continued long after 1961 (when other East European countries were liberalizing again), suggests this approach. By 1963, the liberal faction had lost most of the important positions held by its adherents in 1957. The crucial point to note here is that with his Politburo divided, Gomulka had to play a game of politics; hence, he was not strong enough politically to impose his own predilections upon Poland's political scene.

Third, the United States had undertaken to extend Poland agricultural aid (under the Food for Peace Program) and most favored nation status, in recognition of the Gomulka regime's efforts to divert Poland from the Soviet-dominated mainstream of Communist politics. A rapid

---

*In the course of this study, five distinct factions were identified in the Polish leadership: (1) the "Natolin group," composed of Moscovites who continued to support the harsh measures of Stalinism; (2) the "Pulawy group," which argued for pragmatism and more humane Communist rule; (3) a "liberal group," which advocated rapid liberalization combining a socialist economy with Western political freedoms; (4) Gomulka's hangers-on, of increasingly hard-line persuasions; and (5) the "Partisan group" (which came into prominence toward the end of the 1950's), known for its authoritarian persuasions, anti-Semitism, and nationalistic tendencies.

withdrawal from the October, 1956, liberalization patterns might have jeopardized this windfall, which at that time was helping to diminish Poland's economic dependence on the Soviet Union and, hence, its susceptibility to such economic pressures as Moscow might have applied to bring that country back into the mainstream.

These three factors were certainly not mutually exclusive considerations in the Polish policy-making process; they probably combined with others to urge a cautious approach to re-Stalinization. As long as this circumspection predominated in the Polish Politburo's decision making, the various groups whom Gomulka sought to bring back under central control had opportunities to resist that were not available elsewhere in Eastern Europe, and resist they did—vigorously.

Poland's re-Stalinization drive accelerated during the 1960's, when some of the other Soviet bloc countries were relaxing theirs, so that in the mid-1960's it was no longer the most liberal country in the bloc. But neither was it the most totalitarian. Nowhere else in the bloc (save perhaps Czechoslovakia) did a regime have more difficulties keeping a tight rein on the creative intelligentsia; nowhere else did a Communist regime face such strong opposition from religious groups to its repressive policies and such strong competition for popular allegiance as was the case in Poland. In a sense, Poland came to stand out as a contradiction in terms: a totalitarian-minded regime that was never quite able to regain full control over the politics of the country.

Notes

1. For concise descriptive treatment of this subject, see pertinent sections of the country chapters in Stephen D. Kertesz, ed., *East Central Europe and the World* (Notre Dame, Ind.: University of Notre Dame Press, 1962). Intellectual ferment in Rumania during this period is well described in Ghita Ionescu, *Communism in Rumania 1944-1962* (London: Oxford University Press, 1964), pp. 259-66.

2. Excellent eyewitness accounts are given in Tibor Meray, *Thirteen Days That Shook the Kremlin,* translated by Howard L. Katzandor (New York: Frederick A. Praeger, 1959); and Flora Lewis, *A Case History of Hope* (Garden City, N.Y.: Doubleday & Co., 1958). See also Zbigniew Brzezinski, *The Soviet Bloc* (New York: Frederick A. Praeger, 1961). For an excellent documentary account of this ferment, see Paul E. Zinser, ed., *National Communism and Popular Revolt in Eastern Europe. A Selection of Documents on Events in Poland and Hungary, February-November, 1956* (New York: Columbia University Press, 1956).

3. *Pravda* (January 19, 1957), as quoted and cited in Howard R. Swearer and Richard P. Longaker, *Contemporary Communism: Theory and Practice* (Belmost, Calif.: Wadsworth Publishing Co., 1963), pp. 205-06.

4. Richard Hiscocks, *Poland: Bridge for the Abyss?* (London: Oxford University Press, 1963), pp. 274-75.

5. See Brzezinski, op. cit., Chapter 12, "The Maoist Reconstruction of the Center."

Part 2: The Dynamics of Communist Political Development

5   Problems and Concepts

The second part of this study departs from the first in scope, detail, and conceptualization. It will focus on three countries of the Soviet bloc: East Germany, Hungary, and Bulgaria. Its task is to examine comparatively the politics of economic reform and its impact on these three Communist political systems during the 1963-67 period, which witnessed more or less rapid liberalization in most of the bloc countries. This restricted focus will permit a more detailed examination of the questions posed for comparative analysis. The conceptualization will become clear later in this chapter, after a brief delineation of some of the major problems that forced the leaderships of these countries to decentralize their economic systems.

Economic Problems of Communism

Throughout the 1950's, most of the Soviet bloc countries registered impressive quantitative growth indexes, even though these often fell short of the ambitious plan targets set by their regimes. These growth rates, furthermore, were achieved through an inordinately high expenditure of resources (detracting from the consumer sector), attributable to the predominance of political criteria in economic planning and to managerial inefficiency. By 1956-57, these problems, endemic to the highly centralized Communist economic systems, had moved some economists to argue for a change in management performance criteria and in the role of central planning, i.e., for more rational economic methods in general and decentralization in particular.[1]

Neither the Kremlin nor the East European regimes were ready at that time to seek remedies in decentralization. This may have been due in part to their fear of losing control (the greater since the Polish and Hungarian upheavals) and in part to the belief that rapid progress could still be made by a more conscientious application of Stalinist methods. Thus, liberal economic reform advocates fell into political oblivion during a period in which the main task was to complete the control structure of the Communist state.

By the early 1960's, however, economic processes in Eastern Europe had become so glaringly inefficient that they stifled even quantitative growth, the index by which Communist regimes had judged the performance of their national economies. A marked decline in industrial growth rates had occurred throughout the Soviet bloc countries. The following table tells part of the story for the three countries in question.

Table 1

Industrial Growth Rates of Bulgaria,
Hungary, and East Germany, 1960—64.

	1960	1961	1962	1963	1964
Bulgaria	13.3%	11.7%	11.0%	10.0%	8.8%
Hungary	12.8	11.0	8.4	7.0	7.0
East Germany	8.2	5.9	6.2	4.9	5.7

Source: J. F. Brown, *The New Eastern Europe: The Khrushchev Era and After* (New York: Frederick A. Praeger, 1966), p. 291, from *United Nations Economic Survey of Europe, 1963:* Part 1, *The European Economy in 1963* (Geneva, 1964), p. 5.

Other aspects of the general economic malaise could be gleaned from complaints by Communist regimes about the low quality of production output, the high cost, the lack of efficiency of production, and the associated decline in the growth of labor productivity. Much of this will be highlighted in the following chapters; here a few pertinent examples are illustrative.

As a lead article in Bulgaria's party daily pointed out,[2] plan overfulfillment was often associated with waste: Bulgaria's plan for industrial production had been overfulfilled by 29 million leva; however, the quality of the products was so shoddy that the State

Purchasing Enterprise had refused to buy many of them (amounting to 3,450,000 leva in state-priced value). Furthermore, the Ministry of Internal Trade had discontinued its purchase from 160 of Bulgaria's state-owned enterprises because of their low-quality production. Poor-quality goods were even more damaging to foreign trade, on which all of the East European economies depend to a large degree. Speaking before the Central Committee plenum in November, 1961,[3] Bulgarian party leader Todor Zhivkov pointed out that Bulgaria's foreign trade would amount to some 9.5 billion (old) leva; but at the same time the Ministry of Foreign Trade had been given eight billion leva in state subsidies. Considering that Bulgaria's foreign trade was divided equally between exports and imports, it was clear that the state subsidy for exports was almost double the amount of the export value. In addition, the Bulgarian state was losing money because profit plans were not being fulfilled.[4] Goods were gathering dust in warehouses and some, for which there was no more room in warehouses, were rotting in the rain.[5]

Basically the same problems were plaguing the Communist leaders of Hungary, perhaps with slight variations in emphasis. Overfulfillment of production plans led to stockpiling, not only because the goods were of low quality but also because designs were outmoded or there was simply no demand for the products in the first place.[6] The most often mentioned economic problem in Hungary, however, was the declining growth of productivity[7] (measured as the amount of labor going into a given unit of production).

Thus, the necessity for change was clearly evident in Eastern Europe. But how does one explain the fact that three countries under consideration, at widely differing stages of economic development, undertook more or less simultaneously to reform their economic structure? First of all, the problems they were facing in productivity and quality became salient in each country about the same time. Because of their isolation from the capitalist West, their foreign trade had been confined mainly within the Communist bloc, where, during the postwar reconstruction and initial period of economic development, goods of all types were in demand, regardless of their quality. Cost was hardly relevant in trade within and among countries where all means of production and distribution were owned by the state. Toward the end of the 1950's, the demand structure of East European markets began to change as a result of market satisfaction of some of the more basic producer and consumer goods.[8] For the consumer it was no longer a question of buying a suit and a pair of shoes or walking the streets

49

without them; he could now wait until either the price went down or a better product was for sale. People tended to save whatever money they had left, rather than spend it on shoddy goods.

Second, at about this time, possibilities for trade with the West were increasing. Both short-term and long-term credits were being extended to East European countries for purchases of capital goods which, with rational management, could improve productive processes, reduce costs, introduce new products, and, most of all, improve the competitive position of East European industries in the world market. But the credits would have to be repaid with interest. Logically, the East European Communists were confronted with a choice: continuing isolation from the rest of the world, or competition. Given their ambitions for rapid economic modernization, their decision was almost a foregone conclusion.

We have suggested that at least two factors (the elimination of basic scarcities and the opening of trade routes to the West) converging upon the East European economic scene made changes in the economic system within the rigid boundaries of the political system little short of inevitable. This did not mean, however, that the East Europeans were about to deviate from Soviet guidelines of political behavior. On the contrary, there is good reason to believe that the Soviet Union, which was facing identical problems,[9] helped spur the economic reforms which germinated in East Europe's Politburos between 1963 and 1965.

Yevsei Liberman's article, published in *Pravda* on September 9, 1962, probably gave the initial impetus to economic reform in the three countries, as well as others in Eastern Europe. The fact that it appeared in the official daily organ of the CPSU meant that the Soviet party leadership approved of Liberman's ideas; indeed, an editorial postscript to the article invited public discussion of these ideas.

Given the continuing subservience of our three East European Communist parties to Soviet policy, one can only speculate how they would have solved their mounting economic problems had the Soviets not pointed the way to permissible reform. They might have engaged in economic reform regardless; they might also have experienced severe economic and political crises. Such speculation aside, the necessity was there, and Soviet doctrine no longer opposed reform.

Analysis of Political Development

Political analysts of Eastern Europe (particularly after the Czechoslovak "spring") generally agree that meaningful economic reform in Communist systems is impossible without political reform. This highly generalized proposition seems valid, but it invites the conclusion that if Communist regimes want to forge an efficient and progressive economic system, they will have to reform the political process at the same time or fail in the attempt; and thus it closes our intellectual senses to the dynamic relationships between economic and political development. It may lead to ignoring those Communist countries which have not made any significant (striking or, from the Western point of view, desirable) political reform because, according to this proposition, any economic reform they may have experimented with or enacted is altogether meaningless unless it is accompanied by "democratization" in the political realm.

Systems theory, combined with structural-functional analysis, offers a more heuristic approach to the study of the dynamics of the changing politico-economic process in Eastern Europe. Integral to systems theory is the proposition that

> ... when one variable in a system changes in magnitude or in quality, the others are subjected to strains and are transformed; the system changes its pattern of performance, or the unruly component is disciplined by regulatory mechanisms.[10]

According to this proposition, one should expect not only that economic reform would generate pressures for change in the political system, but also that the ruling organs of the several Communist systems would respond in different ways—mixtures of resistance and accommodation—to these pressures for change.

The difference between these two approaches, essentially, is that the latter leads us to take a close look at the process of change in the making, whereas the former is more likely to leave us impervious until the change has taken place.

The following chapters explore the thesis that socioeconomic development places demands upon the political system, requiring adjustments in prevailing processes, structures, and institutions. Three working hypotheses provided the point of departure for this exploration:

1. A rise in demand articulation leads to change in the structure and functions of the political subsystem to which the demand is presented.

2. Change in one subsystem (economic reform, for instance) gives rise to demand and change in other subsystems.

3. The nature and scope of the demand for change, as well as the

rate and scope of consequent change, varies directly with the level of socioeconomic development in each country.

In the following chapters it will become apparent that these hypotheses are "ideal" stimuli-response patterns which the real world does not always exhibit. But they are useful in that they direct our thinking toward what we really want to know, and thus they help us to ask pertinent questions about what is relevant.

This comparative examination will focus on three subsystems: the economy, the trade unions, and the national legislature. The countries to be examined are East Germany, Hungary, and Bulgaria (listed in descending order of socioeconomic development). Among the great variety of indicators which have been developed to measure socioeconomic development, five have been chosen to document what is actually common knowledge—i.e., that East Germany is the most highly developed country in the Soviet bloc, Bulgaria is the least developed, and Hungary ranks between these two. These indicators are (1) the percentage of the working population engaged in industry, (2) the percentage of the working population engaged in agriculture, (3) the percentage of the population living in cities over 100,000, (4) the percentage of the population living in rural areas, and (5) the percentage of the population enrolled in postprimary education. Table 2 and Table 3 give the figures for these indicators from the three countries under consideration.

The Conceptual Framework

The conceptual framework of this analysis concerning the relationship between socioeconomic and political development is based on the theoretical foundations contained in *Comparative Politics: A Developmental Approach,* by Gabriel Almond and George Bingham Powell.[11] For the present purpose a brief explanation of basic terms and conceptual elements pertaining to this analysis is presented.

An organized society (a polity) is a system of interdependent parts, structured according to the functions it must perform in order to maintain itself, adapt to its changing environment, attain its goals, and integrate its various elements for coordinated action. Looking at the three polities in Eastern Europe as systems, the following elements are particularly relevant to this study.

1. Every system has its boundaries, that is, the limit which circum-

Table 2

Level of Industrialization and Urbanization
in Bulgaria, East Germany, and Hungary, 1961

Country	Pop. in Industry	Pop. in Agriculture	Pop. in Cities over 100,000	Pop. in Rural Areas
Bulgaria	18.6%	64.2%	15.0%	66.4%
East Germany	36.0	17.0	20.8	28.0
Hungary	29.3	36.3	23.6	68.0

Note: The Bulgarian figure for percent of population in industry was taken from a 1956 census. In 1964 Bulgaria claimed that 32 percent of its work force was employed in industry and construction, but the Bulgarian *Statistical Yearbook* for 1966 specifically excludes collectivized peasants from the working population (see p. 68, Table 2). Although there has certainly been an increase in the industrial proletariat of Bulgaria, the high figure of 32 percent cannot be considered comparable with the other figures listed in this table.

Source:The Worldmark Encyclopedia of the Nations (New York: Harper & Row, 1963).

scribes its structure and functions. In organic systems—*Homo sapiens,* for instance—these boundaries are clearly delineated by visible features. The boundaries of political systems, however, are much more amorphous; hence, they are more difficult to define. The difficulty is compounded by the fact that there is no comprehensive, universally accepted definition of exactly what the term "political" may or may not describe. The present study hews to David Easton's definition:

> The boundary of a political system is defined by all those actions more or less directly related to the making of binding decisions for a society; every social action that does not partake of this characteristic will be excluded from the system and thereby will automatically be viewed as an external variable in the environment.[12]

Clearly, political systems vary greatly as to their boundaries. In the United States, for instance, the boundaries of the political system are fairly narrowly circumscribed in normal times but can expand suddenly and tremendously in times of war or civil unrest.

For purposes of comparison, it might be useful to introduce a

Table 3

Enrollment in Post-Primary Education in Bulgaria, East Germany, and Hungary, 1956–66 (approximate percentage of population)

	1956	1957	1958	1959	1960	1961	1962	1963	1964	1965	1966
Bulgaria											
Secondary, Technical Education	.77								2.00	2.20	2.12
University Education	.56					.89			1.26	1.33	1.34
Total	1.33								3.26	3.53	3.46
East Germany											
Secondary Education		.52	.51		.47	.47	.45	.45	.47	.51	.54
Technical Education		3.38	3.82	3.51	2.99	2.73	2.90	3.09	3.32	3.50	3.72
University Education		.48	.47	.51	.59	.67	.66	.67	.65	.63	.63
Total		4.38	4.80	—	4.06	3.87	4.01	4.21	4.44	4.64	4.89
Hungary											
Secondary, Technical Education	1.69	1.87	1.74	1.93	2.05	2.40	2.82	3.31	3.81	4.14	4.05
University Education	.49	.47	.38	.37	.38	.45	.53	.66	.66	.90	.92
Total	2.18	2.34	2.12	2.30	2.43	2.85	3.35	3.98	4.62	5.04	4.96

Source: Computed from *Statistical Yearbook* of each country.

gradation from "hard" to "soft" boundaries, in order to distinguish more clearly between those aspects of national life which are either more or less directly related to authoritative, binding decision making (i.e., direct or indirect control).

2. Every system is composed of subsystems which are more or less autonomous. We use the term "autonomy" rather than "independence" because in the modern political system, every subsystem, even the individual citizen, is more or less dependent upon other parts of the political system. By "autonomy" we mean the range of freedom granted to the subsystems to act independently (free from central control), to take independent initiatives, and to coordinate among themselves in pursuit of their own interests and those of their members. In Communist authoritarian systems, this freedom is extremely restricted; in democratic systems it is far wider.

3. Within the context of our model, functions are performed by people who play roles in the political system.* The structure of a political system is essentially the relationship of the role players to each other. This concept of role player relationships, though highly fluid, focuses our attention upon the dynamics of the political system without distracting us from the powers and functions of institutions. It also keeps the crucial variable of autonomy clearly in view. The functions of the Minister of Health in the Soviet Union, for instance, are very similar to those of his counterpart in Great Britain, but the relationships of these role players to other ministers and to higher organs differ widely in their respective countries.

Political development entails an increasing diversity and specificity of functions.† This increasing diversity and specificity is common to the political development of both democratic and authoritarian political systems. Therefore, it cannot be regarded as an indicator of even the likelihood of democratic political development. The essential difference between authoritarianism and democracy, it would appear, lies in the relative degree of autonomy characterizing the relationships between the role players.

---

*Functions have been alluded to in previous parts of this chapter. Superficially, functions and roles might appear to be synonymous terms. However, a role player can perform a variety of separate political functions. Implicit in the concept of role-playing, aside from functions, are a number of other important attributes, such as status and power.

†Theoretically and historically, of course, retrogressive development, i.e., a decrease in diversity and specificity of functions, cannot be ruled out.

4. Every organic system formulates and seeks its own goals. Goal-seeking is an integral part of the system's maintenance and preservation functions. Political systems have been known to progress, stagnate, or decay according to their goals and their success in pursuing them.

Successful goal attainment depends in large part on the degree of consensus within the boundaries of the political system, not only on the goals but also on the methods, for goal-seeking in the modern nation-state requires integrated, coordinated mass action.

5. Closely related to goal seeking are the concepts of input, output, and feedback—essential components of any system. Input, as defined by David Easton, consists of both demand upon, and support of, the political system. It can take the form of either action (as when the people of East Germany "vote with their feet") or communication (such as interest articulation). Output is the demand and support transformed into authoritative decisions (policy, law, or goal). Feedback is the term we use to describe the flow of that information which tells the decision maker about the effectiveness of his output or goal steering.[13] Ordinarily it is often impossible to distinguish clearly between input and feedback because many of the demands channeled into the decision-making apparatus arise from previous output.

We should hasten to add that anyone within the boundaries (hard and soft) of the political system can, theoretically, make inputs into the political system. This includes specifically the top leadership of the polity. In fact, as a rule, the higher the role player in the structure of the political system, the more likely his demands are to have an impact upon the decision-making apparatus. On the whole, political systems vary according to the flow (quantity) of inputs admitted into the political system, the differentiation and autonomy of demand articulation channels, the degree of screening of inputs along the way to the decision-making apparatus, and the degree of restriction imposed on input generation at various levels of the political system. A virtual prohibition of autonomous demand generation, for instance, is characteristic of a highly authoritarian system below the superstructure; only support, clearly identified with previous outputs, is permitted to flow upward. In a democratic system, on the other hand, the channels for demand flow are widely proliferated; indeed, demand articulation has become a highly specialized function of the political system (interest groups), and demands are aggregated and integrated at various levels of the political structure (by political parties in electoral platforms and in the legislatures). We might say that the more autonomy prevails among the component parts of the political system, the more likely there is to be effective demand articulation and a structure for demand aggregation.

Several other elements of the political system should be mentioned, although we will not deal with them in as much depth in this study. For instance, the political system, like all organic systems, renews itself—in this case through the continuing recruitment of role players into the political structure. It maintains its basic patterns through "political socialization." Most importantly, in this connection, all political systems more or less tend to resist rapid or radical change and demands for such change. This leads us to another, equally important, point: If the political system tends to resist change and demands for change, pressure and stress are likely to build within the system—i.e., dissatisfaction is likely to grow among the population and political groups, resulting in alienation and the search for alternatives of leadership and/or structures. The extent of such alienation is likely to vary with the ability of the political structure to absorb the demand input (either expanding its structure and functions, or transforming the input into output). If demand articulation is not permitted into the decision-making apparatus or is too heavily screened on the way, the stress is likely to be great.

On the other hand, political systems vary also according to their capacity to resist demands for change. Communist systems, for instance, have maintained impressive police, military and paramilitary forces for this purpose, thus foreclosing alternatives to the regime in power.

This, in bare outline form, is the conceptual framework within which our empirical analysis will proceed. We have already shown that the Communist political system, as developed in Eastern Europe under Stalin's auspices, stood at the totalitarian extreme of the continuum of political development:* its hard boundaries encompassed all aspects of national life; it permitted very little or no autonomy to its component subsystems; though its functions were fairly well differentiated, its structure was highly centralized; output predominated over input, and the latter was severely restricted to the system's highest echelons; recruitment was almost exclusively ascriptive; and socialization was

---

*We use the word "totalitarian" here to denote a political system which (1) "allows no recognition of or representation to other political parties" or group interests, and (2) seeks to "control all aspects of national life." From *Webster's Collegiate Dictionary,* 5th ed. and 7th ed., respectively.

politically controlled. In all of these aspects the political systems of the three countries under consideration were virtually identical. They were artificially constructed according to the Soviet blueprint regardless of the socioeconomic development which these countries had achieved. Political development, in the sense discussed in this chapter, began only after the period of the construction of Communist control was over.

We have established our search pattern. At this point, then, we can begin our description and analysis of the political systems of our selected three Communist countries of Eastern Europe as they embarked on their economic reforms.

Notes

1. Yevsei Liberman published his basic ideas for economic reform in 1956. *Kommunist,* No. 10 (1956); cited in Marshall I. Goldman, "Economic Growth and Institutional Change in the Soviet Union," *Soviet Policy Making* Peter H. Jungler and Henry W. Morton, eds. (New York: Frederick A. Praeger, 1967), p. 81, n. 1. The Polish economist (and erstwhile Professor of Economics at the University of Chicago) Oskar Lange argued for decentralization and rationalization in various articles published in 1956 and 1957, as did Friedrich Behrens and Arne Benary in East Germany. See Carola Stern, *Ulbricht,* translated by Abe Farbstein (New York: Frederick A. Praeger, 1965), p. 212.

2. *Rabotnichesko Delo* (August 1, 1963); cited in Radio Free Europe, *Bulgarian Background Report* (August 3, 1963). Hereafter cited as BBR.

3. BBR, (March 13, 1963), p. 3.

4. BBR (October 19, 1963).

5. "Expensive Furniture in the Rain," *Rabotnichesko Delo* (May 20, 1960); Radio Free Europe, *Bulgarian Press Survey* #245. Latter is hereafter cited as BPS.

6. Radio Free Europe, *Hungarian Background Report* (August 24, 1961); ibid. (January 26, 1963). Hereafter cited as HBR.

7. HBR (September 6, 1962; August 7, 1963).

8. Wolfgang Eschricht and Joachim Granitza, "Bedarfsforschung—Wichtige Aufgabe des industriellen Absatzes," *Einheit* (March, 1963).

9. A brief but vivid account of this trend in the Soviet Union and its impact on the Soviet economy is given by Goldman, op. cit., p. 71. For a comprehensive analysis of the Soviet economic system, see Nicolas Spulber, *The Soviet Economy: Structure, Principles, Problems* (New

York: W. W. Norton & Company, 1962), especially Chapters 1, 12, and 13. East European Communist economic structures are analyzed in an earlier work by Spulber, *The Economics of Communist Eastern Europe* (Cambridge, Mass. and New York: The Technology Press of the Massachusetts Institute of Technology and John Wiley & Sons, Inc., 1957).

10. Gabriel A. Almond and G. Bingham Powell, *Comparative Politics: A Developmental Approach* (Boston and Toronto: Little, Brown and Company, 1966), p. 19.

11. For a complete exposition of this approach, the reader is referred to Almond and Powell.

12. David Easton, "The Analysis of Political Systems," *Comparative Politics: Notes and Readings,* Roy C. Macridis and Bernard E. Brown, eds. (Homewood, Ill.: The Dorsey Press, Inc., 1961), p. 83.

13. We are departing here from Easton's model and borrowing from Karl W. Deutsch, *The Nerves of Government* (New York: The Free Press, 1963), especially pp. 88-91, 128-31.

6 Bulgaria

Economic Reform

Bulgaria was, along with East Germany, among the countries of the Soviet bloc that began to reform their Communist economic structures (at least experimentally) even before the Soviet Union did. Like all of the other bloc countries, however, Bulgaria did not move toward economic reform before the publication of Liberman's article in Moscow's *Pravda* had legitimized the idea of decentralization. Although the Bulgarian leadership publicly gave credit to Soviet guidance in the formulation of its economic decentralization program and its blueprint for reform bears a strong resemblance to that of the USSR, Bulgaria is among the few countries in the bloc in which a genuine public debate occurred on the reform issues before the actual reform program was published.*

The Bulgarian reform program did not comply with the full scope of some of the economists' demands for decentralization. But, in view of the fact that it went beyond the degree of decentralization envisaged by the USSR's own economic reform blueprint, one must suspect that the influence of indigenous economists in the forging of Bulgaria's new economic system was significant. At the same time, the initial impetus for Bulgaria's economic reform came from above. The economists did not begin to issue ideas on the subject until the Bulgarian party government had committed itself to reforming the economic structure;

---

*The others were the USSR and Czechoslovakia.

and, perhaps just as important, the Bulgarian party government did not move in this direction before the Soviet regime had (symbolically) removed some of the doctrinal fetters from Stalin's economic system by printing Liberman's article in *Pravda.*

The Eighth Congress of the Bulgarian Communist Party (BCP), which was convened in November, 1962 (two months after Liberman's article appeared), issued a resolution hinting broadly at the need to improve planning and to increase the scope of worker participation in both the formulation and the implementation of plans.[1] This resolution also stressed the importance of both moral and material incentives as a means to this end.* By May, 1963, the Politburo of the BCP had already prepared some general guidelines for reform of the economic structure for approval by the Central Committee. Experimentation with these guidelines began during the summer of the same year in a small number of individual state enterprises.[†] At the same time, Bulgaria's enterprises continued to be merged rapidly into giant associations ("trusts"), probably in order to create an intermediate administrative level which would help to insure the party-government's continuing control in the coming decentralization.

In April, 1964, some 50 enterprises in a variety of industries, construction, and trade were drafted into the experiment; and in 1965 their number was further enlarged. By the end of 1965, some 44 percent of Bulgaria's total industrial productive capacity was operating under the experimental system.

Demands for Reform

Among the three countries under consideration, Bulgaria was the only one which experienced what appears to be a genuine, albeit low-key, public debate about economic reform during the two years preceding the official commitment of the party-government as to the nature and scope of the reform. The debate was rather one-sided, in that the reform advocates were doing most of the writing; but occasionally an

---

*In Communist countries the practice has been to reward labor with as little pay as possible and to compensate for the resulting apathy with "moral incentives,' such as competition, or overtime work mobilization in honor of an important political or historical event. This evidently has not produced the desired results; hence the recognition of the utility of "material incentives."

†Which would pay each employee according to his work and let the workers share in the profitability of the enterprise.

article appeared which defended the old economic system or some of its features that were under attack.

In general, the debate focused on the relationship of the central control and planning organs to the enterprise and their respective functions. Most frequently the blame for Bulgaria's economic malaise was heaped on the shoulders of the central planning organs or on the excessively centralized economic system itself. Central planners were condemned for having issued faulty plan indexes which resulted in gross waste, because they did not correspond to "objective economic laws."[2]

Not only was centralized planning called inefficient, but it was also claimed to be unnecessary. Liberal reform advocates contended that most of the work of central organs in the economy could be carried on better by the enterprises themselves. Party-government control over the economy could be just as adequately and more efficiently maintained through indirect (fiscal and other regulatory) means.[3]

Under the prevailing (Stalinist) system, the interests of the state and the enterprises were deemed at odds.[4] But if profitability were to become the key index of enterprise performance and the governing criterion of management, the interests of state and enterprises would be identical and would render most of the prevailing plan indexes superfluous. Enterprise managers and workers could be expected to work more efficiently if their own interests rather than those of the state were involved.

But if profitability were to become a workable concept in Bulgaria's new economic system, then enterprise autonomy from the state would have to extend beyond mere plan targets. Most of the participants in the debate appeared to agree on the necessity of a price reform. In Communist Bulgaria, as in all other Communist countries of Eastern Europe, prices had always been artificially set; they bore no direct relationship to the costs of production—indeed, production cost analysis had never been a highly developed practice in Communist economics. There were economists in Bulgaria who thought that the state ought to leave price determination entirely to the enterprises. Those who advocated this radical departure from Communist practice also emphasized the necessity for competition among enterprises, which would lead to price determination according to supply and demand.[5]

The advocacy of free competition between enterprises on the basis of consumer choice led almost inevitably to an attack on the party-government's policy of amalgamating enterprises into trusts, which

... can impose on the citizen goods for which there is no demand, which are of poor quality or at high prices, as sometimes happens in practice.

Under these conditions, the normal market relations are impossible, the law of cost cannot play its stimulating and regulating role.[6]

Trust monopolies, according to this opinion, would rob enterprises of all incentive to increase their productivity, quality, and design and to lower their prices.

The attack on the trusts was vigorously supported by collective farm chairmen as well as district party and government organizations.* They expressed their grievances against the disadvantageous position of collective farms in relation to the state purchasing monopolies and demanded equal rights.[7]

Demands for economic reform were by no means one-sidedly in favor of decentralization. Although liberal ideas such as those summarized here dominated the Bulgarian press, there were some writers who felt that a mere improvement in central planning methods and greater worker discipline would pull Bulgaria out of its economic rut.† According to this view, the regime should avoid far-reaching decentralization. Bulgaria is the only country among the three under consideration whose media published such competing concepts for economic reform.

---

*The attack on state purchasing monopolies by collective farm chairmen may be very significant in view of a (then) recent ruling of the Bulgarian Council of Ministers that these chairmen shall be elected by secret ballot in a number of districts. *Kooperativno Selo,* (January 20, 1966), cited in Radio Free Europe, *Bulgarian Situation Report* (January 27, 1966. Hereafter cited as BSR.) It was impossible to ascertain whether or not those who demanded the abolition of monopolies in the agricultural sector (or a curbing of their powers) were newly elected cooperative farm chairmen; but it is probable that incumbent chairmen wanted to improve their record among their constituencies with a view to coming elections.

† Those who argued against decentralization were inclined to attack the liberal reform advocates. Petrov's article (op. cit.) thus became the object of particularly sharp controversy, unusual for Bulgaria's ordinarily submissive public media. On the one hand, it gave rise to further demand articulation from the countryside for the abolition of monopolies which the party-government was then still in the process of establishing. On the other hand, it was the object of severe attacks by conservatives who wanted to maintain the centralized economic structure. Among the latter, see Atanas Lyutov, "A New Way of Planning, or Rejection of Planning—What Does Assistant Professor G. Petrov Suggest?" *Rabotnichesko Delo* (January 16, 1966); and Georgi Baburski, "A New Way of Planning, or Economic Chaos," ibid. (January 20, 1966). For coverage of both articles, see BBR (January 25, 1966).

Needless to say, this intellectual awakening in the economic sector represented a challenge to the Stalinist economic system such as Communist Bulgaria had never experienced in the 20-odd years of its existence. But the available evidence is not sufficient to allow a definitive interpretation of the role of the economists and other writers in the economic reform of that country. It is impossible to say with certainty, for instance, that these writers acted as independent thinkers expressing their own views, even though many of them demanded reforms amounting to a reversal of the regime's policies (such as the abolition of the trust monopolies). Two alternative interpretations are equally possible. The first one is that the writers acted as agents of competing factions within the Bulgarian leadership, as often happens in Communist systems. The second interpretation is that Moscow's changing attitude on economic management (symbolized by *Pravda's* publication of Liberman's article) and the ensuing debate in the Soviet Union encouraged by Bulgaria's economic thinkers to speak their own minds, taking their cues from their Soviet colleagues.

Neither of these interpretations is mutually exclusive. The true one may well be a combination of these, such as that the economic debate in the Soviet Union was interpreted in Sofia as a signal to start thinking about change, which may have bolstered the arguments of reform advocates in the Bulgarian ruling circles, who in turn encouraged the economists to articulate their own ideas for decentralization.

There is little doubt that the Bulgarian leadership was serious about generating and experimenting with new ideas for reform. In July, 1964, for instance, the Council of Ministers issued a decree according to which specialized enterprises subordinate to the People's Councils (local administrative units) and cooperatives producing small items would (on an experimental basis) be almost entirely autonomous of state control. These enterprises, apparently not a part of the more general reform experiment, would be allowed to fix their own indexes on output, labor, and costs on the basis of contracts signed by them according to the prevailing (and growing) demand for their products. They would be able to determine the price for their products in agreement with the trade enterprises or, failing this, through the mediation of the competent district People's Council. According to this decree, the only plan index centrally determined for these enterprises would be "the profits and payments made into the budgets of the respective peoples' council and the state."[8] This decree was basically in line with a more liberal revision of policy toward private artisans, intended to improve the supply of goods and services in the countryside.[9] In view of this decree, even the most liberal reform demands mentioned here (save those calling for the abolition of trusts) did not appear to be irreconcilable with the new outer parameters the regime had set for the economic reform.

Although the Bulgarian regime appears to have been in favor of instituting liberal economic reform, there are also indications that it was internally divided on the scope of the reform. The party chief, Todor Zhivkov, admitted that while most people were eager to rush into economic reform faster than even the regime was ready to proceed, "certainly some people will not be delighted."[10] Disagreement at high levels was further indicated by several postponements. The regime promised to publish its theses on the economic reform in August, 1965, and they were to be discussed throughout the country before final enactment. The publication of the theses, however, was delayed until December 4, 1965.[11] A Central Committee plenum had been scheduled for January, 1966, to discuss and approve the theses on economic reform. It was twice postponed, and finally convened in April, 1966.

Bulgaria's Economic Reform Theses

The theses reveal that the autonomy of the role players in Bulgaria's economy would increase, especially at the enterprise level. But this autonomy would be provisional, in the sense that most enterprise decisions and actions would remain subject to approval and control at higher levels. The trust was to be the administrative pillar of the new economic system.

The most significant change introduced by the new economic system was the approach to economic planning. According to the theses, each individual enterprise would make contracts with its suppliers and customers without central direction. These contracts—provisional and subject to approval at various points within the administrative-hierarchical ladder—would form the basis of the enterprise's annual production plan. Enterprise plans would then be approved and consolidated by the trusts; thereupon they were to be submitted to the relevant ministries. Once approved by the ministries, enterprise plans would form the basis of the national economic plan. At any step in the hierarchical ladder from the trust to the state planning agency, contracts concluded by the enterprise could be disapproved. The state thus sought to assure the continuing production of essential but nonprofitable goods in the new economic system. Enterprises engaged in the experiment apparently had shown themselves too eager to shift their production lines to those commodities which were most profitable.

Central planning, thus, would continue in Bulgaria, but its process would be reversed. Four obligatory planning indexes would remain: (1) the volume of the basic production, (2) the limit on capital investment, (3) the limit of some basic materials of production, and (4) the spending and earning of foreign currencies in external trade.

The theses envisaged a comprehensive price reform according to criteria and principles yet to be determined. It was clear, however, that price determination would continue to be largely but no longer exclusively the prerogative of the state. There would be three types of prices: (1) inflexible—for capital goods and some essential consumer goods, prices would be fixed by the state; (2) flexible—on a wide range of products, the state would fix the upper and lower limits of the price and leave the rest to the enterprises; (3) free—on seasonal and locally produced goods the price would be at the discretion of the producer. There was some room for competition.

Under the new system the enterprise would be required to establish and maintain a variety of separate funds for (1) technical improvement, (2) research for new production, (3) social and cultural programs, and (4) remuneration. The state would determine the percentage of enterprise income to be paid into these funds.

The new economic system provided for a number of indirect economic controls in the hands of the state. The turnover tax on the various stages of production (always a basic fiscal measure in Communist economies) would help to regulate the price of commodities and, thus, the profitability of production. Production funds would be taxed to encourage their rational use. Enterprises were encouraged to deposit idle production funds with the State Bank and receive interest. There would also be a tax on income distribution, enabling the state to exercise indirect control over the remuneration of labor. In addition, the state would directly regulate the basic wage norms. Subject to these controls, and after the obligatory fund deposits, the remaining profits could be distributed as material incentives to the workers and staff.

The new economic program fell far short of the measures the more liberal economists and administrators would have liked to see adopted. Nevertheless, if implemented, Bulgaria's new economic model would allow a degree of enterprise autonomy from the state such as had not been in existence since the Communists came to power. The importance of this will be analyzed in a later chapter.

Developments in the Bulgarian Labor Sector

Bulgaria's new economic system would significantly increase the prerogatives and responsibilities of the enterprise managers. How would the workers fare under the new rules? This was a question in which there was, undoubtedly, widespread interest among the people.

At the beginning of Bulgaria's experiment with economic reform, some six months after the initial guidelines were issued, an article appeared in the theoretical monthly journal of the BCP which raised the demand for a significant extension of "democracy" to the workers. Fearful that the increased powers of enterprise managers contemplated in the new economic model would not be balanced by a concomitant growth of "enterprise democracy," and observing that some managers were abusing their powers to the disadvantage of the workers, Miloshevsky made the following suggestion:

> Parallel with the rights of the directors, the rights of the working people of the individual enterprises must be increased. It can be considered that the conditions are already ripe for the creation of such an organ in our state enterprises, through which the workers shall participate in the solution of many questions of production, connected with the organization of labor, with the labor remuneration, with the distribution of the profit; that they shall have a word to say even in the appointment of the director of the enterprise, etc. [12]

It will be noted that these ideas are the very essence of the Yugoslav Workers' Council system. The public appeal of this article, or for the Workers' Council system in Bulgaria, however, is difficult to assess. No further public demands for worker management were uncovered in the course of the research on Bulgaria. In all probability, the regime felt that the propagation of the idea of genuine workers' participation in management was too dangerous to be tolerated.*

The variety of competing public demand articulation which was brought to bear on the subject of economic reform in Bulgaria was not duplicated in the labor sector. Unlike the Hungarian trade unions, those in Bulgaria continued throughout the period under consideration as the obedient transmission belts of the party-government. Characteristic of

---

*Significantly, however, the author of this article was allowed to continue articulating his liberal persuasions on economic reform.

their subservience to party control was the resolution issued by the Trade Union Congress held on May 9, 1966, which called for the continuing "struggle for mobilizing the creativeness and the energy of the working collectives through the further unfolding and enriching of socialist competition and a movement for Communist labor. The struggle for speedy and continuous rising of productivity of labor must be placed in the center of attention."[13] The resolution, however, criticized individual trade union organs for their lack of zeal in the continuing struggle against "the violators of labor and technological discipline and the squanderers of socialist property," as well as against "all forms of bourgeois ideology and against the unthinking worship of anything that comes from abroad."

In Bulgaria, as elsewhere in Eastern Europe, economic reform, aimed at increased efficiency, brought in its wake a certain amount of economic dislocation as more efficient methods of production were introduced and some workers became superfluous. In Bulgaria, however, this problem was less acute than in more highly developed countries such as Hungary. Nevertheless, it is worth noting that the Bulgarian Council of Ministers issued a decree on January 20, 1967, setting forth measures for indemnifying, retraining, and reemploying workers dismissed because of job obsolescence.[14] No public demand articulation was observed in connection with this measure, but in view of this decree, it must be assumed that the Bulgarian leadership was made aware of the problem through channels other than the public media. Evidently, then, with respect to labor problems, Bulgaria's public media were not an important vehicle of demand articulation.

It should be added that in Bulgaria there was a dire shortage of labor in certain industries, notably mining and construction. A number of legislative decrees on labor have been issued, each containing preferential clauses for workers in mining and construction. Similarly, the decree on obsolete workers set forth additional indemnification for workers willing to take jobs in these industries.

This suggests that, in view of a labor shortage, worker dislocation through job obsolescence was not yet likely to lead to a conflict situation. As will be observed on the Hungarian scene, the dislocation problem there was more acute and may have contributed significantly to the evolution of the Hungarian Trade Union Council into an associational interest group.

The Formation of Production Committees

In May, 1963, the session of the Bulgarian Central Committee session which issued the guidelines for economic reform also issued a decree for the establishment of Production Committees. These committees, composed of elected representatives from each production team within an enterprise, were to participate in a consultative capacity in the management of the enterprise. The procedure for election was by open (as opposed to secret) ballot, leading to the assumption that the workers had little or no choice in the selection of the committee members.[15] Furthermore, the director of the enterprise, the president of the trade union, the undersecretary of the local party committee, and the secretary of the local Komsomol (youth organization) were ex officio members of the Production Committee.[16]

The Bulgarian Communist Party theses on economic reform, published in December, 1965, describe the functions of the Production Committees as follows:

> Through the Production Committees the workers' collectives participate in deciding on the basic problems connected with the development and improvement of production, the timely commissioning of production capacities, the improvement of the quality of production and increasing the profitability of the enterprise, the correct distribution of the income and the systematic improvement of the working and living conditions for the workers, the selection of the managing and other cadres, etc. The managers of the enterprises ensure the fulfillment of the decisions of the Production Committees and take into consideration their suggestions, while observing the legal provisions.[17]

According to Doroinov, the Production Committees meet about once every month.

> The usual question to be discussed is an appraisal of the work of shops, departments, and some individual comrades during the past month. The director of the factory informs the committee on the state of the plan fulfillment of each department and workshop, and suggests their rates. The Production Committee discusses these rates and reports their acceptance of them. A report on the factory plan for the coming month follows, questions concerning it are discussed, and decisions are made.[18]

To say that the Production Committees are only consultative bodies and that enterprise directors' decisions are final would probably be an oversimplification of one-man management combined with plant democracy. "It is much more complicated than that . . . *the Production Committees, as managing bodies, make decisions which are obligatory for the directors."*[19] To be sure, "only the director has the power to issue practical instructions to the operative management. However, should the director disregard an instruction by the production council committee, the latter has the right to appeal before higher organs of the administration, the party, and the trade unions, depending on the issue in dispute."[20]

It may be surmised from the above elaboration of the functions and powers of Production Committees that their primary purpose is to act as checks and balances upon the management of enterprises. Neither of the authors who have written on the subject mentions the interests of the workers as coming within the purview of the Production Committees. Their functions appear to be primarily economic-managerial. The extent to which Production Committees will be able to perform these functions effectively will, of course, depend upon their technical competence. In this connection, one writer[21] complained that the Production Committees were still unable "to understand the economics of the factories" and were not even conversant in economic terminology; hence, their activity had not been particularly impressive.

The Bulgarian Legislature

In the legislative realm, Bulgaria's political development proceeded very slowly during the period under consideration. By the end of this period (1967) it could be said that the institutional framework for parliamentary action had been visibly widened, but the degree of sustained parliamentary activity had not increased commensurately.

The liberalization of Bulgaria's National Assembly began with a speech by Politburo member Encho Staykov, Chairman of the National Council of the Bulgarian Fatherland Front, to a Central Committee plenum in March, 1962.[22] In this speech, Staykov argued that legislation should be the prerogative of parliament and decrees should be issued only in exceptional cases. Draft bills should be promptly submitted to the legislative commissions for study prior to debate on the floor of the House. Furthermore, Staykov insisted, it was the constitutional right of the deputies to question the ministers of the government.

As far as we know, this was the first time such demands had been aired publicly at such high levels in the Bulgarian Communist Party. It is interesting here to speculate that, in the wake of the Twenty-Second Soviet Party Congress, the party leadership might have been moved to increase the scope of parliamentary activity slightly and that Staykov was given the task of addressing the Central Committee on the subject, but in doing so, Staykov may have gone beyond the limits intended by his colleagues in the Politburo.* This speculation aside, the resulting net gain for the Bulgarian parliament was the introduction of an optional question period and an increase in the number of parliamentary commissions from six to eleven. During the question period, deputies could, upon prior notification in writing, interrogate the government.

For the next three years no significant events connected with the Bulgarian legislature were reported. If the increased number of commissions had any effect on parliamentary activity, it was not overtly reflected on the floor of the House. Parliament met two to three times a year, two or three days each session, rubber-stamped the decisions of the regime put before it, and dispersed again without any visible ripple in public attention. As far as is known, no questions were asked of the government during the legislative sessions in 1963 and 1964.

At the Tenth Session of the Fourth National Assembly (elected in November, 1962), for the first time in Bulgarian Communist history two government ministers (of Home Trade and Public Health) presented accounting reports.[23] According to a UPI dispatch from Sofia, dated June 22, 1965, the Minister of Home Trade submitted his report in response to a formal interrogation. His report was followed by one from the National Assembly Commission for Trade, after which there was an unusually lively debate of both reports in which 19 deputies made speeches critical of the many deficiencies in the Bulgarian economic system. The resulting resolution (voted unanimously) approved the policy of the Ministry of Home Trade but called for greater efforts to satisfy consumer demands.[24] It recommended further that

---

*We must emphasize that this is speculation based on a very few events. For one thing, the Bulgarian Parliament gained no more than an "optional" question time in 1963 and used it only once during the next two years. To suggest that Staykov's demands, voiced at the March, 1962, Central Committee plenum, might have been acceptable to Bulgaria's leadership would stretch the limits of credulity, considering the record of that leadership.

Staykov was, however, reelected to the Politburo and the Central Committee at the Eighth Bulgarian Communist Party Congress in November, 1962, and retained his chairmanship of the National Council of the Fatherland Front. This indicates that either he had not yet lost favor with the leadership or it was simply inopportune to drop him at that time. (This was the time in which the Stalinists—such as Chervenkov and Yugov—were being deprived of their posts in the Bulgarian Party). Nevertheless, Staykov lost both of his party posts at the Ninth Bulgarian Party Congress in November 1966, and in May, 1967, he was replaced as Chairman of the National Council of the Fatherland Front. He was 66 years old, and there was no evidence that his retirement was voluntary.

accumulated, unsalable stocks of consumer goods be sold at discount prices and that the ministry discontinue its purchases of low-quality goods. Similarly, the report by the Minister of Public Health was followed by a report of the National Assembly Commission for Public Health and a subsequent critical debate on the floor.

These debates, together with a number of rubber-stamping formalities, made this an unusually busy session. It was the subject of a laudatory lead article in the party daily, which put this milestone of Bulgaria's socialist development into the following perspective:

> ... for the first time ministers appear with accounting reports in the National Assembly, submitting to broad and highly competent evaluation the activities of the department which they head, uncovering the shortcomings and difficulties in their own work and asking for the assistance of the deputies to give them a new impulse in their work.[25]

According to this article, many deputies had suggested that this practice be continued in future sessions.

Except for an occasional, vague hint by Todor Zhikov that the role of the National Assembly should be strengthened, public demand articulation regarding an increase in legislative activity was notable only by its absence. Behind the scenes, however, the question was obviously being debated. For in July, 1966, several noteworthy (in the context of Bulgaria's political system) amendments were made to the rules of the National Assembly. First, the hitherto optional question period was made mandatory at each session. Second, the option of secret voting was introduced (by adding to the old rule that "voting in the National Assembly is done openly" the new clause "unless it decides that the voting shall be secret"). Third, the number of National Assembly Commissions was again increased from 11 to 13.[26]

Earlier in the same year it was reported that the local People's Councils were electing their executive committees by secret ballot.[27] The significance of this development is questionable, inasmuch as the First Secretary of the District Party Committee, usually a member of the People's Council, presents the list of the candidates for the executive committee. "Under such circumstances it is natural that nobody dares to make a different suggestion. The people's councillors approve the suggestion and by secret ballot elect unanimously the whole executive committee as suggested."[28]

Since then—at least until 1968—no events of comparable significance have been reported concerning the Bulgarian legislative process. In his Accountability Report to the Ninth Bulgarian Communist Party Congress in November, 1966, Todor Zhikov listed some outstanding tasks for the future. Among these were (1) drafting a new constitution; (2) increasing the role of the National Assembly; (3) giving some legislative initiatives to the mass organizations, such as the trade unions, the Fatherland Front, and the Komsomol; and (4) strengthening the role of the People's Councils.[29] At the end of the time for this study, none of these projected role expansions had been initiated by the Bulgarian regime.

Summary of Bulgaria's Political Development

The final enactment of Bulgaria's new economic model was preceded by a variety of publicly articulated demands for reform. Many of these demands went beyond the scope of the reform legislated by the regime, particularly in the realm of role-player autonomy. Some of the demands competed not only with each other but also with the institutions of the political system. Of the three countries under consideration, Bulgaria is the only one in which this type of public demand articulation occurred.

At this time it is impossible to define precisely the extent to which the Bulgarian leadership was influenced by the demand articulation in the public media. The fact that the actual scope of economic reform fell short of the scope of the demand is not, by itself, an indicator of the influence of demand articulation, for political systems seldom conform to the full scope of the public demand. But that the type of demand articulation does exert some influence upon change in the political system will become clear later in the study, where a comparative analysis of the data presented in this and the following two chapters will be made.

The essence of Bulgaria's economic reform was to grant the role players at the various levels increased independence of action. But much of this independence was provisional and subject to approval by higher authority. Nevertheless, the new economic model was designed to promote some independent initiatives among the enterprise managers, staffs, and workers, by making the enterprise a self-supporting economic unit and basing material rewards of all role players on the profitability of the enterprise. Thus the pursuit of personal material interests (albeit controlled at higher levels in the hierarchy) was embodied in Bulgaria's economic reform. This has the potential to open further possibilities for further political development.

74

Contrary to the expectations of the postulated hypotheses, there was no parallel development in the trade unions or the legislature of Bulgaria. Both of these subsystems remained the obedient tools of the party leadership. Although, during the period under examination, there was an increase in parliamentary activity and an expansion of parliamentary committees, the activity itself did not manifest a significant increase in autonomy. Nevertheless, the new economic model has been in operation for only a very short time, and the expected spillover effects may yet reach these institutions. Indeed, Zhikov's promise that the role of the legislature, the local councils, and the mass organizations would be expanded in the future may be a sign of latent forces already at work.

Notes

1. Published in the Bulgarian party's daily, *Rabotnichesko Delo* (November 16, 1962), see BBR (December 16, 1965).

2. Ivan Mironov, "The Efficient Use of the Basic and Turnover Funds and of Material Incentive," *Ikonomicheska Misal*, Mp/5 (1964), translated in BPS #542. See also D. Nachev, "Profit—A General Economic Index," *Partiyen Zhivot*, No. 13 (1964), translated in BPS #551; and P. Kunin, "The Systematic Development of the National Economy According to Plan and the Principle 'From Each According to His Abilities, to Each According to His Work' Under Socialism," *Novo Vreme* (December 12, 1963), translated in BPS #503.

3. Mironov, op. cit., adduced the following example of central planning inefficiency: Between 1959 and 1962, capital investment had grown by 38 percent, while unfinished construction financed by this investment had risen 108 percent. To remedy costly discrepancies such as this, Mironov suggested that indirect controls, such as a property tax on unused reserves and interest-bearing loans for investment, would encourage optimum use of resources at the disposal of enterprises.

4. D. Nachev, op. cit., observed: "The enterprises are interested in withholding some of their reserves when making draft plans, so as to be given power over planned targets, thus making it easier for them to fulfill these targets at an earlier date. The interests of the state are the exact opposite." He also contended that, since the state takes 75 to 97 percent of the enterprise's profit, and since the personal income of the manager and worker is not affected by an increase or decrease in profit, there is no incentive to make production more efficient.
Kunin, op. cit., argued in the same vein that the Bulgarian party government was managing the economic system as if the society had already developed to the highest stage of Communism, where abundance for everyone made material incentives superfluous. On the contrary, Kunin maintained, during the transition stage, the conscience

of socialist man is unreliable, for man is still motivated primarily by material remuneration according to his work.

5. See, for instance, Georgi Petrov, "For a New Way of Planning," *Rabotnichesko Delo* (January 13, 1966), summarized with extensive quotations in BBR (January 25, 1966). Kunin, too, advocated price determination through market forces. Miloshevsky, on the other hand, was more equivocal on this issue. While he contended that free price determination would violate "established proportions of the national economy," he also thought that it might be feasible to leave the price of certain products entirely at the discretion of the enterprise. Nachev argued only that prices be realistically fixed so as to make the concept of profitability feasible.

6. Petrov, op. cit.

7. See BSR (February 10, 1966), p. 2.

8. From a Bulgarian Telegraph Agency report of July 11, 1964, cited in BBR (August 26, 1964).

9. See, for instance, the decree of July 6, 1964, cited in BBR (May 13, 1965).

10. Interview with correspondents from *Le Monde* (Paris), published February 26, 1966, cited in BBR (March 1, 1966).

11. See BBR (December 16, 1965).

12. Professor Angel Miloshevsky, in *Novo Vreme* (November, 1963), cited in BBR (December 10, 1963).

13. "End of the Trade Union Congress," BSR (May 17, 1966).

14. *Darshaven Vestnik,* No. 8 (January, 1967); BSR (February 9, 1967).

15. Ivan Doroinov, "Production Committees—New Committees in the Industrial Plants," *Chervino Zname*, (November 20, 1964); BPS #555.

16. Jacques Calderon, "A New Form of Worker Participation in the Management of Factories," *Partiyen Zhivot*, No. 7 (1965); BPS #576.

17. "The Bulgarian Theses on Economic Reform," BBR (December 16, 1965), p. 11.

18. Doroinov, op. cit.

19. Calderon, op. cit.

20. Ibid.

21. Doroinov, op. cit.

22. "Sixth Congress of Fatherland Front Ended," BSR (May 18, 1967).

23. "National Assembly Session," BSR (June 24, 1965).

24. "More Discussion Than Usual in National Assembly Session," BSR (June 29, 1965).

25. *Otechestven Front* (June 25, 1965), cited in BSR (June 29, 1965).

26. "Old Hacks Still Enjoying Priority," BSR (July 19, 1966).

27. "Secret Ballot in Election of District Executive Committee," BSR (March 3, 1966); "Secret Ballot in People's Councils Elections Confirmed," ibid. (March 10, 1966).

28. "More Secret Ballot in People's Councils Elections," BSR (April 26, 1966).

29. "The Ninth Bulgarian Party Congress—An Appraisal," BBR (November 25, 1966).

7   Hungary

Economic Reform

In Hungary, the need for economic reform was more pressing than in Bulgaria. Its annual growth in labor productivity had slowed from seven percent in 1961 to 3.6 percent in 1964.[1] With a high foreign trade turnover—36 percent of its national income in 1965—Hungary was in a poor competitive position in world markets. Furthermore, it had contracted a huge foreign debt, largely during the aftermath of the Hungarian Revolution of 1956, and the notes were due almost simultaneously.[2]

Aside from the foreign trade factor, domestic demands were changing, thus necessitating greater flexibility in output.[3] Hungary's economic development had apparently reached a transition stage from a seller's market to a buyer's market.

In March, 1964, Reszo Nyers addressed the party Central Committee's Political Academy on the importance of technical development to the Hungarian economy.[4] He asserted that Hungary's technical development fell far short of that prevailing in capitalist countries and candidly cited a number of interesting reasons for this shortcoming. First, the prevailing Communist belief that technical obsolescence was a feature peculiar only to capitalism had helped retard Hungary's economic development. Second, centrally planned targets had given priority to socialization and control of the economy, to the exclusion of technical development. Third, heavy emphasis on quantitative plan fulfillment had drawn attention away from the need to improve quality and design of the output. Fourth, complete lack of competition between enterprises operating according to a central plan, which guaranteed the sale of their products to state-owned purchasing agencies, had obviated the need to modernize plants. Consequently, Nyers asserted:

> As the low standard of our technical development is the chief reason for our backwardness, it must also become the chief factor in our progress .... Technical development constitutes an economic juncture in Hungary upon which all our economic-political efforts converge. Therefore, if we are able to attain a general rise in the level of technical development, we will approach the solution of the major part of our economic problems.

Technical development of the Hungarian economy, Nyers suggested, required some bold initiatives at the enterprise level. It involved research and experimentation, not all of which would pay in the long run. But the risk factor, in Nyers' (erroneous) opinion, was much greater in capitalist than in socialist countries because, in the former, the enterprise had to assume all of the risks, while in the latter most of the risk was absorbed by the whole society (through the state budget). Nevertheless, he called upon enterprise managers to invest sums in research and development in excess of the funds allocated to them by the state for this purpose, meaning that they should assume a greater part of the risk themselves.

Although the need for economic reform was clearly evident to Hungary's party leadership, there was also an equally evident reluctance to hasten into the problem haphazardly. There was little overt evidence of division within the leadership on the subject; rather, one could see an inclination to cautious deliberation. It was not until December, 1964, that the Hungarian Politburo presented its preliminary reform guidelines to the Central Committee for approval. These guidelines, however, were never published. Two months later, on February 11, 1965, Hungary's party chief and (then also) Premier, Janos Kadar, gave the Hungarian Parliament an indication of the party-government's approach to the formulation of a comprehensive economic reform program.[5]

First he roundly criticized the faulty implementation of essentially correct party directives at all levels of the administration, up to and including the ministries. Then he announced that the "mechanism of economic management" would be reappraised, with a view to its more rational development. The regime, he said, would proceed with deliberation and avoid "adventurous experimentation." It would be ready within a year to introduce a revised "economic mechanism."

Several weeks later, Reszo Nyers revealed in an interview with the party daily, *Nepszabadsag,* that

> Broad and concrete preparatory work was started in the wake of the Central Committee resolution passed in December 1964. For examining the various problems of economic management, *we set up eleven work groups made up of approximately 130 economists, engineers, lawyers, factory experts and scientific researchers.* Each work group makes use of the knowledge of additional experts. Thus, even at the initial stage of the work, the number of participants is relatively large and is going to get larger [emphasis added].[6]

After these initial announcements, there appeared a large number of articles in Hungary's party and theoretical journals pertaining to economic reform. By and large, these articles contained more systematic, comprehensive, and sophisticated analyses of economic problems and associated ideological issues than those which appeared in Bulgarian periodicals. The difficulty arises in deciding whether one can properly categorize the ideas expressed in Hungary as demand articulation. For, with few exceptions, these contributions were more descriptive of problems and proposed solutions under consideration within the party-government (presumably the study groups of experts) than they were demands for solutions which the government should consider. Competing and conflicting demands for economic reform were absent from Hungary's public media.

Aside from occasional allusions to the fact that expert discussion groups had been established to debate the direction of Hungary's economic reform, the news media, as far as we know, were silent on the proceedings of these groups. Since not even the preliminary guidelines were published, one is entitled to the assumption that the regime wanted to forestall public debate on economic reform issues. The gathering of the country's experts into closed discussion groups fits this assumption: behind closed doors they could air their views and debate with party-government leaders without danger of public agitation.

Looking back to the revolution of 1956, the leadership had every reason to be sensitive to the potential volatility of Hungarian public sentiment. This sensitivity can be seen in the defensive attitude of the leadership lest the public get the impression that fundamental changes were under way or the corollary impression that past patterns of action had been wrong. Thus, Hungary's public media insisted that the economic reform currently in the making would not result in a new economic system, but in a new economic mechanism. Reszo Nyers, among other leaders, went out of his way to defend past policies, saying:

> One . . . erroneous interpretation, of which I would like to speak right at the beginning, is the conception according to which everything that we have done thus far has been incorrect and wrong and that we need a new economic mechanism, because the basic line adopted in the past has proven to be unsuitable.[7]

On the contrary, Nyers asserted, the present economic reform was made necessary by the transition of the Hungarian economy from its "extensive" (quantitative) to its "intensive" (qualitative) stage of development. The latter stage requires different techniques and objectives.[8] This explanation was often echoed in the Hungarian press as the standard justification for economic reform.

Considering the pressing need for economic reform, the Hungarian regime's deliberate approach to the problem would suggest that the leadership wanted a new model that would work from the very beginning. Thus, there is good reason to believe that the experts were allowed to speak their minds freely behind closed doors, i.e., that the *in camera* demand articulation was autonomous. This is indeed reflected in the new economic model, adopted in 1967, which will be described below. It turned out to be the most "liberal," in the sense that it granted the greatest degree of autonomy to the economic role-players.

The debate on Hungary's economic reform in the public media was largely consensual; presumably it reflected the progress and consensus reached behind closed doors by the party leaders and expert groups.* At this point, we will briefly summarize the more important reform issues debated in the public media.

Consensual Public Debate

Excessive centralism was roundly blamed for Hungary's economic

---

*This impression is confirmed by Politburo member Jeno Fock's authoritative statement: "One of the important features of work connected with the economic mechanism is that, already at this stage, we can start to prepare the cadres for the new system. This means that the recognition that our methods of economic management have to be transformed and further developed in the direction we plan to follow, is rendered unambiguous and general. We have to inform a broad circle of people of the new requirements made by the introduction of the new mechanism upon the various levels of leadership and economic management. Increased efforts have to be made to advance the theoretical knowledge of leaders." Op. cit.

malaise. In an article appearing in the Hungarian party's ideological monthly,[9] it was pointed out that enterprises had been hanging on to the central apparatus, to the detriment of their own initiative. There were several crucial functions which the central institutions simply could not administer effectively. Among these were (1) more effective exploitation of reserves which were located at the local level;[10] (2) production coordination, which, if administered centrally, would only lead to an enlargement of the bureaucratic structure without solving the most basic problems;[11] (3) regulation of supply and demand of manpower, which had defied all attempts at centralized administration.

The solution to these problems lay in delegating functions and responsibilities to the enterprise that would allow it to operate for profit. This, Nyers told the Hungarian party's Central Committee in November, 1965, must be acknowledged as a fundamental principle of a socialist planned economy. He went on to say that obligatory plan indexes would be gradually reduced, and he envisaged that they would eventually be abolished altogether. Enterprises would be allowed to formulate their own yearly and longer-term plans on the basis of their customers' requirements in terms of quantity, quality, and delivery dates, with the ultimate aim of increasing profits. Jeno Wilscek saw a rather far-reaching implication for production-trade relationships arising out of the profit role: enterprises should be allowed to select the market for their domestic and/or foreign products in order to maximize their profits without central interference.[12] In this respect, however, Nyers cautioned that enterprise independence should not be misinterpreted to mean that the enterprise could place its interests above those of the community. They would continue to be guided and influenced by the center, but through economic rather than administrative means. Essentially, however, enterprises should be free to manage their own affairs to such an extent that they could no longer blame extraneous factors beyond their control (i.e., centrally determined factors) for their inability to perform their essential tasks. Wilscek also was particularly emphatic on this point. Enterprises, though owned by the state, should be self-managing, self-supporting, and self-developing.

Since modernization of productive processes was deemed an essential prerequisite to achieving a competitive position in foreign markets, Hungary's enterprises should be encouraged to take calculated risks with a view to increasing their profitability. In Nyers' opinion, the role of the state bureaucracy in investment decisions should be reduced. Dr. Thomas Nagy, Professor of Economics, opined in a radio address that firms should be able to determine the growth of their fixed and working capital in order to increase their future incomes as well as those of their workers.[13]

In another radio broadcast, Finance Minister Timar indicated that in the future, the state's banking institutions should have the power to lend or refuse money to an enterprise for development projects.[14] In the past, banks had to grant credits to enterprises if investment plans had been approved by central authorities. This new proposal apparently gave rise to some anxiety lest the banks become too powerful and take over the role of the central authorities.[15] As a compromise, it was suggested that if an enterprise could not get a loan from one bank, it could turn to another.

As in other countries of Eastern Europe, the financial remuneration of management and labor was to depend upon the profits earned by enterprises. But there should be a limit to enterprise discretion in profit distribution. Although the regime's guidelines concerning wages and profit distribution still remained to be worked out, one commentator noted:

> It is obvious that the division of the profits cannot be left to the decision of the firm, because it is feared that in such a case the aims of development would suffer. Thus, it is reasonable that the maximum ratio of the profit [which the firm could add] . . . to the share fund should be centrally fixed. Finally, it is also necessary centrally to regulate and restrict wage increases, because too big wage increases would diminish profits and the net income of society, thereby slowing down the development of the people's economy and causing inflation.[16]

Price reform could not be carried out until 1968, but future prices would be designed to promote harmony between supply and demand. They would reflect both social outlays on production and the extent of fixed and working capital used by enterprises, so as to develop a more economical structure of consumption. Furthermore, export and import prices should exert an influence on the cost and income of producing and marketing enterprises. While the new price-fixing practice would not surrender the principle of state control, it would become more flexible. Nyers, in a speech to the Hungarian Central Committee in November 1965 predicted that a threefold pricing structure, similar to Bularia's new economic model would be developed for Hungary's economy: (1) centrally fixed prices, (2) flexible prices within limits fixed by the state, (3) free prices.[17]

In Hungary, however, world prices would have a direct influence on domestic prices:

> It ·is desirable that the system of price and incentives be capable . . . at least until full-scale introduction of new foreign trade prices, i.e., until 1 January 1967—to give an idea of the trends of the socialist foreign trade prices. This is necessary above all, in the case of firms using mainly import products or firms producing mainly for export. In both these cases, changes in market conditions (including price) ought directly to orient the development of the qualitative and quantitative factors of production. The future rate of such impulses will be greater than in the past.[18]

In this connection, Nyers, in his Central Committee speech, was critical of the monopolistic position of trading enterprises, which made them impervious to consumer demand. He asserted that foreign trade would continue to be centrally directed, but by means of foreign exchange regulations. He advocated that an increasing number of producing enterprises be allowed to carry out direct dealings on foreign markets (thus bypassing the trade enterprises). Nyers further suggested that retail shops in the domestic economy should be allowed to buy from the wholesale firm of their choice and even directly from the producing enterprise. Then, he continued, "Any clash between the interests of the sellers and buyers should further the assertion of the social interest."[19]

It would appear, in the final analysis, that the price-commodity relationship should stimulate production, according to demand for the quality and design of the product; it should also stimulate an increase in the productivity of the enterprise.* In this connection, it is interesting to note that during 1965 the Hungarian party-government resorted to the capitalist expedient of selling its substandard goods at a discount in order to reduce its stocks. As reported by Premier Gyula Kallai to the Parliament in November, 1965:

---

*Tallos complains: "Even if, after comparison with world market prices, our foreign trade organizations admit that some of our export goods are—to put it mildly—obsolete and require modernization, nothing is done to induce the producers to take notice of this. . . ." Op. cit.

This year the internal trade network organized 13 sales of cutrate clothing and sundry industrial articles. This enables the public to buy at prices one billion forints cheaper than at the original fixed prices .... Profits derived from the sales were such that, while reducing stocks and freeing storage space, they also brought to light certain weaknesses in production and marketing. No proper coordinating exists between consumer needs and production.[20]

From this discussion of Hungary's public debate on the economic reform issues, it is readily apparent that a decisive shift had taken place in the thinking of the Hungarian leadership. This shift had not left the ideology untouched, as will be seen in the following discussion of an article by Central Committee member Istvan Friss in the party ideological monthly, which will summarize this discourse.[21]

According to Friss (basing his argument on the authority of Friedrich Engels), one of the assumptions underlying the Communist economic system had been that

anarchy within social production is replaced by conscious organization according to plan. Nobody had—and even could not have had—definite concepts about how much time would be needed until the change signalled by Engels would be completed and until ... people would make in full conscience their own history, until the social forces brought into motion would have the desired effect, and the leap of humanity from the realm of necessity into the realm of freedom would be completed.

Obviously, Friss pointed out, the time factor had been underestimated.

As Lenin had once been forced to concede, so the Hungarian Communist Party had to recognize "that the commodity-money relations had not stopped."

In our society, too, the sales activity inserted itself between production and utilization. For a long time we believed that, if according to the plan every produced item were utilized, this would have to be so in reality, too. But it is not so. In our country, too, goods must prove their utility on the market. Socialist planning and the socialist economic plan restricted to a great extent the anarchy and spontaneity of the capitalist market, but could not fully eliminate them. ...

We had to learn at our own expense that these laws cannot
be left out of consideration.

If Friss's article genuinely reflects the party's attitude, then the
ruling Communists of Hungary had apparently learned that impersonal economic forces govern the relationships between the role
players in the economy and, hence, govern economic progress.
Moreover, these impersonal forces were not amenable to central
control at the will of the Communists. The Hungarian party leadership had learned, furthermore, that there are only certain general
economic processes and trends susceptible to central planning and,
even under the best of circumstances, "planning inevitably contains
elements which are unknown or not very well known and which
can only be estimated with a greater or lesser degree of accuracy."
Among these unknown elements are weather conditions, the price
evolution in foreign markets, changes in consumer tastes, and the
like. On the top of that, Friss suggests, planners are human, and
humans often make mistakes.

> It follows that . . . it is not at all certain whether what was
> consciously planned is good and desirable from the viewpoint
> of society, or that the unplanned, the spontaneous, is bad
> and harmful for society. We could only consider things in this
> way if we were certain that what the plans stipulate is not
> only based on good intentions, but also on correct percep-
> tion, consideration, and foresight . . . . Our plan does not al-
> ways have those advantageous qualities.

As a consequence, the party's guiding role suffered. But under the
new economic mechanism to be instituted in Hungary, the party's
guiding role would be strengthened. It would be based on a more
scientific foundation. The party was better aware of its limited
capacity for manipulation—i.e., that there are some things better
regulated by market forces than by party directives. Thus, if market conditions developed differently from what the plan foresaw,
the party would make appropriate adjustments in the plan because
the party had learned that it could not know everything. As for
the implications for the managers of this commendable rise in
humility within the party leadership, Friss pointed out:

> In the course of our work on the mechanism, many people
> raised the question: How far can we go increasing the inde-
> pendence of enterprises, lower level bodies and managing

units, without jeopardizing the plan? The general opinion is that it is the correct thing to grant maximal independence to the managing units, but in the meantime to establish circumstances and conditions, under which—in possession of their full independence—they will consider it worth while, to the purpose, and financially interesting, to execute matters that suit the central plan without any instruction.

The Economic Model

Hungary's new economic mechanism was put into law by a degree of the Hungarian Revolutionary Workers and Peasant Government.[22] This decree sets forth the relationship between the state enterprise, state authorities, and the workers. Its most notable feature is the degree of autonomy granted to the enterprise and, more specifically, the enterprise director, as summarized in the second section of Paragraph 8:

> The director decides—within the context of the provisions of law—independently and by assuming individual responsibility in enterprise affairs. Notably:
>
> (a) In the determination of the enterprise plan
> (b) The exercise of employers' rights according to the Labor Code
> (c) In matters of technical development
> (d) In credit matters
> (e) In the drawing up of contracts
> (f) In the determination of products and choice of products
> (g) In questions of development by the enterprise's own resources (investments)
> (h) In the establishment of the enterprise balance
> (i) In matters of association with other economic bodies (common enterprise, merger, etc.).

New enterprises can be established by competent ministries or other "bodies with nationwide authority," or by the Executive Council Commission. The founding agency must endow the new enterprise with the assets to begin operation. Once an enterprise is thus established and a director has been appointed, according to the decree, the enterprise and its director enjoy the full scope of autonomy granted by the decree. It is accountable to the founding agency, but if its performance is satisfactory—i.e., if it operates profitably—the powers of the founding body to interfere in its operation appear to be quite limited.

Paragraph 15 of the decree states that the enterprise must divide its profits in three ways:

1. commitments to the state (taxes, interest on capital, etc.)
2. development and reserve funds (investment capital, and insurance against temporary deficits)
3. profit sharing fund, as well as contributions to social and cultural purposes.

The first two commitments are defined by "a special provision of law," not stipulated in the decree. What is left may be deposited into the profit-sharing fund, in the distribution of which the trade unions will have a voice.

Should the enterprise run a deficit beyond the capacity of its reserve fund, and "provided a profitable operation of the enterprise cannot be guaranteed in some other way," the founding agency may "initiate supervisory control."[23] It can do this only by establishing a reorganization commission, composed of three to five members, to take charge of the enterprise. If no way can be found to run the enterprise efficiently, or if the enterprise's functions can be performed more efficiently by another enterprise, the founding agency may terminate the enterprise.

Otherwise, the limits of state power to interfere in the operation of the enterprise are striking:

The founding enterprise can issue instructions to a factory for some specific activities *only in exceptional cases,* if the economic interest (the solution of a military task, fulfillment of inter-state commitments, etc.) cannot be guaranteed *through economic means or are not suitably efficient* [emphasis added].[24]

There are, however, several safety clauses in the decree which give some indirect control powers to the founding agency. It can, at its own discretion, establish trusts, consisting of a number of enterprises and headed by a director-general with supervisory powers over each constituent enterprise, although the enterprises keep their own separate accounts. Alternatively, the founding agency may establish a control commission "in larger enterprises."[25] The commission, however, can only make suggestions and reports regarding the operation of the enterprise. Both of these measures impinge upon the autonomy of the enterprise at the discretion of higher authority, but they fall far short of giving state organs the direct control powers they enjoyed under the old economic model.

On the other hand, the decree allows enterprises, at their own initiative, to pool their resources in mergers or more limited functional associations. This must have the approval of the founding agency or agencies of the enterprises concerned. The head of such an association would be selected by the member enterprise directors, subject to approval by the competent minister. Such an association, however, could in no case affect the operational independence of the enterprise.

One additional safety clause endows the competent ministry with the power to control and/or terminate any activity by associations which it deems to be "contrary to the public or economic interest."[26] This may refer to such activities as price collusion or other monopolistic operations, but the decree is no more specific on the meaning of public or economic interest.

Although the decree is a curious mixture of ambiguity and specificity, it leaves little doubt that the powers of the state vis-à-vis the enterprise have been drastically curbed. It does not once mention a state economic plan, but it is quite explicit about the enterprise director's prerogative to formulate the enterprise's production plan.

Even in the formulation of prices the autonomy of the enterprise director appears to have been considerably enhanced. A separate decree on consumer price regulation, published on December 14, 1967, divided Hungary's consumer goods into four price categories: (1) fixed prices, (2) maximum prices, (3) regulated prices, and (4) free prices.[27] This decree does not give any details as to the types of goods in each category, but reports prior to this decree stated that fixed prices would cover about 20 percent of consumer goods.[28]

It was clear, however, that most of Hungary's goods (about 60 percent) were priced below actual cost of production, while some (30 percent) were priced above cost.[29] This would entail a net rise in prices, which the Hungarian party-government was extremely reluctant to enact rapidly. It would, according to official estimates, take 10 to 15 years to reform the price structure of the Hungarian economy.

Hungary's "new economic mechanism" was promulgated as the law of the land in 1968. Since then official assessments of its workability have been guardedly optimistic. On paper it looks as

90

though far-reaching development has occurred within the hard boundaries of the political system: all the means of production are still owned by the state, but they are entrusted to autonomous role players whose powers of discretion are somewhat analogous to those of ships' captains at sea, who are solely responsible to the owners of the merchantmen they command. Perhaps the most encouraging signs for the future of this development are reports of reductions in ministerial staffs concurrent with the phasing out of the old economic model. In 1967, some of the economic ministries lost 40 to 50 percent of their personnel.[30] Henceforth, it would seem to be up to Hungary's managerial elite, more than the party-government, to make the new economic system work.

The Hungarian Trade Unions

The debate about economic reform (conducted for the most part *in camera*) gave rise to a genuine soul-searching about the role of trade unions in Hungary's new economic system. Early in the discussions within the party-government circles and the 11 study groups working on economic reform, it was recognized that whatever improvement the new economic system could be expected to bring about would depend in part on the participation of the workers in the factories. Such participation, it was realized, could best be promoted by increasing the workers' interest in the factory's performance under the new economic model—i.e., by giving the workers a material, moral, and participatory stake in the new system.

The Yugoslav model of worker participation in factory management had attracted the Hungarian workers in 1956. During the Hungarian Revolution, workers' councils had sprung up spontaneously in Budapest and had become virtually the only real organization of economic activity and local government.[31] For some time after the revolution had been quelled by Soviet tanks, the workers' councils remained a serious obstacle to the reimposition of Soviet-dominated Communist rule, calling strikes in response to Kadar's moves to curb their powers. Only in January, 1957, did Kadar feel that his regime was established securely enough to move against the workers' councils: during that month their leaders were arrested, and reliable party members were put in their places.

By the end of 1957, the Hungarian workers' councils were defunct. Kadar's regime had dissolved them and established in their place new "works councils" (or shop councils, as Ferenc Vali calls them).[32] These works councils carried on worker participation in management but left the power in the hands of the party. Two-thirds of their members were drawn from the Communist-dominated trade union ranks; the rest were elected by the workers. With the introduction of the new economic model in 1967, the regime announced that these works councils would not be re-elected.

In view of the experiences of less than a decade before, it is not surprising that the Yugoslav model of worker participation in management was resolutely rejected by the Hungarian leadership.[33] However, although the enterprises would remain under state ownership and the new economic system would give greater power to the managers, collective participation was also thought to be essential. As Nyers explained to the Central Committee in November, 1965, there would be greater coordination between management and workers' representatives on all important decisions affecting the workers. Trade unions should organize the more efficient involvement of the workers in the affairs of the enterprise.

In March, 1965, for the first time local trade union leaders were elected by secret ballot, the list of candidates having been nominated some 10 days before. This new procedure had been established at the Twentieth Hungarian Trade Union Congress in May, 1963. The election returns were not announced; hence it is not known how many incumbents were voted out or how many candidates were rejected. But speaking about the 1965 trade union elections, Zoltan Fabok, a Trade Union Council Secretary, said that the elections had pointed to virtues and defects of the incumbent leadership. Many incumbents had not been reelected because of laxity and failure to avail themselves of their rights, "causing both productive work and the income of the workers to suffer."[34]

It may be that the election by secret ballot of trade union officers at local and intermediate levels gave rise to pressures (or added to existing pressures) for a meaningful role as workers' representatives in the factory. It may also be that the forthcoming abolition of the works councils left a vacuum in worker representation which the trade unions wanted to (and were probably intended to) fill. Perhaps the Hungarian workers were aroused by the announced elimination of the works councils and found ways of conveying their feelings to the trade union leadership. The available information on any of these factors is not sufficient to permit an evaluation of their possible contribution to the stir that became evident in the Trade Union Council of Hungary in 1966. With respect to the trade unions the evidence that autonomous demand articulation was channeled through public media was much more convincing than it was in economic reform debate. That conflicts of interest could—and did—arise between the workers, on the one hand, and management, the state, and the party on the other, was readily acknowledged.[35] "Could there be . . . contradictions between the trade unions and the state organs . . .?" asked Edit Soter, correspondent of the party daily *Nepszabadsag*. "Certainly," said Sandor Gaspar, Secretary General of the National Council of Trade Unions, "in our country, the general interests of the state and the workers, as well as of the trade unions representing the workers, are identical. But there could be, and are, differences of interests and opinions on concrete questions."

Gaspar contended that in the new economic system the trade union officers must be asked to express their opinions before a decision is made, at all levels of state administration, in questions concerning the workers. "In some cases, where there is a disagreement between the trade unions and the state offices, the trade unions should be allowed to publish their contrary opinion. This will be a new feature in the work of the trade unions."[36]

A number of major problems were of grave concern to trade union officials.

1. The drive for higher productivity had, as early as 1965, led to the dismissal of some 13,000 workers.[37] This was a topic of concern at a Trade Union Council meeting where demands were raised that the trade unions make provisions to find new jobs for workers falling prey to efficiency drives.[38] Later, in a published interview, Tivadar Nemeslaki, Chief Secretary of the Steel and Metal Workers' Trade Union, expressed the contrary opinion that

> the trade unions should . . . influence the economic managers in such a way that they will not consider reduction of the work force as the only means for increasing productivity. They should use the means of cutting the work force only at the very worst, and they should create adequate new jobs in the interests of employment.[39]

2. Disposable income and purchasing power had been stagnating in Hungary since 1964. Statistically, however, wage levels continued to rise as the regime included a variety of social benefits in the calculated wages of the workers. Undoubtedly, some of these hidden wages were of real value to the workers; but by 1966 the trade unions had adopted the view that the state ought to call a spade a spade. They maintained, furthermore, that in the future the disposable wage level ought to keep pace with the rising price level of consumer goods and foods.

In preparation for the introduction of the new economic system, the regime had begun to increase prices toward the end of 1965, resulting in a net decrease in purchasing power. Sandor Gaspar acknowledged the necessity of price reform, but evidently he thought that some of the price boosts had been "spontaneous and unwarranted":

> If we fail to take care in the weeks and months ahead, and leave room for such spontaneous and unwarranted economic interests, this may have some harmful consequences.[40]

3. Overtime work had been a standard means for plan fulfillment, but with the drive to increase productivity, the regime was trying to eliminate it. Naturally, this would mean a decrease in the income of the workers involved. The trade unions, Nemeslaki opined, should see to it that the worker earned as much in an eight-hour day as he currently did with overtime. The chief of the Metal Workers' Union implied, however, that this would necessitate an increase in the worker's productivity.[41]

4. Nemeslaki complained also that in some factories the shop stewards had good reason to fear reprisals by management if they took up the cause of the workers too vigorously.

Demands for a Solution

A permanent solution to the four problems discussed above would require a far-reaching reorganization of the trade unions in the factories and a change in their relationships to management and state institutions at all levels. This was the essence of persistent demand articulation throughout 1966, in which the top-level trade union leadership played a conspicuous role.

Most of the writings on the subject ascribed a dual role to the trade unions: (1) educating and mobilizing the workers in social consciousness for greater productivity and (2) defending the interests of the workers. Significantly, however, the stress was almost invariably on the latter function.[42]

In order to protect the interests of the workers and reconcile the conflict of interest between the proletariat and the state, Gaspar suggested that there must be a clear division of functions between the trade unions and their state-managerial counterparts. As a specific example, Gaspar stated:

> The practice whereby the leader of the trade union, as an *ex officio* member of the steering committee of the ministry, should attend all the meetings and approve of decisions, must be abandoned. The leader of the trade union should not be an *ex officio* member of the steering committee of the ministry, just as the minister or deputy minister should not be an *ex officio* member of the Board of the Trade Unions, but the principle should be that the minister, as well as the Secretary General of the trade unions should consider all questions from their special situation and point of view and only after this should the questions concerning the conflict be discussed.[43]

In his speech to the Ninth HSWP Congress, Gaspar asserted that "the safeguarding of [workers'] interests has a new meaning in the work of the trade unions."

> By safeguarding of interests we mean, in the first place, that the trade unions work constantly to strengthen the ruling power of the working classes.[44]

It was clear from the tone and content of his speech that this was more than the usual doctrinaire Communist chatter. Gaspar demanded, among other things, that if a conflict of interest should arise between the government and the workers, it was the trade unions' job to see that the conflict was resolved in the interests of the working class.

Gaspar demanded further that "the Party, as the ideological and political leading force, should ask for the opinion—even in setting the goals—of the class forces assembled in the trade unions."[45]

Perhaps the most persistent issue in the trade union debate in Hungary was that of the rights of the workers (represented by the trade unions) in their relations with management and higher administrative offices. The unions demanded the right to be consulted on all decisions affecting the workers, and veto power on the more important categories of decisions. Thus, Sandor Beckl, a Secretary of the National Council of Trade Unions, stated in an article published in the trade union monthly, *Munka,* that the unions must be consulted "on every question concerning the work and living conditions of the workers."[46] Conflicts arising between unions and management should be aired and, if necessary, resolved at higher levels. "Questions of labor relations should be decided upon only in agreement with the trade unions." The unions should have sole decision-making powers on issues affecting the welfare of the workers, such as work conditions, insurance, safety, holidays, and the like. On management decisions which violate provisions in the "collective contract" (to be discussed below), the unions should have veto power. Beckl stressed the necessity of determining unambiguously "what rights, at what level the trade union bodies and individual functionaires have. If possible, this should be done in such a way that trade union bodies and functionaries may have the same rights at every level as their partner, the economic manager."

In this connection, Tivadar Nemeslaki welcomed an increase in the competence and authority of subordinate managers (at lower levels within the enterprise). He hoped that this would bring about an improvement in worker-management relations because the subordinate manager would then be able to handle conflicts and grievances on the spot, in cooperation with shop stewards and higher union functionaries, whereas under the old system the manager or foreman could avail himself of the convenient excuse that the workers' grievance was beyond his authority.[47]

Contracts. Apparently the Politburo and Central Committee resolutions concerning economic reform had called for the periodic conclusion of agreements between enterprise management and labor—so called "collective contracts."[48] These were not new to the Hungarian communist scene; contracts had been in practice before 1956 but had fallen out of favor after the revolution. Now that they were to be reinstituted, the trade unions wanted to make sure that all of their desired rights would be legally defined. (The contracts, it appears, were to have the force of law.) An article in the Hungarian trade union daily opened with the following passage:

Before long, the collective contract will again become the constitution of our plants. But still, we cannot just take out of the archives and dust off the old one. We need something new and different.[49]

The author of this article then mentioned most of the previously cited demands—the division of functions between management and labor, the rights of the unions as representatives of the workers, and relationships of the trade unions to management and higher administrative organs—as subjects to be included in the contract.

Appointment and Dismissal of Management. Perhaps the most vigorously contested issue not yet covered in these pages was the demand of the trade unions for a voice in the selection, appointment, evaluation, and dismissal of enterprise managers at all levels. This was a demand expressed by virtually everyone connected with the trade unions who wrote or spoke publicly about the future worker-management relations.

On this issue there appeared to be a serious conflict within the Politburo between the representatives of the trade unions and the state. Nyers was quite emphatic about the state's interests when he wrote in October, 1966:

> The state as the owner of state enterprises exercises every sphere of competence connected with the appointment of directors, the account of their activities, and the evaluation of the whole work of the enterprise.[50]

Apparently this did not end the matter, for in his speech to the Ninth HSWP Congress, Gaspar reiterated the demand:

> The measure which states that the opinion of the workers on the judgement, appointment and replacement of economic managers is represented by trade unions, has the purpose of developing plant democracy and increasing the rights of the workers.[51]

Ironically, Nyers was chairman of the Congress session at which Gaspar spoke.

Summary and Evaluation. The debate concerning the role of the trade unions in the new economic model was quite lively and, in this respect, highly unusual for a Communist system. On the whole, however, it was a rather one-sided debate: hardly anyone would argue with the trade union writers. There was only one conflicting demand—on the question of appointment and dismissal of managers—against which the party-government's economic reform chief registered a counter-claim for the state. Thus, while most of the workers' demands on these issues were made by the trade union leadership, there must have been a large reservoir of sympathy for these demands within the party-government. This, indeed, is reflected in the new Labor Code, which broadly defines the relationship of the trade unions to the enterprise managers and the state.

The New Labor Code

The Labor Code was enacted into law by the Hungarian Parliament at its September, 1967, session.[52] It reflects the spirit of Hungary's new economic model in that it prescribes only the general legal framework within which the worker-management relationships will be established, leaving the details to "enacting clauses" to be worked out by agreement between representatives of the state and labor at various levels.* These "enacting clauses" would have the force of executive decrees. At the enterprise level, "collective agreements" between management and trade unions were to be among the enacting clauses of the Labor Code. Significantly, insofar as the collective agreement between management and labor conforms to the provisions of the law, the resulting contract is not subject to approval by any higher authority.

The most significant single element in the Labor Code is its explicit statement on the role of the trade unions, which describes them "as the organs representing, and protecting the interests of the workers," and assigns them certain broadly defined legal rights.[53] No mention is made in the Code of the hitherto primary function of the trade union: "to intensify production, to organize work competitions, and to make secure the leadership of the Party."[54]

---

*At the government level, the state representative would be the competent minister, and labor would be represented by the National Council of Trade Unions. At the enterprise level the representative of the state would be the director, whose counterpart for labor would be the enterprise trade union council. Trade union councils for enterprises and constituent units (factories and plants) were newly established and elected in March, 1967, in order to protect the interests of the workers under the new economic mechanism in which authority and prerogatives of the director and his subordinates in the management of the enterprise would vastly increase.

Questions concerning living and working conditions may be decided on ministerial or lower levels only with the consent of the trade unions; at the Council of Ministers' level, the Central Council of Trade Unions has an advisory role on these questions.[55] Similarly, labor safety rules can be established only by the enterprise director in agreement with the trade union council. The trade unions have the right to check on the implementation of these regulations, and management is bound to honor their request for information on these matters. Should managerial action in these matters be found to be faulty by the trade unions, the latter may ask for remedial measures and, failing this, they may institute proceedings themselves. The unions may exercise a suspensory veto on any managerial decision or action which infringes on the contract or constitutes "treatment offending against socialist morality." This veto will remain in force until judgment is passed by higher authority. The right to participate in the formation of labor dispute tribunals is granted the unions.

In the enterprise, the trade union council has the right to decide on the use of the social and cultural fund, after hearing the opinion of the management.[56] The intriguing question here is whether this clause empowers the trade unions to decide on the way profits are to be distributed among the workers. Paragraph 15 of the decree on state enterprises (on the distribution of enterprise profit into the various funds) states that part of the profits "can be utilized for the increase and supplementation of the workers' income, i.e., *for social and cultural purposes* [emphasis added]," which indicates that profit-sharing is included in "social and cultural funds." Nevertheless, even this interpretation would still leave in doubt the power of the trade unions to decide on profit-sharing. In June, 1967, the Economic Committee passed a decree regulating the sharing of distributable profits among managerial staff workers and other employees. According to this decree, the managerial staff would receive the lion's share (80 percent of their yearly income), whereas the workers' share would amount to only 15 percent. Unless the trade unions can overcome these limitations, there would seem to be severe limitations to their decision-making powers on this matter.

Presumably to ward off retaliatory action by management against trade union officials (shop stewards or workers on the enterprise trade union council) in conflict with management, paragraph 16 states that "the agreement of the immediately superior trade union body is requisite for assigning an elected officer of the trade union to another place of work, and also for the termination of his employment by the enterprise. . . ."

A great many more framework rules are set forth in the Labor Code which are beyond the immediate focus of this study. Some of these are common in the West (such as laws against discrimination, regulations on child labor and pregnant women); others reflect state ownership of the means of production in Communist systems (such as regulation of work time, liability of the worker for willful and unintentional damage, disciplinary measures, and the like). The peculiarity of the latter stipulations is that they are dignified as the law of the land in Communist countries.

The question of the trade union role in the appointment and dismissal of the enterprise director is not mentioned in the chapter of the Labor Code dealing with union rights. But paragraph 10 of the decree (11/1967) on state enterprises is explicit enough:

> After listening to the opinion of the competent trade union body, the director and his deputy (deputies) are appointed and dismissed by the founding body.
> In judging the activities of a director and his deputies, the opinion of the trade union body has to be considered.

This means that the trade unions gained no more than a consultative voice on this issue, which as we have seen, was the subject of a prolonged struggle between them and the state leadership, or, more specifically, between Gaspar and Nyers.

On the whole, the rights of the trade unions mentioned above amount to a favorable outcome of the two-year-long debate on these issues. They endow the unions with real powers and prerogatives to protect the interests of the workers; henceforth much would depend on the aggressiveness of the trade unions in the exercise of their rights on behalf of the workers.

The intention of the trade union leadership to defend the workers' interests seems evident. However, the possibility that they would at some time in the future again defend the interests of the party could not be ruled out. In fact, to say that the vigorous assertion of trade union rights represents a switch of allegiance from the party to the workers would be to stretch this analysis beyond the elasticity of the data. We have seen no evidence that the top leadership of the trade unions was subject to election or recall by the rank and file. Four of the top trade union leaders held seats in the Central Committee;* three of them were noted in this chapter as champions of increased trade union powers.

The fact that these four were elected (or reelected) to the Central Committee in November, 1966, as trade union representatives, precisely during the period of the debate, indicates that the party leadership looked favorably upon their arguments for the protection of the workers' interests.‡

There were strong indications that the Hungarian Communist Party intended to maintain its control over the trade unions; it would be surprising if it did not wish to do so. The party stated that it would continue to guide the trade unions ideologically and politically, but it has forsworn organizational and administrative means. The trade union leaders pay at least passing lip service to the party's guiding role.† This leading role is to be exercised in the future through vigilance and persuasion of the party members within the trade unions, and by introducing "some important questions on the agenda which are being discussed by the trade unions."[57]

When Janos Kadar spoke to the National Congress of Trade Unions in May, 1967, he, too, took pains to reaffirm the independence of the trade unions. Recognizing possible differences of opinion ("otherwise, why would we need two separate organiza-

---

*The four are Sandor Gaspar, Secretary General of the National Trade Union Council (also Politburo member); Sandor Beckl, Secretary of the National Trade Union Council; Gabor Somoskoi, Secretary of SZOT; and Tivadar Nemeslaki, Secretary General of the Metal Workers Union. See HSR (December 6, 1966); HBR (February 6, 1967).

‡Perhaps an even more striking indication of this is the fact that Sandor Gaspar, a former First Secretary of the Budapest City Party Committee (Budapest has provincial status in the territorial organization of the Hungarian party), was switched to the top post in SZOT in June, 1965; and Tivadar Nemeslaki, a former First Secretary of the Kamarom County Party Committee, assumed the leading post in the Metal Workers' Union in the summer of 1966. These two functionaries, together with Sandor Beckl, pumped new life into Hungary's trade unions. Assuming that they were appointed to their posts by the party leadership and that the leadership did not misjudge their sentiments, their appointments would seem to indicate a leadership attitude favorable to the revitalization of the trade unions.

†Said Sandor Gaspar to the Ninth HSWP Congress (in the paragraph of his speech following his above-mentioned demand that the party consult the trade unions in setting the goals): "To say the least, up until now we have to do the same things but in a different way according to the original functions. In short, the party is guiding and activating all the bodies in the system of the dictatorship of the proletariat but it does not work in their stead." "The Work of the Trade Unions Will Become Broader."

tions?"), Kadar stated that the decisions of the party regarding trade unions were "only mandatory for party members working in the trade unions and not for the independent, elected trade union bodies."[58]

An authoritative article in *Partelet* stated: "On the other hand, the Party members are responsible for the acceptance and enforcement of the resolutions of the Party offices and organizations, as a result of their convincing work on the trade union boards."[59] Presumably, this rule would apply from top (Politburo member Sandor Gaspar) to bottom. At lower levels—up to the newly created enterprise council—however, officials are elected by secret ballot with two-thirds majority vote.[60] Theoretically, at least, the union leaders at this level need not be party members.

How much persuasive or manipulative power the party membership in the enterprise and trade unions will retain only the future can tell. A more important issue is how much discipline prevails in the rank and file of the Communist party that could be applied in the execution of party directives. Only the years ahead can yield definite answers to these questions.

The Hungarian Legislature

In 1962 it could still fairly be said that the Hungarian Parliament was a "constitutional fiction," a "rubberstamp" of the party-government's legislative policy, a "pale shadow of what it should be."[61] By the end of 1967 the Hungarian Parliament was well on the way to becoming a real, albeit limited, representative of the electorate and a participant in the national legislative process.

It is clearly evident that Hungary's party leadership was intensely aware of the necessity to facilitate and encourage the active (albeit controlled) participation of the people in the political process, as it had been in the reform of the economy. In April, 1965, for instance, the party's theoretical monthly, *Tarsadalmi Szemle*,[62] published the draft of the Central Committee's "Ideological Guidelines." This, it will be remembered, coincided with the beginning of the economic debate in Hungary. One chapter of this document advocates the extension of socialist democracy in three ways:

(1) A modernization of the institutions through which the people exercise their democratic rights, particularly the Parliament and the People's Councils. The Ideological Guidelines call for clear-

er definition of their functions and call upon scholars to study the question.

(2) A redress of the balance between centralism and local autonomy, aiming at a harmony between general and local interests.

(3) Popular participation in public affairs, to be promoted particularly through better communication between leaders and people at all levels: leaders should supply more detailed and timely information, on the one hand, and on the other, they should show greater willingness to listen to the advice of the workers.

Demands for Reform

Radio and press commentaries in connection with Hungary's Constitution Day (August 20,1965) revealed some of the ferment, particularly in scholarly circles, on the question of popular representation.[63] There appeared to be a consensus that Hungary's Constitution no longer reflected the nation's socialist development, particularly in view of the promised economic reform. Since no revision of the Constitution was then contemplated by the party-government, however, several commentators thought that popular representation in the governmental process could be significantly increased within the current framework.

The demand for reform focused particularly on two problem areas: electoral reform and revitalization of Parliament. One of the most outspoken public advocates of reform, Otto Bihari, Professor of Law at Pecs University and a member of the Communist Party, suggested in the August-September issue of *Tarsadalmi Szemle* that the present procedure of electing parliamentary representatives was "obsolete" in that it did not establish any clear relationship between the deputy and his electors.[64] In parliamentary elections the voters were presented with a single list of candidates, which they could either approve or reject. Bihari suggested that a procedure be adopted whereby each deputy would represent his own district. More audaciously, Bihari advocated that the people be given a genuine choice of more than one candidate at the polls.*

---

*Single-member constituencies were already in practice in local elections of the People's Councils. In the local elections of February, 1963, the electors "had a fair chance to debate the record of the candidates. In 3,800 cases this chance was taken to such an extent that the officially proposed candidate was rejected and had to be replaced by another and in 300 cases no agreement could be reached on a single candidate. So two are being put up, this giving the electors the rare novelty of a choice on February 24." HBR (February 5, 1963). Bihari's proposal,

Addressing himself to the activities of Parliament, Bihari deplored the fact that this (constitutionally supreme) legislative body in practice lacked clear definition of its powers and functions. The Presidential Council made most of the laws, relegating to Parliament such functions as discussing the annual economic plan and the budget. Bihari contended that many of the Presidential decrees were .of such fundamental importance that only Parliament should be empowered to legislate them. The powers and prerogatives of Parliament should be so defined that all legislative issues affecting the interests of the people should come under its direct purview. This would, of course, entail longer and more frequent parliamentary sessions.

Furthermore, Bihari wrote, the powers of the parliamentary committees should be augmented. Drafts of governmental decrees should be submitted to the appropriate committee during the planning stage and in ample time for study. This procedure would enable Parliament, through its committees, to exercise some control over the activities of the Presidential Council, even while Parliament is not in session. Beyond this, Bihari advocated that the parliamentary committees be given independent decision-making powers on certain questions; but he did not elaborate on this point.

All of these recommendations, Bihari wrote, could be adopted without changing the Constitution. There was one additional suggestion, however, which would require constitutional amendment; Bihari thought that in order to draw the people more intimately into the legislative process, the more important legislative issues should be decided by popular referendum. This demand, one may be sure, went far beyond the limits envisaged by even the most liberal of Hungary's party leaders. In fact Istan Szirmai, the party's chief ideologist, Politburo member, Secretary of the Central Committee in charge of the party's agitation and propaganda (AGITROP) section, and presumably the principal architect of the "Ideological Guidelines," downgraded the importance of the reforms proposed by Bihari (without, however, specifically referring to him):

In some places the idea of an election reform has already been raised. It was suggested that we should nominate several

therefore, is not without precedent, at least not on the local scene. Actually, later reports of the local scene stated that electoral contests between two candidates took place in 179 local constituencies. See HSR (March 7, 1967).

persons in each electoral district among whom the voters can choose. We are deliberating this matter and are also trying to find ways and means of rendering parliamentary life more lively. We have also been asked whether, it would not be timely to draft a new constitution. These are significant, but not the most important elements of the democracy of our system.

Let us not create the illusion that we can only broaden socialist democracy with the help of an election reform. More important preconditions of socialist democracy are freedom to criticize and freedom of speech which, in turn, require that the information we provide be comprehensive. During the last few years we have made a considerable advance in this respect; in Hungary, information, freedom to criticize and freedom of speech are guaranteed.[65]

At first glance this statement would seem to imply that Szirmai thought all was well with Hungary's socialist democracy. This, however, would be an oversimplification of Szirmai's position. What was at issue here was a concept of democracy—socialist democracy—which is peculiar to Communist thinking. It amounts to this: Socialist democracy is based on the participation of the people in the vital tasks of national progress, as determined by the Communist Party. The party alone expresses the will of the people and recognizes that widespread popular participation of the people is essential in the execution of the people's will. It is interesting to note that Hungary's party leadership was acutely aware of continuing, sharp differences between its own conception of the people's will and that of the population at large. It was the party's job—i.e., the job of every party member—to bring this dissonance into the open and endeavor to establish harmony by changing the minds of the people to the party line. The Ideological Guidelines were quite explicit about this, and openly critical of Hungary's party organizations for their deplorable laxity in this endeavor. Given the assumption that the people accepted the party's policies and conscientiously engaged in their pursuit, Hungary's leadership was willing to listen to their views about the best way to implement these policies. It was also prepared to encourage popular criticism of government leaders and party leaders at lower levels for the way they executed the party's policy. Such criticism could only serve to keep all of the role players on their toes. But unless the people were properly informed, they could not evaluate the activities of their leaders, nor make constructive suggestions for improvement. Hence, the Hungarian media frequently exhorted local party and economic leaders to draw the people—presumably committed to the party—into the decision-making process, to inform them of the problems at hand and listen to their advice.

At the November, 1965, session of Parliament, Premier Gyula Kallai was quoted saying: "Parliament is the chief depository of the development of socialist democracy." Some MP's had urged the government to intensify parliamentary work. Kallai endorsed this demand as justified, even though, in his opinion, Parliament was "developing continuously, getting richer, [and] its democratism growing stronger."[66]

At the same session, an unusual event took place. A deputy from County Fejer made a formal interpellation to the Minister of Heavy Industry concerning the work conditions of the bauxite miners in his county. Deeming the minister's reply unsatisfactory, the deputy refused to accept it, and the entire House joined him in casting a negative vote. Interpellations are not uncommon in the Hungarian Parliament, nor are negative votes by interpellating deputies; but a unanimous rejection of a ministerial reply by the entire House had occurred only once in Communist Hungary—in August, 1956, two months before the revolution. The present case earned laudatory comment for Parliament in the party's daily, *Nepszabadsag*, to the effect that such action helped to raise the prestige of the House in the eyes of the people.[67]

Bihari's demands for parliamentary reform were echoed in an article by Janos Szentkiralyi, editor-in-chief of the farmers' weekly, *Szabad Fold*,[68] Szentkiralyi recalled Kallai's remark to the November, 1965, session that "Parliament is the chief depository of the development of socialist democracy," and agreed that its activities are improving. Unfortunately, he contended, "this mainly holds true if we compare the present situation with that prevailing 10-15 years ago." He lamented the lacklustre activity of Parliament in plenary sessions, question periods, and committees. "In other words," Szentkiralyi continued:

> We should fully transform into practice Paragraph X of our Constitution which says "Parliament is the highest body of state power of the Hungarian People's Republic. Parliament should exercise all its rights deriving from the people's sovereignty." If we examine the activity of Parliament from the point of view of the above quotation we have to admit that

in many respects, our Parliament is still in its infancy. Excuse me for the expression, but, sometimes, it could be compared to a serious conference rather than a body which is truly the highest organization of state power in a socialist country.

On October 13, 1966, the Hungarian Politburo convened an "enlarged" plenum of the Central Committee and submitted to it a draft of principles for electoral reform. The Central Committee approved this draft and left it to the Council of Ministers to draft an electoral reform bill in accordance with these principles. A month later, on November 11, 1966, the Hungarian Parliament approved the bill unanimously.

The Electoral Reform Law

The essence of the electoral reform law was to create single-member constituencies for members of Parliament, such as were already in existence for members of the People's Councils. The voters would be allowed to nominate candidates at meetings organized by the People's Front. The nominations would then be forwarded to higher headquarters of the People's Front, where, with help of party representatives and nonparty members, the conflicting nominations would be "harmonized," i.e., the final selection would be made.

The possibility for multiple candidates for any constituency was not ruled out; but Ferenc Erdei, Secretary General of the People's Front, who introduced the electoral reform bill into the House, went out of his way to dispel any illusions regarding the political commitments of the candidates. There would be only one platform in future elections: the party's platform. The voters might have a choice of representatives but not a choice of programs. Erdei explicitly ruled out any "stepping back" to a multiparty system.

Speaking for the party on behalf of the election reform bill was Antal Apro, Politburo member and Deputy Premier. He expressed the regime's determination to promote further democratization of political life in Hungary. The competence of Parliament would have to be increased to include preparation of legislative bills. In addition to its legislative activity, Parliament should help to control the implementation of economic reform and address itself to the more important problems of socialism. In the short debate which followed the introduction of the bill, one MP voiced concern about the possibility that not all interested voters would have an opportunity to put forth candidates, since the nomination meetings were to be held in factories, collectives, and shops—which did not include all of the qualified voters. He suggested, therefore, that people who did not work at these institutions be invited to the nomination meetings.

The reformed electoral system was put to the test in February, 1967, only three months after it was enacted into law. Nomination committees met in February (February 2-21), with nearly half of the total electorate participating.[69] Unfortunately, the liberalized nomination procedure did not live up to its full promise: in 340 out of a total of 349 constituencies the electors accepted the official nominee of the People's Front. At an election rally in the Budapest Sports Hall, Janos Kadar was mildly critical of the few multiple-candidate constituencies and predicted that in the future, one would have to get used to contests at the polls. Kadar attributed the lack of contested nominations to the leading cadres' "conscious and revolutionary democratic discipline" at the nomination meetings. Though he added that this attitude was "extremely heartening," the tone of his speech betrayed his feeling that this time it had been somewhat misplaced.[70]

The same "conscious and revolutionary democratic discipline" was in evidence at the elections on March 19, 1967. The returns indicated that the official candidates of the People's Front had received 95-99 percent of the valid votes. In the nine two-candidate constituencies, the official People's Front candidate, appearing first on the ballot, had been elected.[71]

The official interpretation of this lack of voter initiative was that the people were skeptical of the electoral reform; many felt that the old system was the only one possible and did not see the necessity for change. *Magyar Nemzet* endeavored to dispel these erroneous views, maintaining that the electoral reform is not just a mere formality but "an important part of the overall development of our democratic institutions and the expansion of socialist public law."[72]

The New Realignment

Amid frequent exhortations, particularly in the Party daily *Nepszabadsag*, the new House did show a greater vitality than had its predecessor. During its first session of April 14, 1967, it approved the nominations to the new Presidential Council, the Council of Ministers, and the Speaker of the House. This was "business as usual," and the most significant fact about this session is to the credit of the party for its nominations, rather than the Parliament: There were extensive changes in the composition of the government which, without going into detail, pointed to a division of functions between party and government and to the importance of the experts in the administration of the new economic system.*

Also at its first session, the Parliament increased the membership in its 10 standing committees so that they might better cope with their increased functions and competence. The usual committee size of the previous Parliament had ranged from nine to 13 members; augmented committees ranged from 11 to 21. As of 1970 it was not yet possible to give an objective evaluation of the activities of these committees, but it was clear that if the attitude of the party leadership was any indication, they would be infused with new life.[73]

The chairmen of the permanent committees met with Gyula Kallai, the new Speaker of the House, to discuss procedures for increasing the competence and activity of Parliament. They asked for a more important role for the plenum of the House in legislative activity and urged that their respective committees be given the right to participate in drafting laws.[74]

On July 12-14, Parliament met for its first "business session," to discuss economic reform measures proposed by the government. Debate was unusually lively, 57 deputies participating. There were some definite indications that several members were speaking for the interests of their constituents, asking speedy solutions for unemployment problems, location of new industries, and the extension of new economic principles to the private artisan sector.[75]

According to Kallai, the Council of Ministers, on August 3, 1967, had passed on for study the suggestions made on the floor to the competent state agencies, with instructions that the deputies be informed within one month about the steps which the government would take. On October 1, 1967, *Nepszabadsag* reported that 52 out of 57 deputies who had raised problems at the August

---

*To mention just a few examples: Jeno Fock, an economic expert, replaced Gyula Kallai as Hungary's Premier. Kallai is better-known for his parliamentary expertise and liberal views in this area of political activity; he assumed the position of Speaker of the House. The four newly elected Deputy Premiers are all economic experts recognized in their respective areas: Antal Apro (Comecon), Lajos Feher (agriculture), Matyas Timar (finance), and Milkos Ajtai (planning). See HSR (April 19, 1967).

plenum had received "satisfactory" and "acceptable" answers from the state authorities.[76]

The September legislative session (September 27-29, 1967) again reflected the vigor of the new Parliament. It also brought into a more realistic light the relationship of the Hungarian legislature to the party-government. The most important legislative issues were a new Labor Code, a comprehensive law concerning economic reform in agricultural collectives, and a bill concerning the ownership and use of land. The introduction of this legislation, basic to the new economic model, into the House had a twofold significance: first, it showed that the party-government was serious about its promise to increase the legislative functions of the new Parliament (other legislation pertinent to the new economic model had been enacted by decree); and second, it provided a good test of the extent to which the MP's would stand up for the interest of their constituents.

Drafts of the three laws had been circulated for public discussion in April, 1967, and had been extensively debated in meetings at factories and collectives in which parliamentary delegates presumably participated. According to Hungary's Minister of Labor, Joszef Veres, the party-government had modified the Labor Code in line with useful suggestions made at these debates.[77] However, as the party daily pointed out, many of the suggestions had been lost on the way up, and it would be up to the parliamentary delegates (especially to members of the appropriate committees) to insist that they be incorporated in the Labor Law.[78]

According to the information available in the press, 20 House members participated in the debate on the Labor Code and made a total of 50 recommendations. Fifteen of these directly concerned the Labor Code; the others were pertinent to associated executive decrees, the texts of which had been submitted to Parliament. (This latter step, too, was a new feature in Communist Hungary's legislative procedure.) Many of the suggestions revealed (and one of the deputies made bold to say) that the speakers were voicing interests of their constituents.

However, of the 15 suggestions made by MP's for modifications in the Labor Code, only two were accepted by the party-government. The People's Front daily wrote of "grumbling" among the deputies because of this, but tried to justify the party-government's action on the basis that the laws before Parliament sought to set the limits of the freedom of action, not to tie the hands of the role-players who would work within the framework of these laws. Apparently the rejected proposals were intended to regulate in detail the extension of the law, whereas the party-government, in the spirit of the new economic model, wanted the people to remain free to apply their "creative energies."[79] *Nepszabadsag* took a similar stand and proposed that many of the suggestions which were not incorporated into the law would find their way into the executive decrees or collective contracts which would be formulated on the basis of the Labor Code.

All three laws were unanimously endorsed in toto, but not without recognition being given to a flaw inherent in the parliamentary statutes which ruled out House votes on individual suggestions or paragraphs. Gyula Kallai admitted before the House that the statutes would have to be rectified in this respect, and *Nepszabadsag* did not hesitate to support this proposal.[80]

Thus, toward the end of 1967, it was clear that Hungarian party-government meant business in revitalizing Parliament. The fact that the labor and land laws were legislated in Parliament rather than (as had been the custom) in the Presidential Council was evidence of the party-government's intentions. On September 30, 1967, *Esti Hirlap*[81] reported an "information leak," according to which more legislative activity would be in store for Parliament at the expense of government decrees. There were justifiably high hopes in Hungary that the members of Parliament would know how to take advantage of their increased freedom of action in the interests of their constituents.

Summary of Hungary's Political Development

At the end of our research time frame (1968), Hungary's political development had progressed significantly in the three sectors originally hypothesized for this study. In each sector the role-players gained a visible degree of autonomy. Demand articulation was notably instrumental in this political development (though in the economic reform debate it occurred for the most part behind closed doors), and the demands showed relatively little orientation to the political system then in existence—they were largely autonomous.

Interestingly enough, there was very little competition or conflict in demand articulation between the party-government and the champions of change. One would have expected much more opposition by conservative elements within the party than came to light in the public debates. Actually, only two cases of conflict (or potential conflict) were noted in this chapter: one between Gaspar and Nyers on a trade union demand, the other between Bihari and Szirmai on the former's demand for constitutional change. This leads to the conclusion that the party leadership was already to a large extent sympathetic to the changes demanded and, one suspects, discriminated (by censorship) against the more conservative forces. The key question concerns the cause and effect relationship between demand articulation during the reform period and the party leadership's commitment to change. This may well be one of those circular questions for which all answers are debatable.

Notes

1. J. F. Brown, *The New Eastern Europe: The Khrushchev Era and After* (New York: Frederick A. Praeger. 1961), p. 291. Comparable figures for Bulgaria are 9.2 and 4.5 percent and for East Germany, 5.3 and 6.5 percent. (The last figure for East Germany was recorded in 1963.)

2. Jeno Fock, "On Some Timely Questions Connected with Economic Development," *Tarsadalmi Szemle* (October, 1965); Radio Free Europe, *Hungarian Press Survey* #1651. Hereafter cited as HPS.

3. Reszo Nyers, "Problems Connected with Our System of Economic Management," (July, 1965); HPS #1621.

4. Reprinted in *Nepszabadsag* (March 12, 1964), under the title "The Role of Technical Development in Our Economic Policy." Reviewed in HBR (March 19, 1964). Nyers was then a candidate member of the Politburo and Secretary of the Central Committee of the Communist Party, in charge of economic affairs. One may assume that his remarks reflected the views of at least a segment of Hungary's top party leadership, since in 1966 he was promoted to full Politburo membership.

5. "Kadar's Important Speech on Home and Foreign Policy," Radio Free Europe, *Hungarian Situation Report* (February 12, 1965). Hereafter referred to as HSR.

6. "On the Transformation of the System of Economic Management," *Nepszabadsag* (April 25, 1965); HPS #1594.

7. Nyers, op. cit.

8. See also Jeno Wilcsek, "The Role of Profit Within the Management of Factories," *Tarsadalmi Szemle* (March, 1965); HPS # 1587.

9. Nyers, op. cit.

10. Fock, op. cit., HPS # 1651, p. 2.

11. Nyers, op. cit.

12. Wilscek, op. cit.

13. Thomas Nagy, "On the Role of Economic Mechanism," *Radio Kossuth,* (December 8, 1965); HPS # 1669.

14. "Interview with Finance Minister Timar," HSR (February 18, 1966).

15. *Nepszabadsag* (February 15, 1966), cited in HSR (February 18, 1966).

16. Nagy, op. cit.

17. "The 'Comprehensive Revision' of the Hungarian Economic System," HBR (November 23, 1965).

18. Gyorgy Tallos, "Price Modifications in Comecon," *Figyelo* (December 15, 1965); HPS # 1672.
   Another economist, Andras Raba, wrote in Hungary's foreign trade monthly that "Market impulses, the flexible perception of price and value relations, and reacting to them, would further our international competitiveness, and make possible a greater exploitation than the present of advantages deriving from foreign trade. It would also make it possible for the stimulating effects of world economy to prompt into greater development our internal production forces, without endangering the stability of our planned economy." Andras Raba, "Export and the Economic Mechanism," *Kulkereskedelem* (July, 1965); HPS # 1626.

19. Central Committee speech (November, 1965).

20. "Prime Minister Gyula Kallai Addresses Parliament," HBR (November 17, 1965).

21. Istvan Friss, "The Plan and the Market," *Tarsadalmi Szemle,* (November, 1966); HPS # 1766.

22. Decree No. 11/1967, published in *Magyar Kozlony* (May 13, 1967); HPS # 1822.

23. Ibid., Paragraph 19. This procedure becomes mandatory for the founding agency "if this was suggested by the Minister of Finance, by the President of Central Control Commission or by the competent bank."

24. Ibid., Paragraph 25.

25. Ibid.

26. Ibid., Paragraph 37.

27. HSR (December 19, 1967).

28. HBR (December 12, 1967). According to the information contained in this report, only three price categories were envisaged before the actual decree was issued, the "regulated prices" being left out. Maximum price ceilings would be imposed on about fifty percent of Hungary's consumer goods and the rest would be free of price control.

29. HSR (January 5, 1968).

30. "Reorganization of Three Economic Ministries," HSR (June 27, 1967).

31. United Nations, Report by the Special Committee on the Problem of Hungary, Ernst C. Helmreich, ed., *Hungary* (New York: Frederick A. Praeger, 1957), p. 362.

32. See Ferenc A. Vali, *Rift and Revolt in Hungary* (Cambridge, Mass.: Harvard University Press, 1961), p. 394. For an excellent survey of the evolution of Hungary's workers' council to works councils, see HBR (October 5, 1963).

33. Nyers, op. cit.

34. "Elections of Local Trade Union Officials," HSR (April 2, 1965).

35. Edit Soter, "Statement by Sandor Gaspar, Secretary General of the National Council of Trade Unions (SZOT)," *Nepszabadsag* (June 19, 1966); HPS #1724, p. 3. See also Tivadar Nemeslaki, interview with Edit Soter in *Nepszabadsag* (October 16, 1966); HPS #1757.

36. Ibid.

37. Nyers' interview in *Partelet* (May, 1965); HPS #1599. Nyers stated, however, that only 7,000 were actually dismissed, while the

others had been transferred or retired. "In the future," Nyers continued, "unjustified increases in manpower have to be avoided and then there will be no need for large-scale dismissals."

38. Nemeslaki, "The Trade Union Council Debates Economic Reform," HSR (March 4, 1966).

39. Soter, "The Reform of the Trade Unions and the Economic Mechanism," *Nepszabadsag* (October 16, 1966); HPS #1757.

40. Sandor Gaspar, "In the Interest of Society, in Defense of the Worker," *Nepszava* (August 14, 1966); HPS #1737. In this context Gaspar wielded a two-edged sword: His statement concerned not only the party-government but also the enterprise manager and the factory trade unions. He feared that the trade unions might feel inclined to support managers who wished to push up the price of their products in order to increase profits, in which the workers would share.

41. Soter, "The Reform of the Trade Unions. . . ."

42. Among the most notable articles in this respect are Soter, "Statement by Sandor Gaspar. . . ."; Sandor Beckl, "The Reform of the Economic Mechanism and the Trade Unions," *Munka* (August, 1966), translated in HPS #1740; Gaspar, "The Increased Role and Tasks of the Trade Unions in Our Country", *Tarsadalmi Szemle* (September, 1966), translated in HPS #1745; and Gaspar, "Speech to the Ninth Hungarian Socialist Workers' Party Congress," translated in HPS #1772.

43. Soter, "Statement by Sandor Gaspar. . . ."

44. Gaspar, "The Work of the Trade Unions Will Become Broader," speech to the Ninth HSWP Congress, excerpted and summarized in *Nepszabadsag* (December 2, 1966); HPS #1772, p. 5.

45. Ibid.

46. Beckl, "The Reform of the Economic Mechanism and the Trade Unions," *Munka* (August, 1966); HPS #1740.

47. Nemeslaki, HPS #1757.

48. Beckl, "Enterprise Democracy in the New System of Economic Management," *Partelet* (August, 1966); HPS #1739. Contractual agreement between management and individual workers was also in vogue in Bulgaria and East Germany. The difference between these two countries and Hungary was that the Hungarian trade unions intended to make the contractual relationships work in the interests of the workers.

49. Gyorgy Lepics, "What the New Collective Contracts Will be Like," *Nepszava* (November 19, 1966); HPS # 1768, p. 4.

50. Reviewed in HSR (October 28, 1966).

51. HPS # 1772.

52. "Law II of 1967 on the Labor Code," *The Hungarian Gazette* (October 8, 1967); HPS # 1877.

53. Labor Code, Paragraph 11. (1): "It is the right of the trade unions—as the organs representing and protecting the interests of the workers—to work consistently for the improvement of the level of the workers' material, social and cultural standards, to protect their rights and interests affecting their living and working conditions and to put those rights and interests into practice; to draw the workers into this activity and to inform them about these matters; and to represent them in contacts with the management of the enterprise and with government organs."

54. Ernst Helmreich, ed., *Hungary* (New York: Frederick A. Praeger, 1957), p. 272.

55. Labor Code, Paragraph 12.

56. Ibid., Paragraph 13 (4).

57. Unsigned, "Party Guidance of Trade Unions," *Partelet* (July, 1966); HPS # 1728.

58. "Trade Union Congress Ended," HSR (May 9, 1967).

59. "Party Guidance of Trade Unions."

60. HSR (April 2, 1965).

61. "A Hungarian Parliamental Session of More Than Usual Interest," HBR (November 6, 1963).

62. "The Hungarian Party's 'Ideological Guidelines,' " HBR (April 13, 1965). The Ideological Guidelines are not to be confused with the guidelines for economic reform, which, as far as we know, were never published.

63. "Constitution Day," HSR (August 20, 1965).

64. "Tarsadalmi Szemle on Electoral Structure," HSR (August 31, 1965).

65. *Tarsadalmi Szemle* (November 1965); HPS # 1661.

66. Quoted by Janos Szentkiralyi, "A National Workshop," *Szabad Fold* (January 30, 1966); HPS # 1683.

67. Joszef Veto, "Before the Entire Nation," *Nepszabadsag* (November 16, 1965); HPS # 1663.

68. Szentkiralyi, op. cit.

69. *Magyar Nemzet* (February 22, 1967); cited in HSR (February 24, 1967).

70. HSR (February 24, 1967). The tone in Kadar's speech was echoed in an unsigned article, "Places with Two Candidates," in *Magyar Nemzet*, (March 21, 1967); HPS # 1810.

71. "New Parliament and Local Councils Elected," HSR (March 21, 1967).

72. Ibid.

73. See HSR (July 18, 1967) and other HSR's cited in this connection above.

74. *Magyar Nemzet* (May 6, 1967); cited in HSR (July 18, 1967).

75. Ibid.

76. "Hungary's Parliament Begins to Assert Itself," HBR (October 9, 1967).

77. *Nepszabadsag* (September 28, 1967); cited in HBR (October 9, 1967).

78. Ibid. (October 1, 1967); cited in HBR (October 9, 1967).

79. *Magyar Nemzet* (October 1, 1967); cited in HBR (October 9, 1967).

80. *Nepszabadsag* (October 1, 1967); cited in HBR (October 9, 1967).

81. Cited in HBR (October 9, 1967).

8   East Germany

Economic Reform

In point of time, East Germany was the first country in the Soviet bloc to begin comprehensive economic reform. The East German new economic model was fully developed as of July, 1963, when it was approved by the State Council (Staatsrat) and published as "Guidelines for the New Economic System of Planning and Management of the People's Economy."[1] Experimentation with economic reform had begun in four industrial branch associations (Vereinigungen Volkseigener Betriebe—hereafter referred to as VVB's) sometime in March, 1963,[2] and these guidelines were to govern the operation of the entire East German economy as of January, 1964.[3]

No public demand articulation regarding the new economic model was invited and, in the course of this research, none was observed. (Of course, we again make a distinction between genuine, spontaneous demands for economic reform, on the one hand, and educative expositions concerning the applications, procedures, and requirements of the new economic model, on the other. Of the latter there is a great deal to be found in East Germany's public media, exhorting, admonishing, and mobilizing all concerned in support of the Guidelines.)

Walter Ulbricht, East Germany's First Party Secretary, showed himself as the supreme authority on East Germany's economy throughout the period. This is not markedly inconsistent with the general pattern of Communist rulers, but it does contrast sharply with the comparative humility which has characterized the political conduct of Janos Kadar. One finds in the exhortative writing on East Germany's economic reform so many references to Ulbricht's speeches as to make one believe that he is the object of a personality cult.[4]

If the Guidelines published in 1963 were intended as the new economic model for East Germany, the practice during the subsequent four years demonstrated that they were merely the basis of a prolonged experiment in economic reform. And, although public demand articulation was notable largely by its absence from the press and journals covered in the course of this research, one can surmise from defensive statements by East Germany's leaders that the regime was subjected to various kinds of pressures from below, particularly from the managerial elite, to give greater scope to economic reform. These pressures became more noticeable, and presumably more effective, as the Guidelines failed to produce the desired results.

The adoption of the Guidelines was preceded by the publication of the "Program of the SED"[5] at the VI Party Congress in January, 1963. It was the first program of the East German Communist Party. Its text reflected the adaption of the Third Program of the CPSU to East Germany's conditions. Aside from its many other similarities to points in the Soviet party's Program, the SED Program (as well as the principal speeches by the party leaders) set forth the ideological foundation and principles of the economic reform. Among these are the "law of value," the importance of material incentives for motivating the working people, and a higher development of planning and management methods.

Hinting more closely at the forthcoming economic reform, Ulbricht told the Sixth SED Congress:

> Above all, we want the heads at every level, whether in the Economic Council, in the VVB, or in the enterprises themselves, to have full responsibility for all questions connected with production at a high technical level. Individual problems can no longer be transferred from one man to another. It is an organizational prerequisite for this that the structure of the leading organs be in accord with the existing division into groups of specialized enterprises or industries respectively.[6]

In this context, Ulbricht emphasized that quantitative plan fulfillment was no longer a satisfactory measurement of economic performance. These indexes would have to be superseded by qualitative ones, such as profitability, quality, growth of labor productivity, and development of new technology. To this end, "economic accounting" would have to be introduced into the management activities of the VVB's. Thus, in January, 1963, Ulbricht's enumeration of new criteria for economic activity indicated that "Libermanism" had penetrated the walls of the Politburo in East Berlin. The significant shift in economic and ideological thinking which was taking place is best summed up in Ulbricht's new slogan: "What benefits society must also benefit the individual socialist enterprise and workers," meaning that "material interests" of all workers (i.e., the profit motive) were being elevated to the rank of ideological respectability.

Ulbricht told the Congress, furthermore, that "democratic centralism" would be expanded in East Germany. The top-level economic organs would henceforth concentrate their attention on long-term planning of tasks and development targets.

> In doing so, the central state planning organs can and must rid themselves radically of the flood of petty work to which they were subjected. They must do so contrary to traditional ideas and, if need be, contrary to wishes of individual members on the staff of these organs. Many problems of detail, moreover, can be decided much better and much more expertly on the spot. In this way we insure more effective state direction of the overall processes of the national economy and a better observance of the economic laws and economic proportions.[7]

As part of this change, the VVB's were to take over important functions hitherto entrusted to the state planning organs. In effect, then, at the Sixth SED Congress Ulbricht forecasted important changes. For a closer examination of these changes, we will now turn to the Guidelines.

Main Features of the Guidelines

What Ulbricht meant by an expansion of democratic centralism, as we learn from the Guidelines, was a filling out of the pyramidal structure of East Germany's political system. This was to be accomplished by delegating many of the detailed planning and coordinating tasks from the center to the 88 VVB's into which the state-owned enterprises, encompassing entire industrial branches, had been administratively amalgamated since 1958. The VVB's were to take over the detailed planning and coordination of the production, supply, and distribution of production for all enterprises within their respective branches.

At the head of each VVB is a director-general who, in the final analysis, is responsible for the operation of the trust and its component enterprises. Under the "principle of personal management," he has wide decision-making powers over all he surveys. Under him in the organization of the VVB superstructure are managers of various sections (sales, technology, production, and the like). According to the Guidelines, the director general would receive the general target indexes from the relevant industrial department in the People's Economic Council (*Volkswirtschaftsrat*). Bound by these target figures, the VVB staff would then delineate the goals of each enterprise (*Volkseigener Betrieb*, or VEB) within its purview and request from the VEB managers a detailed plan outlining how their enterprises would meet these goals. These prospective enterprise plans were subject to approval at the VVB level, where, in addition, the plans would be coordinated and the supply and distribution of products at various stages in the process worked out. Much of this "balancing" had formerly taken place at the central level, particularly within the Central Planning Commission. The VVB's were, furthermore, given the responsibility for marketing the products of their enterprises; they would, therefore, have to coordinate their plans with the trade organizations and do some market research of their own.[8] They would also have to assure adequate service facilities for maintenance and repair of these products.

One of the obvious aims of economic reform was to rid the state of the burden of subsidizing unprofitable enterprises. To this end, the VVB's were directed in the Guidelines to introduce rational economic accounting principles and to apply "economic levers" in the administration of their component enterprises. A far-reaching price reform was envisaged, beginning with a reevaluation of existing capital equipment, in order to arrive at a more accurate idea of the true costs of production. This cost and price reassessment was to proceed in three stages over a period of three years. Although eventually prices would reflect the real costs of production, the Guidelines emphasized that "comprehensive price control by a special state organ" would continue. Nevertheless, the VVB's (but not the enterprises themselves) did gain a significant degree of financial autonomy from the central state organs.

The "economic levers" to be introduced consisted largely of a number of funds to be established and administered by the VVB's and, presumably, filled through enterprise contributions from their proceeds. The most important of these funds were the overhead fund to finance the personnel and activities of the VVB,* the technology fund to finance research and development of new productive processes,[†] the credit reserve fund to tide over enterprises in financial difficulties,[‡] and the disposition fund for financial incentives in socialist competitions and other special drives.[φ] The proportional payments by enterprises into these funds were to be determined by the state.

The establishment of such funds was common to the economic reform in all three countries and the purpose was the same—to force the economic units to become self-sufficient and to eliminate state subsidies to them. But in East Germany the VVB's appear to have been assigned a much greater role in the management, collection, and redistribution of proceeds of the constituent enterprises than have their counterparts in Bulgaria, for instance.[‡]

The VVB was to be in charge of the financing of enterprise projects and, to this end, it could shift resources from one enterprise to another within its given industrial branch; it could give or withhold premium payments to enterprise managers at will or in accordance with the desiderata of the state economic organs; it could determine which enterprise was to get the benefit of new investments; and it could choose among research and development projects to be promoted within the industrial branch. The scope of autonomy called for in the Guidelines, therefore, extended to the intermediate level of the VVB's and not to the enterprises. It stood in contrast with Bulgaria's new economic model, which, though it maintained the trusts as the most important economic organizations, gave greater autonomy to the enterprises in this respect; it contrasted even more sharply with the Hungarian model, in which the trusts did not figure prominently.

---

*Since the VVB is a nonproductive superadministrative organization, it has to be financed by the constituent enterprises.

†This fund is financed by the constituent enterprises according to a certain percentage of their production costs. Hence, logically, the less efficient the production, the larger the fund and the greater the amount of money spent on research and development.

‡Punitive interest rates are charged to enterprises forced to draw on this fund, the rates being determined by the German Bank of Issue.

φOther funds are the contingency fund, the premium fund, the profit distribution fund, and the social and cultural fund. The latter was established in December, 1964, and will be discussed in another context below. See *Neues Deutschland* (December 29, 1964).

‡Actually, the Guidelines cover this distribution and redistribution system in elaborate and complicated detail, describing the rights of the enterprises and VVB's. This, however, is of greater interest to the student of Communist economics than to the student of political development; hence, we will confine this discussion to general relationships between these two economic units.

Above the VVB's in the hierarchical structure was the People's Economic Council, which had created a number of industrial departments, to supervise the VVB's and assure their plan fulfillment. The People's Economic Council was to formulate the annual plan for all of East Germany's industrial facilities and submit this plan to the State Planning Commission for approval. The Council's annual plan then would serve as the basis for longer-range perspective plans ("a profoundly prepared scientific document") to be worked out by the State Planning Commission, setting forth the basic norms of East Germany's industrial and technological development.

In addition to the state-owned industrial complex, the jurisdiction of the People's Economic Council was extended to cover the activities of the private and semiprivate (enterprises with state participation) enterprises still operating in East Germany. These units were hitherto under the immediate authority of local economic councils at the town, city, county (Kreis) and district (Bezirk) levels.* In his speech to the Sixth SED Congress, Ulbricht already envisaged some centralization measures that would widen the scope of the authority of the People's Economic Council over the locally directed private and semiprivate industries. He said:

> Extensive tasks in enforcing the production principle arise in the local industries. Here the dispersion of managerial functions in local enterprises must be overcome gradually. We propose for this purpose that all enterprises previously under local direction, except the local-authority and public-service enterprises, which are only of local importance, be placed under the Bezirk economic councils. The Bezirk economic councils will receive their directives and instructions for the development of industries directly from the People's Economic Council. They should no longer come under the Bezirk Council.[9]

---

*Kurt Seibt, Minister of Direction and Control of the District County People's Councils, stated in *Neues Deutschland* (December 9, 1964), that there were a total of approximately 150,000 of such enterprises under local jurisdiction. These employed about 520,000 workers out of a total working population of approximately 6,000,000. According to the East German *Statistical Yearbook,* the percentage of the total industrial product manufactured in private and semiprivate establishments was the following for the years indicated.

	Private	Semiprivate	Total
1963	7.6%	8.1%	15.7%
1964	6.7	7.9	14.6
1965	6.3	8.0	14.3
1966	6.1	8.4	14.5

The Guidelines envisaged the execution of Ulbricht's proposal. Accordingly, the Bezirk Economic Councils established industrial sections which were then supervised by the relevant industrial departments of the People's Economic Council.

Aside from the probably long-range purpose of consolidating state control and ownership of the remaining private sector, the more immediate purpose underlying this centralization measure was to bring about better coordination and standardization of production and technical development between the state and private industrial sectors. To this latter end, "product groups" were established within the VVB's and charged with the coordination of product standardization between state and local industries.[10] Furthermore, at the Seventh SED Central Committee plenum (following the Sixth SED Congress) in December, 1964, Alfred Neumann directed the Bezirk Economic Councils to request from the VVB's "technical and economic parameters, development trends for main products, as well as target figures typical for the industrial branch."[11]

In effect, then, the Guidelines envisaged a curious mix of decentralization and centralization, with the evident aim of improving coordination and information processing concerning the multifarious functions of a highly industrialized economy.

The rationale of the East German economic reform program, granting extensive autonomy only to the VVB's, may lie in the fact that, finally, profitability was only a secondary criterion of enterprise performance. The most important consideration was technological innovation, with the aim of achieving the highest standards (*Hochstniveau*) in product design and production processes, surpassing even those of the most advanced of the "capitalist countries." (East Germany's labor productivity was 20-25 percent below that of West Germany.)[12] Thus, it mattered relatively little whether the enterprise showed a profit at year's end; it mattered much more whether the enterprise had made use of its intellectual and material resources to improve its technology, for advancements in technology and productivity were the primary targets stipulated in the perspective plans of the state. Presumably, such development would ultimately enhance profits.

This duality of purpose—profit and technology—is apparent in the bonus system. The Guidelines proposed that a percentage of the employees' salary be tied to the fulfillment of plan indexes.* The size of the bonus fund each year would depend entirely on the profitability

*Ten to 20 percent of salaries was the figure suggested in the Guidelines.

of the enterprise,[13] but within this limit the yearly bonus paid to the employees would be calculated on the basis of various indexes: "fulfillment of the profit plan of the VVB; fulfillment of state plan categories; fulfillment of the export plan; fulfillment of the new technology plan." The distribution of the bonus fund would remain at the discretion of the VVB director general, not the enterprise managers. The regime's preoccupation with this incentive fund seems to focus on the "leading cadres," virtually to the exclusion of the workers. For the latter, the most prevalent slogan is "new technology—new norms" (Neue Technik—Neue Normen). According to this principle, as technology improves, the worker will have to produce more for the same wages.[14]

New Techniques, New Tasks

The new economic model in East Germany, it would appear, was based on the proposition that new techniques would minimize the necessity for far-reaching structural change. While the state would continue to set the economic goals and issue compulsory norms for the VVB's and their component industrial units, the directors general and their subordinate managerial cadres would be governed by "mathematical-technical" and "scientific-technological" management methods. The importance of this change for East Germany's political development lies in the implication that despite the low increase in role player autonomy, decision making in the economic realm was to be based on rational criteria dictated by science, mathematics, and technology. To this extent, then, the powers of arbitrary political decision making would presumably be curbed at all levels of the economic sector of the East German political system. In order to make these new criteria operative within the old totalitarian-bureaucratic frame, the managerial cadres up to and including the directors general would have to change their methods and learn to apply new techniques.

At the Fifth SED Central Committee plenum in February, 1964, Ulbricht had much to say on this subject. He warned the cadres, particularly at the VVB level, that they must shed their sectarian attitudes and modus operandi in the management of their respective productive processes. Concerning the material aspects of VVB management, Ulbricht said:

> To solve the main tasks I have outlined, a director general must make use of modern methods of VVB leadership. This includes: information analysis, planning, organization, coordination,

control. These themes are parts of VVB science and big enterprise leadership.[15]

In this connection, Ulbricht stressed the application of mathematics and electronic data processing. Admitting that East Germany was still far behind in computer technology, he urged rapid progress in this field and called for technological cooperation with the Soviet Union. The managers, for their part, would have to go back to school. According to Ulbricht,

> This could be achieved by the establishment of an institute for the post-graduate education of leading economic cadres. I emphasize: This concerns the post-graduate training of leading economic cadres who have years of managerial practice.
>
> For the time being, such an institute could have two functions: The transfer of knowledge of socialist economic management to the general directors of VVB's, managers of large state-owned enterprises, and to an able, new generation of cadres.[16]

But there was more to good management in the new economic system: the managers would have to change their ways with their subordinates and workers. They would have to learn to combine personal management and responsibility with worker participation. This latter requirement was also stressed in Hungary and, to a lesser extent in Bulgaria; its overriding purpose is to increase the responsiveness of the managers to imaginative suggestions by their subordinates, with a view to improving efficiency and productivity and eliminating waste. In this connection, Ulbricht urged specifically an intensification of collaboration between the VVB directors general and their scientific-technical councils and, on the enterprise level, between the managers and their production committees.

East Germany's party writers lost no time elaborating Ulbricht's proposals in exhortative and explanatory articles,* all of them stressing

---

*Die Wirtschaft, East Germany's weekly economic journal, is particularly notable for its participation in this educative and exhortative endeavor. But Einheit, the ideological monthly of the SED, also published many articles on purely economic subjects, elaborating Ulbricht's teachings. Representative of these articles are Herbert Wolf, "Zu einigen Fragen der bewussten Ausnutzung der oekonomischen Gesetze des Sozialismus," Einheit (April, 1964); and Alfred Lange, "Oekonomische Weiterqualifizierung und neues Oekonomisches System," ibid. (June, 1964).

the inseparable interrelation between ideology, politics, and economic science.

In the new economic system of East Germany, special consideration was given to the inventors and innovators (Neurer), the brain trust of progress. Much depended on the speedy translation of their ideas into practice.[18] "Success," said Ulbricht,

> now primarily depends on our ability to plan, manage, and organize scientific-technical work properly from basic material research up to the innovator movement, from long-range planning up to the production and the sale of the products.[19]

Only in this way could the "technical revolution" be mastered in East Germany and the highest level of production attained.

Problems with the New Economic Model

East Germany's new economic model did not fulfill the hopes of its designers. During the first two years of its implementation it proved to be too highly centralized for efficient operation. Bureaucratic habits were difficult to break, especially inasmuch as the politico-economic structure continued to invite their application. At all levels of the economic system, the implementation of the new economic model left much to be desired.

At the Ninth SED Central Committee plenum, Ulbricht complained that

> the implementation of our plan tasks is quite burdened by the fact that various offices to an increasing extent practice formal-administrative management methods of letter and report writing and increasingly waste time and money. This extreme paper work above all burdens the VVB's and enterprises and reduces our successes in many fields.
>
> In the activity of the Economic Council in particular there are incidents in which bureaucratic perfectionism reigns wherever the managers fail to tackle the new problems of socialist economic management theoretically. In this respect directors general and managers face serious obstacles.[19]

A director of the planning section of one of the VVB's protested publicly against the quantity and scope of central directives which required detailed elaboration in about 350 pages each year.[20]

If this quantity of directives and regulations burdened the VVB staffs, it burdened even more the staffs of the component enterprises, which had to break down the VVB plans for their own operations. This led one frequent contributor to the SED ideological journal to lament that continuing centralization in East Germany was a serious impediment to reaching the highest effectiveness of the economy because it forced VVB's and enterprises to plan for the superior organs rather than for their own best achievements.[21] Another author counseled the enterprise directors not to interpret central plan indexes too rigidly: in the final analysis, the new economic system and its laws should be interpreted in the best interests of the socialist society. However, such flexibility of interpretation presupposed "correct cognition of the economic laws of socialism."[22]

Although our research uncovered no publicly articulated criticism of the powers granted to the VVB's in the new economic model (as was the case in Bulgaria), there was enough opposition to the VVB's to put even Walter Ulbricht on the defensive. For instance, in February, 1964, Ulbricht asserted:

> The VVB's and their directors general play an outstanding role in the new economic system of planning and managing the economy. Therefore, we cannot agree with people who demand a weakening of the functions of the VVB's. The executive boards of some big chemical enterprises, for example, repeatedly brought up the question as to whether it is not possible to exclude them from the association of the VVB and give them—in coordination with other enterprises—the position of "united enterprises." Such a regulation is not a solution. With the support of our big enterprises the VVB's must be strengthened in such a way that they will be able to completely fulfill their tasks.[23]

With the continuing bureaucratic interference of both the state organs (industrial departments in the Economic Council) and the VVB's, opposition at the enterprise level to centralism had presumably increased. One desirable alternative, obviously demanded, because it was rejected in an article in *Wirtschafts—Wissenschaft*, was to substitute "economic levers" for central directives. While the article did not minimize the problems inherent in the new economic model, it attributed the inadequacies of performance to problems in planning still to be overcome, to be expected in the transition period.[24]

Toward the end of 1965, the People's Economic Council was abolished and its industrial departments transformed into ministries. One should be careful, however, not to attach too much significance to this organizational change, despite Ulbricht's already cited criticism of continuing "sectarian" practices in the People's Economic Council. For one thing, the change coincided with a similar reorganization in the Soviet Union; for another, seven of the 15 heads of industrial departments within the former Economic Council were appointed as ministers, with functions virtually identical with those they had performed before.

But toward the end of 1966, one could notice a shift in emphasis from the VVB to the enterprise as the basic unit in East Germany's economic system, accompanied by a reluctant curbing of the powers and functions of the VVB's. Most of the articles appearing in the public media under review stressed the importance of enterprises rather than that of the VVB.[25]

In short, then, East Germany's new economic system was leading the economic process in the opposite direction from that intended by its designers. It had been intended to eliminate much of the bureaucratic paper work so characteristic of the old system and to make room for creative initiatives at the production level. Instead, it increased the bureaucratic work load at each level, inasmuch as it burdened the managing units with the "scientific elaboration" of plan indexes, with which they had not been concerned under the old system.[26] Thus, the VVB's were hamstrung by central plan directives, and they in turn stifled initiative at the enterprise level with their own directives and requests for "scientific elaboration." The new economic system was not bringing the East German economy closer to its main goal: reaching the highest standards of technology and productivity.

The Fourteenth SED Central Committee plenum set the stage for a most thorough appraisal of the performance of the new economic system. Ulbricht's speech at this plenum was unusually defensive; its tone suggested that he had lost some of his self-confidence in his infallible authority as chief problem-solver of East Germany's economic system. One could discern a note of frustration as Ulbricht uncovered the many inadequacies in the administration of the new economic system, from the highest level down to the enterprises and locally managed private and semiprivate industries. Among many other shortcomings of the new economic system, Ulbricht pointed out:

> The crux of the matter is that superior organs have to an increasing extent interfered in the economic activities of enterprises. The result was often enough that enterprises were forced to violate the principles of business-type accounting. This practice of interference was linked with a great deal of red tape, which

130

placed great demands on the working strength of many important economic cadres.[27]

The principal culprit here was apparently the VVB management.*

A new set of regulations defining the role and rights of state enterprises had been published in draft form.[28] Ulbricht said that these new regulations would enable the enterprises to defend themselves against such administrative interference, but suggested that the pertinent protective clauses be fortified so as to make superior organs financially liable to enterprises "for losses resulting from their forcing them to violate business-type accounting."

At the same time, Ulbricht cautioned against the erroneous conclusion that the changed emphasis in favor of enterprise autonomy would lead to the abolition of the VVB's.

> ... the independence of enterprises with regard to VVB's is of a relative character. The directors general have the right to guide the activities of enterprises, especially their technical policies in accordance with the requirements resulting from the objective economic law of production concentration.

This guidance, however, should be exercised within the enterprise plan, and administrative interference not connected with plan implementation should be avoided. In the near future, Ulbricht said, the Council of Ministers would draft guidelines for the VVB administrations.

The essential result of this reevaluation, summarized by Ulbricht for the Central Committee, was a streamlining of the relationships between the role players at the various levels of the East German economy: no more fundamental change was promised. According to this diagnosis, the flaws in the new system were rooted in the faulty perceptions among the role players of their roles and functions; hence, a more precise delineation of these roles and functions were required. The central planners were interested in too many goals, which, though interconnected, placed excessive burdens of elaboration and coordination on the shoulders of the VVB planners. The latter, in turn, were unable to coordinate the multifarious functions and production

---

*Several paragraphs earlier in his speech Ulbricht said: "If some criticism was voiced here about the work of the VVB's, it was because they had violated the basic idea of the new economic system, because they had interfered in the area of responsibilities of enterprises with administrative means no longer corresponding to the new economic system, and because they had violated the principles of business-type accounting."

relationships among the many enterprises under their control. The solution of these problems would require a more extensive delegation of autonomy at each lower level.

The Streamlining of East Germany's New Economic System

The results of the reevaluation of the new economic system at the Fourteenth SED Central Committee plenum are most aptly summarized in two documents which appeared in March, 1967. One of these is the "Draft Regulations Concerning the Tasks, Rights, and Duties of the VVB."[29] The other is the "Regulations Concerning the Tasks, Rights, and Duties of the People's Production Enterprises."[30]

According to these documents, the VVB would remain as the leading organ of the economy, directing and controlling the enterprises within its industrial branch. On the basis of central perspective plan indexes, the VVB director general would continue to be responsible for the effective development of the industrial branch, which he would have to plan in detail, in cooperation with the managers of the constituent enterprises. The VVB would continue to be accountable to, and subject to the directives of, the competent ministry. Thus, the VVB would remain as the kingpin in the new economic system. The structure of the system had not changed significantly. However, the functions had been redistributed in the course of the reevaluation, as will be seen in the regulation on state enterprises.

The enterprise director, in cooperation with his staff, would henceforth have to work out a detailed perspective plan and annual plan for the operation of his enterprise on the basis of centrally determined plan indexes, and to justify these plans to the management of the VVB. The enterprise would have to elaborate alternative plan variations (Planvarianten) which would promise the most efficient attainment of central plan indexes (presumably to give the VVB some choice in the selection of plans).

One of the problems discussed at the Fourteenth SED Central Committee plenum was the contractual relationship between enterprises. (Gerhard Schurer, the head of the Central Planning Commission, had called this the "Achille's heel of plan-fulfillment, lowering costs, and raising quality.")[31] It was to be solved by granting the enterprises the freedom and responsibility to develop their own cooperative relations with other enterprises on the basis of central plan indexes and to base their yearly and longer-range plans on these relationships. These cooperative relationships had formerly been coordinated by the VVB's and would, under the present law, be established independently of VVB direction.[32] In other words, the enterprise was now free to establish its own horizontal relationships without vertical direction (by the VVB's), but these relationships had to conform to, and promote the implementation of, central plan indexes. The enterprise was granted similar freedom to establish relations with banks, in order to obtain credits for expansion or improvement of the production process, in accordance with plan directives and on the basis of its ability to project greater profitability.

At the same time, the enterprise would lose all claim to state subsidies. Within the fulfillment of central plan indexes, the enterprise must be self-supporting and organize its financial and managerial affairs accordingly. It must furnish its own means of expanding, acquiring new technological levels of production, and renewing plant equipment (with the help of bank credits), and see to it that its annual intake was sufficient to meet its financial obligations to the various compulsory funds.

According to the new regulations, the enterprise would have the right to protest state-imposed tasks which do not conform to its own plans (which have been approved by higher organs—i.e., the VVB). But this right to protest was limited: it could not be exercised against tasks imposed by the Council of Ministers regarding the development of science and technology and the production of commodities essential to the structure of the economy.

The sale of the product was made the responsibility of the enterprise, which would, in cooperation with its partners in production and the trade organizations, assure the marketability of its products. Market research was stressed, particularly for exports. The enterprise was charged with the task of steadily increasing the scope and profitability of its exports.

Even price-determination functions—but little power—were assigned to the enterprise. Prices would have to be calculated according to the cost of production. World market prices of comparable products would have to be taken into account in the price formation. The price suggested by the enterprise would be provisional and subject to approval by higher authority. Once the price was set, the enterprise should be concerned with lowering its production costs. This eventually would result in a reevaluation of the product price, but in the meantime the enterprise would stand to make a profit from the reduction of production costs.[33]

Many of the clauses in the enterprise regulations are concerned with administrative directives and duties (such as packaging, bookkeeping, managerial behavior with regard to the workers, and the like) which are not directly pertinent to this discussion.

Thus, when all was said and done, the enterprise managers of East Germany had gained a net increase in functions but little leeway to exercise their own initiatives. They would continue to be bound by central plan directives emphasizing new technology as a higher criterion than profitability. The VVB's would continue to direct the enterprises, although some of the control functions had been taken away from them. The East German leadership had obviously learned that the goals it sought were not attainable within the former, highly centralized framework, but, as we have observed, it was extremely reluctant to relinquish its control.

The East German Trade Unions

The trade union movement in East Germany was no less essential to the implementation of the new economic system than were its counterparts in Bulgaria and Hungary. However, very much like Bulgaria, and in sharp contrast with Hungary, East Germany did not experience any ferment among the trade unions in connection with the new economic system. Throughout our research time frame, the FDGB (Freier Deutscher Gewerkschaftsbund, i.e., Free German Trade Unions) remained the obedient tool of the party-government, mobilizing the workers for the implementation of the plan directives. This obedient spirit is exemplified in the pledge by the FDGB Presidium to the SED Central Committee soon after the Sixth Party Congress, which was published in the FDGB daily:

> The Presidium assured the SED Central Committee, headed by Comrade Walter Ulbricht, as elected by the party congress, that the labor unions, as loyal party helpers, will make the program of socialism the basis of all actions by labor union members.
>
> General promotion of creative activity by the working people, inspiring them to implement the SED program and achieve greatest labor productivity, all this is real representation of labor union interests because this is the most important prerequisite for further improving the standard of living of working people.[34]

Like Bulgaria and unlike Hungary, East Germany established production committees in the enterprises as a means of worker participation in the decision making at the management level.[35] These production committees corresponded closely to the Hungarian works councils, which were abolished during the initial implementation stage of the new economic model in Hungary. In Bulgaria and East Germany the production committee may have mitigated some of the latent or potential worker unrest which might otherwise have come to the surface during the implementation of the new economic model and (as it did in Hungary) stirred the trade unions into action. Their intended purpose, however, was "to insure cooperation of the worker representatives in the management of the enterprise."[36]

Although "elected" by the workers of the enterprise,[37] the composition of the production committees tended to favor the experts, highly skilled workers, and members of the Communist party. One such committee of 25 counted among its members two with doctoral degrees, 19 graduates from technical institutions, and four graduates from specialized schools (Fachschulen). Nineteen of these 25 were party members. The relationship of the production committees to the trade unions remained to be worked out.[38]

Perhaps another safety valve for worker unrest in East Germany is the institution of "conflict committees" (Konfliktkomitees), semijudicial arbitration courts before which workers can bring their grievances against management.* Although the decisions of the conflict committees can be—and often are—overruled by higher authorities, they do serve as a grievance outlet. This may help keep some equilibrium in the relations between workers and management.

As for the trade unions, the available information indicates that they are preoccupied largely with work competitions which they organize to fulfill the plan indexes of the enterprise—quantitative and qualitative targets—raise labor productivity, and meet the deadlines.† In this connection, it is noteworthy that since 1966 the FDGB has been participating in the planning process of the enterprises and VVB's.[39] This elevation of trade union functions was in all probability designed to increase the plan commitments of the enterprise, for it came within a few months of a published complaint that the managers of enterprises were reluctant to mitigate the faulty methods of the central organs by committing themselves to additional, compensatory duties.[40]

The announcement of FDGB participation in the planning process

---

*Descriptions of cases before the conflict committees are a regular feature of the biweekly *Arbeit und Arbeitsrecht.*

†On the average, *Arbeit und Arbeitsrecht* published an article on this subject about once every month.

was followed by the news that another socialist work competition would be organized, this time under the slogan "Onward to the Twentieth Anniversary of the SED with Good Deeds in Socialist Work Competition." The author added:

> The creative initiative of the workers in this competition is an expression of its trust in the party as the leading force of our socialist establishment.[41]

But even though the trade unions are clearly the servants of the state, one can often find articles interspersed in the journals which are of genuine human interest. For instance, the FDGB intervened on behalf of a worker who had been convicted of a crime and sentenced to one year in jail. Released from confinement, he was refused his former job by the enterprise. Through the intervention of the FDGB, the manager was compelled to reemploy the worker, on the grounds that he had not been fired prior to his imprisonment.[42] Many similar stories can be found in *Arbeit und Arbeitsrecht*, describing trade union efforts to defend the grievances of invalids, pensioners, and workers whose rights had been violated.

There has also been some improvement in the work conditions of the East German proletariat, in which the trade unions may have been instrumental. In April, 1966, for instance, the weekly work schedule was reduced from 48 to 45 hours, with alternating five-day workweeks. The announcement was published jointly by the Council of Ministers and the FDGB.[43] At the same time, however, the FDGB stressed that within this shorter working period, the work norms must be upheld.[44]

Since July, 1966, enterprise managers have been required to include in their planning provisions for the improvement of working and living conditions.[45] Several months later an article stated that the workers in one factory would have much preferred getting their part of the cash which the enterprise was spending to improve their living and working conditions. The author sought to show, however, that a plant heater here and a water faucet there would soon improve the health of the workers and reduce absenteeism due to illness. He concluded:

> It is well demonstrated that good working conditions and a high production-culture raise the joy of working, the interest in the enterprise, as well as the interest in social-political work.[46]

Thus, the work of the trade unions is sometimes two-sided: it allows for the representation of workers' interest when those interests coincide with those of the state—or when, at least, the two are not in conflict. But this has always been the role of the trade unions in Communist systems. The East German trade unions have not changed their role any more than the Bulgarian ones did. Therein lies the glaring contrast between them and their Hungarian counterparts.

The East German Legislature

The Volkskammer (People's Chamber) of East Germany showed no signs of reviving from the inert docility which had characterized its activity since the consolidation of Communist power. Although the Volkskammer is composed of representatives from five parties (including the SED) and the mass organizations, neither debate on, nor opposition to, the policies of the regime has been in evidence.

A redistricting of parliamentary and local election districts was undertaken in 1963, in connection with the new economic system. The districts were made smaller, with the announced purpose of making them coincide more closely with the economic centers of gravity (Schwerpunkte).[47] This, however, did not lead to an increase in legislative initiatives in the Volkskammer (although it may have improved the jurisdiction of the people's councils over private and semiprivate industry). Two years later, in the local elections of October, 1965, more candidates appeared on the single-list ballots of the National Front than there were positions available. This, however, was accompanied by an intensive propaganda barrage which stressed that the list of the National Front represented the candidates approved by the people in nomination meetings. [8] Since voters would have to enter a special booth in order to cross out candidates or amend the list, there were very few who would make themselves so conspicuous.*

Thus, the composition of the People's Chamber in East Germany—as in Bulgaria and, to a somewhat lesser extent, in Hungary—continues to rest on a fictitious consensus of the population.† One of the more important functions of the deputies, as stated in the Politburo Report to the SED Central Committee on July 6, 1967, is to continue to promote this consensus, and, perhaps to make it more real:

---

*A reporter for *Neues Deutschland* wrote that he was told by the supervisor of one election district: "If you are looking for a quiet place to sit, pick one of these two election booths. No one will bother you there. *Neues Deutschland* (October 11, 1965).

†The July 2, 1967, elections resulted in 99.93 percent of the total votes cast in favor of the National Front list of candidates. *Neues Deutschland* (July 4, 1967).

One of the most important tasks of the newly elected deputies will be to consolidate contact with their voters, constantly to justify their trust, to account to them, but above all, to develop their initiatives and their participation in the completion of socialism in the GDR—for which the population made a free decision on July 2.[49]

And yet, sometimes the SED leadership was disturbed, particularly during election campaign periods, by the demands of the people, with which the candidates sometimes tended to identify themselves. Thus, for instance, Hans Modrow, First Secretary of the District Committee of Berlin-Kopenick, complained in an interview with *Neues Deutschland*:

Some comrades believe that they can win the favor of their fellow citizens by raising unrealistic demands or by passionately defending such demands of the citizens. This is painful, especially when other comrades contradict them and explain to the citizens why we are presently not yet in a position to act on certain plans.[50]

Since one of these demands concerned a reduction of the workweek to five days, and since the workweek was subsequently reduced, one can surmise that, at times, popular pressures do find an effective outlet even in East Germany. As yet, however, the Volkskammer did not appear as an effective interest articulator or aggregator of the people.

Summary of East Germany's
Political Development

At the end of this research time frame the East German political system remained more output-oriented than that of the other two countries we have reviewed. Its political process was concerned primarily with the mobilization and regimentation of the role players and the people at large.

The economic reform turned into a long experiment, lasting about five years. It led to a delegation of functions from the center down to intermediate and lower levels, but since these functions remained tied to central plan indexes and control, the role players could not be said to have gained autonomy commensurate with the augmentation of their functions. One of the most notable phenomena (from the point of view of this thesis) was the reluctance displayed by the regime in delegating these functions downward to the enterprise level.

If there was any significant effect of the economic reform upon the functions of trade unions, it was to increase their efforts to mobilize the workers to greater feats in work competition. Otherwise we have not seen any efforts made by the trade unions to become the real representatives of the interests of the workers. The Volkskammer, similarly, showed no signs of stirring away from its position of subservience to the demands of the regime.

Thus, the most highly developed of the three countries under study experienced the lowest degree of political development during the reform period.

Notes

1. "Richtlinien fuer das neue oekonomische System der Planung und Leitung der Volkswirtschaft," *Neues Deutschland* (July 16, 1963), supplement.

2. Gerd Friedrich, "Zu den Aufgaben und der Verantwortung der VVB," *Einheit* (April, 1963).

3. "Richtlinien."

4. See, for instance, Gunter Mittag, "Das neue oekonomische System der Planung und Leitung—Ergebnis schoepferischer Arbeit unserer Partei," *Einheit* (April, 1963). This article, by a Politburo member, is dedicated to Walter Ulbricht, whose guiding spirit gave both concept and reality to East Germany's new economic model. Further indications of Ulbricht's cult of personality are adduced in a later chapter.

5. Lead article in *Einheit* (January, 1963). SED stands for Sozialistische Einheitspartei Deutschlands, i.e., the Communist Party.

6. Walter Ulbricht, "Das Programm des Sozialismus und die geschichtliche Aufgabe der Sozialistischen Einheitspartei Deutschlands," speech before the Sixth SED Congress, *Neues Deutschland* (January 16, 1963).

7. Ibid.

8. See Wolfgang Eschritt and Joachim Granitza, "Bedarfsforschung—Wichtige Aufgabe des industriellen Absatzes," *Einheit* (March, 1963). Appearing some four months prior to the publication of the Guidelines, this article is interesting for its condemnation of dogmatic thinking connected with the *Tonnenideologie* ("tonnage ideology") and its advocacy of sales techniques which are common in capitalist countries. The study and adoption of capitalist techniques were openly advocated in East Germany during this period. One of the more interesting articles on the subject was written by Gunter Kohlmey, "Neue Aufgaben fuer die Erforschung der kapitalistischen Wirtschaft," *Einheit* (August, 1963). Kohlmey maintains that even though the capitalist system is

exploitative and will eventually go out of existence (while the socialist system is nonexploitative and will perpetuate itself), the Communists have much in common with the capitalists—the profit motive, among other things—and should study the capitalist system with a view to borrowing some of its more useful features. See also Ulbricht's speech to the Fifth Central Committee plenum of the SED, where he said: ". . . I refer to the inquiries of the Soviet author I. Bykov concerning the organization of research in capitalist trusts. He writes that research financing in the Du Pont de Nemours trust is primarily designed to maintain the competitiveness of the enterprise divisions, to raise their profitability, to cut down the amortization time for the invested funds, to find new profitable capital investment spheres, and to develop basic research still further. Basic research in that case accounts for about 19 percent of the total research expenses. We consider it correct to draw some conclusion from these facts for our own country." *Neues Deutschland* (February 6, 1964). This was only one of the many approving references Ulbricht made to the capitalist system.

9. Ulbricht's speech to the Sixth Party Congress. The Bezirk Economic Councils were under the jurisdiction of the Bezirk Council, the administrative organ of the district. (East Germany is divided into 15 districts.) According to Ulbricht's proposal, the Bezirk Economic Council would be separated from the Bezirk (administrative) Council and come directly under the jurisdiction of the People's Economic Council.

10. "Was sind Erzeugnisgruppen?—Notizen von einem Gespraech mit dem Generaldirektor der VVB Eisen-Blech-Metallwaren, Genossen Rudi Georgi," *Neues Deutschland* (November 24, 1963).

11. "Volkswirtschaftsplan 1965 in der Industrie und weitere Durch-fuehrung des neuen oekonomischen Systems," speech by Politburo member Alfred Neumann to the Seventh plenum, *Neues Deutschland* (December 8, 1964).

12. See Ulbricht's speech to the Fifth Central Committee plenum, *Neues Deutschland* (February 5, 1964). Judging by the many references in East German media to West Germany in connection with this drive to technological superiority, it would probably not be far afield to interpret this as a politico-psychologically conditioned endeavor to "keep up with the (West German) Joneses"—that is, to show the people of West Germany and the rest of the capitalist world that a Communist country could do as well or better. On the other hand, more objective economic criteria can be seen at work here also: If East Germany could attain world standards in industrial and technological designs and achieve a productivity higher than that of the capitalist countries, her position in international markets would be markedly improved. This consideration has special significance, keeping in mind that East

Germany is still diplomatically ostracized by all of the non-Communist countries of the world, and that the achievement of a competitive position with West German industry could well put a crack in the "Hallstein Doctrine."

13. See Siegfried Bohm, "Einige Aufgaben der Grundorganisationen bei der Durchsetzung des Systems der oekonomischen Hebel," *Einheit* (May, 1964). According to Bohm, deposits into the profit fund can be made only if and to the extent that the profit plan is overfulfilled; short of overfulfillment, profits have to be reinvested into VVB and enterprise projects.

14. See "Direktive Neue Technik—Neue Normen 1965: Direktive zur Verwirklichung des Grundsatzes 'Neue Technik—neue Normen' und zur produktivitaetswirksamen Gestaltung des Arbeitslohnes in der volkseigenen Wirtschaft und in den Betrieben mit staatlicher Beteiligung," *Arbeit und Arbeitsrecht*, No. 3 (1965). See also Werner Rogge, "Neue Technik—neue Normen und gewerkschaftliche Interessenvertretung," *Einheit* (January, 1966).

15. "Referat des Genossen Walter Ulbricht auf der 5. Tagung des ZK: Die Durchfuehrung der oekonomischen Politik im Planjahr unter besonderer Berucksichtigung der chemischen Industrie," *Neues Deutschland* (February 5 and 6, 1964), Parts I and II, respectively. This quotation is taken from Part I.

16. Ibid.

17. For a representative article on this subject, see Rudolf Gertsch and Heinz-Dieter Haustein, "Die Neuerer und das neue oekonomische System," ibid. (July, 1963).

18. Speech at the Fifth SED Central Committee plenum, *Neues Deutschland* (February 5, 1964).

19. Walter Ulbricht, "Die nationale Mission der Deutschen Demokratischen Republik und das geistige Schaffen in unserem Staat," *Neues Deutschland* (April 28, 1965).

20. *Die Wirtschaft* (October 14, 1965).

21. Herbert Wolf, "Probleme der oekonomischen Theorie in der zweiten Etappe des neuen oekonomischen Systems," *Einheit* (February, 1966).

22. Otto Reinhold, "Die politische Oekonomie in unserer Zeit," *Einheit* (February, 1966).

23. Walter Ulbricht, "Die Durchfuehrung der oekonomischen Politik im Planjahr unter besonderer Beruecksichtigung der chemischen Industrien," Part II, *Neues Deutschland* (February 6, 1964).

24. *Wirtschafts-Wissenschaft* (October, 1965), cited in *Bericht ueber die Entwicklung in der Sowjetzone* (Bonn: Ostburo der SPD, October, 1965).

25. Compare, for instance, two articles by Politburo member Gunter Mittag. In May, 1965, he wrote "The VVB's are the fulcrum (*Drehpunkt*) of the new system." "Das neue oekonomische System der Planung und Leitung der Volkswirtschaft wird planmaessig verwirklicht," *Einheit* (May, 1965). In February, 1967, he wrote: "The enterprise in socialist production process is the basic unit (*grundlegende Einheit*). . . ." "Ueber die kontinuierliche Verwirklichung des neuen oekonomischen Systems der Planung und Leitung, *Einheit* (February, 1967).

26. See Gunter Mittag's article in *Einheit* (February, 1967). "The processing (Ausarbeitung) required of the enterprises is more elaborate than it used to be under the old system."

27. "Das neue oekonomische System und der Perspekitivplan," *Neues Deutschland* (December 20, 1966).

28. "Entwurf zur Verordnung ueber die Aufgaben, Rechte und Pflichten der Volkseigenen Produktionsbetriebe," *Die Wirtschaft*, No. 48 (November 30, 1966), supplement.

29. "Entwurf zur Verordnung ueber die Aufgaben, Rechte und Pflichten der Vereinigung Volkseigener Betriebe," Supplement to *Die Wirtschaft*, No. 13 (March 30, 1967).

30. "Verordnung ueber die Aufgaben, Rechte und Pflichten des volkseigenenen Productionsbetriebes," *Gesetz-Blatt der DDR*, II, 21 (March 9, 1967). The draft version of this law, which does not differ significantly from the final version, was published in *Die Wirtschaft* No. 48 (November 30, 1966); supplement.

31. "Zu einigen Grundfragen des Perspektivplanes und seiner Durchfuehrung," *Neues Deutschland* (December 17, 1966).

32. See Manfred Herold und Hans Wittik, "Oekonomie und Planung der sozialistischen Kooperation," *Einheit* (March, 1967). According to these authors, "inter-enterprise relationships are no substitute for—but prerequisites for—rational, well-founded planning."

33. See Günter Hartmann und Wolf-Dietrich Lankrer, "Preisbildung

und wissenschaftlich-technischer Fortschritt," *Einheit* (April-May, 1967). In his speech to the Fourteenth Central Committee plenum, Ulbricht said that prices would eventually be flexible. The clause concerning prices in the enterprise regulations (Par. 28) permits the inference that some flexibility already exists. It says: "The enterprise must propose prices for new products and submit these to superior organs, insofar as it has not the right to determine the prices itself or to agree with the distributor on such prices."

The procedure of price determination is described in "Ueber die Preise hat der Leitzer zu entscheiden," *Die Wirtschaft*, No. 45 (November 10, 1966). The article explains that in line with the reevaluation of industrial costs and prices, the state continues to subsidize consumer goods in order to avoid rising consumer prices. Enterprises try to get the optimum price for their product, which often has to be adjusted downward. Price inspection at the VVB level would continue to be strengthened, the article stated. In one case, the Minister of Trade, Rudolf Lorenz, made an inspection tour of the clothing industry and was promised, among other things, that during the third quarter of the following year, production costs would diminish so as to permit lower prices for children's clothing. He directed the enterprise to lower the price immediately and to plan to recoup the costs of its investments over a longer priod of time.

34. "Kampfatmosphaere fuer hoeschste Arbeitsproduktivitaet! Kommunique des Praesidiums des Bundesvorstandes des FDGB," *Tribüne* (January 20, 1963). This sentiment was echoed five years later in an open letter by the FDGB Presidium in the same paper. Supplement in *Tribüne* (September 11, 1967): "The active participation (Mitarbeit) in the building of socialism, the fulfillment of our people's economic plans—that is the best representation of the workers' interests, for it leads, step by step, to the improvement of the workers' living conditions.

35. Ulbricht's speech to the Sixth SED Congress.

36. See Fritz Rosel, "Zur Bildung der Produktionskomitees in den Volkseigenen Grossbetrieben," *Einheit* (December, 1963).

37. Ibid.

38. Gunter Rohrlack, "Aus den Erfahrungen eines Produktionskomitees," Einheit (August, 1964).

39. Gerhard Muth, "Aufgaben der Gewerkschaften im Planjahr 1966 und Probleme der Gewerkschaftsarbeit bis 1970," *Arbeit und Arbeitsrecht*, No. 6 (1966).

40. *Wirtschafts-Wissenschaft*, No. 10 (1965).

41. Muth, op. cit.

42. Hans Anschrat, "Kuendigung Inhaftierter," *Arbeit und Arbeitsrecht*, No. 2 (1964), p. 43.

43. *Die Wirtschaft*, No. 11 (1966).

44. Muth, op. cit.

45. H. Stobel and G. Winkler, "Plan zur Verbesserung der Arbeits und Lebensbedingungen," *Arbeit und Arbeitsrecht*, No. 17 (1965).

46. Gunter Grosche, "Verbesserung der Arbeits-und Lebensbedingungen," *Arbeit und Arbeitsrecht*, No. 23 (1965).

47. (Unsigned), "Die Volkswahlen 1963—ein neuer Hoehepunkt in der Entwicklung unserer Republik," *Einheit* (September, 1963).

48. Representative of this propaganda effort is *Neues Deutschland* (October 2, 1965).

49. "Aus dem Bericht des Politburos an die 2. Tagung des ZK," *Neues Deutschland* (July 7, 1967).

50. "Vertrauensmann oder Kampfer?," *Neues Deutschland* (October 1, 1965).

9 The Dynamics of Political Change

We come away from our descriptive analysis of political change in the three East European countries with our working hypotheses severely disciplined. The three countries under examination have not accommodated our original postulates of direct covariance between socioeconomic and political development. Only Hungary has shown significant movement in all three of the hypothesized sectors; Bulgaria and East Germany confined their reform to the economic sectors alone.

At this point we must take another searching look at our thesis, with a view to determining just what impact socioeconomic development has had on the political development of each political system and what other factors have been at work to help channel political development in different directions. This is the purpose of the present chapter. Again the analysis will be comparative, pointing to the presence and/or absence of relevant variables in one or more of the three countries and suggesting the probable effect.

In organizing this discussion, a retrospective approach seems appropriate. First, we shall compare the findings of the preceding three chapters, which traveled the road of political development in each country separately from the beginning to the end of our time frame. Second, we shall examine the different ways adopted by the three political systems to arrive at their respective reform models. Finally, we shall look at some additional factors which have developed differently in each country and may have, together with socioeconomic factors, offered different options to the decision makers in their planning of reform.

Similar Problems, Different Solutions

The problems which necessitated reform of the economic sector were essentially similar in all three countries. They arose mainly out of the command structure which governed the relationships between the state and the enterprise. This structure lacked the capacity to deal with the changing relationships of the producer to the consumer, not only at home but also abroad. Goal-seeking—concerned mainly with the creation of distributable wealth—had become more difficult: piled-up inventories in the warehouses told the decision makers that the wealth created had become less and less distributable. Here, then, we have an example of change in one set of relationships giving rise to change in another.

And yet, in each country this problem was of different dimensions. The Bulgarians, for instance, were concerned mainly with raising the quality of their production, whereas the Hungarians worried about both quality and technical development in order to become competitive with other countries. In East Germany, on the other hand, the emphasis was on reaching the world standard in productivity, specifications, and diversification, from which they were not very far removed.

In a way, the solutions adopted by the three countries reflect not so much the different dimensions of the problem as the capacity of the several political systems to cope with the problem. One change common to all three countries, and of potentially great importance, was the shift from political-administrative to economic-pragmatic criteria of decision making for the economic sector. This "secularization," in the abstract, amounted to a net decrease in the power of the decision maker: his actions were increasingly bound by rational laws, and to this extent the power of arbitrary decision making was curbed. To this extent, also, the influence of the expert increased; he could make demands upon the decision maker and argue with him on rational grounds.

This change is reflected and institutionalized in one feature of economic reform which all three countries have in common: a net increase in the autonomy of the role players in the economic sector. Theoretically, to the extent that economic decision making is governed by economic criteria, it matters little who makes the decisions. In the reality of Communist systems, however, any change in the structure of the economic subsystem is a matter of conscious political choice entailing certain predictable (and some not so predictable) consequences. Thus, the delegation of autonomous decision-making power to role players at lower levels entails some net loss of this power at the center (depending, of course, on the degree of control or supervision the center chooses to retain). As a matter of conscious political choice, then, the scope of structural change is subject to many considerations and variable interactions. The level of socioeconomic development is only one of these.

Understandably, then, we find some striking and unexpected differences in the development of role-player autonomy from central control. We can distinguish two separate roads of political development, one followed by East Germany and Bulgaria (respectively the most- and least-developed countries under examination), the other by Hungary. The road pursued by East Germany and Bulgaria led to a streamlining and expansion of the existing pyramidal structure. An intermediate layer of control was inserted into the structure: the associations of state enterprises (trusts), each headed by a director general who had wide decision-making powers but was accountable to central organs of the state for his actions. This streamlining entailed increased participation by the role players in the operationalization of pertinent central plan directives—hence, an expansion of autonomous functions and responsibilities. However, the enumeration and coordination of functions at any given level was subject to review and approval at the next higher level. Thus, the streamlined structures led to progressively detailed information processing at each level of the pyramid, with a minimum loss of control at the center. In essence, then, there was little significant change in the vertical relationships between the role players attending economic reform in East Germany and Bulgaria. Nor was there any noticeable spillover effect upon the role of the trade unions or legislatures and their relationships to state and society.

By contrast, Hungary's road to economic reform led to a significant increase in role-player autonomy, a substantial change in relationships between role players horizontally and vertically, and a noticeable spillover into the trade unions and legislature. Although the amalgamation of enterprises into trusts was begun in 1963, there has been little news of its progress since then; and as far as can be seen from the reform laws, the trust is not a key element in the economic structure of Hungary. Instead of the expansion and streamlining of the central economic structure which we observed in Bulgaria and East Germany, Hungary's reform led to a contraction in the economic ministerial staffs.

In Hungary, for the most part, the relationships between ministries and enterprises were direct, i.e., without intermediary role players. But the powers and functions of the ministries vis-à-vis the enterprise managers were drastically curbed, and those of the enterprise managers were correspondingly enhanced. As long as the enterprise made a profit sufficient to meet its fiscal obligations and remained solvent, it experienced little or no interference from the state. The central planning agency would continue to formulate economic goals, but the enterprise manager would no longer be bound by obligatory plan indexes.

The corresponding change in the roles and functions of the trade unions and Parliament evolved during the debating period concerning economic reform. We witnessed in Hungary simultaneous evolution in three interconnected parts of the Communist political system. It is impossible, therefore, to identify a cause-effect relationship between the three movements. In our search for an explanation of this triple-change phenomenon, we will have to look for factors whose presence in Hungary could have an impact on all three subsystems (or factors which might have brought about the observed movements in each subsystem separately), and which were either absent in Bulgaria and East Germany or were rendered impotent by countervailing forces.

In the search for an explanation of the variants of political development, we propose to use the political style characterizing the formulation of economic reform in each country as the key to the intervening variables. The most notable difference in this respect was the type of demand articulation admitted into the decision-making apparatus. To the extent that demands are admitted into the system, the political choice is influenced by the demand syndrome.

Typical of the political style of the East German leadership is the fact that only a few months intervened between the first vague hints at the necessity for economic reform (at the Sixth Party Congress) and the formal issuing of a fully elaborated blueprint for structural reform which became the basis for extensive experimentation. No public demand articulation was observed during or after this intervening period. East Germany's new economic model was forged by a small group of party experts and apparatchiks within the central leadership. Once it was proclaimed, the public media concentrated their efforts on mobilizing the experts, managers, and workers within the economic structure into making the new economic system work. The emphasis was on science—scientific thinking, planning, accounting, and action. The new economic system extended a relative increase in role-player autonomy to the intermediate level of the trusts; and only after two years' experience had demonstrated the inability of the trusts to manage their industrial branches with the desired results could the enterprise managers effectively make demands upon the central leadership for greater autonomy. These latter demands were task-oriented—to wit, the managers complained that they could not execute their assigned tasks because of excessive administrative interference by the trusts. The effect of this demand articulation, combined with the unsatisfactory performance of the new economic system, was to introduce a second stage of economic reform (with a further streamlining of the structure) to bring a better balance of autonomous action into the vertical relationships among the role players. Still, the trusts remained the vital intermediate control agency of enterprise action.

Bulgaria's political style differed from that of East Germany in that, during the experimentation period, the regime allowed ideas for further reform to be publicly articulated. The Bulgarian leadership, apparently, was not as rigidly committed to its own economic guidelines as was the East German regime. In the aggregate, the confluence of demands for economic reform in Bulgaria's public media called for more role-player autonomy than the regime was prepared to grant, particularly in goal setting (planning), market orientation (pricing), and horizontal contracting. The trusts became an object of particularly sharp controversy involving competing demand articulation through public media. The reformed economic model resulting from this political style was structurally similar to that of East Germany (the trust remained as the pillar of the structure), but enterprise autonomy was comparatively greater, particularly in areas such as freedom to contract (horizontally), price formation, and goal setting, in which the enterprise manager appeared to have provisional autonomy, subject to approval at higher levels.

Hungary's political style was strikingly different from that of both East Germany and Bulgaria. The regime did not publish its own reform guidelines. Rather, it sought to formulate a new economic model based on a consensus among representatives of the most important professions, a model which could gain broad support. The Hungarian approach to the problem was to gather the experts into discussion groups to debate the direction the reform should take, as well as the numerous potential pitfalls that could be anticipated along the way. The burden of this debate did not enter the public media; instead, the public was continually kept informed of the emerging consensus and of outstanding problems still to be resolved. Though we know little about the *in camera* proceedings, we assume that the discussants argued autonomously from the perspective of their individual expertise and experience. The assumption of autonomous demand articulation is supported by a separate, public debate conducted by *Nepszabadsag*, the party daily, and its published summary of conflict and consensus among participating experts on a variety of issues. The assumption of autonomous demand articulation is further supported by the economic model resulting from the *in camera* debates, which, compared with those of the other countries, has the least common base with the structural patterns of the past and calls for the greatest enterprise autonomy. To recall an already quoted passage from an article by Central Committee member, Istvan Friss: "The general opinion [was] that it is the correct thing to grant maximal independence to the managing units. . . ."

We have, then, a fairly direct relationship between the type of demand articulation observed and the degree of autonomy granted to the role players within the economic subsystem, as shown in Table 4.

Table 4

Demand Articulation, Autonomy, and Spillover
in East Germany, Bulgaria, and Hungary

	Type of Demand Articulation	Degree of Autonomy	Spill-over
East Germany	Nonautonomous Task-oriented	Low	Low
Bulgaria	Semiautonomous Competing	Medium	Low
Hungary	Autonomous	High	High

Some Intervening Variables

The notions which we are about to present in explanation of the variants of political development are based on data which are largely a by-product of the research done. In some cases the data are admittedly insufficient to lend empirical support to comparative analysis, and sometimes we have had to bridge the gaps with theoretical links or comparative inferences.

Scanning the history of the three political systems, one can single out several variables which have had a bearing on the political style and which developed differently in each country. One can distinguish here between endogenous (internal) and exogenous (external) variables.

Endogenous Variables

Authority Orientation. This variable is subsumed under the concept of "political socialization." But here we will confine ourselves to the more limited and precise concept of orientation to authority because at this time we know little or nothing about the degree to which the process of political socialization has advanced in the political systems under consideration. Political socialization is a concept which, most scholars would agree, involves the transmission of a value system, including an orientation to the political culture. The Communist regimes of Eastern Europe have tried ambitiously to indoctrinate their peoples to accept the ruling political party or individual and to respect its political authority. The degree to which they have been successful is highly problematical. The Communist press in all three countries publishes a continuous barrage of instructions, exhortations, and admonitions to the functionaries on acceptance and respect, leading one to believe that in all countries political socialization is far from satisfactory. But with respect to authority orientation we can at least make some factually based assumptions concerning the peoples of Bulgaria, Hungary, and East Germany.

By authority orientation we mean, then, behavior patterns based on the mix of obedience to and expectations from those who manage the political system. Needless to say, authority orientation conditions the kinds of demands which are made upon the political system. One does not, for instance, air demands which might provoke violent retaliation by those in authority.

We can distinguish, at least theoretically, between the degree of authority orientation prevalent among the Communist Party membership and that prevalent among the population at large. The former is, presumably, higher than the latter. Indeed, the Communist Party is the primary transmission agent of orientations to political authority among the population at large. It is backed in this endeavor by the secret police and other control agencies. All other things being equal, therefore, the degree of the citizenry's orientation to political authority should vary with the size of the Communist Party relative to the total population, the dedication of the Communist Party membership to the party's values and goals, and the historical time span during which the transmission process has taken place.

What we are suggesting here is that there is no one-to-one relationship of the availability of coercive means in the political system to the extent of authority orientation. As Karl W. Deutsch has suggested, power is a currency, and the relationship of political power to the political behavior of the citizenry is somewhat analogous to that of a bank to its depositors.[1] It depends in large part upon the level of confidence and expectations, based on the way the power currency is administered. As the Hungarian Revolution of 1956 has demonstrated, even in the presence of ample coercive means, there can be a "run on the bank" of political power. Once there has been such a "run," confidence has to be reestablished all over again.

The Availability of Authority-Oriented Experts Relative to the Need. That the need for expert role players varies with the level of socioeconomic development in any political system is axiomatic and needs no further elaboration. Whether the available expertise need be authority oriented is more problematical; and this is a crucial consideration in the choice of political action available to the political leadership. The assumption, which is often made, that the infiltration of experts into the political system will change the system may be true in the long run; in the short term its validity depends on the demand-supply function, i.e., on the extent to which the system needs the expert for goal steering, relative to the available supply of desirable (in this case, politically reliable and authority-oriented) experts.

If, in a Communist system, the disparity between the need and the availability of experts is so great that the party is forced to abolish the requirement of party membership in its recruitment of role players, then the authority-orientation syndrome is bound to suffer. The expert is then in a position to make demands upon the system with less regard for conformity with established political-ideological patterns. His bargaining position is enhanced commensurately.

The "Conflict of Generations" Between Continuity and Change. The old party apparatchiks who obtained leadership positions within the various subsystems posed a dilemma to the central decision-making apparatus when goal seeking became more complex. These old stalwarts obtained their positions on the basis of their proven loyalty to the party and their commitment to its values and goals at a time when the consolidation of Communist control was more important than economic progress.

To the extent that these apparatchiks remain in positions of power, they tend not only to retard economic progress but also to stand in the way of any reform measure which they feel might jeopardize their vested interests or challenge their limited adaptive capabilities with new functions or procedures. They are, thus, a force supporting patterns of control which the leadership can ill afford to alienate.

The remaining apparatchiks are opposed by the new generation of experts, who are qualified by formal education and training to manage the multifarious goal-seeking process and, as such, are becoming increasingly indispensable to the political system. Even if the "experts" are politically socialized sufficiently to be trusted by the party leadership in management functions, their more pragmatic ideas may run counter to the processes to which the old guard has grown accustomed. This "conflict of generations," as it is known in the Communist countries of Eastern Europe, leads to competing demand articulation and impinges upon the political choice. Thus, depending on their aggregate power and influence in the political system, the party stalwarts of the old generation can have an important bearing on the political style which conditions political development.

The Incumbent Leadership. Closely connected with the conflict of political generations is the tenure, outlook, and flexibility of the highest decision maker (First Secretary of the party) in each country. His political choice is, of course, conditioned by a great variety of endogenous and exogenous factors, but the transformation of the input variable interactions into outputs depends to a large extent on the disposition, temperament, predilections, and past experiences of the incumbent.

Exogenous Variables

Among a large number of potentially influential exogenous variables, we shall consider only two.

The Influence of the West. Western influences may help to condition the political choice for change, depending on the reaction of the leadership to these influences. If the attraction of the Western way of life is high among the people of a Communist country, the regime may be reluctant to liberalize or decentralize its structure and patterns, fearing that such changes might arouse hope and ferment for more far-reaching liberalization. On the other hand, if the leadership is confident that the attractions of the West can be overcome by liberalization (or humanization) of the Communist political system, the influence of the West may well be positive.

The Influence of the Soviet Union. During the 1960's the East European Communist systems have become increasingly autonomous from the Soviet decision-making center in their domestic affairs. Although, as we have suggested, the Soviet Union may have provided the immediate impetus to economic reform in Eastern Europe, the variations in economic models suggest that the three East European countries we have focused upon went their own separate ways. We have found no empirical evidence that Soviet directives guided economic reform in these countries. Nevertheless, the relative importance of these countries to Soviet national interests may have helped the political choice. Soviet power and authority can be (and has been) used to bolster a Communist regime against popular pressures for change.

Comparative Analysis of the
Intervening Variables

At this point, let us make a rapid comparative survey of the development of these six intervening variables in the three countries and assess their relative impact upon the systems' capacity for change.

Endogenous Variables

Authority-Orientation Patterns. The salient difference between the three political systems with respect to authority orientation lies in the fact that in Bulgaria and East Germany its transmission was a continuous, uninterrupted process, whereas in Hungary it broke down completely during the revolution of October, 1956. This is reflected in the membership of the three Communist parties relative to the total populations. Since attitudinal data—which would enable us to make a more accurate assessment of the authority-orientation syndrome—are not available, we shall take variations in party membership over time as an indicator. This seems a reasonable approach, inasmuch as the party is the primary transmittor of authority patterns and agent of political control in the Communist systems. Continuity and change of party membership in the three countries can be compared in Table 5.

Table 5

Communist Party Membership as a
Percentage of the Population, 1955-66

	Bulgaria		East Germany		Hungary	
	CP Membership	App. Pop.	CP Membership	App. Pop.	CP Membership	App. Pop.
1955	455,251	5.9%	1,413,313	7.5%	800,000	8.6%
1957			1,500,000	8.5	100,000	1.09
1958	484,255	6.1			400,000	4.3
1962	528,674	7	1,556,650	9.2	400,000	4
1966	611,179	7.4	1,700,000	10	585,000	5.7

Source: Figures taken mainly from Radio Free Europe reports.

The table shows that whereas Bulgaria and East Germany experienced a steady growth in and consolidation of party membership, Hungary's party was decimated by the October, 1956, Revolution. Although Hungary's party was able to increase its membership rapidly in 1957 (by making membership a requirement for the more desirable jobs), it had to relax its screening process. The fact that the membership of the Hungarian Communist Party remained at the level of 400,000 from 1958 to 1962—i.e., half of its original size in 1955—is indicative of the leadership's dissatisfaction with the caliber of the people it had recruited into the party. Thereafter, the selection of new recruits proceeded more slowly, so that by 1966, the party had risen only to 75 percent of its size in 1955.

Compared with Bulgaria and East Germany, the capacity of the Hungarian Communist Party to transmit stable authority-orientation patterns has indeed been very low over the past 10 years. Its membership relative to the total population (at four to six percent) was far below that of the other two parties; the caliber of its membership was, by all indications, less than adequate for the political functions required to maintain a totalitarian political system. This inadequacy was reflected in the general apathy of the population and in the alienation of the creative intelligentsia (from 1957 to 1959, the best of Hungarian writers refused to write anything for publication), which contributed to a change in the Hungarian regime's policy in the direction of an "alliance" between the party and the people. From this point of view alone, then, the Hungarian political system was more susceptible to the pressures of change than were the Bulgarian and East German ones.

Goal-Seeking and Capacity for Change. Another striking contrast between Hungary and its two sister countries can be seen in the educational composition of their respective party memberships and its influence on the goal-seeking process.

One of the most detrimental consequences of the 1956 Revolution for the Hungarian political system's capacity for goal-seeking was the subsequent inability of the party to recruit competent people into its ranks. Of a total membership of 400,000 in 1961, only 21.3 percent had a secondary or higher education and 47.1 percent had not even graduated from primary school.[2] These statistics are particularly significant in view of the fact that some 58 percent of the Hungarian party membership held jobs in the party (apparatchiks), government, or security police. Little progress was made in subsequent years to redress this imbalance: by 1966, out of a total membership of 585,000 only seven percent of the party membership had been enrolled in institutions of higher learning and 20 percent had graduated from secondary school.[3] The percentage of those without a primary education had dropped from 47.1 in 1961 to 39 percent in 1964.[4]

With this low composite level of formal education and expertise, the Hungarian Communist Party could not effectively manage and control the political system in totalitarian fashion. As of 1961, therefore, the Hungarian leadership actively pursued an "alliance" policy under the slogan "who is not against us is with us," and launched an extensive recruitment drive for experts, regardless of party affiliation or political views, to assume important managerial positions in the economic sector which had hitherto been open only to party members. In many cases incumbent party apparatchiks were replaced by nonparty experts.

As a result of this recruitment of expertise regardless of party affiliation, the expert gained a bargaining position vis-à-vis the establishment that was unparalleled in the other two countries. Authority-orientation patterns suffered commensurate with the political system's inclination to compromise the maintenance of its political patterns in order to increase its capacity for goal-steering.

The position of the old-line party apparatchiks had been seriously weakened by Kadar's "anti-dogmatist offensive" in 1962. This weakening of the apparatchiks resulted in an additional improvement of the experts' capacity for effective demand articulation—i.e., the leadership was more responsive to the demands of the experts. It resulted, moreover, in the emergence of conflict between apparatchiks and experts—between party and nonparty at intermediate and lower levels of the political system—which could be mediated, but not resolved, through political processes.

While comparable data on Bulgaria and East Germany are not available, the Communist parties of these two countries appear to be in a much· better relative position. Neither of these governments had to resort to the expedient of relaxing its standards of political reliability. In Bulgaria, still an "underdeveloped" country, expertise is only gradually becoming indispensable to the system's goal-seeking functions. To be sure, the demand for competent people is greater than the supply, and the party-government has found it necessary to streamline the education system in order to close the gap. According to data published in Bulgaria (current in November, 1964), 64 percent of the 184,000 positions requiring a higher education were filled with qualified people; those requiring secondary education were filled to the level of 85 percent.[5] On the other hand, some 8.7 percent of the country's engineers and economists with a higher education and 10.2 percent of the available manpower with a secondary education were not employed in positions for which they were qualified. On the strength of these data, one can surmise that the need for experts in Bulgaria's economy was not acute as of the late 1960's.

Judging by its level of economic development alone, East Germany's need for experts in economic positions is even greater than that of Hungary. The available evidence suggests, however, that the SED is in a better position to recruit experts from within its own ranks than is the HSWP (Hungarian Socialist Workers' Party). By 1963, the SED claimed that it had succeeded in filling 75 percent of its leading positions at the central level with graduates from institutions of higher learning, compared with 50 percent at the district level, and 25 percent at the local level.[6] Whether this claim was true at the time it was made is impossible to say. Ernst Richert, from whose book these data were taken, estimated (on the basis of his calculations of the influx of graduates from higher institutions into the party and the demise of functionaries since 1954) that the SED had some 250,000 "active" and presumably competent functionaries in key positions, leading the more "nominal comrades." Richert thought that an active cadre base representing at most two percent of the population was rather low for purposes of political control, but it compares very favorably with Hungary.

Of the three countries, then, only Hungary resorted to the expedient of significantly lowering its political reliability criteria for recruitment of managerial personnel. We surmise from this that the "managerial class" in Bulgaria and East Germany remained more homogeneous in its orientation to authority. According to the evidence available in the public media, whatever conflict of interests existed between the political and administrative elites of these two countries remained submerged, indicating that it was probably less acute than in Hungary. The political systems of Bulgaria and East Germany were, therefore, less susceptible to the pressures of change than was that of Hungary.

The Conflict of Political Generations and Capacity for Change. The three countries under consideration show significant differences as to the status of the old revolutionary party apparatchiks in the political system. These variations help to explain the divergent paths of economic and political development.

In Hungary after the Revolution, the apparatchiks of the old generation who had obtained their places in the party through the patronage of Matyas Rakosi were essential to the new leadership of Janos Kadar in order to reconsolidate Communist control and speed the collectivization of agriculture to completion. Aside from their Stalinist outlook and modus operandi, however, these party stalwarts had little to recommend them. Lacking education and training, they were ill-qualified to manage the Communist economy—indeed, they were found to do more harm than good.

Once the collectivization of Hungary's agriculture had been accomplished, Kadar's ruling group saw the necessity for a conciliatory approach toward the people, if only to obtain their cooperation and participation in the essential tasks of the nation. The Revolution had put the Hungarian regime heavily in debt to the Soviet Union and other bloc countries, a debt which could be repaid only through a rapid rise in Hungary's national income. Kadar's regime, more perhaps than any other Communist regime, needed the cooperation of all people. Moreover, Kadar was anxious to show the many Hungarians who had fled the country during the Revolution that under his leadership, Hungary had become a good country in which to live. The old apparatchiks threatened the implementation and success of this new approach.

Soon after the 22nd CPSU Congress, Kadar's ruling group launched an "anti-dogmatist" offensive which gained momentum throughout

1962, leading up to the Eighth Congress of the Hungarian Communist Party (held in November, 1962). This offensive was aimed not so much at the removal of the Stalinist apparatchiks from their positions of power throughout the country as, it would appear, at depriving them of much of their power, at discrediting their "administrative methods," and at forcing them to conform to Kadar's political style. Perhaps to put the old Stalinists at a disadvantage, perhaps also to bridge the gulf dividing the party from the population at large, the local party organizations (presumably on central instructions) invited nonparty people to their election meetings preparatory to the Eighth Congress.[7] Significantly, this procedure was not repeated in the pre-Congress meetings of 1966.[8]

It is impossible to estimate the number of Stalinists who lost their positions between the end of 1961 and the Eighth Hungarian Party Congress, either by central administrative action or in local party elections. It is known that the elections of local party committees resulted in a 20 percent turnover of party secretaries and a 30 percent turnover of executive committee members; and indications are that a similar turnover rate may have resulted from the pre-Congress elections held from September 1 to October 31, 1962. However, the emphasis was not on purge but on education of the Stalinist incumbents; this, at least, was the dominant theme of the party press.[9] Repentant Stalinists who were willing to embrace Kadar's "centrist" policies were welcome.

As part of its "anti-dogmatist" drive, the Hungarian leadership renounced much of the privileged status attending party membership.

> There are still people who believe that their particular position entitles them to special rights and privileges. There are no special positions. Leaders and employees are equally subject to the statutes of the Party and the laws of the State.[10]

The numerous articles defending this policy which have since appeared in the Hungarian press lead to the conclusion that the leadership has succeeded neither in eliminating the old Stalinist apparatchiks nor in persuading them to change their outlook.* But the Hungarian leadership evidently did succeed in emasculating the old guard

---

*Articles alluding to the dissatisfaction of apparatchiks with the status accorded them are too numerous to cite here. One example, picked at random must suffice: "In various Party organizations, at membership meetings, a recurring phenomenon is frequently and increasingly passionately mentioned. Many of the comrades complain that nowadays the Communists, Party activists and Party work in general are not respected as they should be and there is neither a moral nor a political appreciation of them." So begins an article by Imre Vertes, "Party Members and Appreciation of Communist Work," in *Nepszabadsag,* (October 17,

sufficiently to recruit competent people from outside the party ranks for crucial roles in the economy. Thus, an additional dimension was added to the "conflict of generations" in Hungary as the old guard struggled against the rising influence of the younger generation, not only within the party but also in the professional fields which the party sought to control.

In the Bulgarian party the old guard remained comparatively stronger than did that of Hungary, despite signs of increasing impatience in the Politburo with the incompetence of the apparatchiks who managed the economic process. Thus, Todor Zhivkov remarked at a Central Committee plenum in 1961:

> Some comrades . . . sometimes claim high posts and high salaries, speculating with their merits in the past, without taking into consideration their training and real possibilities.[11]

Similarly, in its June, 1964, issue, *Novo Vreme*, the party's theoretical journal, addressed itself to the problem of party stalwarts who "in the past have worked well, but their forces and working capacity have decreased and they still do not want to realize it," and recommended that they be replaced by younger, more qualified cadres.[12]

By 1965, the need for competent managers had become more acute, and Bulgaria's leadership evidently entertained the hope that the old guard could be put out to pasture. In November of that year a decree was issued by the Council of Ministers concerning pensions to "old revolutionary cadres." This hope turned out to be somewhat premature. The resistance of the old revolutionaries to the government's retirement plan proved so strong that the regime decided to temporize. Addressing himself to this problem in his speech to the Ninth Party Congress in November, 1966, Todor Zhivkov adopted a conciliatory tone:

> The raising of specialists to leading work in no way means disregard for the old revolutionary workers. We must also in the future aim at not pensioning off prematurely those of them who are still able to work, while the pensioners should, according to their possibilities, be used for nonpayroll work.[13]

The conflict of political generations was only beginning in Bulgaria's political system. Under the circumstances, it would seem that Zhivkov's strategy was to allow competing demand articulation on the subject of economic reform in Bulgaria's public media. Zhivkov, who himself was

---

1965); HPS #1655. The author, of course, defends the Kadar line, but criticizes some erroneous ways of implementing this line.

evidently not strong enough to remove the old guard from power, may have welcomed whatever help he could get from the experts in his effort to weaken the position of the apparatchiks.

During the period under review, East Germany did not show symptoms of cadre malaise as acute as in either Hungary or Bulgaria. Occasionally Ulbricht would warn against habits and views left over from the Stalin era, but on the whole there was no effort to move against the apparatchiks. The following factors may help to account for this: (1) East Germany was at a much higher stage of economic development when the Communists assumed control of the country and hence had a much larger pool of expertise relative to the available management positions; (2) the destruction of East Germany's industry during World War II, combined with the wholesale shipment of many of the still remaining industrial plants to the Soviet Union, left a larger supply of expert manpower than was needed in the remaining industrial establishment; and (3) the expropriation of private industrial establishments by the state proceeded more gradually in East Germany than it did in the other two countries. Bulgaria and Hungary had virtually completed their industrial nationalization by 1950, whereas in East Germany, even in 1952 some 30 percent of the total industrial products, all of the craft production, and 55 percent of the labor force remained in the private sector. Having adopted a more gradual approach to nationalization, the East German regime had more time to recruit managers who were both expert and politically reliable. Since then, technical education has been a paramount issue. If there was in East Germany a conflict of generations between the party apparatchiks and the experts at the management level, it was not a prominent issue in the sources researched during the time period under investigation. One could observe, however, concurrent with the "secularization" of economic decision making, an increase in the autonomy, power, and functions of the party expert.

Some Characteristics of Incumbent Leadership. Among the three leaders of the political system in question, Janos Kadar was the last to rise to the position of First Secretary. He was the only one to have experienced the injustice of imprisonment under Rakosi's Stalinist rule. Kadar came to power as a result of Soviet military intervention in the Revolution of 1956. Presumably, he was hand-picked by the Soviets because the qualities of loyalty to Moscow and domestic pragmatism "were so mixed within him" that under his rule, Hungary might survive as a Communist state and remain a loyal ally to the Soviet Union. Kadar's political style lent credibility to the words of one of the more seasoned observers of Eastern Europe, who wrote about him:

> He was always a flexible, tolerant, even sentimental man with a good deal of warmth and human feeling. Yet his flexibility lay in the methods he used to reach the goal; about the goal—socialism and, eventually Communism—he showed himself to be strictly orthodox.[14]

There appears to be a difference in styles of rule according to the political training received by the incumbents. Those who spent the war years in Moscow, for instance, were inclined to be much more repressive in their domestic policies than the ones who spent the war years at home. Of course, the lines of distinction are often blurred by the political behavior of subleadership elites at national and local levels. As for Janos Kadar, he was one of those Communists who had spent the war years at home. He rose to prominent leadership positions only during the later 1940's and early 1950's. He was arrested in April, 1951, and confined in prison until July, 1954, the victim of a purge of the "home Communist" faction by the "muscovites."[15] With the fall of Matyas Rakosi in 1956, Kadar was elected again to the Central Committee, its Politburo and Secretariat.

Kadar's repressive policies during the immediate postrevolution period and his subsequent switch (after 1961) to a more humane course show him to be adept at both types of political leadership—perhaps a more pragmatic individual than Zhivkov or Ulbricht.

Bulgaria's Todor Zhivkov rose to the post of First Secretary in 1954, in the wake of Stalin's death and the resultant Soviet change to "collective leadership," which was soon emulated by all of the East European party-governments then still ruled by one man. Zhivkov's continuing tenure in office is probably due more to Soviet support than to the strength of his own power position. This assumption is indicated and supported by several visits to Sofia by high-level Soviet delegations at times of leadership crises in Bulgaria. One of these occasions was a reported conspiracy against Zhivkov's leadership in which several high-ranking army officers and intermediate-level party functionaries are known to have been involved. It brought a Soviet party delegation, headed by Suslov, to Bulgaria, touring the country for several days and displaying their unconditional support of Zhivkov.

Zhivkov's record as a ruler is that of a rather unimaginative apparatchik whose policies have reflected greater response to inputs from the Soviet Union than those from within the Bulgarian political system. Zhivkov's servility to the Soviet leadership was, as far as is known, the primary cause of the above-mentioned conspiracy.[16] This is reflected in the fact that, of the three countries under discussion, Bulgaria's economic reform style—from demand articulation to the new economic model—parallels that of the Soviet Union most closely, even though experimentation with the new economic model was begun a year earlier in Bulgaria.

In stressing Zhivkov's servility to the Soviet leadership, we do not wish to negate the "Bulgarianness" of Bulgaria's political system nor the individuality of Zhivkov's political style. In imaginativeness and vitality Zhivkov's style was dull in comparison with that of Nikita Khrushchev. In terms of flexibility, Zhivkov's political style compared favorably with that of Walter Ulbricht, if only because Zhivkov demonstrated a higher capacity for response to change in both the Soviet Union and his native country than Ulbricht did; but it fell far short of the flexibility demonstrated by Janos Kadar. Thus, interacting with other variables described in this chapter, Zhivkov's political style and the degree of its flexibility helped to condition the nature and scope of political development and to circumscribe the Bulgarian system's capacity for change.

East Germany's Walter Ulbricht is distinguished from his above-described colleagues in at least two respects: (a) he is the only First Secretary in the Soviet bloc who has held supreme power since 1945; (b) he alone among the three leaders served his political apprenticeship in the Soviet Union, i.e., he is the only Muscovite in the group still holding power. This apprenticeship and his subsequent selection by Stalin as ruler of East Germany is indicative of a "dogmatic" or "Stalinist" outlook which is probably not shared, or at least not to the same degree, by Kadar or Zhivkov. Judging only by the many references to his name and speeches in a large portion of the articles on economic reform, one would say that Ulbricht has developed a "personality cult" of his own. As the "most hated man in Europe" he has little else to recommend him as a leader other than his proven ability to keep the East German population in line, a job perhaps even more demanding in East Germany than in the other East European countries.

Ulbricht's inclination to "de-Stalinize" the authoritarian political process in East Germany is low indeed. In 1953 his reluctance to introduce the "new course" (consisting mainly of a temporary halt in the process of socialization in the economy and an attempt to raise the standard of living at the expense of heavy industry) had brought Ulbricht into difficulties with the new Soviet leadership. Instead of raising the standard of living, he had decided to raise the work norms. In June, 1953, Moscow forced the issue, but not in time to prevent the revolt of the workers, which had to be quelled by Soviet troops. For Ulbricht this event confirmed his thesis that a loosening of the reins, represented by the new course, could only lead to ferment. Khrushchev's denunciation of Stalin's personality cult and acts of terror produced ferment among party and people of East Germany little less acute than it did in Poland and Hungary, but Ulbricht managed to isolate the workers and intellectuals and deal with each separately. This feat of political acrobatics preserved political stability in East Germany at a time when Poland and Hungary were succumbing to popular upheavals, and won Ulbricht a good deal of respect from Moscow. His thesis of the necessity to continue Stalin's methods in East Germany was once again confirmed and probably gained some credence in Moscow. In February, 1958, Ulbricht overcame the last challenge to his leadership, the opposition of a political faction in the Politburo (led by Karl Schirdewan) which endeavored to remove him. Since then he has held a tight rein in true Stalinist style. "He who gives reactionaries a small finger," he said to the National Assembly (Volkskammer) on November 3, 1956, "will in the end lose his life."[17]

Ulbricht was by no means the only leader in Eastern Europe who held this view of totalitarian politics. Chervenkov in Bulgaria and Rakosi in Hungary acted in a political style very similar to that manifested by Walter Ulbricht; and both, incidentally, had received their preleadership training in the Soviet Union during World War II and before. Their tenure in office, however, ended in 1956 (Chervenkov was demoted to Deputy Prime Minister and Rakosi was ousted), leaving Ulbricht as the only one of his kind in Eastern Europe. His longevity in office and his ability to overcome any threats to his leadership have doubtless helped to condition the orientation of East Germany's role players and people to his personal authority. Poets write odes to him; songwriters create hymns to his name.[18]

What we have tried to suggest in this brief discussion is not that the First Secretary of the party is omnipotent, but that his *Weltanschauung*, temperament, and personality have an important bearing on the political style, and hence on the system's capacity for change. The imprint of these qualities tends to deepen over time. When all of the variables discussed in this chapter are considered in the aggregate, one gets the impression that the First Secretary is as much the master of the political forces within the system as he is their slave. Indeed, since the Communist system has not yet developed a process of periodic leadership rotation, the First Secretary's position is usually more powerful than that of any head of party or government in non-Communist political systems.

Exogenous Variables

Western Influences. The influence of the West is present in all of the East European countries, perhaps to varying degrees and dimensions. Our interest in this variable is limited to the perceived threat of Western influences to the patterns of the Communist system, as demonstrated by the public reactions of the several leaderships. Some striking differences in the anti-Western propaganda themes of the three countries can be noted, and on this basis we can make some tentative inferences of the degree to which the individual leaderships feel their system threatened by Western influences.

Demonstrative of Hungary's domestic propaganda offensive against the West are several articles published in 1965, following President Johnson's April, 1964, "bridge-building" speech. The bridge-building policy is seen as a realization by the U.S. Administration that the policy of "liberation" has failed; that capitalism can no longer be reinstated by armed force.[19] Therefore the capitalist West, and particularly the United States, has switched to psychological warfare. Among its instruments are the radio and tourism. Western radio programs beamed into Hungary, these authors admit, have vastly improved in sophistication and appeal. Many of the Western tourists, the Hungarian propaganda media claim, do not enter Hungary for legitimate purposes, but for spying and propaganda activities.[20] The articles, however, close with the encouraging note that although the new tactics of bridge-building present novel challenges to the ideological work of the Hungarian Communist Party, they can be met successfully by persuasion. Writes Laszlo Gyenes:

> The more effectively we fight the ideological heritage of the past [that of Rakosi?—author], the less firm will become the ground on which the propagators of "relaxation" intend to build.
> And really, this ground is becoming increasingly weak. The

trends of our development leave very little opportunity for the disrupting views of imperialism to spread. And if we make good use of our ideological weapons, we will have great success in the ideological battle, and in the neutralization of the relaxation endeavors.[21]

This quotation, as well as the tone of this and other articles, leads one to believe that the Hungarian leadership is confident that the challenge of Western influences is not only susceptible to ideological-persuasive counterreaction but, more importantly, that this challenge will lose its momentum as Hungary's liberal political development progresses. Hungary's Communist officialdom is worried about the influence of the West, but it also appears to be confident that in time the Hungarian citizenry will come to see the superiority (or comparative desirability) of the Hungarian political system, not through propaganda but through conviction. For the time being, the Hungarian leadership remains reluctant to close its borders: the answer to the problem is not stopping the flow of tourism in and out of Hungary, but a stepping up of the ideological counteroffensive.[22]

Disregarding the relative lack of sophistication of Bulgarian propaganda, the anti-Western offensive in Bulgarian media is essentially similar to that of Hungary.[23] The populations of both countries are apparently susceptible to the quality of Western material goods (automobiles, watches, etc.), which the domestic manufacturers cannot match. Hence, one finds in the media of both countries numerous allegations of lure and blackmail exercised by the Western propaganda machine on gullible citizens. These allegations are usually accompanied by gross distortions of life in the West: working conditions, lack of social security, lack of political freedoms, and the like. The influence of Western broadcasts, particularly by Radio Free Europe and the Voice of America, have apparently become a source of major concern to Bulgarian ideologists. As of 1968, these were still being jammed in Bulgaria, whereas other East European countries had abandoned this practice sometime in 1963 or 1964.

In Bulgaria, as in Hungary, the emphasis is on ideological work to overcome the challenge of Western influences. Bulgaria's propaganda on this subject, however, is more critical of the low state of ideological education, particularly among the youth. Moreover, it does not show the confidence we have seen in Hungarian media that the citizenry will eventually become immune to Western influences.

East Germany's anti-Western propaganda contrasts sharply with the

166

other two countries in that (a) it focuses primarily on West Germany, and (b) its favorite subject is West German militarism, revanchism, and neofascism, with distortions of life and conditions in West Germany running a close second.[24] Almost invariably the United States is tied to West German imperialism. The most consistent single message to the East German people on this subject is that the GDR is the peace state doing everything possible to prevent West Germany from starting another war. Almost every political event in West Germany is grist for the hostile East German propaganda mill. The Soviet Union, understandably, is upheld as the epitome of virtue, exemplary in everything that leads to peace, progress, and human happiness. This admiration of the Soviet Union is also characteristic of Hungarian and Bulgarian propaganda, but compared with East Germany, these latter two countries' propaganda is somewhat sedate. If there is a paradox between socioeconomic development on the one hand and the uncritical charismatic cult of a foreign, hegemonial power on the other, it is manifested in the most striking dimensions—on the surface, at least—in East Germany.

Undoubtedly, part of the explanation of this paradox can be found in East Germany's peculiar position in the international arena. Until May, 1969, when the GDR won diplomatic recognition from Syria, Cambodia, the U.A.R., and Southern Yemen, Sudan, and Iraq, the Pankow regime had diplomatic relations only with the Communist countries of the world.* Part of a divided country, East Germany is "independent" only in the fictional terms of Soviet semantics, where words like independence, democracy, and freedom have meanings different from those we accord them in the West. While one has difficulty finding concrete evidence that the Soviets interfere in East Germany's internal affairs any more than those of other East European countries (except, of course, Yugoslavia and Albania), it is clear that East Germany cannot make a move in the international arena without Soviet backing.

Ulbricht's regime, therefore, lacks widespread diplomatic recognition and the legitimacy such recognition provides both domestically and internationally. West Germany's "Hallstein Doctrine" was the single

---

*As of 1966, Hungary had diplomatic relations with 70 countries, Bulgaria with 62, East Germany with 13. In addition, East Germany maintained consular relations with nine countries. See R. Barry Farrell, "Foreign Policy Formation in the Communist Countries of Eastern Europe," *East European Quarterly* (March, 1967), p. 44.

most important factor inducing most of the governments of the world to desist from recognizing Pankow.* East Germany's gargantuan efforts to win diplomatic recognition are beyond the scope of this study, but they are indicative of the importance the regime attaches to the establishment of relations with non-Communist countries and the frustrations caused by consistent failure in this regard. Ulbricht's visit to Cairo in 1965 was played up in the East German news media as a major diplomatic breakthrough, a sign of the growing esteem accorded to Pankow; but the claim turned out to be vastly inflated, since Cairo could not be persuaded to show its esteem of Pankow in the usual diplomatic terms. The exchange of open letters between West Germany's Social Democratic Party (SPD) and East Germany's SED and the proposed public debate between the two in 1965 can be seen in this light as another East German offensive gone wrong. The SPD raised some very embarrassing questions (such as why East Germany continued to shoot people who tried to escape to West Germany), which soon put Ulbricht on the defensive and led him to abort the planned debates.

The East German regime is, thus, the prisoner of its own patterns, its diplomatic isolation, and its lack of popularity. It cannot afford to relax its hold lest its own slaves break loose.

Our inferential conclusion from this study of contrasts is that, regarding the influences of the West, all three political systems are on the defensive. But of the three Hungary seems to be the most confident, East Germany the most apprehensive. The different political styles certainly reflect these variants in leadership attitudes toward the influences from the West; more importantly, they may also be conditioned by these attitudes.

Soviets Interests in the Three Countries. Although the Soviet Union remains actively interested in the internal developments and foreign affairs of the three East European countries, we may assume that it is more interested in East Germany than in the other two. This is to suggest not that the Soviets interfere in East Germany's domestic affairs, any more than in those of the other two, but that, in case of internal turmoil, the Soviets would probably rush to the aid of the East German regime more quickly than to that of Bulgaria or Hungary. Presumably the 20 combat-ready Soviet divisions deployed in East

*The "Small Coalition" under Willy Brandt, which came to power in West Germany after the September 28, 1969, elections, publicly disavowed the "Hallstein Doctrine."

Germany would be adequate to quell any popular upheaval in that country.

This, then, must be counted as an additional factor on the minds of the East German people, a factor reinforcing authority orientation. The history of the past 20 years provides ample evidence that the Soviet leadership supports Ulbricht, however it regards him as a person or leader. Ulbricht is the only man in East Germany with the proven ability and inclination to keep the country closely tied and subservient to Moscow. His associates are unknown quantities in this respect. Nationally, ethnically, and culturally drawn to West Germany, the East German population (and perhaps some of its elite groups) is not one the Soviets can afford to take chances with: the spectre of reunification is too ominous. Of all these considerations the East German people are presumably very much aware.

Notes

1. Karl W. Deutsch, *The Nerves of Government* (New York: The Free Press, 1963), pp. 120-22.

2. "Party Recruitment After Abolition of Candidate Membership," HSR (June 9, 1967).

3. "On the Eve of the Hungarian Party Congress," HBR (November 24, 1966).

4. "Party Recruitment After Abolition of Candidate Membership."

5. "Old Hacks Still Enjoying Priority," *Narodna Mladesh*, (January 8, 1966); cited in BSR (July 19, 1966).

6. Ernst Richert, *Macht ohne Mandat* (2nd ed.; Cologne und Opladen: Westdeutscher Verlag, 1963), pp. 262-63.

7. "Hungarian CP Renewal Gains Impetus," HBR (October 5, 1962).

8. "Preparation of IXth Party Congress; a Departure from the 1962 Pattern," HSR (August 23, 1966).

9. "Hungary Stamps out 'Personality Cult,'" HBR (September 28, 1962).

10. "Winds of Change in the Hungarian Communist Party," HBR (March 15, 1962).

11. "Decree on 'Old Revolutionary Cadres,'" BSR (November 9, 1965).

12. Ibid.

13. "The Ninth Bulgarian Party Congress—An Appraisal," BBR (November 25, 1966).

14. J. F. Brown, *The New Eastern Europe* (New York: Frederick A. Praeger, 1966), p. 42.

15. Ibid., pp. 270-71.

16. Brown, op. cit., p. 19.

17. Carola Stern, *Ulbricht* (Cologne: Kiepenheuer & Witsch, 1963), p. 197.

18. Some of these are reproduced in ibid., pp. 249-51, 285-89.

19. This theme is representative of much of the anti-Western propaganda literature of this period. We are drawing here specifically on two articles which are almost identical in their views: Laszlo Gyenes, "In the Spirit of Relaxation," *Komarom Megyei Dolgozok Lapja*, (October 8, 1965), HPS #1650; and Erno Gulyas, "On the Policy of Relaxation," *Nograd*, (November 21, 1965); HPS #1666.

20. In this connection, two other articles are notable: Janos Bolygo, "An Odd Case: What Did Professor Montias Investigate in Hungary?," *Magyar Nemzet* (July 3, 1966), HPS #1726, which accuses the noted Yale economist of spying during his research trip to Hungary in the summer of 1966; and T. K., " 'Missionary' Tourists," *Del-Magyarorszag* (September 19, 1965), HPS #1648, a story of two tourists who allegedly passed out religious leaflets in an unidentified Hungarian town.

21. Gyenes, op. cit.

22. See "Ideological Clear-sightedness is one of the Most Effective Weapons for Overcoming our Errors," *Tolna Megyei Nepujsag* (September 22, 1965); HPS #1647.

23. Representative of the Bulgarian's efforts to counter Western influences are the following articles: V. Teodorov, "We Know Where to Draw the Line," *Vecherni Novini* (January 30, 1964), HPS # 510: ". . . The children of workers and peasants in capitalist countries remain ignorant all their lives because the secondary school fees are beyond their means; working class people in the West receive no paid holidays, neither are there rest homes for them, workers' canteens or free medical care. And God forbid the worker left without work (a threat always hanging over him), or becoming seriously ill. . . ." See also Ivan

Bachvarov, "Revolutionary Vigilance—A Foremost Duty of Every Patriot," *Novo Vreme* (February 2, 1964), BPS #515; and I. Vulov, "The Fight Against the Anti-Communist Propaganda of Imperialism," *Partyien Zhivot* (November, 1965), BPS #597. Many more could be cited which are specifically directed to the task of emasculating the Western influence, aside from the more general ideological treatises which include this task as one of several subjects.

24. See, for instance, the front page of *Neues Deutschland*, (December 23, 1964), on which the following articles appeared: "Existenz der DDR nutzt Europa" ("The Existence of the GRD Is Useful to Europe"), "Kein Vertrauen zu Nazi-generalen" ("Never Trust Nazi Generals"), "Bonn's Plaene gefaehrden alle" ("Bonn's Plans Put Everyone in Danger"), and "Kaempfen Sie mit uns gegen den Atomwahnsinn" ("Fight with Us Against the Insanity of the Atom"). Of course, not every issue of the official organ of the SED carries such a proliferation of fear-propaganda on its front page; nevertheless, articles such as these are a predictable feature of the East German media.

10 Summary of the Variables

Let us now summarize the variables for each political system and highlight their probable impact in conjunction with socioeconomic development on the systems' capacity for change.

Hungary

Compared with Bulgaria and East Germany, Hungary had reached an intermediate level of economic development at the time when the economic reform movement began in the Soviet bloc. The Hungarian Communist Party was numerically weak, relative to the total population. The 1956 Revolution had broken the orientation of the population to Communist authority and the caliber of the new party membership was below that required for the effective inculcation of authority-orientation patterns among the population. Moreover, with a very low aggregate education composition, the Hungarian Communist Party lacked the capability to manage the economic sector.

The party-government under Janos Kadar successfully emasculated the old generation of party apparatchiks still entrenched within the political system (particularly in managerial positions of the economy), whose outlook and modus operandi had helped stimulate the revolutionary ferment in 1956. Simultaneously, the party-government recruited competent people outside the party to help manage the multivariate economic processes and endeavored to form an alliance with the people, in hopes of increasing popular participation in the economic functions of the nation. Kadar's alliance policy was also calculated to obtain a measure of popular support for his regime, in order to compensate for the lack of support of the distrustful apparatchik elite.

The political necessity for this approach in Hungary is readily apparent, but it is also easy to envisage a different course of action under a different leadership. Had a man like Rakosi—the Ulbricht type—remained at the helm of the Hungarian political system, the dogmatist apparatchiks would have retained far greater freedom of action at intermediate and lower levels, and the approach to Hungary's problems would have been less flexible and imaginative. Under Kadar, however, the variables described in the previous chapter had relatively free rein, compared with the other two countries.

Among these variables was the influence of the West, which was probably stronger in Hungary than in Bulgaria and (since the erection of the Berlin Wall) East Germany. Hungary's borders to the West having been opened, many Hungarians were permitted to visit relatives who had emigrated after the Revolution, and many émigrés returned to visit Hungary. This reunion of Hungarians from East and West is one of the dominant themes in the propaganda literature on the problem of Western influences. In contrast with Bulgaria and East Germany, however, the Hungarian literature on this subject manifested a feeling of confidence that the East-West ideological gulf could be bridged, that the images would converge as Hungary drew away from the Stalinist tradition, and that Hungary's people would develop a positive outlook on Kadar's political system. In the meantime, patient persuasion rather than closing the borders seemed the best approach to the fight against Western influences.

This, then, was the political environment—i.e., the climate created by prevailing patterns of interaction between the regime and the people—in which Hungary's economic reform took place. It was an environment conducive to change not only in the economic sector but also in other sectors of the political system. Indeed, with the emasculation of the Rakosi-ite apparatchiks and the recruitment of the nonparty experts—with the attempt at an alliance between party and people—the stage had been set for a change in the political process. The reform of the economic structure, it was emphasized, would be based on a consensus of the experts within and outside the party. At the same time, however, the basic features of the Communist system—i.e., state ownership of the means of production and essential control of the state by the party—had to be preserved, and popular ferment had to be avoided, especially during the debating period. This helps to explain why the regime foreclosed competing demand articulation in Hungary's public media, why it confined the reform debates *in camera* and informed the public only of the consensus emerging from the debates. Hungary's deliberate approach to economic reform, the shunning of "dangerous experimentation," reflects a desire to forge a comprehensive economic model that would function smoothly from the start. One senses here a fear of mistakes and possible failure, a desire to mend the often torn cloak of infallibility which is so essential to Communist rule.*

One senses also in the Hungarian approach a desire to bring about a consensus among the population on national goals and on the methods by which these goals might best be achieved.

Although we know virtually nothing about the proceedings of the *in camera* debates, it seems reasonable to assume that the interests of the workers were raised in these discussions. Fortuitously, perhaps, there was a change in the upper-level leadership of the trade unions during the period of these debates. This new leadership (primarily Sandor Gaspar and Sandor Beckl) took the initiative to gain greater freedom of action and more power for the trade unions vis-à-vis the enterprise managers and the state, resulting in conflict between Gaspar and Nyers (both Politburo members), which only Kadar could resolve. Gaspar is known to be, next to Nyers, one of the most capable and trusted men in Kadar's entourage. Gaspar's appointment in 1965 as head of the National Trade Union Council, therefore, can be interpreted as a sign of Kadar's recognition of discontent among the proletariat and of the necessity for an effective interest-articulation mechanism that would

---

*This impression is confirmed by the Hungarian leadership's defensive statements on the subject of economic reform—to wit, that the reform does not represent a departure from basic party policy, but a change in method necessitated by a new phase of economic development. Furthermore, one can see the Hungarian party leadership's sensitivity to (potential) popular criticism of its alleged infallibility in statements such as the following: " . . we must dispel a few incorrect views. The most frequently recurring among them is the one that the Party and the Party organizations have to decide directly on every question, have to define every detail, and that the task of the other bodies (state and mass organizations) is merely the implementation. The continuation of such practice would result, first of all, in two harmful consequences. The independence of the responsibility of state and mass organizations would not develop suitably and Party activities would be wrongly interpreted by the masses, who would make the Party organizations and the CC directly responsible for the slightest mistake." Bela Bliszku, "More Effective, More Modern Party Work," *Nepszabadsag* (March 20, 1966); HPS #1696.

give the workers a voice in the political process. One is reminded of Gaspar's demands to the Ninth Party Congress that "the Party . . . should ask for the opinion—even in setting the goals—of the class forces assembled in the trade union movement."[1]

The demand for a greater role for the national legislature in Hungary's political process was less directly connected with the substance of economic reform; hence there is little reason to believe that it was a matter for debate in the reform councils. Nevertheless, it can be traced again to the regime's over-all objectives of increasing popular participation and confidence in the political process. In the development of both the trade unions and the legislature the notion was reflected that popular participation could be enhanced only through an improvement in the representation of popular interests and views. Kadar's regime possessed the flexibility to respond positively to these forces and to expand the political structure accordingly, without at the same time departing from the basic parameters of Communism.

Lest we overstate the case of Hungary's political development, let us hasten to emphasize that the Communist system continues to prevail in that country. The party leadership retains the initiative of policy and decision making. It would not permit the formation or existence of a competing political party, nor would it allow any public opposition to its rule. The party-government is in no way responsible to Parliament, nor is it legally bound by the advice or demands of the trade unions.

But compared with that of the other Communist countries, Hungary's political development has been significant. Within the Communist framework there has been a transfer of influence, if not of political power, to major institutions (legislature and trade unions) representing the people; and election procedures have been liberalized to such an extent that these institutions can be more accurately representative of the people. That the people have not yet taken full advantage of these opportunities has, as we have seen, been a source of some regret to the party leadership. For the time being, Hungary's Communist Party admits it is neither omnipotent, nor omniscient, nor omnipresent. It has, further, made some encouraging attempts to bridge the gulf between ideology and pragmatism—between what is orthodox and what works, and between political power and popular consensus.

Bulgaria

Of the three countries, Bulgaria had the lowest level of economic development during the reform period. The numerical strength of the

Bulgarian Communist Party was higher than that of Hungary, but not as high as that of East Germany. Authority-orientation patterns in Bulgaria were among the most stable in Eastern Europe (Bulgaria is the only one of the three countries that has not experienced a popular revolution during the two decades of Communist rule). In the aggregate, the membership of the Bulgarian party left something to be desired in competence and expertise, but in relation to Bulgaria's low level of economic development, lack of expertise did not yet seem to be a critical factor. The Bulgarian leadership never had to resort to alliance tactics or recruit expert help from outside the party. The authoritarian and doctrinaire integrity of Bulgaria's Communist system, then, remained relatively unimpaired. Nevertheless, the Bulgarian leadership was moved to admonish the leading apparatchiks at intermediate and lower levels to admit a higher proportion of educated applicants into the party.

In Bulgaria the old Stalinist apparatchiks were still firmly entrenched in intermediate and lower-level leadership positions. By virtue of their outlook and political power, they tended to inhibit change. Zhivkov lacked both the imagination and the political support among party and people inside Bulgaria to emasculate the old guard. Whatever political flexibility he possessed was conditioned more by Soviet stimuli than those from within his own political system. The appearance of competing demands for reform in Bulgaria's public media runs parallel with the great debate on the subject which was begun in the Soviet Union with the publication of Liberman's article in *Pravda*. On the one hand it can be seen as a sign of continuing covariance of Bulgaria's political style with change in the USSR; on the other hand, it may have been calculated to bring pressure on the old guard and, thus, to weaken its resistance to reform. At the same time, public interest in the economic debate was not so high as to develop a ferment of ideas on the issues. This may reflect the relatively low composite level of Bulgaria's intellectual development (compared with Hungary and East Germany), and it may also be attributable to the high level of authority orientation among the Bulgarian people.

As it was, at Bulgaria's relatively low state of economic development, and with Bulgaria's economy still managed largely by old-generation apparatchiks, the experts were not yet sufficiently strong to make their demands impinge upon the political choice of the direction and scope of economic reform. The influence of the West, insofar as it was a visible source of concern to the Bulgarian leadership, was confined largely to the young generation; hence it was a problem for the youth organizations (Komsomol) to immunize Bulgaria's youth against the material attractions of Western life. Bulgaria's adult generation, for the most part still rurally based, was not yet caught up in the Western magnetic field. In another decade, when Bulgaria's young generation has matured and become participant in the political and economic processes of the nation, the complex of pressures on the political system might develop different dimensions and the regime might have to increase its capacity for change or, alternatively, its capacity for repression.

Pressures arising from the labor sector were probably not as high in Bulgaria as they were in Hungary. For one thing, the working population was still engaged largely in agriculture. The industrial workers, for their part, were more inclined to vent their dissatisfaction by quitting and looking for other places of work. The practice was so widespread that the Bulgarian party-government was compelled to issue legislation designed to inhibit this freedom of movement in the job sector, and thus to assure some stability and continuity in the performance of industrial functions.[2] Thus, at least until 1964, the industrial proletariat of Bulgaria was making use of other means to improve its livelihood, working conditions, and other desiderata.

This does not mean that the workers in Bulgaria would not have preferred labor unions that could effectively articulate their interests to management and the party-government. But that was not the function of the Bulgarian trade union; and existing patterns of political authority and popular orientation to this authority were such as to forestall any expectations that the functions of trade unions would change. In Bulgaria, apparently, there were other ways for workers to satisfy their interests until the amendments to the labor code appeared. With the more confined environment of these amendments to the labor code (if they can be effectively enforced), some time will probably elapse before pressure builds up within the Bulgarian labor force to such an extent as to become a serious source of concern for the regime. At the end of our research time frame, the party-government appeared to have little difficulty in maintaining the status quo.

As to the developments in the role and powers of the Bulgarian national legislature, it reflects little overt popular pressure. Zhivkov's repeated promise to grant greater powers to the legislature, however, may be in response to subterranean popular pressures upon his regime. During the time frame under discussion, the structure of the Bulgarian

Parliament was augmented twice by the addition of new legislative committees, whose influence on the legislative process, however, continues to be minimal. The introduction of the question period undoubtedly enhanced the role of the Parliament, not as a legislative body but as a forum before which the individual ministries could be held accountable for their actions. This accountability, however, remained limited indeed. The Bulgarian legislature could not call spontaneously for the removal of an incompetent minister, but it could embarrass the minister by a negative vote, and thus keep him on his toes. This expansion of Parliament's role could only have helped Todor Zhivkov in maintaining a greater degree of efficiency and responsible operation in his ministries; it certainly did not impede the authoritarian powers of his regime.

At the end of our time frame, then, Bulgaria's political development was largely confined to the economic sector. If pressures were building in the other sectors as a result of the economic reform, they found no expression in the public media and they were evidently not strong enough as yet to force the Bulgarian regime to change direction.

East Germany

At the highest level of socioeconomic development of the three countries, East Germany's political system manifested the lowest capacity for change. Our description of the variables intervening in East Germany's socioeconomic and political development relationship suggests that Ulbricht's party-government had at once the least compelling reasons for change and the most compelling reasons for continuing the status quo.

East Germany's labor productivity had been growing at a respectable average level of 6 percent with only minor fluctuations, i.e., the country was continuing to achieve impressive growth rates in output with only minimal increases in employment even before economic reform got under way.[3] This fact alone may initially have convinced the East German leadership that in order to do better, the participants in the economic process would have to be motivated to greater efforts, but that there was nothing fundamentally wrong with the economic system per se.

Numerically, the SED was the strongest party (relative to the total population) in Eastern Europe. To all appearances it had a sufficient number of technically qualified cadres to manage the economy. With totalitarian patterns of rule stable since 1953 (the year these patterns were briefly interrupted by the workers' revolt) and some 20 Soviet divisions stationed in the country, the East German population knew what to expect from political authority. The erection of the Berlin Wall in 1961 and the subsequent shooting of those caught in the attempt to escape to West Berlin probably reinforced the authority orientation of the population. If totalitarian rule thrives best in an atmosphere of crisis, East Germany was perhaps the ideal country in Eastern Europe for its perpetuation.

Although the popular orientation to political authority was high, it could be maintained at this level only by continuity in rigid authoritarian patterns of rule. A relaxation of control, such as even a partial opening of public demand channels, might have reawakened latent ideas for change which would have been difficult to contain. In this respect, the influence of the West, particularly of West Germany, must be regarded as a real threat to the stability of the East German political system. Ethnically and culturally based identifications of the East German population with that of West Germany widens the dimensions of this problem. Lack of international recognition of East Germany as a sovereign state deprives the Pankow regime of much of the legitimacy which the Hungarian and Bulgarian regimes can claim. This lack of legitimacy has to be compensated for by coercive means.

This is how it must look to Walter Ulbricht, the only "little Stalin" still ruling in Eastern Europe. A man possessed of an authoritarian personality par excellence, his *Weltanschauung* conditioned in Stalin's Comintern, Ulbricht would by temperament be loath to loosen the authoritarian reins even if the psychopolitical conditioning of East Germany's population at large were less threatening to his throne. He is now 75 years old, and all of his life's political experiences have probably deepened his conviction that his authoritarian style is the only one conducive to stability in a Communist political system.

In the background there remain the 20 "fraternal" Soviet divisions stationed in East Germany to defend Ulbricht's regime against encroachments from the capitalist world. Ulbricht would undoubtedly be loath to let any situation develop in East Germany that might require the deployment of Soviet troops against the population, such as occurred in 1953. But the very presence of such a sizable Red Army contingent in East Germany is a continual reminder to the people of the futility of fomenting popular upheaval.

So much for the factors which inhibit the East German regime's susceptibility to the forces of change. On the other side of the coin, the necessity for change does not appear to be nearly as great as in the other countries of Eastern Europe. At the time the East German Communists assumed power they inherited a large pool of skilled manpower and expertise. The changeover from private industry to state industry—i.e., the process of nationalization of the country's means of production—was more gradual in East Germany than in the other East European countries, allowing the regime more time to select competent people with suitable authority orientation for crucial role-playing positions in the economy. Economic goal seeking and maintenance of political patterns, therefore, did not conflict as much in East Germany as they did, for instance, in Hungary or as they were beginning to in Bulgaria. Although we find a great proliferation of educative articles in the dailies and periodicals, replete with illustrative examples of VVB's and VEB's applying the right methods with good results, actually the technical competence of the managers does not appear to be a problem of concern in the public media. On the other hand, there is a great emphasis on postgraduate education to the extent that VVB's have been asked to establish special schools for their technical cadres in cooperation with various universities and scientific institutes. The focus here is primarily on new products and productive processes, with the aim of reaching or surpassing the most developed countries of the West in world markets. This ambition itself reflects East Germany's high level of industrial development.

The stress on cybernetics indicates that East Germany has a potential for information processing at central and intermediate (VVB) levels which Hungary and Bulgaria cannot hope to acquire in the near future. Thus, while a reduction in the role of the central planning agencies is a feature of all three economic models, this central role remains greater in East Germany than in the other two countries. The need for autonomy—for autonomous, creative, responsible planning and action—at the enterprise level may, therefore, not have appeared as great. Although there were task-oriented demands for greater autonomy for the VEB's (as could be seen from rebukes by the leadership), the capability of cybernetics offered viable alternatives to these demands, which would, at the same time leave greater control of the enterprises at the center. East Germany's economic reform, therefore, offered the least autonomy to the role players at the enterprise level.

East Germany's economic reform produced no visible stir in the labor sector. The trade unions continued their functions, transmitting the party-government's demands, mobilizing the workers to greater efforts, and educating them in the socialist spirit. The creation of production committees as part of the new economic model appears to have some significance if only in contrast with Hungary, where the abolition of production committees led to a transfer of their functions to the trade unions. But since the East German production committees were never intended to represent the interests of the workers, but rather to help organize and coordinate short-term production tasks, and since these committees were composed predominantly of scientific-technical cadres and skilled workers, their mediating role in the conflict of interests between managers and workers could easily be overemphasized. From the little information available, the East German production committees may, in time, develop a capacity for coordination of production functions and thereby alleviate some of the stresses in this area of worker-manager relations; but the actual representation of worker grievances is beyond their powers and functions. The power of the enterprise manager was not significantly enhanced in East Germany's new economic model; hence, the relationships between management and workers remained largely the same. The workers had little more to fear from management under the new system than they did under the old. This contrasts sharply with Hungary's economic reform, where increased power of the manager presented serious threats to the interests of the workers. When we combine these factors with other variables we have discussed in this chapter (authority orientation and leadership disposition), the lack of movement in East Germany's trade unions is more readily understandable.

The lack of political development in East Germany's legislature can be attributed to the factors briefly described in this chapter. As long as Ulbricht remains in power, he is not likely to let his decision making be influenced by any legislative assembly. Popular expectations in this regard are probably not high: the East German people have lived under some kind of totalitarian dictatorship since 1933, and legislative assemblies serve as a forum for the articulation of the party-government's policy rather than the articulation of popular interest. Hitler's Third Reich was no different in this respect from Ulbricht's Communist system. Popular orientations to political authority seem to have been thoroughly conditioned by more than a generation of rigid authoritarian rule.

Potentially, there may be many latent expectations of change in popular representation once Ulbricht departs from the throne of political power, and these may rise to the surface, particularly if his death is followed by a leadership crisis.

Notes

1. HPS # 1772.

2. See HBR (February 7, 1964). The amendments to the labor code called for enterprise management to sign a contract with every new worker, stipulating a term of employment. Should the worker violate the contract by quitting before its expiration, he could not be hired again by another employer; furthermore, he would lose all rights and privileges, such as social security, housing, sick benefits, and the like. Apparently during the first half of 1963, 188,313 out of a total of 700,000 industrial workers had changed their jobs. *Rabotnichesko Delo*, (August 28, 1963).

3. See J. F. Brown, *The New Eastern Europe* (New York: Frederick A. Praeger, 1966), p. 291.

11 Conclusions and Prospects

Conclusions

From what was said in the last chapter, it follows that the impact of socioeconomic development upon political development depends upon a number of historically conditioned factors which evolve differently in each country and evoke different stimulus-response relationships in the several political systems. One vital link between these intervening variables and socioeconomic development is the capacity of the political system for steering toward its goals, for this capacity appears to be conditioned by the interactions between these two variable clusters.

In East Germany, for instance, a high level of socioeconomic development, already attained before the Communist takeover, provided Ulbricht's political system with a labor pool sufficient in skill and expertise to steer the economic subsystem in the direction of progress even under relatively tight central control. Authority-orientation patterns were so well developed that the population did not expect to be able to make effective alternative demands for change upon the regime. Other variables (Ulbricht's authoritarian personality, extreme fear of Western influences—indeed, fear of any change that might produce ferment among the people—and the security interests of the Soviet Union) inhibited change. In Hungary the cluster of intervening variables had evolved entirely differently, so that, at a level of socioeconomic development lower than that of East Germany, the Hungarian political system's capacity for goal steering was seriously

185

impaired. On the other hand, Kadar's personality allowed much greater flexibility and pragmatism than Ulbricht's did. As a matter of pure speculation, one could substitute the East German political system upon the Hungarian scene and find that the goal-steering mechanisms would break down entirely, resulting in political chaos and perhaps popular revolt.

In Bulgaria, on the other hand, the variable mix of low-level socioeconomic development, high authority orientation, low expertise, and stubborn entrenchment of old-guard apparatchiks (combined with an unimaginative, inflexible leadership) still left the political system with a relatively high capacity for goal steering and thus weakened those pressures for change which otherwise might have been compelling.

Thus, depending upon the conglomeration of intervening variables and their interactions with the socioeconomic development complex, the pressures for political development and the political system's susceptibility to these pressures may not bear any direct relationship to the level of socioeconomic development at all. This, of course, does not mean that the impact of socioeconomic development upon political development is minimal, but rather that it is exerted by way of other variables whose influence upon political development appears to be more direct and immediate. Socioeconomic development may be a necessary condition for political development, but by itself it is not sufficient to determine the direction of change in the political system.

Prospects

We have examined in this study three Communist systems over a very short period of time. It was a period of rapid change, to a large extent consciously manipulated by the incumbent leaderships, probably under an initial stimulus from the Soviet Union. Toward the end of our time frame, new economic models had been signed into law, but the new relationships between role players still had to stand the test of time and practice. Conceivably, the new economic models could again be revoked, although this appears most unlikely. At this point we will simply have to assume that the changes which have occurred so far in the three countries set the stage upon which future political development will take place. In all three political systems this stage is a relatively novel one which gives rise to some interesting speculations for the future.

Regardless of the scope of political autonomy granted to the role players in the new economic models, the ideological determinants of the political process are giving way to more pragmatic ones. The political decision-making process, particularly for the economic sector, is being based upon increasingly rational foundations, and subsystem role players at various levels have been drawn into this process as more or less autonomous participants. Although the extent to which the new economic models have increased role-player autonomy varies from country to country, the relationships of the role players to the state organs and to each other have changed visibly. In all systems, for instance, the role players at trust and enterprise levels have gained sufficient autonomy to establish relationships (contracts) with each other independently, whereas under the old rules, these relationships used to be centrally directed. These autonomously established, horizontal relationships now govern to a large extent the long-range decisions and plans of the central state organs. Insofar as rational criteria, such as profitability, technical development, and labor productivity, have become predominant in the decision-making process, the arbitrariness which has been so characteristic of Communist decision making has been drastically curbed. The hard political boundaries encompassing the economic system have by no means contracted, but they may have softened somewhat as the role players have become more autonomous and the political system has become more susceptible to impersonal economic forces or laws.

Coincidental, and perhaps commensurate, with the increased autonomy, the influence of the economic role player upon the decision-making process at the center has increased. Based on rational criteria—with which he, as the expert, is presumably most familiar—he is now in a better position to make demands upon the political system. In the long run, the most likely and significant effect of this will be an expansion and institutionalization of demand channels leading upward into the political decision-making center, giving rise to more fluid and pragmatic political processes.

All other things being equal (and, of course, they are not), we would expect, according to the findings at hand, some variations in demand objectives in the three countries. In Hungary, for instance, where the dominant criterion of economic performance is enterprise profitability (based, of course, on rising labor productivity and technical development), one would expect an increase in profit-oriented demand articulation, which might focus on a further liberalization of price determination, competition with domestic and foreign enterprises, market forces, and the like. One would expect a similar demand syndrome in Bulgaria (indeed, we have seen similar demands publicly articulated during the debating period in that country). But since Bulgaria's political development did not yield the same degree of enterprise autonomy, demands in that country may continue to focus on weakening the inhibitive powers of the trusts on the freedom of action of the enterprises. In East Germany, at its present stage of political development, the demands by the enterprise managers are likely to remain largely task-oriented, since profitability is a criterion subsumed under higher goals of attaining or surpassing the highest technological standards of the most developed capitalist countries.

Under present circumstances, then, Hungary's political development appears to have reached the stage where demands from the economic sector are likely to propel the system in the direction of further liberalization. Furthermore, Hungary's political development was not confined to the economic sector alone (as it was largely in Bulgaria and East Germany), but it spilled over into the labor and legislative sectors of the political system. The role players in both of these sectors gained a significant measure of autonomy and, more importantly, their relationships to the people were visibly strengthened. Though trade unions and Parliament are still dominated by the Communist Party leadership, their new role and functions have moved them into an intermediary position between the rulers and the ruled. Thus, caught in the middle between a mellowing totalitarian regime and the rising expectations of the Hungarian people, the effectiveness of these two institutions may well hinge on their ability to bridge or narrow the gulf between the two. Failing this, the trade unions and Parliament may well succumb to paralysis, with unforseeable consequences for the political system. But if they succeed, they will help the Hungarian political system through the coming period of conflict—which seems inevitable with the increasing fluidity of the political process and is, indeed, already visible to an increasing extent in the Hungarian press—to a further stage of political development, which, hopefully, will be based on a better consensus between party and people.

Turning our attention once more to Bulgaria and East Germany, in both countries political development was confined largely to the economic sector. We have already suggested that the respective new economic structures and dominant performance criteria will give rise to different demand objectives in the two countries (profit-oriented ones in Bulgaria and task-oriented in East Germany). The prospects for more liberal political development, under present conditions, are therefore better in Bulgaria than in East Germany.

However, present circumstances are likely to change, especially in East Germany, in the near future. Ulbricht is nearly 80 years old and may soon have to give up his throne. It would be futile here to speculate who his successor will be; whoever will inherit Ulbricht's mantle is not likely to be powerful enough, initially, to fill the huge political power vacuum which Ulbricht will leave behind. A leadership crisis, the usual pattern of political succession in Communist systems, is almost inevitable.

Inevitable also, at East Germany's stage of economic development, has been the rise of expert apparatchiks into leadership positions at all levels below the Polituro. Barring the unlikely assumption that Ulbricht's successor can or will base his political power entirely or largely on the political and military support of the Soviet Union, he will have to seek political support among his colleagues in the Central Committee and the district party executive committees. There he may find that the hitherto stable orientation to Ulbricht's political authority has vanished and a new set of psychopolitical variables have come into play. Although the apparatchiks have, presumably, developed their own vested interests in the Communist system (and would not, in any case, abandon Communism for fear of Soviet intervention), they will probably demand a greater participatory role in the political decision-making process.

The hitherto suppressed creative intelligentsia will almost certainly raise its voice, and the population at large will, at the very least, demand an atmosphere free from oppression. It is unlikely that a new leadership will be able to continue screening out these popular demands, as Ulbricht has been able to do.

The long and short-range consequences of these and other new variable interactions cannot be foretold. It seems certain, however, that they will bring greater fluidity into the political process of East Germany's Communist system, barring massive military intervention by the Soviet Union. Relations between East and West Germany may also become more rational and give rise to additional forces for change in the political system.

Zhivkov, at the time of writing, is 59 years old. Although he is politically much weaker than his counterpart in East Germany, he continues to enjoy the support of the Soviet Union. At Bulgaria's present level of socioeconomic development, the pressures for change do not yet appear to be so strong as to impinge seriously upon the regime's freedom of political choice. This situation, however, is already now beginning to change. Bulgaria's economy is approaching the level of development where the expert role player will become indispensable to goal steering; and soon a different kind of popular participation (i.e., voluntary, conscientious, and responsible—the kind for which even authoritarian regimes have to make concessions) will be essential to further progress. Whether Zhivkov is sufficiently astute and flexible to manage the political system in the presence of these emerging forces must remain an open question; but if he is not, there may well be crises during the 1970's.

For the present, as we have already suggested, the stage is set for a variety of demand articulation from the economic sector, which may cause more liberalizing political development and thus prepare the ground for the conflicting forces which will, almost inevitably, arise in the future. Perhaps in the meantime Zhivkov will fulfill his promise to give the Bulgarian legislature a greater role as an intermediary between party and people.

In the final analysis, one should not leave out of account the potential reciprocal influences of the three countries upon each other, as well as those of the other East European countries undergoing similar political development—particularly the Soviet Union. These influences may give rise to additional potent forces for change within the several political systems. If political development in Eastern Europe continues to be a gradual process (unlike that in Czechoslovakia in 1968) which does not seem unduly to threaten the underlying foundations of the Communist systems (although it may erode them imperceptibly), then the several Communist regimes may be less fearful of granting concessions for more liberal political development.

Part 3: The Changing Framework of Soviet Hegemony

12 East European Relations with the Soviet Union: From Pawns to Participants

When one considers the Soviet totalitarian system (totalitarian here defined as a system in which the central authorities seek to control totally every facet of national life), it would seem logical that the Soviet Union, insofar as it controls the countries of Eastern Europe, would seek to mold their political systems in its own likeness and to make their policies conform to its own. That this is indeed the ideal Soviet aim (even if reality does not always accommodate Soviet policy makers) is amply demonstrated by the history of Soviet-East European relations during the postwar period. From the Soviet point of view, to make Communism in Eastern Europe an extension of the Soviet political system and its policies was not only logical, it was an imperative dictated by the nature of Communism and its goals in the international environment in which it sought to survive and grow.

The foregoing parts of this book, focusing on the forces at work in the domestic evolution of East European Communist systems, have traced the trend from *Gleichschaltung* under Stalin to increasing diversity of domestic politics under Khrushchev and his successors. It will be remembered that soon after Stalin died, the new Soviet leadership sought to contain the potential popular ferment in Eastern Europe through concessions, particularly in the consumer sector. We have already briefly described signs of reluctance among satellite leaderships to follow post-Stalin Soviet policy through its several gyrations, which they apparently felt might destabilize their own regimes. As it turned out, the pent-up frustrations and disaffections of the captive peoples could not be contained everywhere. Terror and blood purges were replaced by concessions and amelioration; fear gave way to recrimination against the executors of Stalin's repressive policies.

Khrushchev had neither the image, the power, nor apparently the personal inclination to perpetuate Stalin's brand of leadership. The power Stalin wielded was not transferable: it had been gradually arrogated through years of careful manipulation, ruthless elimination of political opposition, and the creation of groups of followers loyal to the personal command of the *vozhd*. Khrushchev differed from Stalin in one respect that was crucial to the evolution of intrabloc relations. A self-confident master of the art of politics, he relied primarily on political maneuver and never became the absolute dictator that Stalin had been. Instead, he found it expedient at the Twentieth CPSU Congress in 1956 to denounce Stalin for his excessive use of ruthless methods in the exercise of his personal power, implying that he (Khrushchev) was going to rule by different methods.

In line with this predilection, Khrushchev attempted to restructure the Soviet bloc on a foundation that could accommodate some of the emerging vital interests (which had been suppressed under Stalin's personal rule) of the several ruling Communist parties without unduly jeopardizing the leading role of the Soviet Union in the Communist camp. In a real sense, Khrushchev sought to rectify some of the damage Stalin had done to the international Communist system.

To this end, Khrushchev flew to Belgrade in 1956, accompanied by Premier Bulganin, to end the Soviet-Yugoslav dispute and bring Tito back into the camp. At the Belgrade airport, he publicly apologized for "mistakes" committed by the Soviet Union in its relations with Yugoslavia in Stalin's time. (At the time, Khrushchev was not yet ready to criticize Stalin directly, so he heaped the blame for these "mistakes" on the late Lavrenti Beria, the infamous former chief of the Soviet Union's secret police who had been executed in December, 1953.) In this encounter, Khrushchev also implicitly conceded that the road charted by the Soviet Union was not the only one leading to Communism, that socialism could develop differently in different countries. This concession was more explicitly stated in the communique on Tito's visit to Moscow a year later, which stated, among other things, that there were several roads to Communism.[1] Needless to say, this concession undermined the already tenuous ideological foundation of Soviet totalitarian control over the countries of the Communist camp. It also acknowledged an existing fact—a significant diminution of Soviet authority in the international Communist movement. For the Chinese, too, were embarked on their own road to Communism, as Khrushchev admitted at the Twentieth CPSU Congress,[2] and Italy's Communist Party leader, Palmiro Togliatti, in his thesis on "polycentrism,"[3] asserted the right of Western Communists to autonomy from Soviet control.

By making these concessions, Khrushchev undoubtedly did not intend to downgrade the Soviet Union's leading role in the world Communist movement or in the Soviet bloc proper; he simply sought to make the Communist international system more viable and manageable than it had been even under Stalin's personal command. Incessant emphasis on the uniting principles of Marxism-Leninism to which all Communist parties adhered, and of which the Soviets continued to regard themselves as the leading interpreters, revealed the assumption that the Soviet Union's political and ideological authority in the bloc was sufficiently great to lead the diverse elements of the international Communist movement into the mainstream. Insofar as this assumption relied on the top-level leaderships of the Soviet bloc countries (most of whom depended heavily on Soviet support for their positions), it was not altogether unfounded. But among lower levels in the several Communist parties and among the populations, ferment increased with every change in doctrine and policy dispensed from Moscow. After Khrushchev denounced Stalin's personality cult, it was no longer so much a question of whether the satellite leaderships would remain loyal to Moscow, as whether they could remain in control of their oppressed populations. For if Khrushchev's admission of different roads to socialism released nationalistic aspirations in Eastern Europe, his condemnation of Stalin's personality cult released anger at the oppression suffered at the hands of the Soviet Union's henchmen, not only unnecessarily (contrary to past propaganda) but also illegitimately. In Poland and Hungary the people rose in revolt; in other East European countries, popular ferment threatened the continuing stability of Communist rule.

In the course of the Polish and Hungarian upheavals of 1956, Moscow felt compelled to confess to "violations and mistakes which belittled the principles of equal rights in the relations between the socialist states" and to promise to base its relations with East European countries on a more satisfactory foundation.[4] Among the remedies the Soviets suggested were a reevaluation of the "desirability of the further stay of Soviet advisers in these countries," as well as of "the question of the Soviet forces stationed in those countries. . . ." Accordingly, most Soviet advisers, who had been the Soviet controlling arm in the bloc countries, were withdrawn and status of forces agreements were concluded with those countries where Soviet troops were stationed (Poland, East Germany, Hungary, and Rumania), regulating the rights and obligations of Soviet forces and the host governments. Among the most prominent victims of this new policy was Soviet Marshal Rokossovsky, who had to leave his post as Politburo member and Defense Minister of Poland. Indeed, for some time after 1956, Poland, whose leadership had successfully defied the Soviet Union in the matter of Gomulka's ascension to the First Secretaryship, became (if only temporarily) the vociferous exponent of national Communism in the Soviet bloc.

Thus, by the second half of the 1950's, the Soviet leadership was making concessions to nationalism in Eastern Europe to the extent of withdrawing at least some of the most offensive features of arbitrary Soviet domination over the satellites. This paved the way for the rulers of Eastern Europe to play an increasingly autonomous and meaningful role in the affairs of their respective states, and to take into account national needs, traditions, and group interests in their formulation of policy. As we have seen, Poland's domestic politics departed in several significant ways from those of the other bloc countries after Gomulka's rise to power (e.g., its refusal to collectivize agriculture, its relatively lively parliamentary legislative process, and its reluctance to crack down on intellectual freedom), while among the other bloc countries, diversity became conspicuous only at the beginning of the 1960's. The seeds of this growing autonomy from Soviet control (relative to the restrictive frame of the Stalin era) had been sown during the period of popular ferment—1953-1957. Aside from the above-mentioned events, considerable importance attaches to the impact of Poland, Yugoslavia, and China on the subsequent course of Soviet-East European relations.

The Significance of Poland to
Soviet-Satellite Relations

Monolithic unity of the Soviet bloc, as seen through the ideological prism of Moscow, means a close identity of ideology, institutions, and political processes in all of its member countries. Gomulka's successful ascension to political power in Poland, against the wishes and in spite of the intervention of the Soviet Union, threatened to end this unity, as well as that of Soviet authority in the bloc. The year 1957 was a time for reevaluating the foundations on which relations between the Communist states rested. The authority once wielded by Stalin in the Communist camp had dwindled in the hands of his successors; indeed, it had been partially replaced by the influence of Communist China and Yugoslavia. Popular nationalism in Poland and Hungary had extracted potentially far-reaching concessions from the Kremlin, leading to a further diminution of Soviet control.

These circumstances made imperative a meeting of the ruling Communist Party leaders to hammer out common rules of conduct, agreement on ideological guidelines and world outlook, and agreement on the extent to which ruling Communist Parties could deviate to either the right or the left (revisionism and dogmatism, respectively) without impairing the unity of the Communist camp. All of these questions were, of course, logically and intimately connected with the reestablishment of Soviet authority in the Communist world through a common recognition of its leading role. For if there was to be unity in the camp, someone would have to set the course.

To Gomulka the reestablishment of Soviet authority may well have meant the reconsolidation of a Stalinist type of Soviet control over East Central Europe, rendering more difficult the perpetuation of concessions he had made to popular sentiment in Poland. Under the circumstances, Gomulka was loath to give public recognition to the leading role of the Soviet Union in the Communist camp.

Until mid-1957 Gomulka could count on the public support of the Chinese and Yugoslav Communists for his stand in favor of national Communism. But by the fall of 1957 the Chinese position on this issue had changed. At the Moscow Conference of Ruling Communist Parties in November, Tito, pleading an attack of lumbago, did not represent the Yugoslav Communist Party. Thus Gomulka stood alone at the conference and, probably unwilling to defy the rest of the bloc alone, submitted to the majority. Perhaps partly in deference to his vigorous arguments, however, the "Moscow Declaration" issued at the conference made reference to the leading role of the Soviet Union only once. Having surrendered on this issue, however, Gomulka continued to insist on the necessity of adapting the central doctrine to Polish domestic conditions. This did not mean that Gomulka's Communism was fundamentally different from the orthodox line pursued and espoused by Moscow; rather, it meant that in his view this line could not be applied in Poland as rigidly or rapidly as in other countries, owing to national conditions which had existed for centuries and which could not be altered overnight. The subsequent history of Gomulkaism in Poland is marked by the gradual withdrawal of concessions made during the "Polish October," at the height of popular unrest.

Despite Gomulka's eventual submission to Soviet authority and his gradual retrogression toward totalitarianism on the domestic scene, the events in Poland during 1956 have had lasting significance in the conduct of Soviet-satellite relations.

First, Gomulka's assumption of political power in Poland against Soviet wishes and in the face of Soviet political intervention showed that the Soviet Union reserved military intervention for a last resort. At the very least, it would appear that a majority of Polish Politburo membership, united behind Gomulka, had convinced the Soviet leadership that Gomulka was the only man who could save Poland from popular anti-Soviet and anti-Communist revolution. Evidently, Khrushchev preferred to wait and see rather than use military force.

Second, if it is true that the Chinese advised the Soviet leadership against using military force against the recalcitrant Poles in 1956, then the Chinese can be said to have exerted an influence upon Soviet decision makers on a matter affecting Soviet hegemony over its satellite empire in Europe.

Third, with Poland embarked upon its own road to socialism, and in spite of the fact that this road gradually led back to the mainstream, diversity had made its appearance in the Soviet bloc. Nationalism was by no means encouraged (and it must be said of the Polish leadership that it did not attempt to sanctify it in its dogma or party theses), but it was tolerated by the Soviets under certain conditions.

All of this, of course, should be seen in the light of Poland's importance in the Soviet bloc. Poland's geographic location makes it strategically vital to the Soviet Union for its national defense and security, for the maintenance of Soviet military control over East Germany, and for any plans Moscow might entertain concerning military aggression against Western Europe. Furthermore, Poland's population of some 30 million represents more than a third of the entire East European Soviet bloc (excluding Yugoslavia). The fighting spirit of the Poles was eminently well demonstrated against the Nazis during World War II. Undoubtedly these considerations, together with those previously mentioned, played a large part in Khrushchev's decision to wait and see.

The Influence of China and Yugoslavia
on the Evolution of Soviet-Satellite
Relations During the 1950's

The influence of China and Yugoslavia on the evolving relationships between the Soviet and East Central European leaderships should be stressed. It is not within the scope of this summary analysis to go into a detailed history of the roles played by the Communist leaders of these two countries during the 1950's; rather, a brief statement of the impact of their respective policies will be made.

Yugoslavia

The impact of Yugoslavia upon Soviet-satellite relations arose initially from Khrushchev's effort to reestablish accord between the CPSU and the League of Communists of Yugoslavia. Toward this end, as has already been mentioned, Khrushchev had to concede that there were several roads to Communism and that Communist parties were equal. The idea was planted and grew quickly in the environment of the post-Stalin "thaw." Having been reaccepted into the Soviet bloc (without having sacrificed their independence), the Yugoslav Communists became the symbol of "national Communism" for all those, Communists and non-Communists alike (specifically in Poland and Hungary), to whom Soviet control was anathema. Tito gave his support to the Polish road to Communism, initially pursued by Gomulka against Khrushchev's wishes, but by 1958 a new ideological dispute had erupted between Moscow and Belgrade which robbed the latter of its political effectiveness in the Soviet bloc. Nevertheless, the concessions made in 1955 and 1956 remained a more or less conspicuous part of Soviet official doctrine, even after the leadership of the CPSU managed to reassert its primacy throughout the Communist camp. The Kremlin was able to reimpose a measure of ideological unity (at least at the public level) throughout the Communist world (excluding Yugoslavia) until 1960. But once open polemics erupted between the Soviet leaders and those of China and Albania, ideologists in the Kremlin began once more to look with increasing favor upon the Yugoslav "revisionists."

China

Like the Yugoslavs, the Chinese Communist leadership supported Wladyslaw Gomulka's initial departure on the "Polish road to socialism." In October, 1956, when the Polish Central Committee elevated Gomulka to First Secretary, the Chinese were reported to have counseled the Soviets against military intervention. Until the summer of 1957, the Chinese press was unstinting in its support of the Polish position, leading Gomulka to believe that he could successfully resist Soviet demands for public recognition of its leading role in the Communist camp. But during the summer the Chinese reversed their position.* At the Moscow conference of the Ruling Communist Parties in November, 1957, the Chinese delegation came down squarely on the Soviet side concerning the primacy of the CPSU in the Communist camp, leaving the Poles in an untenable position, supported only by Yugoslavia. The Polish delegation, as earlier mentioned, apparently had no choice but to sign the "Moscow Declaration;"† the Yugoslavs refused to sign the document.

Ironically, although in the short run the Chinese Communist stand on the issue of Soviet primacy was detrimental to the interests of the Polish leadership, in the long run it had the opposite effect. For to the Chinese Communists, the leading role of the Soviet Union entailed not only rights but also responsibilities. These included sharing Soviet economic wealth, such as technology and nuclear weapons, and the support of military ventures in pursuit of national goals of socialist countries, such as Chinese attacks on Quemoy-Matsu and the Indian borderlands. Clearly, the leading role of the Soviet Union did not mean that Moscow could control China's internal or external policy. Under these circumstances, Khrushchev apparently preferred to exclude mention of the leading role of the Soviet Union in the Communist camp, and instead increasingly emphasized the responsibilities of Communist parties to the international Communist movement. Thus, Khrushchev said in his speech to the Twenty-first CPSU Congress in 1959:

> . . . reference is made to the well-known thesis of the Declaration of Moscow conference that the camp of socialist countries is headed by the Soviet Union . . . this is a tribute to our country and working class. . . .
> At the same time it is necessary to stress that in the Communist

---

*Donald Zagoria associates this shift with a factional struggle in the Chinese leadership, primarily concerned with domestic policy issues. In this struggle the "Left" won over the "Right," resulting in the launching of the "Great Leap Forward." See Zagoria, op. cit., Ch. 2, pp. 66-74.

†The "Moscow Declaration" set forth a unified Communist view of the world and general guidelines for future action as well as some overall rules of conduct in intraparty relations.

movement and in the socialist camp complete equality and independence of all Communist and Workers parties and socialist countries has existed and does exist. . . . All Communist and Workers parties are equal and independent and all of them are responsible for the fate of the Communist movement and for its failures and victories![5]

Two years later, in his address to a meeting of party organizations in Moscow on January 6, 1961, Khrushchev gave an account of the CPSU position expressed at the Moscow Conference of Eighty-one Communist Parties, which had met in November, 1960, to arrive at a common line for the international Communist movement. Khrushchev asserted in this speech that the Soviet delegation had asked the conference to delete all references to the CPSU's leading role in the Communist movement:

. . . it is not possible for leadership over socialist countries to be exercised from any center at all. . . . If we are called the leader it gives no advantage either to our Party or to other parties. On the contrary it only creates difficulties.[6]

Soviet Attempts to Reassert Bloc Control

That Khrushchev's position was never really meant to apply to the Soviet bloc proper (i.e., that part of East Central Europe controlled by the Soviet Union) is clear from Moscow's continuing attempts to promote "unity" in the bloc under Soviet auspices. But having publicly renounced its leading position, it was more difficult to maintain it over any unwilling "satellite."

Aside from the relative diminution of Soviet authority in the bloc after Stalin's death, the most pressing problem Khrushchev had to face was the economic bankruptcy which threatened East European countries after years of Soviet exploitation. It was no longer possible for the Soviets to disregard the economic plight of the satellites. Initially, after 1953, Moscow directed the satellites to embark on a "New Economic Course" to create a better balance between heavy and light industrial production in favor of consumer goods. But by 1956 the Soviets felt compelled to extend large-scale credits to East Central European countries. According to a Czechoslovak source, from December, 1955, to February, 1957, Moscow gave 5,776 million rubles in credits to these countries.[7] The post-Stalin Soviet leadership may have become aware of the contradiction between excessive political control and economic progress in domestic as well as in intrabloc affairs.

The withdrawal of Soviet advisers from satellite capitals gave greater autonomy to the East European governments and represented a commensurate loss of direct control by Moscow. Khrushchev had to find a way to restore Soviet control over East Central Europe's economies and at the same time promote economic progress. To attain both of these objectives, a new framework was needed for the conduct of Soviet bloc economic relations, one that would lead to faster economic development and at the same time assure Soviet control.

The Council for Mutual Economic Assistance (Comecon or CMEA) appears in retrospect to have been an ideal core around which a new structure for the bloc economic system could be built.

The Council For Mutual
Economic Assistance

The Council for Mutual Economic Assistance (CMEA, or Comecon) was formed in 1949 by the Soviet Union, Albania, Bulgaria, Czechoslovakia, Hungary, Poland, and Rumania (East Germany joined in 1950), in response to the Marshall Plan, which in the West gave rise to the Organization for European Economic Cooperation (OEEC). The Soviet Union and East European Communist countries had been invited to participate in the Marshall Plan, but at Stalin's behest they declined. Retrospectively, it appears that CMEA was created by the Soviets as a palliative of more psychological than material value to its members. Under Stalin the national economies of the Soviet bloc were being developed along "autarkic" lines (of industrial self-sufficiency, relying on the Soviet Union for raw materials) with little regard to economic interdependence. Initially, then, the attention of Comecon was directed toward the organization of international trade among its members. The Council itself did not convene at all between 1950 and 1954.

Toward an International Socialist
Division of Labor

It was only after Stalin's death that the Soviet Union began to realize the potential economic and political values inherent in CMEA. As already mentioned, part of Stalin's legacy to the Soviet Union and its satellites had been a major economic crisis brought on by his faulty economic policies of overinvestment in heavy industry and underinvestment in primary production, light industry, and farming. It was with the "New Course," introduced during Malenkov's leadership, that the idea of economic specialization among the countries of the

Soviet bloc began to gain currency in the USSR. At the CMEA meeting in East Berlin in 1956, Soviet proposals for industrial specialization and coordination were adopted. Henceforth there was to be no more economic duplication among the countries; rather, the economies of the Soviet bloc would complement each other. The Soviet proposals provided for the redistribution of production centers, affecting some 600 groups of engineering manufacturers throughout the bloc.

To give structural reality to this division of labor, 12 standing commissions were established in 1956. These commissions were to coordinate bloc activity in such major fields as agriculture, coal, electric power, engineering, and foreign trade. Each member country's capital city (except Tirana) became the seat of at least one of these commissions, usually reflecting the importance of the country's major industry to the blocwide specialization endeavor. In the intervening years, each commission has usually been headed by the minister of the economic branch under the host country's purview.

Blocwide Integration vs.
National Sovereignty

A multitude of specialization agreements have been signed among the bloc countries. It is important to note, however, that all of these agreements have been bilateral or trilateral and that until 1962 the Soviet Union did not participate in this specialization endeavor. These agreements, therefore, do not represent an attempt at blocwide integration; rather, they appear to have been adopted by the bloc countries in an effort to develop and maintain sovereignty over their own economies within a framework of growing blocwide inter-dependence.

Nevertheless, real progress was made in building an infrastructure for Comecon. Such things as joint investment efforts toward a common rail transport system (a freight car pool), an electric power grid joining most of the Comecon countries, and an oil pipeline leading from the Urals in the Soviet Union to refineries in most member countries were soon in existence. Furthermore, in early 1964 a Comecon bank was established to act as a clearing house for trade between the countries. Thus, some progress was made in creating a structure for coordination, even though functional integration lagged far behind. At best, however, the many bilateral specialization agreements represented only token efforts toward achievement of the integration goal.

The absence of real progress in functional integration within

Comecon is a reflection (one of several) of the lack of agreement among member countries which already existed by the latter half of the 1950's. Council sessions have been cloaked in secrecy, so that only agreements expressed in communiqués become known to the world outside. But the debates were often lively and prolonged.[8] Judging from the evident reluctance of some Comecon countries to give up existing production facilities (or the development of such facilities) in order to adhere to the Comecon specialization framework, one can surmise that in many of the Council and committee debates at least some of the participants were motivated by the desire to preserve (if not to enhance) their existing degree of economic independence from other Comecon members and/or the Soviet Union.

The Comecon Charter, which was drafted in 1959 (a full decade after Comecon was organized), supports this view. It upholds the principle of national sovereignty and equality among member states and in Article IV, Paragraph 3, bestows upon them some specific rights:

> All recommendations and decisions by the Council shall be adopted only with the consent of the interested member countries of the Council, and each country shall be entitled its interest in any matter considered by the Council. The effects of recommendations and decisions shall not extend to countries which have declared their lack of interest in the questions concerned. Each such country may, however, accede subsequently to recommendations and decisions adopted by the other member countries of the Council.

In effect, this establishes the option for any CMEA member country to disassociate itself from any decision of the Council. It could be interpreted, moreover, that any member could block a proposed resolution by declaring itself interested but opposed. Furthermore, the Charter allows any member country to withdraw from Comecon with only six-month's notice.

In 1962, Khrushchev tried to overcome the bottleneck that had developed in functional integration (and perhaps also the veto power of member countries) by attempting to establish what would have amounted to a supranational planning agency which Moscow would undoubtedly have dominated. The opposition offered this plan by Rumania, a country whose industrial development was just then going into full swing, is by now well documented. Hence, a brief summary of the sequence of events leading to the failure of supranationalism in Comecon will suffice.

Khrushchev set forth his views about a supranational planning agency for Comecon in *Kommunist* (August, 1962), and it was reprinted in English in the *World Marxist Review* the following month.[9] It was reported that in November the Rumanian leadership notified Moscow that it would leave Comecon should a supranational agency be established.[10]

Two subsequent Council sessions (February and July, 1963) discussed Khrushchev's proposals, with the Rumanian delegation in opposition. (Since the sessions were held in the usual atmosphere of complete secrecy, one must look to other, sometimes esoteric, reports for information about the discussions.) In March, 1963, the Rumanian Party Central Committee publicly endorsed the instructions it had given to Alexander Birladeanu, the Rumanian representative to the Comecon, and the way he had executed these instructions. This may be interpreted as a purposeful gesture on the part of the Rumanian leadership to show the Soviet Union and other bloc countries that the Rumanian Workers' Party was united on this issue and was determined to safeguard the principle of "sovereignty" (whatever reality that principle possessed in Comecon).

The Comecon Council session of July 24-26, 1963, issued a communiqué in which it reaffirmed the principles of "equality, strict observance of sovereignty, and mutual comradely assistance. . . ." It further stated that "the best possible basis for a mutual coordination of economic plans is provided by bilateral consultation between member nations." Thus, by July, 1963, a decision had been reached: the Soviet proposal for a supranational planning agency was defeated.

Subsequent events have shown that it is perhaps more correct to say that the Council session of July, 1963, and its resolution in favor of bilateralism was only the first round in a continuing fight between Rumania and the Soviet Union. In April, 1964, the Rumanian Communist Party issued a lengthy statement which has since become known in the West as its "Declaration of Independence." Concerned largely with the Sino-Soviet dispute and problems of interparty relations, the Declaration offered the first detailed statement of Rumania's position with respect to Comecon integration. On the subject of a supranational planning authority, the Declaration was adamant:

Our party has very clearly expressed its point of view, declaring that since the essence of the suggested measures lies in shifting some functions of economic management from the competence of the respective state to the competence of superstate bodies or organisms, these measures are not in keeping with the principles which underlie relations among the socialist countries. . . .

The planned management of the national economy is one of the fundamental, essential, and inalienable attributes of the sovereignty of the socialist state. . . . The sovereignty of the socialist state requires that it effectively and fully avail itself of the means to practically implement these attributes, holding in its hands all the levers of managing economic and social life. Transmitting such levers to the competence of superstate or extrastate bodies would make of sovereignty an idea without any content.[11]

Cooperation Within Comecon

Since 1962, no significant progress has been made toward multilateral integration of the bloc economies. Bilateral specialization continues to develop, although slowly. The output under specialization arrangements still represents only an insignificant fraction of the gross national product of the countries concerned. This was exemplified by Czechoslovakia, whose specialization agreements for the manufacture of engineering products have usually been concluded on a short-term basis, leaving the parties relatively free to shift ties according to their economic advantage.

There are other forms of economic cooperation between countries within the Comecon framework. One of these consists of joint investments, in which the industrially developed countries (primarily Czechoslovakia and East Germany) invest in the raw material industries of other bloc members (notably Poland, Hungary, and Bulgaria). These investments are then repaid in the form of raw materials. The country receiving such investments profits through the development of its raw material industries at little capital expense to itself; the investing country gains the needed raw materials for its industries. Ownership of the enterprise remains in the hands of the recipient country.

Another form of cooperation occurs through the establishment of joint enterprises, in which two or three countries pool their resources to build a plant which they jointly own and manage, and from which they share profits proportionate to the size of their respective investments.

Neither of these forms of economic cooperation has been as extensively developed to date as bilateral specialization. Joint enterprises began to be established only in the 1960's. By 1965, Michael Kaser, an authority on Comecon, knew of only two of these.[12]

This lack of progress on integration, which runs against much of the exhortative propaganda and officially expressed enthusiasm not only in the Soviet union but also in most of the East European countries, points to a significant development in Soviet bloc relations. A decision-making process has evolved for blocwide programs and policies in which East European leaderships have risen to the de facto status of participants, rather than the pawns they once were in the Soviet design. No doubt, the Soviet Union remains much more equal than any of the East European countries in the decision-making councils of the bloc, but the latter have gained the ability, individually and collectively, to advance or protect their own national interests against those of the Soviet Union and other bloc countries.

Soviet efforts to supranationalize Comecon have been renewed under Brezhnev and Kosygin, and with particular vigor after the invasion of Czechoslovakia. But with the enactment of economic reform programs (some of which have been elaborated in previous chapters), the integration issues have become vastly more complex than they were under Khrushchev. While most East European leaderships are continuing to pay lip service to the idea of integration, the models of integration advanced in individual countries of the bloc vary to such an extent that it seems difficult to reconcile them into one scheme that would be acceptable to all leaderships concerned. It seems particularly difficult, for instance, to reconcile Hungary's predilection for direct and autonomous enterprise-to-enterprise agreements (with little or no governmental interference) with the Soviet predilection for centralized decision making for an integrated Comecon structure. On Hungary's part, of course, this conflicting predilection arises directly out of its decentralized economic model, which allows more freedom to enterprise management than any other model so far enacted in the Soviet bloc. This conflict of interests has brought Hungary squarely into Rumania's camp on the issue of supranationalization, making it even more difficult for the Soviets to make headway in this aspect so vital to the institutionalization of its control over the bloc countries.

The Warsaw Pact

The Warsaw Treaty Organization was created on May 14, 1955, by the Soviet Union, Albania, Bulgaria, Czechoslovakia, East Germany, Hungary, Poland, and Rumania. Its stated purpose was to offset the increased likelihood of war posed by the remilitarization of West Germany and the accession of that country to NATO.[13] The coincidence of this event with the signing of the Austrian State Treaty (one day later) has led some observers to conclude that the real Soviet purpose in creating the Warsaw Pact was to provide the Red Army with a different justification for maintaining units in Rumania and Hungary after the Soviet troop withdrawal from Austria obviated the necessity for protecting the supply line through these countries.* Nevertheless, throughout the remainder of the 1950's, the Warsaw Pact's activities did not display the urgency one might have expected from its hasty formation and its stated purpose. In time, however, it was to become one of the more effective instruments of Soviet control over Eastern Europe.

In 1956, Hungary's withdrawal from the Warsaw Pact provided a justification (if not the impetus) for the Red Army's cruel repression of the popular revolt. Unlike the Comecon Charter, the Warsaw Treaty has no fixed duration or provision for dissociation by any of its members: its only provision for dissolution is the abolition of NATO.† Twelve years later, as will be discussed in more detail below, the Warsaw Pact Council made the Czechoslovak crisis its own affair (Rumania not participating), and in August, 1968, the armies of five Pact countries invaded Czechoslovakia in a well-coordinated *Blitzkrieg* that surprised the world.

From the Soviet point of view, the military integration of the bloc, though far from trouble-free, worked much better than the economic one. Part of the reason is undoubtedly the discipline of command and control that is more common to military organizations than to political or economic ones. This discipline lends itself well, one may assume, to the structure of the Warsaw Pact, where the commander-in-chief is a Soviet officer and all defense ministers of the member countries (military officers without exception) are deputy commanders-in-chief. The chief of staff, too, has always been a Soviet officer, and many of the higher-ranking personnel of the member countries have undergone military (not to mention political) training in the Soviet Union.

During the 1960's (during the period of East-West détente and coincidental with the eruption of the Sino-Soviet dispute), joint military maneuvers became commonplace; occasionally, they were

---

*While this may have been a consideration in the minds of Soviet policy makers at the time, it must be stated that the Warsaw Treaty makes no mention of Soviet force deployments in the member countries. It will be recalled that in 1956-57 the Soviet Union concluded bilateral status of forces agreements with the countries then under its occupation.

†In contrast with Hungary, Albania ceased to participate in the Pact's activities as of 1961 (when it defected to the Chinese camp), and formally withdrew in September, 1968, one month after the invasion of Czechoslovakia.

commanded by a general officer of a participating East European country. The scenarios included nuclear warfare with NATO, the hypothetical adversary. During the same period, the Warsaw Pact forces were modernized with up-to-date Soviet weapons. While it is not known whether the Soviet Union has placed nuclear warheads anywhere in Eastern Europe, there is little reason to doubt that the delivery systems in the hands of Warsaw Pact forces can accommodate nuclear projectiles.

Yet, with all of these accomplishments, the Warsaw Pact has not been living up to the Soviet Union's expectations, largely because the political leaderships of the bloc countries are somewhat less obedient to Moscow than the military is. As of 1965, the Soviet Union was facing problems of policy making for the Warsaw Pact much like those it had been experiencing in Comecon, although not of such a nature or scope as to disrupt the functioning of the military alliance system.

In September, 1965, two years after Khrushchev's supranationalization scheme foundered on the rock of East European nationalism, Brezhnev proposed the formation of a policy-coordinating mechanism for the Warsaw Pact that had the earmarks of a supranational institution to be dominated by the Soviet Union.* As was to be expected, this proposal intensified the already existing friction between Rumania and the Soviet Union to the point where, on May 7, 1966, Rumania's new party chief, Nicolae Ceausescu, issued a blanket denunciation of Europe's division into military blocs, calling them "barriers in the path of collaboration among the peoples." In another phrase that made one wonder whether the Soviet Union might have been exerting military pressure on dissident Rumania, Ceausescu asserted that "the existence of blocs as well as the sending of troops to other countries is an anachronism incompatible with the independence and national sovereignty of the peoples and normal relations among states."[14] Amid frequent Soviet calls for a strengthening of the Warsaw Pact, the Rumanian regime circulated its own position paper to the member countries, in which it held that Soviet troops in Eastern Europe were no longer necessary nor justifiable; and should any country feel the need for their presence, it should bilaterally come to an agreement with the Soviet Union on this issue. In any case, Rumania

---

*Brezhnev voiced this proposal to the Soviet Union's Central Committee in the following terms: "Judging the problem of improving the activity of the Warsaw Treaty Organization, it is necessary to establish, within the framework of this Pact a permanent and operational mechanism for evaluation of current problems." *Krasnaya Zvesda* (September 30, 1965).

served notice that it no longer regarded the Warsaw Pact as a legitimate framework for the Soviet occupation of Eastern Europe, and it would no longer help to pay for the maintenance of Soviet troops in the occupied countries. Moreover, the Rumanian position paper argued that there should be a rotation of the office of commander-in-chief among the member countries, and that these countries should be allowed to participate in the making of decisions on the use of nuclear weapons.[15]

Despite obvious political pressures exerted by the Soviet Union, particularly on the Rumanians, Brezhnev's idea for a "permanent and operational mechanism for evaluation of current problems" was not adopted by the Warsaw Pact's Political Consultative Committee in its meeting of July, 1966. Thereafter, Rumania became a frequent absentee from such high-level bloc leadership meetings, thus making it impossible to formulate binding decisions or resolutions in the making of which Rumania had no voice.

Another equally important aspect of the Bucharest conference of Warsaw Pact leaders was an appeal for an all-European conference on peace and security. Three years before the 20th anniversary of NATO, when its members could opt to withdraw from the alliance, it seemed opportune in the eyes of the Warsaw Treaty powers to promote sentiments in Western Europe for the dissolution of NATO and the withdrawal of American troops from the Continent. In the propagandized Soviet view, the primary threat to peace and security in Europe was West Germany's refusal to recognize the situation that had resulted from World War II (i.e., the division of Germany, with West Berlin on East German territory, and the Oder-Neisse line, behind which lie 40,000 square miles of former German territories) and its alleged quest for a military establishment, including nuclear weapons, that would enable it to alter this situation. Evidently the Soviet leadership and its allies hoped that West Europeans would come to realize the danger to peace inherent in this situation, and that they would exert pressure on West Germany to abandon its "militarism and revanchism." This, then, would make NATO and the U.S. presence in Europe superfluous.

To this end, the foreign ministers of the Warsaw Pact countries convened in Moscow on June 6, 1966, for the purpose of reaching agreement on a joint declaration on European peace and security. The meeting was expected to last two or three days.[16] Instead, it turned into a 12-day marathon of acrimonious debate over deep-seated policy differences.[17] The differences in views were said to be so great that some of the foreign ministers had to fly back to their respective capitals for consultations with their governments.

One of the bones of contention was the treatment to be accorded to West Germany in the proposed declaration. According to East European diplomatic sources, the Soviet Union proposed a strong denunciation of West German policies and encountered strong opposition from the Rumanian delegation. In the heat of the debate on this issue, East Germany's Foreign Minister, Otto Winzer, reportedly derided Rumania's obduracy on this issue as "treason to the Communist cause."[18] Rumania's Foreign Minister, Corneliu Manescu, thus provoked, threatened to walk out of the meeting. The crisis was resolved in a private audience between Manescu and Brezhnev, in which the Soviet party leader conceded that Rumania's differences with the Warsaw Pact allies would be discussed only bilaterally in the future—i.e., Rumania would no longer have to endure the collective pressure of its pro-Soviet allies.

Undoubtedly, there were many other issues in dispute to prolong the foreign ministers' meeting in Moscow, but these have not been reported to the public. Nor are there any reports about the positions of other member delegations, except that Hungary was said to have been allied with East Germany in the charge of treason against Rumania. But from the unusually long duration of the session one may assume that many other differences of interest and political strategy had to be resolved or compromised, and that Rumania probably did not raise the only dissenting voice; it was only more adamant and, hence, more conspicuous. Furthermore, one can only speculate on the impact of Rumania's independent position on the text of the Warsaw Pact's "Declaration Strengthening Peace and Security in Europe," which was issued at the Political Consultative Conference of the Pact's party and government leaders in Bucharest on July 5, 1966.

This document claimed that the imperialist policy of the United States, "in collusion with the militarist and revanchist forces of West Germany," was promoting tensions in Europe. West Germany was allegedly seeking to revise the postwar territorial division of Europe and to acquire nuclear weapons for this purpose. In the process, West Germany was "directly prodding the U.S.A. to a still more dangerous course in Europe."

At the same time there were, according to the declaration, peaceful and progressive forces on the rise, "complicating the implementation of military ventures in Europe, and capable of paralyzing those that were generating tensions." These progressive forces were seeking the "complete independence of their countries and the preservation of their national identities." Therefore, the declaration concluded, "the problem of European security can be solved through the joint efforts of all the European states, of all social forces that are for peace, regardless of their ideological views and religious and other persuasions." To this end, it appealed to all European states to convene a security conference for the solution of the problems causing tension on the Continent.

The Warsaw Pact's prescription for European security consisted of the following specific elements (listed here in the order in which they appear in the declaration):

1. The development of "good-neighbor relations" between the countries with different social systems, based on "principles of independence and national sovereignty, noninterference in internal affairs, and mutual advantage." Contacts and cooperation in trade, science and technology, culture and art should be promoted without discrimination.

2. The dissolution of military pacts. The Warsaw Pact declared its readiness for the simultaneous liquidation of itself and NATO.

3. "The withdrawal of *all foreign troops from other countries' territories* to within their national frontiers" (emphasis supplied) and the liquidation of all foreign bases. At the same time, both German states should come to an agreement between themselves for mutual force reductions.

4. The preclusion of West Germany's access to nuclear weapons in any form. Even the participation of that country in any nuclear grouping, such as the multilateral nuclear force then being contemplated within NATO, should be prohibited.

5. The recognition of the finality of postwar frontiers in Europe, particularly those of Poland (the Oder-Neisse line) and between the two German states.

6. A peace settlement with Germany, based on the recognition of two separate German states. Reunification was held out as a possibility for the future, through gradual rapprochement between the two "sovereign" German states and through "agreement on disarmament in Germany and Europe," with the aim that a reunited Germany "will be peace-loving and democratic and will never again pose a threat to its neighbors or to peace in Europe."

The proposal was puzzling in several respects. First, the suggestion of simultaneous pact liquidation was inconsistent with the constant exhortation by the Soviet Union to strengthen the Warsaw Pact. One explanation for this inconsistency was, of course, that the Soviet Union sought to strengthen the Warsaw Pact as long as NATO continued to function as an anti-Soviet alliance (as, indeed, the declaration stated). This explanation, however, could not account for the evident Soviet desire to enhance its control over the Soviet bloc through a transformation of the Pact structure (the permanent and operational mechanism that Brezhnev proposed in September, 1965).

Even more puzzling in this context was the proposal of a complete foreign troop withdrawal, which would have affected Soviet forces in East Germany as well as American, British, and French forces in West Germany. Insofar as Soviet troops helped to maintain Soviet control over Eastern Europe, their withdrawal would undoubtedly lead to a diminution of that control—precisely when the Kremlin sought to consolidate its position in the bloc. Past Soviet proposals aimed at eliminating the U. S. presence from Europe usually held out the quid pro quo of a Soviet troop withdrawal from East Germany for a U.S. withdrawal from West Germany, which would allow Soviet troops to continue their occupation of the other East European countries (e.g., Poland and Hungary at that time).

If these two proposals would result in a weakening of Soviet control over Eastern Europe, then the proposal to cultivate contacts and interactions between the countries of East and West could only lead to more rapid diversification and autonomy among the East European countries. Gradually, as trade with Western Europe made the bloc countries less dependent on the Soviet Union, and as Western ideas in science, technology, and management became more influential in Communist countries, their interests would be less closely tied to those of Moscow. Already in 1966, there was a good deal of evidence from the economic reform movements to support this conclusion. (See Chapters 6-10.)

In other words, the Bucharest Declaration held the seeds of erosion of Soviet control over Eastern Europe at a time when Moscow was visibly eager to strengthen its control. There were several plausible explanations for this contradiction—among them the contention that the security system advocated in the Bucharest Declaration would enhance Soviet power in Europe once the United States had withdrawn, or that it would assure stability in Europe (even a *Pax Sovietica*) at a time when Moscow was becoming increasingly concerned over the growing Chinese threat in the East. Even so, it is difficult to believe that this declaration, in all of its manifestations, was the original Soviet blueprint for a European security system. It is more likely that it reflected the input of ideas and predilections of various East European regimes (most notably, of course, those of Rumania) in the 12-day-long meeting of Foreign Ministers in Moscow.

There was little, if any, positive response from the West to the Bucharest Declaration in 1966, and the Warsaw Pact did not again pursue the subject until the Budapest summit in March, 1969.* In the meantime, Rumania continued to upset the united front of the Soviet bloc by establishing diplomatic relations with West Germany (in January, 1967) and ostentatiously improving its relations with Israel after the Arab-Israeli war of 1967, while the rest of the bloc countries followed the Soviet lead and severed theirs. In addition, there were other problems to preoccupy the Soviet Union and its allies—among them the preparatory meetings for a world Communist Party conference aimed at censuring the Chinese and the crisis in Czechoslovakia, which began in January, 1968. The latter was to become a crisis for the Warsaw Pact, as will be seen in Chapter 14.

Some Conclusions

Since this chapter is intended for historical background to the one that follows, and since the Czechoslovak spring is to be summed up in the

---

*European peace and security was again the subject of discussion at the conference of European Communist and Workers' Parties at Karlovy Vary (Czechoslovakia) in April, 1967, at which parties from both Eastern and Western Europe were present. Rumania absented itself from this meeting because "no previous common agreement was reached regarding the character, aim and way of unfolding of the conference," and because its regime had an approach to European security different from what it anticipated the Karlovy Vary conference to pursue. See Laszo Hadik, et. al., "East European Views on European Security: A Chronological Survey," IDA Research Paper (July, 1967), p. 254 (mimeographed). A comparative reading of the Bucharest Declaration and the Karlovy Vary Statement (both in ibid., pp. A-62 ff.) reveals two major differences: the Karlovy Vary statement deemphasized the most interesting points of the Bucharest Declaration (mutual pact liquidation, complete withdrawal of foreign forces from all European countries, and the development of East-West contacts), although it did mention all of these points in passing and gave approval to the Bucharest Declaration; and it laid much greater stress on the role of Communist and workers' parties, in cooperation with other progressive forces, in defeating the forces of imperialism and revanchism that allegedly continued to threaten peace and security in Europe.

succeeding chapter, we will end the narrative here with a few pertinent conclusions.

First, since the death of Stalin, the Soviet Union has, under successive leaderships, sought to maintain its control over Eastern Europe. Its success has been partial, at best. Albania (not within the purview of this study) withdrew from the Soviet bloc in 1961, and Rumania has become a troublesome ally. The Soviet Union's diminishing ability to dominate the East European countries has been due, in part, to its political strategy in the bloc—to create and maintain a fiction of equality and to persuade rather than command. This strategy was dictated by the realization that Khrushchev and his successors did not possess the political power and prestige wielded by Stalin, and by the growing necessity to make the Communist systems of the bloc perform and compete with those of the West. The recognition of national conditions and peculiarities was to alleviate anti-Soviet tensions in Eastern Europe; the common ideology and goals of Communism and the prestige of the Soviet Union were to keep the "satellites" in the mainstream of Soviet interpretations and goals.

Second, out of this evolved a "conciliar" structure of decision making for the Soviet bloc. The "satellites" did become more equal, to the point where they could make their views prevail (given sufficient determination) in Comecon and Warsaw Pact councils. The Soviet Union lost its ability to command across the board. It had to compromise its objectives with those regimes that were determined to pursue their own interests. The unanimity vote rule was written into the Comecon Charter in December, 1959; but in practice it also came to apply in the Warsaw Pact. Rumania became the outstanding exponent of the pursuit of national interests; but if we are ever to understand the international politics of the Soviet bloc, it is important to decipher the inputs of the other East European countries to the decision making of the Soviet bloc. All that could be said on this point up to 1968 was that few of the known Soviet programs were adopted in the councils of the bloc, and that Rumania was the most publicized opponent of those that failed.

Third, if one chose to conclude from this that one bloc country could hamstring all of the Soviet Union's proposals that did not win endorsement in the councils of the bloc, the data would certainly confirm this assumption. But it is doubtful that all of the other countries voted the Soviet way on all of the issues in question. Subtle differences of views could be detected in the state-controlled presses of the several countries, even while all of their leaderships supported the various programs under consideration in bloc councils. But seldom was the curtain of secrecy surrounding the council debates lifted enough to permit a glimpse of conflicting lineups on the issues and the compromises that were being made in the formulation of blocwide decisions.

Forth, bloc "unity" remained one of the primary interests of the Soviet Union; and except for Rumania, the rest of the bloc countries were at pains to maintain the facade. In the final analysis, they had little other choice, given the power of the Soviet Union over them and the various pressures it could bring to bear upon them. But when one speculates that, given the choice, other bloc countries might have wanted to opt for the Rumanian way of independent policy making, one also has to consider that the dynamics of Soviet bloc politics that has evolved since Stalin's death has made it easier for these countries to bring their own interests and views to bear on the bloc's decision-making process.

The following chapter will test some hypotheses of relationships of internal and external factors to the observed degree of the several bloc countries' conformity to Soviet policy.

Notes

1. See "Declaration on Relations Between the Yugoslav League of Communists and the Communist Party of the Soviet Union, June 20, 1956," reprinted in Paul E. Zinner ed., *National Communism and Popular Revolt in Eastern Europe* (New York: Columbia University Press, 1956), pp. 12-15.

2. Translated in Leo Gruliow, ed., *Current Soviet Policies—II: The Documentary Record of the 20th Communist Party Congress and Its Aftermath* (New York: Frederick A. Praeger, Inc., 1957), pp. 29-37.

3. See Donald S. Zagoria, *The Sino-Soviet Conflict, 1956-1961* (Princeton, New Jersey: Princeton University Press, 1962), p. 55.

4. "Declaration on the Principles of Development and Further Strengthening of Friendship and Cooperation Between the Soviet Union and Other Socialist States," *Pravda* (October 31, 1956).

5. David Floyd, *Mao Against Khrushchev* (New York: Frederick A. Praeger, 1963), p. 258.

6. Ibid., p. 310.

7. M. Choluj, "Soviet Credit Aid to Socialist Countries," *Predvoj* (Prague) (November 7, 1959), cited by Zbigniew Brzezinski, *The Soviet Bloc* (New York: Frederick A. Praeger, 1961), p. 457, note 26.

8. Michael Kaser, *Comecon* (London: Oxford University Press, 1965), p. 66.

9. N.S. Khrushchev, "Vital Questions of the Development of the Socialist World System," *World Marxist Review* (September, 1962), pp. 1-19.

10. Kaser, op. cit., p. 94.

11. *Bucharest Agerpres*, (April 27, 1964).

12. Kaser, op. cit., p. 107.

13. The text of the Warsaw Treaty appears in Ruth Lawson, ed., *International Regional Organizations: Constitutional Foundations* (New York: Frederick A. Praeger, 1962), pp. 205-10; and also in a more informative discussion of the Pact, *The Warsaw Pact, Its Role in Soviet Bloc Affairs,* a study submitted by the Subcommittee on National Security and International Operations to the Committee on Government Operations, United States Senate, 89th Cong., 2nd Sess. (Washington, D.C.: U.S. Government Printing Office, 1966).

14. Excerpts of Ceausescu's speech appeared in *The New York Times* (May 14, 1966).

15. Ibid. (May 17, 1966). Subsequently, a Rumanian government spokesman "denied the form in which the proposals were said to have been circulated," but he reiterated some of the proposals and did little to challenge the rest. Ibid. (May 22, 1966), IV, p. 3.

16. Peter Grose, "East Bloc Aides Meet in Moscow," ibid. (June 7, 1966).

17. Raymond H. Anderson, "Warsaw Pact Sets Bucharest Meeting for Early in July," ibid. (June 18, 1966).

18. David Binder, "East Bloc Clash on Bonn Reported," ibid. (June 16, 1966).

13 East European Conformity to Soviet Policy

The last chapter examined some of the qualitative changes that have helped to transform the relations of the East European countries with the Soviet Union, on the one hand, and with the West, on the other. It suggested a number of factors that have contributed to a mixed trend of increasing East European domestic autonomy from the Soviet Union and to the growth of relationships with Western countries.

The present chapter will test some hypotheses developed by the previous one with data pertinent to the 13-year period of 1956 to 1968. The variable relationships to be examined here can be summed up in the proposition that East European countries' subservience to Soviet leadership is associated with factors inherent in either the domestic or the bloc framework, i.e., that these factors either induce or enable East European countries to conform to or deviate from Soviet policies. The following hypotheses will be tested with rank-order correlations:

1. The greater an East European country's trade dependence on the Soviet Union, the more it will conform to Soviet policy.
2. The easier it is for the Soviet Union to apply military force in an East European country, the more subservient that country will be to Soviet leadership.
3. The more cultural interactions an East European country maintains with the Soviet Union, the more it will conform to Soviet policy.

The following three hypotheses stipulate the complement, that relationships with the West tend to diminish East European countries' conformity to Soviet policy:

4. The greater the East European countries' trade interactions with the West, the greater will be their deviation from Soviet policy.

5. The greater the East European countries' intergovernmental interactions with the West, the greater their deviation from Soviet policy.

6. The greater the East European countries' cultural interactions with the West, the greater their deviation from Soviet policy.

The last two hypotheses postulate a relationship between domestic socioeconomic development of the countries in question and their conformity to Soviet policy:

7. The higher an East European country's level of socioeconomic development, the greater its deviation from Soviet policy.

8. The greater the relative difference between the level of an East European country's socioeconomic development and that of the Soviet Union, the greater the deviation from Soviet policy.

These hypotheses cover only a small fraction of the total range of variable interactions that might govern relations among states. What we present here, then, is something of a pilot test of hypotheses which generally "make sense" to the student of international relations, but which may or may not be true.

The variable relationships to be explained in this chapter should, ideally, have universal validity (i.e., the factors posited to explain conformity to Soviet policy should be important in explaining conformity of any subordinate states to a dominant state at different places and points in time). The use of inferential statistics to test the validity of the hypotheses would seem to call for a random sample from all the countries of the world. The focus of our attention, however, is on Eastern Europe. Admittedly, the relationship between the Soviet Union and the countries of this area is unique: there is no other area of the globe where one power dominates several lesser powers to a comparable extent. This relationship, then, makes Eastern Europe a most interesting testing ground for our hypotheses—a testing ground where the dominance-subservience relationship has already been clearly established. In short, although our sample of countries was not randomly selected, we have reason to believe that it is not so biased as to obscure relationships which actually exist or to cause relationships to materialize which in fact do not exist.* Admittedly, the number of countries (i.e., the N) to be examined is small, but if we use nonparametric statistics applicable for a small N, the results can be meaningful. The inclusion of Albania and Yugoslavia in this limited sample not only increases the N but also adds two former bloc members that have successfully withdrawn from the Soviet orbit.

As will become apparent in the following discussion, the indicators we use to measure the independent and dependent variables in question are not very sensitive. They are somewhat analogous to a primitive seismograph that can measure only subterranean vibrations of certain fairly high levels of magnitude. But we believe they provide a useful beginning on what we hope will be a long trek toward empirical validation. As long as we are mindful of the limitations of the techniques we use, our findings should be closer to reality than reasoned assumptions can bring us.

Measuring East European Conformity
to Soviet Policy

In every hypothesis examined in this chapter, conformity to Soviet policy serves as the dependent variable. Conformity, as used here, means the adoption, pursuit, or articulation of policy positions by East European countries in accordance with related Soviet policies or objectives.

Table 6 lists seven indicators which together form an index for measuring the relative degree of East European countries' conformity to Soviet policy during the 13-year period. The absence of data on Soviet policy expectations and East European reactions has forced us to resort to indicators which only indirectly measure East European conformity.† The rationale underlying each indicator in the index will be discussed briefly below.

The seven indicators are not treated equally. Each has been subjectively assigned a weighted score which we calculate to be

---

*In effect, our sample is restricted largely to those states of the world which are, or once were, within the Soviet sphere of influence. If we were to take a random sample of all the countries of the world, the variability of the dependent variable, conformity to Soviet policy, would increase substantially in the direction of less conformity. But the same would happen with respect to the independent variables. For example, most other states of the world would score lower on trade dependence than would any of the East European states.

†Ideally, in order to measure conformity to Soviet policy fully and without error, one would require complete information on (1) the number of policy objectives and actions to which the Soviet leadership sought conformity; (2) the importance

proportionate to its relative importance as an indicator. Strict conformity (i.e., no known deviation) is assigned a score of zero; the lower the score, the higher the conformity rating of the country in question relative to the others.

Rationale for the Selected
Conformity Indicators

Since the limited data availability forced us to work with less than ideal indicators of conformity, it is necessary to explain how these indicators measure conformity and why we assigned each the weight we did.

Membership in the Soviet Bloc

To this indicator we assigned the greatest weight, a score of 20, because the Soviet Union so clearly dominates the bloc. Membership in the bloc carries an obligation to cooperate with the Soviet Union and other bloc members, if not blindly to follow the Soviet lead. A country determined to formulate its policies independently of the Soviet Union and other bloc members would withdraw from the bloc, as Albania did in 1961, or be expelled, as Yugoslavia was in 1948. If it cannot withdraw from the bloc on peril of Soviet military sanctions, as may be the case with Rumania at present, then it has to continue to operate within the bloc's political framework; and its deviations from Soviet policy, though admittedly more conspicuous, are less weighty in the total context than its conformity.

Membership in Comecon
and the Warsaw Pact

Since these two organizations have been serving the Soviet Union as instruments to coordinate the bloc's economic and military policies, we have assigned each a score of eight. It might be objected that

---

attached by the Soviet hierarchy to each instance of expected conformity (instances would be weighted accordingly); and (3) the extent to which each East European state conformed to or implemented the Soviet expectations. To obtain "perfect knowledge" of this sort, one would have to be present at all meetings between Soviet and East European decision makers and have access to all communications between them. Conceivably, many examples of deviation from Soviet policy occur that are never known about in the Western world. There have also been instances, some of which were alluded to in the last chapter, where East European leaderships have dissuaded the Kremlin from pressing its desiderata on the bloc countries. Then again, one often finds variations in interpretation or emphasis among the leaders or official media of the bloc on subjects where the Soviet position is not clearly defined and one can only guess at the Kremlin's predilections. As will become clear, only those cases of deviation from conformity that become part of the public record are recorded.

membership in these institutions is synonymous with membership in the Soviet bloc and that they should, therefore, not be included in the index. Theoretically, however, it is possible to be a member of the bloc without participating in these institutions. The Comecon Charter, for instance, stipulates that "any member country of the Council shall be permitted to withdraw from the Council six months after notifying the depositary of the Charter of its intention to do so."[1] While the Warsaw Pact makes no similar stipulation, it is conceivable that a member country might denounce the treaty (as Hungary did in November, 1956) and withdraw (as Albania did formally in 1968). Furthermore, Yugoslavia's associate membership in Comecon since 1964 signifies that it is possible to be affiliated with this institution without being a member of the Soviet bloc as such.

If a country deviates from Soviet policy objectives regarding Comecon or the Warsaw Pact, or criticizes the aims or methods of these institutions (as Rumania has been doing occasionally since 1962) such indicators of deviation are perforce less weighty than if that country were to withdraw from these institutions. Continuing membership and participation in these institutions require a certain level of cooperation. Therein lies the rationale for including these two indicators into the conformity index.

Use of Military Force by the USSR

This indicator measures deviation from Soviet desiderata of such scope and determination as to be remediable only by Soviet military force. We assigned this indicator a weight of 10.

Criticism by the USSR and
Criticism of the USSR

Each reported instance of criticism of an East European country by the USSR, or by an East European country of the USSR, is assigned a weight of two. (For data source, see Appendix B.) Actually, public criticism of a "fraternal" country's policy indicates a serious dispute; but it still permits a compromise of policy or attitude on either or both sides. Therefore, it rates less importance than withdrawal from the bloc or either of its institutions.

For the purpose of this investigation, we were not interested in the direction of the deviation criticized—toward the "dogmatist" or "revisionist" extreme—but only in the deviation itself. Because of the low weight assigned to the indicator and the difficulty in judging the

Table 6

Indicators, Including Assigned Weights
for Index of Conformity to Soviet Policy

Indicators and Indicator Breakdowns	Assigned Weights
1. Membership in the Soviet Bloc	0 to 20
a. Considered* a member of the Soviet Bloc	0
b. Considered a nonmember, maintaining a neutral stance relative to the bloc and the Western world	10
c. Considered a nonmember, adhering to a rival bloc of Communist states	15
d. Considered a nonmember, adhering to a non-Communist, rival bloc of states	20
2. De Facto Participation in Comecon	0 to 8
a. Participates as a full member	0
b. Participates as an observer or on a limited basis	5
c. Eschews participation	8
3. De Facto Participation in the Warsaw Pact	0 to 8
a. Participates as a full member	0
b. Participates as an observer or on a limited basis	5
c. Eschews participation	8
4. Use of Military Force by USSR Against East European States	0 to 15
a. No use of Soviet military force	0
b. Use of Soviet military force	15
5. Criticism by the USSR of East European States	0 to 2
a. No criticism by the USSR	0
b. Criticism by the USSR	2
6. Criticism by East European States of USSR	0 to 2
a. No criticism of the USSR	0
b. Criticism of the USSR	2
7. East European Conformity to Soviet Policy Regarding Relations Among Communist States, Relations Between Communist States and the West, Major Developments Within the USSR	0 to 3.5
a. East European stand identical or nearly identical with that of the USSR	0

b. East European stand varies considerably from that
of the USSR   1.5
c. East European state avoids taking a stand   2.0
d. East European stand contrary to USSR   3.5

*By "considered," we refer to the consensus among scholars of East
European-Soviet affairs.

degree of reported public criticism, we made no attempt to
differentiate among varying degrees of intensity or to attach different
weights thereto.

Soviet Policy Regarding Relations
Between Communist States, East-West
Relations, Major Developments within
the USSR

Appendix A, Table 1, lists for each year of the 1956-68 period the
policy positions and actions taken by the Soviet Union upon which the
East European states are scored for conformity to Soviet policy.
Possible scores on this indicator range from 0 to 3.5.

The assignment of a score of 2 to a country which avoids taking a
stand on an issue put forward by the Soviet Union is based on the
rationale that such avoidance expresses a definite reluctance to accept
the Soviet policy. If all the East European states chose to take no
position on a particular issue to which the Soviets expected conformity,
it would be impossible to score them, unless the Soviets made us aware
of their deviation by publicly criticizing them. However, it is possible to
recognize cases of deviation when several East European states take a
public stand on the issue, with one or a few maintaining silence.
Accordingly, we scored for this indicator only when at least several East
European states have publicly responded in some fashion to the Soviet
Union's expressed position.

Results of Scoring on the Index
of Conformity to Soviet Policy:
1956-68

Appendix A, Table 2, presents the results obtained when the East
European states were scored for the Index of Conformity to Soviet
Policy during the 1956-68 period. The sum of all scores for each state
on each indicator and every year determines its ranking on the Index of
Conformity. These results are reported in Table 7 and in Appendix A,

225

Table 2. Over the 13-year period East Germany deviated the least from Soviet policy, being closely followed by Bulgaria. Hungary follows somewhat further behind, its near-perfect score having been upset by the 1956 Revolution. Poland's score reflects the liberal policies of the early Gomulka regime, which began to conform to Soviet policy only after 1958. Czechoslovakia, which follows Poland, does not manifest noticeable deviation on the Index until 1968.

Since our data are rank-order only, we cannot claim that a country receiving the overall score of 63 (i.e., Poland) is four times more conformist than one whose score is 15.5 (i.e., Bulgaria). The Index only establishes that Bulgaria deviates less from Soviet policy than Rumania does and that any other country which scores between Bulgaria's 15.5 and Poland's 63 is more conformist than Rumania but less than Bulgaria. Also, our Index does not indicate the direction of deviation from Soviet policy. We do not measure whether a country is more "Stalinist" or more liberal in its policies than the Soviet Union. The Index orders the countries of East Central Europe only in terms of their ranking on a conformity scale regardless of the direction of deviation. Thus, "Stalinist" Albania ranks next to "liberal" Yugoslavia, their total scores being 640 and 588, respectively (see Table 7).

Accordingly, Albania ranks lowest on the Index of Conformity (first). Yugoslavia ranks second, Rumania third, Czechoslovakia fourth, Poland fifth, Hungary sixth, Bulgaria seventh, and East Germany eighth. This rank-order on the Index of the dependent variable will be correlated with the rank-order of the indexes of the various independent variables in order to ascertain their measures of association.

Independent Variables, Measurements, and Correlations

Having established our index for East European conformity to Soviet policy and ranked each country accordingly, we can proceed to discuss pertinent assumptions underlying our hypotheses, to measure the independent variables, and to test each hypothesis through rank-order correlations.

East European Trade Dependence
on the USSR

The hypothesis is that the greater an East European country's trade dependence on the Soviet Union, the greater its conformity to Soviet policy. The Soviet Union has a wealth of raw materials, energy resources, and some advanced technology that is more or less vital to the economies of the East European countries. Thus, the Soviet Union is in a position, at relatively little cost to its own economy, to threaten or to apply either sanctions or rewards to East European countries in order to obtain their conformity to its policies. Since hard evidence is scarce on whether or how the Soviet Union has applied this potential source of power to influence the policies of its East European allies, this must remain a reasoned assumption. No doubt, threats and promises are made which go unreported. However, if we can devise an index for measuring the extent of trade dependence of the East European countries, we will have an indirect measure of the potential power available to the Soviets for making threats and promises. It is likely that in some situations the mere existence of certain levels of dependence makes the necessity for threats unnecessary, the leaders of the state being sensitive about their vulnerability. We would expect, then, to find trade dependence positively correlated with conformity to Soviet policy. In the following pages, then, we will present an index of East European trade dependence on the Soviet economy in order to measure this potential source of Soviet power, and correlate this index with the already described index of conformity.

This index consists of four indicators. The first is the percentage of total trade value (exports and imports combined) conducted with the USSR. If an East European state conducts 40 percent of its total trade with the USSR, we assume that it is more susceptible to Soviet pressure than if it conducts only 10 percent of its trade with the Soviet Union. (Appendix A, Table 3 reports the data on percentage of total East European trade conducted with the Soviet Union between 1956 and 1967.) The mean value for each state has been computed as a summary measure, and is presented in Table 8. It serves as the indicator value for the states for the 13-year period. On the basis of the scores for all states, we have rank-ordered them in terms of trade dependence. The rank-order of 1 is assigned to the state which had the lowest indicator value of total trade with the Soviet Union. The state having the second lowest indicator value is ranked 2, and so on.

Our second indicator of trade dependence is total trade value with the USSR as a percentage of net material product. This indicator serves as a corrective to the first indicator. State B may have a very large percentage of its total trade with State A, but if the value of that trade represents a very small percentage of its net material product, then

Table 7

Conformity to Soviet Policy Index Scores for the East European States: Yearly Scores, Total Scores, and Consequent Ranking, 1956-68

Year	A	B	C	EG
1956	1.5	1.5	1.5	0.0
1957	5.0	1.5	1.5	0.0
1958	9.0	3.0	3.0	0.0
1959	6.0	1.5	1.5	0.0
1960	12.0	0.0	0.0	0.0
1961	28.5	0.0	0.0	0.0
1962	60.0	0.0	0.0	1.5
1963	68.5	0.0	0.0	0.0
1964	69.5	0.0	0.0	0.0
1965	60.5	2.0	2.0	0.0
1966	89.0	4.0	0.0	0.0
1967	121.0	0.0	0.0	0.0
1968	110.0	2.0	106.0	0.0
Total	640.5	15.5	118.0	1.5
Rank	1	7	4	8

A = Albania   C = Czechoslovakia
B = Bulgaria   EG = East Germany

Note: In this table, a high score indicates low conformity relative to other states. A low score indicates high conformity. Consequently, in ranking the states, a rank of 1 means low conformity, whereas a rank of 8 signifies high conformity.

State A cannot hurt State B seriously by restricting trade or substantially aid it by offering improved terms, unless the goods exchanged are vital and not obtainable elsewhere. (Appendix A, Table 4, reports the data for total trade value with the USSR as a percentage of net material product for the years 1956-67.) The mean value of each state during the period is computed and is presented in Table 8. The mean values are used to rank-order the eight states from lowest to highest in terms of total trade value with the USSR as a percentage of net material product.

H	P	R	Y
17.0	7.5	0.0	32.5
19.0	15.5	0.0	43.5
0.0	31.5	1.0	77.5
0.0	3.5	1.5	33.5
0.0	0.0	0.0	37.5
0.0	0.0	0.0	36.0
0.0	0.0	0.0	30.0
0.0	0.0	12.0	26.0
0.0	1.5	33.5	24.5
0.0	2.0	28.5	26.5
0.0	2.0	25.5	31.5
0.0	0.0	27.0	48.0
7.0	0.0	64.5	141.0
43.0	63.0	193.5	588.0
6	5	3	2

H = Hungary   R = Rumania
P = Poland   Y = Yugoslavia

Sources: See Appendix A, Tables 1 and 2, and relevant discussion in Appendix B.

Indicators three and four for the trade-dependence index are repetitions of one and two, respectively, except in this case the data concern each East European state's trade with all other East European states except the USSR. The rationale for including indicators three and four is as follows: Throughout the 1956-67 period, most East European states were susceptible to pressure from the USSR by virtue of their close economic, military, and other relations with the Soviet Union. If one state chose to deviate from Soviet policy, and if a sizable amount of trade was conducted with other satellite states, the Soviet Union could possibly exert pressure upon it indirectly through these other East European countries. In short, an East European state's trade dependence is a result of both its trade pattern with the USSR and its trade patterns with other East European states. No doubt the former is more important, but the latter can make a difference as long as the other East European states toe the Soviet line. (Appendix A, Tables 5 and 6, present the data for the indicators on trade with other East European states.) Table 8 presents the mean and rank-order values of the countries on the trade dependence index.

Our basic assumption is that all four of these indicators are partial measures of an East European state's trade dependence—the first two more direct than the latter. Therefore, all four indicators should

Table 8

East European Trade Dependence on the USSR:
Mean Values and Rankings of Four Indicators, 1956-67

Indicator	A	B
1. Mean Trade Value with the USSR as a Percentage of Total Trade Value: 1956-67	32.3	51.7
Consequent Ranking	4	8
2. Mean Trade Value with the USSR as a Percentage of Net Material Product: 1956-67	n.a.	15.1
Consequent Ranking		7
3. Mean Trade Value with East Europe as a Percentage of Total Trade Value: 1956-67	39.3	27.2
Consequent Ranking	8	4
4. Mean Trade Value with East Europe as a Percentage of Net Material Product: 1956-67	n.a.	7.4
Consequent Ranking		7

A = Albania   C = Czechoslovakia
B = Bulgaria   EG = East Germany

Sources: See Appendix A, Tables 3-6, and relevant commentary in Appendix B.

intercorrelate. We can statistically test this assumption, which is central to the validity of our index, by computing the degree of association or correlation among the four indicators. The correlation value should be high. The appropriate statistical formula for our data is the Kendall coefficient of concordance.[2] It is a nonparametric measure of correlation designed for ordinal scale or rank-order data, small N, and not requiring that the variables have underlying continuity. All these characteristics describe our data.

Table 9 presents the rankings for seven of the eight East European states on the four indicators.* These rankings are summed, with the

*It was necessary to omit Albania, since the absence of data on Albanian national income precluded determination of Albanian scores on indicators 2 and 4.

C	EG	H	P	R	Y
35.2	44.3	31.8	31.5	40.4	9.9
5	7	3	2	6	1
6.1	6.3	5.4	1.0	3.4	1.9
5	6	4	1	3	2
31.3	26.7	33.7	28.1	23.8	17.5
6	3	7	5	2	1
5.5	3.8	5.6	0.9	2.0	3.2
5	4	6	1	2	3

H = Hungary   R = Rumania
P = Poland   Y = Yugoslavia

Table 9

Index of East European Trade Dependence
on the USSR, 1956-67: Combined Ranking
Scores on Four Trade Indicators

Indicator	B	C	EG
1. Mean Trade Value with the USSR as a Percentage of Total Trade-Value: 1956-67			
Ranking	7	4	6
2. Mean Trade Value with the USSR as a Percentage of Net Material Product: 1956-67			
Ranking	7	5	6
3. Mean Trade Value with East Europe as a Percentage of Total Trade-Value: 1956-67			
Ranking	4	6	3
4. Mean Trade Value with East Europe as a Percentage of Net Material Product: 1956-67			
Ranking	7	5	4
Sum of the Ranking Scores	25	20	19
Trade-Dependence Index Ranking Score	7	5.5	4

B = Bulgaria   EG = East Germany
C = Czechoslovakia   H = Hungary

Note: Albania is not included in the rankings and index, since data were lacking on indicators 2 and 4. The change in the ranking of indicators 1 and 3 relative to Table 8 reflects the omission of Albania.

H	P	R	Y
3	2	5	1
4	1	3	2
7	5	2	1
6	1	2	3
20	9	12	7
5.5	2	3	1

P = Poland   Y = Yugoslavia
R = Rumania

Source: Table 8.

sum of each country's ranking scores determining its overall ranking on the resulting index. In order to ascertain whether or not a meaningful relationship exists among the four indicators, we determine their degree of association. The four indicators intercorrelate at .64, which is significant at the .01 level (i.e., the probability of this result occurring by chance is less than .01). Consequently, we accept the four indicators as representative measures of the same phenomenon.

Having established an index of trade dependence, we can now test our hypothesis relating trade dependence and conformity to Soviet policy by correlating the two variables. The actual correlation between the two is .52.† This result is significant at the .068 level. Thus, the data tend to validate the hypothesis: The greater the East European trade dependence on the USSR, the greater the conformity to Soviet policy.

Military Capabilities of the
Soviet Union Vis-à-vis East Europe

Our hypothesis is that the greater the military capabilities of the Soviet Union vis-à-vis the East European states, the greater their conformity to Soviet policy. If important Soviet policy goals regarding East Europe are at variance with those held by the East European states, the ultimate recourse of the USSR in seeking to exact conformity is to threaten to and/or actually employ military force. We know that the latter occurred in Hungary in 1956 and in Czechoslovakia in 1968. How frequently threats to utilize armed force have been made by the Soviets we do not know. However, we can estimate the ease with which the USSR could employ its armed forces against the various East European states, and then test for the existence of a relationship with conformity to Soviet policy.

The relative ease with which the Soviets can deploy armed forces against another state depends on the accessibility of the target country to the Soviet Union. Ideally, the accessibility can be measured in (a) geography (number of miles); (b) topography (mountains, water, desert, or other natural barriers); (c) communication (available roads and railroad lines facilitating access); and (d) political barriers (states lying between the threatened state and the Soviet armed forces). The greater these obstacles, the more difficult it becomes for the Soviet

---

†The Kendall rank correlation coefficient was utilized here and in all bivariate correlations in this chapter analysis. For explanation of this correlation coefficient, see Siegel, op. cit., pp. 213-23.

Union to wage aggression. Similarly, other things being equal, the target state will find the threats more credible if the obstacles are minor than if they are great.

We have selected three indicators to estimate the relative ease with which the USSR could deploy its armed forces against the East European states during the 1956-67 period. If Soviet troops are already stationed in a country, it is easier for the Soviets to employ military force against the country. Such states are scored the highest. We differentiate among these according to the number of Soviet divisions deployed in each. The Soviets maintained approximately 20 divisions in East Germany, four divisions in Hungary, and two to three divisions in Poland between 1956 and 1967. Between 1956 and 1958 the Soviets maintained upwards of three divisions in Rumania. Accordingly, we rank East Germany 8, Hungary 7, and Poland 6. Since Soviet troops were deployed in Rumania for three years of the period, we rank it 5. For the remaining states we use as indicators the geographical distance separating them from the USSR and the number, if any, of intermediary states which must be crossed (unless air or sea power is used to deploy all forces) if the Soviets were to employ their troops.

Accordingly, Albania ranks 1, since it is the farthest from the USSR and since the Soviets would have to send their divisions through Rumania and Yugoslavia, the latter of which is not a member of the Soviet bloc. Yugoslavia ranks 2: it is second farthest away in terms of distance, and Soviet troops would have to move across Rumania or enter Yugoslavia from Hungary. Bulgaria ranks 3: it is farther away from the USSR than Czechoslovakia, closer than Albania and Yugoslavia; Soviet troops would have to move across Rumania or be transported by water over the Black Sea. That leaves Czechoslovakia with a ranking of 4. It is geographically contiguous with the USSR on the east. Soviet troops, additionally, could enter Czechoslovakia from East Germany, Hungary, and Poland.

The ranking, then, of the eight East European states in terms of the ease with which the Soviets could employ military aggression against them is as follows, with 8 representing the least difficulty and 1 the greatest: East Germany, 8; Hungary, 7; Poland, 6; Rumania, 5; Czechoslovakia, 4; Bulgaria, 3; Yugoslavia, 2; and Albania, 1. The correlation between the ranking on the military variable and conformity to Soviet policy is .64. This is significant at the .016 level. Consequently, the data seem to confirm our second hypothesis: the greater the ease with which the Soviets can utilize armed force against an East European state, the greater that state's conformity to Soviet policy.

East European Cultural Interaction with the USSR

Our hypothesis is the greater the East European cultural interaction with the USSR, the greater the conformity to Soviet policy. This hypothesis is based primarily on the assumption that East European states bent on deviating from Soviet policy will seek to mobilize popular support by diminishing Soviet input in the public consciousness, or (like Rumania) exploit prevailing Russophobia. In view of the importance Moscow attaches to projecting its cultural image in Eastern Europe (through friendship societies and the like), it seems likely that the less the Soviet cultural input in an East European country, the less willing the regime would be to impose Soviet culture on the population and, hence, the more willing the regime may be to deviate from Soviet desiderata in other matters.

Three indicators have been selected to measure the degree of East European cultural interaction with the USSR: (1) number of East European tourists to the Soviet Union; (2) number of Soviet tourists to the East European states; and (3) number of book translations from Russian into the native language of the East European states. With each indicator we have sought to make the data comparable for all countries. Data on tourists from each East European state to the Soviet Union are expressed as a percentage of the total population of each state. Similarly, data on Soviet tourists to East European states are expressed as a percentage of each state's total population. Consequently, we have a measure of relative extent to which the people of each state interact with the people of the USSR. Book translations from the Russian language are expressed as a percentage of each state's total translations from foreign languages. (Appendix A, Tables 7-9, presents the data for each of the three indicators.) Absence of data on Soviet tourists to East Germany and Russian book translations for East Germany forced us to omit this state from our intercultural index. Data were also lacking on Soviet tourists to Albania for the 1961-67 period. In this case, however, we assigned Albania a rank of 1 relative to the other states. This seemed to be a safe procedure in view of Albania's low ranking (i.e., 1) on tourists to the USSR and in view of Albania's militant estrangement from the Soviet Union throughout the period.

The East European mean scores for these three indicators are

236

presented in Table 10, along with the corresponding rank-order scores of the seven East European states. The intercorrelation of the three indicators is .54; consequently, we accepted the three as suitable for an intercultural index. Table 11 presents combined ranking scores, from which the seven states are ranked to form the index. The country showing the least cultural interaction with the USSR was assigned the lowest rank.

The correlation between the intercultural index and conformity to Soviet policy is very high, .76. This result is significant at below the .001 level. The data, then, confirm our third hypothesis: the greater the East European intercultural contact with the USSR, the greater the conformity to Soviet policy.

East European Trade Interaction
with the West

Our hypothesis is that the greater the East European trade interaction with the West, the greater the deviation from conformity to Soviet policy. Trade interactions bring East Europeans into contact with the products, values, and ways of life of the West. Trade with the West enables the countries, potentially at least, to be less dependent on the economy of the Soviet Union. All other things being equal, the more trade partners any one country has, the less it is susceptible to economic and political pressures by any one of its partners.

However, unlike East European countries' trade interactions with the USSR, East European-West trade cannot be meaningfully discussed as a matter of trade dependence. Compared with Soviet-East European trade, that trade is very low, as shown in Tables 12 and 13 (the only exception being Yugoslavia).

We selected 15 Western countries to represent trade with the Western world: Austria, Belgium-Luxembourg, Canada, Denmark, Finland, France, West Germany, Greece, Italy, Netherlands, Norway, Sweden, Switzerland, the United Kingdom, and the United States.

The correlation between our two indicators of trade interaction with the Western world, i.e., percentage of total trade and trade value as a percentage of net material product, is too low to warrant their use as an index of trade interaction. Therefore, the rankings of the East European states on each of the indicator variables (see Table 14) were separately correlated with the index of conformity to Soviet policy. The correlation between East European trade value with the Western world as a percentage of total trade and conformity to Soviet policy is

Table 10

East European Cultural Interaction with the USSR: Mean Values and Rankings for Three Cultural Indicators 1956-67

Indicator	A	B	C
1. Mean Value: Tourists to Soviet Union from the East European States, as a Percentage of Their Total Respective Populations, 1957-67	0.860	6.882	4.747
Consequent Ranking	1	8	6
2. Mean Value: Soviet Tourists to the East European States as a Percentage of Their Respective Total Populations, 1961-67	n.a.	6.992	3.556
Consequent Ranking	1	6	5
3. Mean Value: Books Translated from the Russian Language into the East European Native Languages as a Percentage of Their Total Translations, 1956-66	47.4	50.8	24.4
Consequent Ranking	6	7	3

A = Albania   C = Czechoslovakia
B = Bulgaria   EG = East Germany

Notes: The percentage figures for indicators 1 and 2 have been multiplied by 1,000 to facilitate reading of the table. Albania has been ranked on indicator 2 despite lack of data.

EG	H	P	R	Y
4.691	4.142	5.007	3.303	0.909
5	4	7	3	2
n.a.	9.447	3.416	2.048	1.048
	7	4	3	2
n.a.	23.3	26.6	33.8	11.2
	2	4	5	1

H = Hungary   R = Rumania
P = Poland   Y = Yugoslavia

Sources: Appendix A, Tables 7-9 and relevant commentary in Appendix B.

Table 11
Index of East European Cultural Interaction
with the USSR, 1956-67: Combined Ranking
Scores on Three Cultural Indicators

Indicator	A	B	C
1. Mean Value: Tourists to Soviet Union from the East European States, as a Percentage of Their Total Respective Populations, 1957-67			
Ranking	1	7	5
2. Mean Value: Soviet Tourists to the East European States as a Percentage of Their Respective Total Populations: 1961-67			
Ranking	1	6	5
3. Mean Value: Books Translated from the Russian Language into the East European Native Languages as a Percentage of Their Total Translations: 1956-66	6	7	3
Ranking			
Sum of the Ranking Scores	8	20	13
Cultural Interaction Index Ranking Score	2	7	4.5

A = Albania   C = Czechoslovakia
B = Bulgaria   H = Hungary

Note: East Germany is not included in the rankings and index, since data were lacking on indicators 2 and 3. The change in the ranking of indicator 1 relative to Table 10 reflects the omission of East Germany.

H	P	R	Y
4	6	3	2
7	4	3	2
2	4	5	1
13	14	11	5
4.5	6	3	1

P = Poland   Y = Yugoslavia
R = Rumania

Source: Table 10.

Table 12

East European Mean Trade Value with the USSR, with the Western
World, and with the USSR and East Europe as a Percentage of
Total Trade Value, 1956-67

Mean East European Trade Value	A	B	C	EG
1. With the USSR as a Percentage of Total Trade Value	32.3	51.7	35.2	44.3
2. With the Western World as a Percentage of Total Trade Value	4.1	15.4	16.5	18.3
3. With the USSR and East Europe as a Percentage of Total Trade Value	71.6	78.9	66.5	71.0

A = Albania   C = Czechoslovakia
B = Bulgaria   EG = East Germany

Note: Appendix A, Table 10, presents East European countries' trade value with the Western world as a percentage of total trade value on a yearly basis for 1956-67.

low, $-.21$. The correlation of conformity with East European trade value as a percentage of net material product, however, is more respectable— $-.43$, significant at the less than .19 level.

Altogether, the results are somewhat ambiguous. While both correlation coefficients are in the predicted direction, one of the coefficients is quite low and the other, though higher, does not attain a sufficiently low level of statistical significance to inspire confidence. The results may be due to the relatively low mean levels of East European trade interaction with the Western world during the 12-year period under examination, Yugoslavia being the only exception. As Table 12 shows, all countries except Yugoslavia conducted less than 30 percent of their total trade with the Western world during the 1956-67 period. Four of the eight countries have a mean value of less than 20 percent.

H	P	R	Y
31.8	31.5	40.4	9.9
23.4	28.5	24.8	57.4
65.5	59.6	64.2	27.4

H = Hungary   R = Rumania
P = Poland   Y = Yugoslavia

Sources: See Appendix A, Tables 3, 5, 10, and relevant commentary in Appendix B.

The results of the two correlations lead us to hypothesize that some minimum level of trade interaction with the Western world is necessary in order to affect conformity to Soviet policy noticeably. We presently lack sufficient information to identify a critical minimum level of trade interaction, but we tentatively conclude that most East European states have not attained such a level.

East European Governmental Interaction
With the Western World

Our hypothesis is that the greater the governmental interaction with the Western world, the greater the deviation from conformity to Soviet policy. The rationale is essentially that of the third hypothesis examined, except that here the contacts examined occur mostly on the governmental, as opposed to the popular, level.

Table 13

East European Mean Trade Value with the USSR, with the Western
World, and with the USSR and East Europe, as a Percentage of
Net Material Product, 1956-67

Mean East European Trade Value	A	B	C	EG
1. With the USSR as a Percentage of Net Material Product	n.a.	15.1	6.1	6.3
2. With the Western World as a Percentage of Net Material Product	n.a.	4.6	2.9	2.6
3. With the USSR and East Europe as a Percentage of Net Material Product	n.a	22.3	11.6	10.1

A = Albania   C = Czechoslovakia
B = Bulgaria   EG = East Germany

Note: Appendix A, Table 11, presents East European countries' trade
value with the Western world as a percentage of East European net
material product on a yearly basis for 1956-67.

Five major states of the West were selected to represent the Western
world: France, Germany, Great Britain, Italy, and the United States.
Four indicators were chosen to form an index of governmental
interaction: (1) number of ministerial visits; (2) number of trade
missions exchanged; (3) number of trade and commercial agreements
concluded; and (4) number of cultural and political agreements
concluded.

Each of these indicators represents, in part, the extent to which each
East European regime has been trying to improve its relations with the
West. This may, in turn, provide alternative options to conforming to
Soviet policy when it conflicts with the national interest of the East
European countries. In addition, contacts between East European and
Western officials can contribute to a modification in existing attitudinal

	H	P	R	Y
	5.4	1.0	3.4	1.9
	3.9	0.9	2.2	10.1
	11.0	2.0	5.4	5.1

H = Hungary   R = Rumania
P = Poland   Y = Yugoslavia

Sources: See Appendix A, Tables 4, 6, 11, and relevant commentary in Appendix B.

patterns at the policy-making level, and stimulate a desire for increased contact and understanding with the West at the expense of close relations with the USSR. (Appendix A, Tables 12-15, presents data on the four governmental interaction indicators for 1957-66.)

Table 15 presents the total score for each state on the four indicators, along with rank-orderings of the East European states on the four indicators. Table 16 presents the rank-orderings again. Here the rankings have been summed for each state to arrive at a combined score. On the basis of these totals, the eight states are rank-ordered from the lowest to highest in terms of extent of governmental interaction with the West. To test the assumption that the four are measures of the same general phenomenon, the degree of association was computed. The resulting intercorrelation was .79, which is

Table 14

East European States Rank-Ordered on Mean Trade Value with the
Western World as a Percentage of Total Trade Value and on Mean
Trade Value with the Western World as a Percentage of Net Material
Product, 1956-67

Mean East European Trade Value	A	B	C	EG
1. With the Western World as a Percentage of Total Trade Value	3.8	15.4	16.5	18.3
Consequent Ranking	1	2	3	4
2. With the Western World as a Percentage of Net Material Product	n.a.	4.6	2.9	2.6
Consequent Ranking		6	4	3

A = Albania   C = Czechoslovakia
B = Bulgaria   EG = East Germany

Sources: Tables 12 and 13.

significant below the .01 level. We conclude that the four indicators are
suitable for combining into a single index.

The correlation between the governmental interaction index and
conformity to Soviet policy is .04. The hypothesis is not confirmed.
However, as with East-West trade interactions, it is possible to surmise
that some minimum level of intergovernmental contacts must be
attained in order to affect conformity to Soviet policy.

East European Cultural Contacts
with the Western World

Our hypothesis is that the greater the East European cultural contacts
with the Western world, the greater the deviation from Soviet policy.
The general rationale underlying this hypothesis is the same as that
given for the third and fifth independent variables, with the added
proviso that popular pressures in East European countries, stimulated
by Western influences, may induce the regimes to depart from Soviet
predilections.

	H	P	R	Y
	23.4	28.5	24.8	57.4
	5	7	6	8
	3.9	0.9	2.2	19.1
	5	1	2	7

H = Hungary   R = Rumania
P = Poland   Y = Yugoslavia

Two indicators were selected as crude measures of the extent of cultural interaction: (1) tourists from Western states* to East Europe as a percentage of the total population of each East European country, and (2) books in the English and French languages translated into the native language of the East European states as a percentage of total translations in each country. (Data for these two indicators are presented in Appendix A, Tables 16 and 17, respectively.) Since data were lacking for East Germany, that country was omitted. Although tourist data were not available for Albania, we feel justified in assigning it the lowest rank (i.e., 1), on the basis that Albania has maintained a highly restrictive tourist policy and Westerners have shown very little interest in visiting that country.

In Table 17 the rank-orders of the East European states on the two indicators are reported. Since the two are not highly correlated, we have not constructed an index of cultural interactions. Each

*The same five Western states used to represent governmental interactions were used to represent tourist interactions.

Table 15

East European Governmental Interaction with Five Western States:
Scores and Rankings on Four Governmental Interaction Indicators,
1956-66

Indicator	A	B
1. Exchange of Ministerial Visits Between East European States and Western States	0	10
Consequent Ranking	1	5
2. Exchange of Trade Missions Between East European States and Western States	7	18
Consequent Ranking	2	6
3. Trade and Commercial Agreements Between East European States and Western States	5	18
Consequent Ranking	1	6
4. Cultural and Political Agreements Between East European and Western States	2	5
Consequent Ranking	2	5

A = Albania   C = Czechoslovakia
B = Bulgaria   EG = East Germany

Note: The five states are France, Great Britain, Italy, West Germany, and the United States.

indicator-variable was independently correlated with conformity to Soviet policy. The variable of tourists from the Western states to East Europe correlates extremely low with conformity, $-.04$. The variable of translations from the French and English correlates $-.24$ with conformity to Soviet policy. While it is negative, i.e., in the predicted direction, the magnitude of the correlation is very low. Cultural interactions with the Western states do not appear to have been related to deviation from conformity to Soviet policy during the period under examination. Once again, we can postulate that there may be some threshold level of intercultural contacts below which their impact on comformity is unimportant.

C	EG	H	P	R	Y
5	1	3	24	15	12
4	2	3	8	7	6
10	5	10	28	21	9
4.5	1	4.5	8	7	3
9	10	10	26	20	10
2	4	4	8	7	4
3	0	6	5	13	5
3	1	7	5	8	5

H = Hungary   R = Rumania
P = Poland   Y = Yugoslavia

Sources: See Appendix A, Tables 13-16, and relevant discussion in Appendix B.

Socioeconomic Development of
East European States

Our hypothesis is that the greater the level of socioeconomic development in Eastern Europe, the greater the deviation from Soviet policy. The rationale underlying this hypothesis is as follows. High levels of socioeconomic development refer to levels of education, science, and technology. Peoples possessing high socioeconomic development will perhaps be less willing to follow blindly the foreign policy dictates of another state and be more inclined directly and independently to formulate their own goals and objectives. This is especially likely to be the case if the dominating country is not economically superior or is even inferior to the other country. People

Table 16

Index of East European Governmental Interaction with the Western World, 1957-66: Combined Ranking Scores on Four Governmental Interaction Indicators

Indicator	A	B	C
1. Exchange of Ministerial Visits Between East European States and Western States			
Ranking	1	5	4
2. Exchange of Trade Missions Between East European States and Western States			
Ranking	2	6	4.5
3. Trade and Commercial Agreements Between East European States and Western States			
Ranking	1	6	2
4. Cultural and Political Agreements Between East European and Western States			
Ranking	2	5	3
Sum of the Ranking Scores	6	22	13.5
Intergovernmental Index Ranking Score	1	6	3

A = Albania   C = Czechoslovakia
B = Bulgaria   EG = East Germany

Source: Table 15.

250

EG	H	P	R	Y
2	3	8	7	6
1	4.5	8	7	3
4	4	8	7	4
1	7	5	8	5
8	18.5	29	29	18
2	5	7.5	7.5	4

H = Hungary   R = Rumania
P = Poland   Y = Yugoslavia

Table 17

East European Cultural Interactions with the Western World: Mean Scores and Rankings on Two Cultural Indicators, 1956-67

Indicator	A	B	C
1. Mean Value: Tourists from Five Western States to the East European States as a Percentage of the Respective Populations of the East European States: 1961-67	n.a.	13.4	13.4
Consequent Ranking	1	5	6
2. Mean Value: Books Translated from English and French into the East European Native Languages as a Percentage of the East European Respective Total Translations: 1956-66	14.6	7.9	14.2
Consequent Ranking	4	1	3

A = Albania   C = Czechoslovakia
B = Bulgaria   EG = East Germany

Notes: The Western world has been represented by France, Great Britain, Italy, West Germany, and the United States. The figures for indicator 1 have been multiplied by 1,000 to facilitate reading of the table. Albania has been ranked on indicator 1 even though data are not available.

EG	H	P	R	Y
n.a.	9.8	2.2	3.2	61.3
	4	2	3	7
n.a.	28.0	33.2	10.0	34.3
	5	6	2	7

H = Hungary   R = Rumania
P = Poland   Y = Yugoslavia

Sources: See Appendix A, Tables 16 and 17, and relevant commentary in Appendix B.

of high socioeconomic development are likely to look down upon people of low standing.

Beyond this, countries of higher socioeconomic development will be in a better position in general to produce essential goods and services necessary to maintain a viable economy and, hence, less vulnerable to the application of pressures upon their economies from abroad. Finally, countries possessing high socioeconomic development will be more likely to seek out trading partners who also possess high socioeconomic development. The more economically developed countries of Eastern Europe, by virtue of their advancement, will have greater reason to seek out the advanced technological products of the Western world. The products and the values associated with them may have an important effect upon the East European regimes and peoples. Our hypothesis concerning overall trade interaction with the Western world may have slighted this important aspect.

Because of the scarcity of reliable statistics, we were limited in our selection of socioeconomic indicators to the following five indicators: (1) infant mortality rate; (2) number of inhabitants per physician; (3) energy consumption per capita; (4) railway passenger kilometers per capita; and (5) employees in manufacturing as a percent of total population. (Appendix A, Tables 18-22, presents data on each indicator for all the East European states and the Soviet Union.) Each indicator's arithmetic mean for the time period under consideration serves as a basis for rank-ordering the countries, as presented in Table 18. For the first two indicators, the country with the highest mean value was assigned a rank of 1, the country with the lowest, a rank of 9, since a high score represents a low level of development. For the last three indicators, this procedure was reversed, since a high score represents relatively high development.

Table 19 presents the rankings of the nine states on the five indicators. The intercorrelation of the five indicators is very high, .82, which is significant below the .001 level. Consequently, the indicators were deemed suitable for combination into an index. After the rank-order scores for each state are summed, the states are rank-ordered for a socioeconomic development index.

The correlation between the socioeconomic development index and conformity to Soviet policy is .57, which is significant at the .031 level. However, the direction of the correlation contradicts the hypothesis. For high levels of socioeconomic development, we find relatively high conformity to Soviet policy.

How are these results to be explained? The partial explanation we have drawn is that the relationship between economic development and conformity to another state's policy is probably curvilinear. States at low levels of economic development are likely to be less susceptible to economic pressure because they are less dependent on other states for necessary products. States at moderately high levels of economic development may be most susceptible to economic pressure precisely because their rather complex and sophisticated economies are dependent on foreign sources for certain essential raw materials and/or finished products. Only states with both a very high level of development, including technologies for producing virtually all desired products, and direct or easy access to vitally needed raw materials can remain independent politically. Our index of socioeconomic development is not capable of differentiating between economic dependence and independence. Yet it is well-known that only a few states in the world are both highly developed and have direct or easy access to vital raw materials and finished products. These include the United States and the USSR, but not the countries of East Central Europe. It is important to note, for example, that Czechoslovakia, East Germany, Hungary, and Poland, which rank high on the index of socioeconomic development, are all now largely dependent upon the USSR for oil, a prime requisite for operating modern technologies. To have Soviet oil supplies suddenly cut off would create serious economic dislocations over the short run, a factor that no East European government could contemplate with equanimity. Rumania, Yugoslavia, and Albania, which rank low on conformity, have been obtaining their oil supplies either from their own resources or elsewhere than the Soviet Union.

Relative Levels of Socioeconomic
Development

Our eighth and final hypothesis is that the greater the relative difference between the level of socioeconomic development in the East European countries and that of the Soviet Union, the greater the deviation from conformity to Soviet policy.

We reason that countries at different levels of socioeconomic development are likely to view their problems from different perspectives and opt for diverse solutions. Goals and methods will differ. We assume that the implementation of different policies does not affect only the domestic sector, but foreign policy as well.

To test our hypothesis, we had to establish an index with which to

Table 18

East European and USSR Mean Values and Rankings on Five
Socioeconomic Development Indicators: 1955-67

Indicator	A	B	C	EG
1. Mean Value: East European and USSR Infant Mortality Rates: 1956-67	82.8	44.3	25.4	34.1
Consequent Ranking	1	6	9	8
2. Mean Value: East European and USSR Number of Inhabitants Per Physician: 1957-66	3488	671	571	810
Consequent Ranking	1	6	8	4
3. Mean Value: East European and USSR Energy Consumption (Coal Equivalent in Kilograms per Capita): 1955-67	297	1768	5066	4894
Consequent Ranking	1	4	9	8
4. Mean Value: East European and USSR Railway Passenger Kilometers per Capita: 1956-67	53	487	1396	1194
Consequent Ranking	1	2	9	7
5. Mean Value: East European and USSR Employees in Manufacturing as a Percentage of Population: 1960-67	4.6	9.2	16.2	15.6
Consequent Ranking	1	5	9	8

A = Albania   C = Czechoslovakia   H = Hungary
B = Bulgaria   EG = East Germany   P = Poland

Sources: See Appendix A, Tables 18-22, and relevant commentary in Appendix B.

H	P	R	Y	SU
47.4	56.0	63.3	81.7	34.5
5	4	3	2	7
635	987	727	1409	526
7	3	5	2	9
2386	3220	1590	932	3115
5	7	3	2	6
1242	1144	687	537	831
8	6	4	3	5
10.5	7.0	6.0	5.6	10.2
7	4	3	2	6

R = Rumania   SU = Soviet Union
Y = Yugoslavia

Table 19

Index of East European Levels of Socioeconomic Development:
Combined Ranking Scores on Five Indicators: 1955-67

Indicator	A	B	C	EG
1. Mean Value: East European and USSR Infant Mortality Rates: 1956-67				
Ranking	1	6	9	8
2. Mean Value: East European and USSR Number of Inhabitants Per Physician: 1957-66				
Ranking	1	6	8	4
3. Mean Value: East European and USSR Energy Consumption (Coal Equivalent in Kilograms per Capita): 1955-67				
Ranking	1	4	9	8
4. Mean Value: East European and USSR Railway Passenger Kilometers per Capita: 1956-67				
Ranking	1	2	9	7
5. Mean Value: East European and USSR Employees in Manufacturing as a Percentage of Population: 1960-67				
Ranking	1	5	9	8
Sum of the Ranking Scores	5	23	44	35
Development Index Ranking Score	1	4	9	8

A = Albania   C = Czechoslovakia   H = Hungary
B = Bulgaria   EG = East Germany   P = Poland

Source: Table 18.

H	P	R	Y	SU
5	4	3	2	7
7	3	5	2	9
5	7	3	2	6
8	6	4	3	5
7	4	3	2	6
32	24	18	11	33
6	5	3	2	7

R = Rumania   SU = Soviet Union
Y = Yugoslavia

measure differences between levels of socioeconomic development. We used the same indicators as in the previous section. Each country's mean score on each indicator was contrasted with that of the Soviet Union (see Appendix A, Tables 23-27). The state that differed most from the Soviet Union received the rank-order number 8, meaning that the smaller the difference between mean scores, the lower the rank-order number. Positive and negative values serve to indicate the direction of divergence from Soviet patterns. Assignment of a positive value demonstrates that the particular country has reached a higher level of development than the Soviet Union. A negative sign represents the reverse. Table 20 summarizes the deviations and rankings for the five socioeconomic development indicators.

Table 21 establishes the index of East European variations from the level of Soviet socioeconomic development. (The variations are presented in Table 20.) Here we are no longer interested in direction of the difference (i.e., plus or minus), but only in the magnitude. For our hypothesis calls merely for the measurement of relative degrees of difference. Countries that are considerably advanced or considerably retarded with respect to the Soviet Union may be more or less equally dissatisfied with Soviet policies. Therefore, in Table 21, having obtained the combined ranking score for each country, we then omit the negative and positive signs, and arrive at the index ranking score by assigning the highest number, 8, to the country with the greatest variation in socioeconomic development from the Soviet Union and the lowest, 1, to the country that differs the least.

The two variables, East European deviation from the level of Soviet economic development and conformity to Soviet policy, correlate at −.71, which is significant at the .007 level. Since the correlation is both high and negative, we conclude that the data confirm our hypothesis: the greater the relative difference between the level of East European socioeconomic development and that of the Soviet Union, the lower the degree of conformity to Soviet policy.

Summary and Conclusions

Having made the long trek through methodology and statistics, it seems appropriate to summarize the end results of the tests of our hypotheses. Table 22 summarizes the correlations.

As admitted at the outset, our instruments for testing these hypotheses are far from ideal. Eventually, we hope, these instruments will be refined or better instruments developed, so that we can measure subsurface vibrations of dissent from Soviet predilections among the East European countries. In future endeavors, a greater availability of data may make it possible to include indicators we would have liked to use but had to discard for lack of information.

Even so, we believe that our findings put into perspective some of the ties that bind the bloc countries to the Soviet Union, and the limitations of Western capabilities (at least in the short term) to loosen these ties. The correlation between governmental interactions with the Western world and East European conformity to (or deviation from) Soviet policy was virtually nonexistent. The correlations with East-West trade interactions were somewhat ambiguous: The correlation of trade with the West as a percentage of total trade was low, whereas trade with the West as a percentage of net material product was fairly respectable. The correlations between cultural interactions with the West and conformity were low or barely existent. Overall, these results suggest that Western practices in these areas have had little causal effect on East European propensities to deviate from Soviet policy. As we have stated on several occasions, the minimal level at which these interactions have occurred may go far in explaining the absence of relationship.

The relatively high correlation with Eastern Europe's trade dependence on the USSR indicates that Moscow can inflict severe economic privation on these countries which their leaderships, bent on economic development, would be loath to incur. Even more significant is the correlation between the accessibility of East European countries to Soviet military power and their conformity to Soviet policy, which needs no further explanation since the invasion of Czechoslovakia.

Cultural relations with the USSR correlates even more highly with the conformity of East European leaderships to the Soviet Union's policies than does the military accessibility variable. Here one may conjecture that these interactions have a significant influence on the popular pressure potential against Soviet domination—where Soviet-East European cultural intercourse is high, popular pressure against Soviet hegemony is likely to be manageable, and hence those regimes that do not wish to "rock the boat" may find it in their interests to continue giving priority to Soviet culture.

The difference in the level of socioeconomic development also correlated quite highly with Eastern European countries' deviation from Soviet policy. This, too, may have an effect on the people, or politically relevant groups among them. It may, for instance, cause widespread aversion to the imposition of Soviet domestic and foreign

Table 20
East European Deviation from Soviet Mean Scores on Five
Socioeconomic Development Indicators and Consequent
Rankings: 1955-67

Indicator	A	B	C
1. Deviation of East European Mean Infant Mortality Rates from Mean Soviet Infant Mortality Rate: 1956-67	−48	−9	10
Consequent Ranking	−8	−2	3
2. Deviation of Mean East European Inhabitants per Physician from Mean Soviet Inhabitants per Physician: 1957-66	−2962	−145	−45
Consequent Ranking	−8	−3	−1
3. Deviation of East European Mean Energy Consumption from USSR Mean Energy Consumption: 1956-67	−2818	−1347	1951
Consequent Ranking	−8	−3	6
4. Deviation of East European Mean Railway Passenger Kilometers from Soviet Mean Railway Passenger Kilometers: 1955-67	−778	−344	565
Consequent Ranking	−8	−4	7
5. Deviation of East European Mean Employees in Manufacturing as a Percentage of Population from Soviet Mean Employees in Manufacturing as a Percentage of Population, 1960-67	−5.6	−1.0	6.0
Consequent Ranking	−7	−2	8

A = Albania	C = Czechoslovakia	H = Hungary
B = Bulgaria	EG = East Germany	P = Poland

Sources: See Appendix A, Tables 18-22, and relevant commentary in Appendix B.

EG	H	P	R	Y
1	−12	−21	−28	−47
1	−4	−5	−6	−7
−284	−109	−461	−201	−883
−5	−2	−6	−4	−7
1779	−729	105	−1525	−2183
5	−2	1	−4	−7
363	411	313	−144	−294
5	6	3	−1	−2
5.4	0.3	−3.2	−4.2	−4.6
6	1	−3	−4	−5

R = Rumania
Y = Yugoslavia

Table 21

Index of East European Deviation from the Level of Soviet
Socioeconomic Development, 1955-67: Combined Ranking
Scores on Five Indicators

Indicator	A	B	C
1. Deviation of East European Mean Infant Mortality Rates from Mean Soviet Infant Mortality Rate: 1956-67			
Ranking	−8	−2	3
2. Deviation of Mean East European Inhabitants per Physician from Mean Soviet Inhabitants per Physician: 1957-66			
Ranking	−8	−3	−1
3. Deviation of East European Mean Energy Consumption from USSR Mean Energy Consumption: 1955-67			
Ranking	−8	−3	6
4. Deviation of East European Mean Railway Passenger Kilometers from Soviet Mean Railway Passenger Kilometers: 1956-67			
Ranking	−8	−4	7
5. Deviation of East European Mean Employees in Manufacturing as a Percentage of Population from Soviet Mean Employees In Manufacturing as a Percentage of Populations, 1960-67			
Ranking	−7	−2	8
Sum of the Ranking Scores	−39	−14	23
Elimination of Positive and Negative Signs	39	14	23
Deviation Index Ranking Score	8	4	6

A = Albania	C = Cezechoslovakia	H = Hungary
B = Bulgaria	EG = East Germany	P = Poland

Source: Table 20.

264

EG	H	P	R	Y
1	−4	−5	−6	−7
−5	−2	−6	−4	−7
5	−2	1	−4	−7
5	6	3	−1	−2
6	1	−3	−4	−5
12	−3	−10	−19	−28
12	3	10	19	28
3	1	2	5	7

R = Rumania
Y = Yugoslavia

Table 22

Summary of the Correlations

Hypothesis Number	Independent Variables Correlated with Conformity to Soviet Policy	Relationship Hypothesized	Correlation Coefficient
1	East European Trade Dependence on USSR	+	.52
2	Accessibility to Soviet Military Power	+	.64
3	Cultural Interactions with USSR	+	.76
4	Trade with the West		
	As a Percentage of Total Trade	–	–.21
	As a Percentage of Net Material Product	–	–.43
5	Governmental Interactions with West	–	.04
6	Cultural Interactions with West Tourists to Eastern Europe	–	–.04
	Book Translations from English, French		–.24
7	East European Levels of Socioeconomic Development	–	.57
8	Difference in Level of Socioeconomic Development Between USSR and East Europe	–	–.71

policies or models that are not suitable to the national culture, tradition, or problems at hand. This certainly seems to have been the case in the recent upheavals in Czechoslovakia; it also appears to be true of Rumania's search for independence.

Notes

1. Article 2, paragraph 3. The Charter is reproduced in Ruth C. Lawson ed., *International Regional Organizations* (New York: Frederick A. Praeger, 1962), pp. 212-22.

2. See, for example, Sidney Siegel, *Nonparametric Statistics* (New York: McGraw-Hill, 1956), pp. 195-328. Elsewhere in this chapter we seek to determine the correlation among three or more indicator variables. In all cases, the Kendall coefficient of concordance has been utilized.

Part 4: The Lessons of Czechoslovakia for Europe's Security

14   The Tragedy of Czechoslovakia

In the eventful decade of the 1960's certainly no event was more significant than the ouster of Antonin Novotny, the ensuing political reforms under Alexander Dubcek, and the final tragedy of the invasion of Czechoslovakia by the armies of the Warsaw Pact. As one of the last chapters in this book, a description of most of the important events would seem to us to be a more vivid summary of the conflicting dynamic forces at work in Eastern Europe than any abstract theoretical treatment we could devise. We will begin by briefly tracing the pertinent features of Novotny's rule.

The Novotny leadership, it will be remembered, had weathered the storm generated by Khrushchev's secret speech at the Twentieth Party Congress better than most of the other East European regimes. Thereafter it had maintained strict, orthodox, Stalinist control over the Czechoslovak population and served the Soviet Union as a model satellite. If there was any factional strife within the Czechoslovak leadership, there was no public knowledge concerning it. Quantitative economic growth had been rapid throughout the 1950's and, relative to the rest of Eastern Europe, the Czechoslovak population lived rather well. At the turn of the 1960's, Czechoslovakia's party-government seemed to be among the most secure in the Communist world. In 1960 it promulgated a new constitution proclaiming Czechoslovakia as a "Socialist Republic," the second one (after the Soviet Union) in the

The first draft of the post-Novotny era in this chapter was written by Wayne H. Ferris, based on a chronology he compiled from reports by Radio Free Europe.

world. Theoretically, that signified its achievement of the requisite material and social base of socialism (as distinguished from the highest stage of Communism, which not even the Soviets could claim to have achieved). This elevation in Czechoslovakia's stature was obviously approved by the Soviets. Its leadership had every reason to be proud and confident.

By 1963 the situation had changed drastically. Orthodox, Soviet-style Communism was retreating, fighting a rearguard action on the political, economic, social, and cultural fronts, and Slovak intellectuals were openly challenging the past and current policies of the Prague regime. Ethnic competition was a factor in Czechoslovakia's ferment that had been absent in the upheavals of Poland and Hungary. Czechoslovakia's population is composed of 66 percent Czechs and 29.3 percent Slovaks. Ever since Czechoslovakia became an independent country in 1918, Slovaks felt themselves discriminated against by the Czech majority. This situation persisted under Communist rule, the Czechs predominating in the ruling organs of party and state and, with the help of willing Slovak stooges, reducing Slovak institutions of party and government to the status of rubber stamps of the Czech-dominated ruling apparat.

Like so many other nationalities in Eastern Europe, the Slovaks have always been proud of their traditions and heritage, feeling themselves ethnically and culturally distinct from their Czech counterparts. It was natural, therefore, that during the initial period under Communism, the Slovak Communist leadership sought to assure some independence from the Czechoslovak ruling apparat. For such "bourgeois nationalism" Rudolf Slanski and Vladimir Clementis (Slovak party chief and Czechoslovak Foreign Minister, respectively), were hanged in 1952. Three other Slovak leaders, Gustav Husak (chairman of the Slovak Board of Commissioners), Laço Novomesky (poet and Slovak Commissioner for Education), and Karol Smidke (chairman of the Slovak National Council), were sentenced to long terms in prison in 1954. Such purges had happened in other East European countries, as we have seen; but to the Slovak Communists they represented not simply a purge of deviants, but an affront of discrimination against their "nation." Although the purge of Slansky and Clementis occurred before Novotny assumed the top party post, the trial and imprisonment of the latter three was without a doubt attributable to his leadership. In 1954 they confirmed his political power and probably helped to cow dissident Slovaks into submission; in 1962 they came back to haunt him.

Two factors, it would appear, gave the immediate impetus to the open expression of public ferment in Czechoslovakia in 1962. The first was the final and complete denunciation of Stalin at the Twenty-second Party Congress (October, 1961), and the removal of his body from the place of honor beside Lenin in the mausoleum on Red Square. Stalin's methods were now discredited and his former protégés and followers in Eastern Europe once again had to scramble to wipe their own slates clean. The history of 1956 repeated itself: factionalism erupted and purges followed.

Novotny's leadership had been able to weather the storm of 1956 without any major visible difficulty, partly because of the rapid economic strides the country was making at that time. But in 1961, and for several years thereafter, Czechoslovakia's economy took a precipitous fall. Agriculture was hardest hit soon after the rapid collectivization drive culminated in 1960. The output of crops fell by 3.1 percent from the previous year in 1961, and by 12 percent in 1962. At the same time, industrial growth (measured in output) declined from 11.7 percent in 1960 to 8.9 in 1961 and 6.2 in 1962; in 1963 a negative growth rate of -0.6 was registered. The immediate effect of this faltering economic progress, one may assume, was a decline of confidence in the leadership.

In the wake of the Twenty-Second CPSU Congress, the first sign of trouble appeared at the Twelfth Czechoslovak Party Congress in December, 1962. It called upon the Central Committee to make a complete investigation into the purges of 1949-54. In April, 1963, Novotny dismissed the First Secretary of the Slovak Communist Party, Karol Bacilek, one of the most loyal of his Slovak Stalinist supporters; five months later, his dogmatistic Premier, Viliam Siroky, another Slovak, was forced to give up his office. Although, in June, 1963, Novotny still maintained that the charge of "bourgeois nationalism" against the Slovak Communist Party had been "correct in principle," the Central Committee, in December of the same year, declared these charges "unsubstantiated *in toto*," and called for the complete rehabilitation of those who had been purged for those charges. The weakness of Novotny's position at the top of the party hierarchy became visible. The erosion of Novotny's totalitarian powers must have been in progress for some time before 1963; but during that year the forces of erosion came into the open. Their public manifestations can be briefly summarized here.

The foundations of Stalinist orthodoxy in Communist economic management had been under serious challenge with *Pravda's* publication of Liberman's article on profitability on September 9, 1962. Undoubtedly, this article combined with Czechoslovakia's economic malaise to give additional stimulus to the desire for economic reform in Prague. Nowhere else in Eastern Europe did liberal reform proponents make such devastating critiques of Communist economic practices or advocate such far-reaching change as did Czechoslovak economists. And, among them, the Slovaks were the most vociferous.

The Slovak economist Eugen Loebl (one of the Slovak leaders sentenced to life imprisonment at the Slansky trial in 1952 but rehabilitated in 1963) argued that in Czechoslovakia, as in the capitalist world, the consumer ought to be "king" of economic planning and output. Repeatedly, Loebl castigated the party-government for its continuing, excessive centralization; repeatedly he called for enterprise independence from the state, the right to fix their own prices, the appointment of competent managers who would know how to take advantage of such independence, and free competition between enterprises. "Why should we not say that the advantage of socialism is that it is able to satisfy the needs of the consumer better than capitalism?" There were others who advocated a similar return to a free market economy; Loebl was only among the most articulate of them.

The effect of this demand articulation was clearly visible in the economic reform program, the first draft of which was issued for Central Committee approval toward the end of 1964.[1] Its basic features were very similar to those of the Hungarian economic reform enacted in 1968 (discussed in Chapter 7), but at the time it was the most progressive program anywhere in the Soviet bloc. However, every attempt at its implementation ran into opposition from hard-line apparatchiks who could not work within its rules; and Novotny's dislike of the new program deprived the reformers of much-needed support by the regime.

Outside the economic sector, similar demands were heard. Julius Strinka, a prominent Marxist theoretician, argued that the changes being contemplated in the economic structure should not stop there, but their impetus should be carried over into the political and social sector. In a scathing critique of dogmatism in Czechoslovakia, he advocated the legitimization and institutionalization of political opposition to the existing regime.[2] The demand for a legitimized political opposition was by then no longer a new one in Communist Czechoslovakia; students had made it on at least two occasions before, and they were to raise it again a month later.

At the national conference of university students, December 18 and 19, 1965, in the presence of Party Secretary Vladimir Koucky, student representative Jiri Mueller advocated that the Czechoslovak Youth League be divided on the basis of age. Those over 18 years old should be formed into a union of political character, to be included in the National Front and allowed to submit representatives to the national legislature. Youth, he said, was disillusioned, unable to express its own interests within the current political framework. Mueller also called for a federative division of the youth organizations into workers, farmers, and students. (Mueller was subsequently arrested and languished in prison until early in 1968.) Novotny rejected particularly the federative idea in his speech to the Czechoslovak Youth League factory organizations on April 18, 1966.

Further support to the legitimization of a political opposition came from Zdenek Mlynar, Secretary of the party Central Committee's legal commission. Writing in the party's daily, *Rude Pravo* (August 16, 1966), he suggested that the class struggle had come to an end and that, therefore, mass organizations should be given more responsibility— especially the task of airing conflicting views in society.

The trade unions, too, wavered between obedience to the state and loyalty to the workers during this period. At the end of the Central Council plenum of the Czechoslovak trade unions, on November 18, 1966, Radio Prague predicted that "new stimuli" would displace the "artificial concord of all interests of production and employees." Radio Prague had issued similar demands for trade union independence from the state before. One of the major problems giving rise to this demand was the dislocation of workers as a result of efficiency drives then under way in Czechoslovakia. Trade union officers suggested that the government tide over those workers who lost their jobs through enterprise efficiency by granting them a "social allowance" until they could find new employment. The government responded favorably.

Nevertheless, although there were clearly visible pressures from the rank and file for a more representative role of the trade unions in the interests of the workers, while Novotny remained in power, the trade unions continued to be obedient tools of the party-government. In one factory ("Karosa" in Horice, Czechoslovakia) pressure for higher wages resulted in the dismissal of the chairman of the trade union and four of his committee members.

The most troublesome ferment (from the party leadership's point of view) existed within the Czechoslovak Writers' Union. It began in 1963, when the weak political position of Antonin Novotny was laid bare; and at that time Novotny evidently decided that discretion was the better part of valor. Although Novotny and his hard-line Stalinist colleagues lost few opportunities to express their distaste for, and warnings against, the unorthodox views and criticisms expressed by the writers in their novels, poems, and articles, Czechoslovakia's publishers issued literary works extremely critical of the more odious policies of the Novotny regime.

At the June, 1967, Writers' Congress, Jiri Hendrich manifested in an emotional outburst the party's determination to force the writers into line. The subsequent plenary session of the party Central Committee (September 26 and 27) decided upon the drastic action to expel three important writers (Ivan Klima, Antonin J. Liehm, and Ludvik Vaculik), and to remove the literary organ of the Czechoslovak Writers' Union, *Literarin Noviny*, from its control and place it under the jurisdiction of the party-controlled Ministry of Culture. Furthermore, according to reports, the Writers' Union's funds for welfare were also to be transferred to the same ministry.

This may have amounted to a last-ditch effort by Novotny's leadership to tighten the party's control over the dissident intelligentsia. To the writers, it may have been the "straw that broke the camel's back." At the July Writers' Union Congress, the rift between Czechs and Slovaks was clearly evident: Slovaks would not speak out against the party's criticisms, which were aimed mainly at Czech writers (the Slovaks being cushioned by their own party leaders in the Czechoslovak party Presidium). But by December, Czech and Slovak writers seem to have joined forces. They alone may not have brought about the downfall of Novotny—but without the support of the intelligentsia the future of the Communist Party in Czechoslovakia was in doubt. By January, 1968, Antonin Novotny had lost the confidence and support of most of the dogmatists in his entourage.

The Quiet Revolution of 1968

The first serious challenge to Novotny's leadership came in a plenum of the Czechoslovak party's Central Committee on October 30-31, 1967, when a group of Slovak and Moravian Committee members accused Novotny of neglecting the economy (and particularly Slovakia's economic development) and demanded that he resign his high party office. In this same session there were also some challenges voiced to Novotny's competence as President of the Republic. Alexander

Dubcek, then First Secretary of the Slovak Communist Party, emerged as the leader of the anti-Novotny faction in the Central Committee. The session ended abruptly without a vote on the issue of Novotny's continuing rule; but it highlighted his vulnerability to progressive forces and, thus, marked the beginning of the end of his political career.

Between the October plenum and early January, 1968, Novotny naturally sought to save his own position. It was probably Novotny who, in his capacity of First Secretary of the Central Committee, extended that Committee's urgent invitation to Brezhnev to come to Prague. Brezhnev's presence reportedly shifted the predominantly anti-Novotny lineup in the 10-member Presidium of the party from the original 8-2 to 5-5. However, a subsequent Central Committee plenum, in session from December 19 to 21, 1967, resolved that Novotny should be ousted from the party leadership and established a commission (composed of the Presidium and a representative from each of the 11 administrative regions of Czechoslovakia) to choose a successor.

On January 3, the Central Committee again convened in a three-day plenary session and resolved to replace Novotny with Alexander Dubcek, thus marking the first time in Czechoslovak Communist history that a Slovak was to hold the highest party post in the land. It also decided on some general principles (to become known as the January Course) to humanize and democratize Communism in Czechoslovakia. Thus began a brief period of ferment—a "quiet" revolution—that was to transform the politics of Czechoslovakia until the massive military intervention by the Warsaw Pact succeeded in gradually restoring Communist orthodoxy. The dynamics of the Czechoslovak revolution had many features in common with that which had briefly transformed Hungary 12 years before; it differed from the Hungarian one basically in that the ferment was guided by a new party leadership that was committed to humanistic reforms and highly responsive to popular demands. The Dubcek leadership managed to give the appearance of being in control of the country, even while it gained immense popularity—a situation quite normal in democracies, but highly unusual in Communist systems—and thus it managed to hold off Soviet intervention for eight months.

A full descriptive treatment of the important events and their impact upon Czechoslovakia's political life would be impossible within the scope of this chapter. Therefore, we will attempt to categorize the important features of Czechoslovakia's quiet revolution into four sets of relationships that were transformed by the course of events, and to give illustrative examples of the process.

The Relationship Between the Ruling Party and Society: Interest Groups and Public Media

The removal of Novotny from his seat of power brought into the open the undercurrents of popular disaffection that had been only partly visible in the writings of Czechs and Slovaks since 1963. Almost immediately, interest groups began to articulate their demands with a spontaneity reminiscent of the Polish and Hungarian ferment of 1956. Many of these groups had existed before as transmission belts of the party's policies; they now proceeded to oust their party-appointed leaderships and replace them with those who would serve the interests of their members. Other interest groups were newly formed.

For instance, toward the end of January, 1968, the Central Committee of the Czechoslovak Writers' Union met to elect new officials, reflecting the predominantly liberal sentiment of its members. It also resolved to publish a new journal to replace *Literarni Noviny* which, as already mentioned, had been transferred by the party Central Committee to the Ministry of Culture in September, 1967. As was to be expected, the Czechoslovak Writers' Union became the most important driving force in the subsequent liberalization of Czechoslovakia, demanding the abandonment of old ways and challenging the positions of old-guard apparatchiks. In March the Writers' Union organized within its ranks the first formal organization of nonparty writers, a "circle of independent writers," to act as a counterweight to the Communist organization.

Students and youth groups reinvigorated their efforts to achieve autonomy from party control that had been denied them under Novotny. The Pioneer Organization, composed of young people between eight and 15 years of age, declared itself independent of the Czechoslovak Youth Union and demanded independent legal status and the transfer of its share of property and funds from the Union's Central Committee. University students were no less autonomy-minded. In February the Youth Union's committee in the philosophical department of Charles University in Prague resigned and was replaced by an Academic Council of Students (ACS) to represent all of the students in that department. A month later, the ACS announced that it would put forth candidates for future elections to the National

Assembly and the municipal council of Prague, and that the interests of the students would be introduced as issues in the election campaigns. The students of other departments of Charles University were not long in following this lead; and on March 19, representatives from 17 University faculties launched an organization to set forth and promote the goals of student groups.

Collective farmers liberated themselves from the shackles of party control when, at their Seventh Congress in February, 1968, the delegates rejected the resolution submitted to them by the Congress Presidium and wrote one in line with their interests. For the first time, the debate at the Congress was unfettered by censorship or other manipulation and the delegates could address themselves to problems of democratization and self-management, and demand cheaper prices for machinery and chemicals, better wages and social security, and better services from the building industry. In the end they resolved to form a statewide interest group of collective farmers.

In the Czechoslovak trade unions, progressive forces scored a major victory when they obtained the resignation of the Central Council's three highest functionaries, all pro-Novotny conservatives, on March 12. At this session, the Council demanded the right of the trade unions to formulate their own positions and programs, and denounced the party's practice of appointing its own reliable recruits to the Council's leadership. A week later, a mass meeting of railroad engineers resolved to form a federation of its own within the Czechoslovak Trade Union Council. Among other autonomy moves within the trade unions, the most prominent was the establishment of enterprise workers' councils that aimed at a transfer of management power to the workers.

An even more striking example of spontaneous interest group formation was the association of non-Communist victims of the early purges, calling itself the Club 321. It was formed in March, 1968, for the stated purpose of pressing the government for the speedy rehabilitation of its members. At the same time, a "club of engaged nonparty people" was formed and applied for legal recognition.

As a result of the climate engendered by Dubcek's "New Course," by March, 1968, preliminary censorship had practically ceased in the public media. On March 5 the party Presidium announced the abolition of preventive censorship. Decisions taken by the government in June and July went a considerable way toward the formal implementation of this decision, prior to the scheduled drafting of an entirely new press law in the fall. The Central Publication Board, the official censorship organ, was administratively neutralized. The burden of responsibility for protecting state secrets was shifted to editors-in-chief of the various media, and the list of secrets was cut from 400 to some 35 pages.

The climate of free expression which emerged had two major fallout effects. First, popular interests which came to be expressed in the media contributed in no small measure to important developments in the Czechoslovak society, including the ouster of Novotny as President of the Republic, agreement by the party to the rehabilitation of the victims of the Novotny era, the dismissal of numerous conservative functionaries in party and government positions, and the mobilization of support for moderate and progressive party members. Second, the media suddenly found that they could report quite objectively on the existing political ferment in Czechoslovakia and on international relations as well.

The Party Leadership's Response to Interest Groups

In general, the most significant response of the party leadership to the emerging interest articulation appeared in the Party Action Program issued by the Central Committee in April, 1968.[3] In this document, the party leadership committed itself, among other things, to permitting the free association of interest groups, their freedom of speech, and their influence on the decision-making process. While it ruled out competing political parties in Czechoslovakia's reform, it explicitly stressed the importance of interest group articulation and public opinion polls in the formation of national policy.

This does not mean, however, that the party leadership was in favor of the spontaneous proliferation of interest groups. There were some, such as Club 321 and the Club of Engaged Non-party People that faced administrative difficulties when they applied for registration.* Furthermore, the party leadership was opposed to the splitting of the Youth Union into separate interest groups. On the other hand, the party leadership conceded that the trade union movement should become autonomous of party control: neither the party nor the government should interfere in their activities, and their right to strike (hopefully as the ultimate weapon) should be recognized. And, though it disliked some interest groups, it did take up some of their

---

*In June, 1968, Minister of Interior Pavel admitted that out of 70 applications by interest groups for legal registration, only one had been approved; the others were still legally regarded as preparatory committees.

causes—most notably that of the purge victims of the Stalin period, whose rehabilitation was to become one of the more sustained efforts of the Dubcek regime.

At the same time, the party leadership began a dialogue with the people of Czechoslovakia, in which leaders sought to explain their policies, to justify or apologize for actions of the past, to inform the people of the present situation—in short, to be honest with the public. This novel procedure for Communist politics had several manifestations.

First, the party leadership exhibited unprecedented candor in revealing the nature of the problems besetting Czechoslovakia. For example, at a public meeting of workers in Prague-Vysocany, on March 28, Ota Sik revealed that the rate of increase of real wages in Czechoslovakia during the past decade had been one-half that in Austria, and one-third that in West Germany. He admitted that the existing standard of living in Czechoslovakia was one-fourth less than that in Austria. Never before had the leadership spoken so frankly to the Czechoslovak people.

A second and related aspect of the new dialogue was a decision of the Presidium on February 7 to publish information of the proceedings at Presidium and Secretariat meetings. In implementation of this policy, the Presidium, on April 16, specified (for the first time in Czechoslovak Communist history) the duties of the individual Central Committee secretaries and of the "inner cabinet."

Third, discredited party and government leaders appeared before the public on radio and television to explain their participation in the policy-making process under Novotny, and to appeal for public sympathy for their present situation. Thus, in March, Defense Minister Buhomir Lomsky issued a statement denying rumors of his involvement in General Jan Sejna's defection to the West. Similarly, on March 18, party Presidium member and Premier Jozef Lenart appeared on television to explain his belated support for the "New Course"; and Presidium member Otaker Simunek appeared on Radio Prague in a similar venture.

A fourth feature of the new information policy was the willingness of the party and government leaders to be interviewed by reporters and to appear before mass rallies, at which they responded to probing questions from the audience. For example, Presidium member Josef Smrkovsky appeared before a mass meeting of politicians, economists, and cultural personalities on March 13, and replied with considerable candor to questions about the reasons for Brezhnev's visit to Czechoslovakia and about Soviet interference in internal affairs during the leadership crisis of December, 1967.

The Relationship Between
the Party Leadership
and the Rank and File

It seems fair to say that none of the above-described transformations in the relationship of the rulers to the people could have been possible had not a similar change taken place within the party. One of the most important changes was a wholesale turnover of party functionaries from the highest to the lowest level.

This turnover essentially favored the moderates and progressives, and was directed against the hard-line elements that had served as the nucleus of the Novotny regime. The conservative functionaries had run the party as a command operation. The progressives who replaced them exhibited a greater attraction to democratic procedures.

It is significant that the housecleaning operation was conducted more or less autonomously at the lower levels of the Communist Party organization and within the many different party organizational groupings. Party functionaries were not removed by higher headquarters; on the contrary, they were either pressured or voted out of office from below. As observed earlier, the public media were instrumental in expressing and formulating the demands for the removal of conservative functionaries. More often than not, discredited party members chose to resign before being formally voted out of office.

In regional party conferences held in March, 1968, there was a 71 percent turnover in membership. In June, some 120 district party conferences were held. The district level, long recognized as the bastion of reaction, registered a major victory for the progressives. For the first time since 1948, genuine debate on political issues occurred, during which scarcely anyone ventured to voice the conservative view. Discussion focused on ways to further democratize the party structure, and suggestions for major changes were frequently expressed.

All of this was reflected in the top-level decision-making process of the Czechoslovak Communist Party. Through successive personnel changes, the composition of the Presidium became liberal. At the same time, the Central Committee became more decisive in the policy-making process. Either because of internal divisions, or in order to conform to previously violated party statutes, the Presidium tended to leave the final resolution of issues up to the Central Committee, or to seek the Central Committee's approval for decisions it had already reached, while keeping the public informed of its proceedings.

Party-Government Relationships

Decisions taken by the party leadership under Dubcek presaged a new set of relationships between the party and the government. The initial character of the changes was increased autonomy for the government in the formulation and implementation of policy.

On April 16 a high-level government spokesman announced that the Inner Cabinet—that is, the Prime Minister and his five deputies—would henceforth directly supervise broad spheres of governmental work, as well as the activities of individual ministers. The spokesman admitted that, previously, the party had directly controlled foreign policy, defense, and security. These would now be delegated to the Inner Cabinet. The Presidium's control would henceforth be indirect, since only one of its members, Premier Oldrich Cernik, was in the Inner Cabinet.

Toward the end of July the party Presidium liquidated the notorious Eighth Department of the Central Committee. In the past this department had served as a superministry responsible for party policy in the administration of defense, justice, and security. There was reason to believe that the government's freedom to act independently of party directives was increased significantly by the removal of the Eighth Department.

The National Assembly also gave indications of asserting its role in the legislative process. In its session of January 10-11, a draft bill on housing, which had previously passed all committees, was deemed inadequate by the plenary session and was returned to the government for amending. This was an important event, since housing construction has been one of the weakest links in the Czechoslovak economy. In a session on March 14-15, the National Assembly Presidium passed a vote of no confidence in the Minister of Interior and the Prosecutor-General. Some 24 hours later both officials were dismissed. On April 19 an election was held for chairman of the National Assembly. Josef Smrkovsky, a prominent liberal in the Dubcek Presidium, was elected in a secret ballot: 188 members voting for and 68 against him. All of this spelled hope for democracy in Czechoslovakia.

The Relationship Between Czechs and Slovaks

Slovak discontent with Czech domination had been one of the paramount factors in Novotny's fall. Dubcek's rise to become the first Slovak to lead the government gave the Slovak people some hope of redress. But it could not be a permanent solution to their problem. The demand for home rule was widespread. There were calls for a confederation of separate Czech and Slovak republics; but more moderate forces favored a genuine federation that would leave essential autonomy to both without destroying the concept of a Czechoslovak nation. The question of how to achieve a federation that would be equitable to both ethnic communities was to preoccupy the Czechoslovak government long after the Warsaw Pact invasion. Its resolution in January, 1969, establishing Czechoslovakia as a federal republic, was to be one of the few lasting accomplishments of the quiet revolution of 1968.

The Balance—and "Two Thousand Words"

All of the categorizations listed above carried Czechoslovak politics along the road toward a Communist democracy. It was a precarious road charted by popular ferment. Except for the eventual federation of Czech and Slovak republics, no feature of this transformation was institutionalized. Too little time, too little public tranquillity, too little unity within the party on the basic issues—all of these are plausible, if only partial, reasons for the ultimate failure of Czechoslovakia's experiment in humanizing Communism. But most important, the Czechoslovak people were growing weary of ferment; they were looking forward to summer vacations; they knew that the new leadership would do what still remained to be done.

It was probably this loss of fervor that prompted a group of intellectuals, on June 27, to issue an appeal, "Two Thousand Words to Workers, Farmers, Civil Servants, Scientists, Artists, and Everyone,"[4] urging the people to help assure democracy in Czechoslovakia. This manifesto warned against popular apathy in the face of conservative elements still in power, arguing that a loss of momentum in democratization might result in a complete halt and a return of the hard-liners. While supporting the Dubcek leadership on the basis that it deserved a chance to transform Czechoslovak politics, it advocated legitimate means of ousting the conservative apparatchiks from their remaining power positions—peaceful demonstrations, strikes, even monetary bribes to obtain their resignations.

Dubcek's Presidium immediately and explicitly dissociated itself from the "Two Thousand Words," but at lower party levels, the reactions were more ambivalent. This manifesto was to mark a turning point in the attitudes of Warsaw Pact leaderships toward the liberalization trend in Czechoslovakia.

The Impact on Czechoslovakia's
Relations With the Bloc

From the very beginning, the popular ferment in Czechoslovakia was a source of anxiety in Moscow and other bloc capitals. Only Rumania's leadership appeared outwardly unconcerned about the crisis, which it regarded as a purely internal affair of Czechoslovakia's, in which no other country had any right to interfere. Other leaderships, particularly in Moscow, Warsaw, and Pankow, faced the possibility of a spillover of Czechoslovakia's popular ferment into their own countries with increasing concern. This fear was perhaps best justified in Poland, when student riots erupted in March, 1968; but in the Ukraine, too, intellectuals were reported to have been more than passively interested in Czechoslovakia's experiment with freedom.

Of equally great concern to Moscow was the increasingly independent orientation of Czechoslovakia's foreign policy under Dubcek, which was in part a reaction to the former regime's subservience to Soviet tutelage over the past 20 years. On the one hand, the Dubcek leadership professed its desire to continue and further improve Czechoslovakia's cooperation with the Soviet Union and the bloc countries; on the other hand, its emerging foreign policy statements and actions were demonstrative of its determination to gain greater independence from and genuine equality within the Soviet bloc.

For instance, on February 22, Dubcek stated before the Central Committee that Czechoslovakia's primary foreign policy concern was Europe, and that it would seek to improve relations with the countries of the Continent, regardless of their social systems. A month later, before an audience in Brno, Dubcek reaffirmed Czechoslovakia's alliance with the bloc countries, but made it clear that within this framework Prague would set forth its own evaluation of world issues. The implication was that Czechoslovakia would no longer be guided exclusively by Moscow's policies or views.

Specifically with regard to West Germany, the Communists' bogey in Europe, the Czechoslovak leadership gave early indications of its desire to change the previous course. In February, 1968, Oldrich Cernik, then Deputy Premier, described the ratification of the West German-

Czechoslovak agreement to exchange trade missions as "an important step toward the normalization of relations"—a development that East Germany and the Soviet Union were particularly anxious to prevent at that time. Although Czechoslovakia did not establish diplomatic relations with West Germany, the visible rapprochement between the two countries became a source of mounting concern in Moscow.

Czechoslovakia's increasingly independent posture and the impact of a free press upon its leadership were reflected at a meeting of world Communist Party delegations in Budapest in April, where the Czechoslovak representative declared that his party would no longer approve of the practice of formulating resolutions or decisions behind closed doors. Even more noteworthy in this respect, however, was Lieutenant General Vaclav Prchlik's press conference of July 15, at a time when Soviet troops were occupying Czechoslovakia under the guise of "maneuvers." Prchlik delivered himself of a number of damaging criticisms of the Warsaw Pact and Soviet domination. For one thing, he challenged the Soviet Union's right to station troops in Czechoslovakia under Warsaw Pact auspices, for there is no clause to this effect in the treaty. Instead, the treaty affirms the principles of respect for state sovereignty and noninterference. Prchlik argued further that all Warsaw Pact member states should treat each other as equal partners and that safeguards ought to be established against the prevailing practice of bringing collective pressure to bear on member countries with opposing views. The role of the Political Advisory Committee should be enhanced, he said, presumably to give greater voice to the East European Pact members. Furthermore, the Pact's joint command, which consisted only of Soviet officers (East European officers having only liaison role) should be changed to give East Europeans a meaningful function in the command structure.

These are only a few examples of Czechoslovakia's increasingly troublesome determination to chart its own course within the Soviet bloc. Needless to say, like all actions of the Dubcek regime, every manifestation of independence from Soviet control was widely discussed in the Czechoslovak press. Although the public media of other bloc countries reported only more or less selectively on developments in Czechoslovakia, the news was accessible to their peoples on Western radio stations. It seemed a reasonable assumption that, in time, the germ of dissent would fall on fertile soil in the Communist countries surrounding Czechoslovakia.

The Warsaw Pact's Efforts To
Deal with Czechoslovakia

Unlike the Hungarian upheaval of 1956, which was dealt with by the Soviet Union alone, the Czechoslovak crisis became a problem for the Warsaw Pact. This fact reflected not only a change in Soviet political strategy within the framework of bloc relations that had evolved since 1956; it also reflected the anxieties generated among some of the bloc leaderships (especially those of East Germany and Poland) by the popular ferment in Czechoslovakia.

On March 23, 1968, Dubcek was summoned to a hastily convened summit meeting at Dresden. (Rumania was absent from this and subsequent meetings dealing with Czechoslovakia.) There he was asked to explain the situation in Czechoslovakia. Apparently, he managed to assuage some of the anxieties of his allies, for the communiqué expressed confidence that the Czechoslovak Communist Party would safeguard and promote the achievements of "socialism." However, it also stressed the need for vigilance and defense against subversion by imperialist forces, and highlighted again the danger to the bloc of "militaristic and neo-Nazi activity in the German Federal Republic." Subsequent reports and rumors in the Czechoslovak press revealed that Dubcek had withstood concerted attempts by other delegations to exert pressure for a change to a more orthodox course.

Beginning in April, 1968, the press of the Warsaw Pact countries, except Rumania and Hungary, began to publish reports and commentaries critical of Czechoslovak internal developments and about some of the leading figures in the reform movement. (Rumania's press remained neutral on the whole, but reported selectively; Hungary's public media often gave favorable commentary about Czechoslovakia's reform, which in many ways resembled its own. Indeed, Hungary's official attitude toward events in Czechoslovakia turned critical only after the publication of "Two Thousand Words.") The intensity of the anti-Czechoslovak press campaign, which was most denunciatory in East Germany, increased throughout the summer of 1968.

Another summit meeting was held on May 8 in Moscow to discuss the Czechoslovak crisis. This time both Czechoslovakia and Rumania were absent. On the following day Warsaw Pact forces massed along Czechoslovakia's borders in Poland and East Germany in "maneuvers"— a first demonstration of the Pact's intention to bring military pressures to bear if necessary. The Prague leadership's assurances that it knew of these maneuvers in advance and saw no cause for alarm could not erase the writing on the wall. Nevertheless, with each increase in pressure by the Warsaw Pact, the people of Czechoslovakia grew more determined to be free.

In June the Soviet Union moved massive troop contingents into Czechoslovakia for joint Warsaw Pact maneuvers. These forces refused to leave Czechoslovakia for several weeks after the maneuvers had officially ended. Logistical problems were lamely cited as the reason for their continued stay; but this could not disguise their real function, which General Prchlik hinted at in his above-mentioned news conference. With each passing week, relations between Czechoslovakia and the Soviet Union became more tense, as the press of both countries traded charges and countercharges.

On July 12, the Czechoslovak Presidium politely declined a summons by the five Warsaw Pact leaderships (Rumania again having excluded itself) to attend a summit meeting in Warsaw, stating that it would prefer to engage its allies in bilateral negotiations that might clear the way to a useful multilateral conference. The Warsaw Pact therefore had another summit with two of its members, Czechoslovakia and Rumania, absent. By this time the anxieties of the assembled leaderships (Hungary's possibly the only exception) had become so great as to prompt them to drop the facade of sovereignty and nonintervention in each others' internal affairs. The summit issued a letter to the Czechoslovak Presidium in which it expressed the rationale for limited socialist sovereignty that was to justify military invasion and became known subsequently as the Brezhnev Doctrine:

> We cannot . . . agree that enemy forces should divert your country from the path of socialism and expose Czechoslovakia to the danger of being torn from the socialist community. This is no longer your affair alone. This is the affair of all communist and workers parties and all countries which are linked by alliances, cooperation, and friendship.

The Czechoslovak Presidium defended itself against the specific charges contained in this letter, reaffirmed its intention to carry through the Action Program issued by the Central Committee in April, and reminded its five concerned allies that each party had the right and duty to choose the policies most appropriate to the problems of the country it rules.

On July 19, the Soviet Union proposed to Czechoslovakia a bilateral summit meeting, to be composed of the entire party Presidium of both countries, as a preparatory step to a multilateral Warsaw Pact conference. Prague agreed, and the meeting was held from July 29 to August 1 in an atmosphere of electrified tension. Two days later, Bratislava was host to a Warsaw Pact summit (again without Rumania). After both of these meetings the Czechoslovak leadership assured the public that it had given away nothing basic to the reform; and indeed, the communiqués lent themselves to interpretation favoring the predilections of both the Warsaw Pact and Czechoslovak reformers.

For the next three weeks there was a lull in Soviet bloc polemics against reactionary forces in Czechoslovakia. It seemed as if the meetings in Cierna and Tisou and Bratislava had resolved the conflict between Czechoslovakia and the Warsaw Pact. In reality, Czechoslovakia was only passing through the analogous eye of the hurricane. On the morning of August 21, the citizens of Prague awoke to the rumble of Warsaw Pact tanks rolling through their streets. For them it was the dawn of a new era: the crisis had only begun.

The Aftermath of the Invasion

Militarily, the invasion of Czechoslovakia was a brilliant demonstration of the mobility and coordination of Warsaw Pact forces. Politically, it at first appeared to be a blunder. At the time of the invasion the Soviet Union claimed that Warsaw Pact forces were responding to the urgent appeals of some unidentified Czechoslovak leaders to help save socialism in their country; but no leader could be found who was either willing to admit to this or able to take Dubcek's place. The Czechoslovak people would not be intimidated by Soviet tanks; indeed, the invasion strengthened their determination to be free regardless of what the Soviet Union might do.

Undoubtedly, the most important reason for the initial political failure of the invasion was that the Soviets could not gain control over Czechoslovakia's communications system—that vital element of totalitarian control. Though Warsaw Pact troops immediately seized and occupied radio stations and press offices, clandestine radio stations continued to broadcast the news as it happened, and to issue instructions to foil the plans of the invaders.

The Fourteenth Extraordinary Czechoslovak Party Congress, which had been scheduled to meet in September, met in secret session on August 22. Its resolution supporting the Dubcek leadership and condemning the invasion was broadcast throughout the country. It also elected a new Central Committee of 150 members, predominantly pro-Dubcek liberals. Since the Czechoslovak Communist Party had spoken through its sovereign congress of duly elected delegates, it was for the time being impossible for the Soviet Union to install a new leadership of its own choosing. There was no choice but to continue dealing with the Dubcek leadership that had already been abducted to Moscow.

The agreement reached in Moscow on August 27, after lengthy and acrimonious negotiations in which the Soviets sought to humiliate and intimidate the Dubcek group, represented a remarkable compromise, under the circumstances. The Soviet Union agreed to the continuing pursuit of the post-January course by the ruling organs of party and government as then constituted. The Czechoslovak leaders had to agree to declare the secret Fourteenth Party Congress invalid, and to schedule a new congress only after the situation had been "normalized." They had to agree further to reimpose censorship on the public media, to accept the "temporary" stationing of Soviet forces in Czechoslovakia, to cooperate closely with the bloc countries in Comecon and the Warsaw Pact, and to protect "friends" of the Soviet Union against possible reprisals.

Again, the agreement between the Soviet Union and Czechoslovakia was highly subject to interpretation, and the interpretation made in Prague differed significantly from that made in Moscow. While the Czechoslovak leadership annulled the Fourteenth Congress, it nevertheless coopted 80 of the newly elected Central Committee members into the old one, thus enlarging it from 110 to 190 and giving it a large majority of liberals. Press censorship was reimposed through the creation of the Office of Press and Information, yet the rules of censorship remained liberal and the implementation so weak that the difference was hardly noticeable—most aspects of censorship were left up to the media concerned.

Reform efforts continued unabated after the invasion. The rehabilitation of purge victims progressed. Trade unions developed into an independent political force. Mass organizations continued to organize and demonstrate in support of the Dubcek leadership. The reorganization of Czech lands and Slovakia into a federation at the governmental level was accomplished by 1969.

But the momentum of the reform gradually slowed under the occupation. People grew weary of the pressures of the occupation. Hard-liners who had lost their positions before and after the invasion again gathered courage to speak out. Many, like Gustav Husak, who had been shocked by the invasion, began to argue for "realism"—the acceptance of the new situation that would not be wished away. Grave economic problems could not be solved without a heavy input of foreign aid. The Soviet Union managed to find ways to keep Czechoslovakia from accepting Western credits, and it would not extend any aid of its own until it was better satisfied with the political situation in Prague. Under these circumstances, the Dubcek leadership, though it remained immensely popular, could not solve any of the basic problems of Czechoslovakia; and it was only a matter of time before it would succumb to internal and external pressures and resign. In the meantime, the Soviet presence continued to strengthen the once-discredited hard-liners in the Czechoslovak Communist Party, who were anxious to return to power and to take revenge on those who had brought about their downfall.

The end of Dubcek's rule came in April, 1969, eight months after the invasion. On March 28, when the Czechoslovak ice hockey team defeated the Soviet team for a second time, massive anti-Soviet demonstrations erupted in several Czechoslovak cities and resulted in some damage to Soviet property. Moscow took this event as a pretext for a full-scale attack on the Czechoslovak leadership, claiming among other things that it could no longer control the country. It demanded a purge of the ruling Presidium and a speedy "normalization"—Soviet style. At the beginning of April, Soviet Defense Minister Andrei Grechko arrived in Prague to issue these demands and to symbolize by his presence Soviet intentions to back them up militarily, if necessary.

On April 17, the Czechoslovak Central Committee voted to reorganize the Presidium. Dubcek had to step down; Gustav Husak took his place. In the new Presidium, "realists" and hard-liners held the balance. The stage was thus set for a return to "normalcy."

The Return to the Status Quo Ante

The pluralization of Czechoslovak society, the most important accomplishment of the Dubcek era, was quickly abandoned by the Husak regime. It undertook to reestablish its control over the interest groups which had freed themselves from party control in 1968 and to liquidate those which had spontaneously formed during 1968.

Wholesale personnel changes occurred in the public media, and preliminary censorship, rigidly applied, brought an end to objective reporting and critical analysis of the news. Through the Ministries of

Culture and Interior (heading the secret police), party supremacy was restored over the cultural sector. In the months to follow, 21 important cultural periodicals were banned; those that remained reflected the subservience of their writers and editors to the party's hard-line commands.

In the trade unions, the return to normalcy was most difficult to achieve. In October and December of 1969, and in February, 1970, the trade union leadership was swept by purges; and in May, 1970, the entire Presidium of the Czech Trade Union Council (some 31 members) had to resign, together with 27 other Council members. According to party pronouncements, the trade unions would revert to their former role of transmission belts of party policies within the enterprises. Legislation passed at the end of 1969 enabled employers to dismiss employees even for causes not directly related to their jobs (i.e., political ones, such as disturbing the socialist system) and robbed the unions of the right to intervene on behalf of the workers in labor disputes with management.

The field of higher education suffered equally severe repression. In Prague and Bratislava, university committees and student unions were banned. The Czech Ministry of Education overturned declarations and decrees of 1968 and 1969 which were aimed at implementing democratization and decentralization in the university system. The ministry employed terror, intimidation, and a system of informers in pursuit of its ends. In October of 1969 it requested all institutes of higher education to ban publication of all student periodicals and to cut off financial support of such organs.

The Husak regime voiced its determination to restore the leading role of the party in all aspects of society. To achieve this aim, large-scale purges at all levels of the party were set in motion. Between May of 1969 and the end of February, 1970, half of the membership of the Czechosolvak party's Central Committee was expelled, and the more orthodox Slovak Central Committee witnessed a purge of one-fourth of its membership. As a result, the liberal complexion of these bodies changed to an orthodox-dogmatic hue. Purges at the Presidium and Secretariat levels achieved similar results.

The Husak leadership established special screening committees to examine the records of all party members during the reform period. This process was to result in the issuance of new party membership cards to those whose records passed the test of reliability. At the time of writing, the exchange of cards was decimating the ranks of the

Czechoslovak Communist Party. Expulsion from the party usually was followed by dismissal from one's job and extreme difficulty in finding another one. Those who wanted to humanize Communism in Czechoslovakia now have to pay the price in human privation and hardship.[5]

At the time of writing, the Husak regime was in the process of refurbishing the economic system into one of "planned management." The structure of the new system was not clearly defined, but it was clear that it would leave sufficient centralization for the party to exercise its leading role. It seemed unlikely that the economic councils would survive the recentralization process—or, if they did, that they would allow the workers any real participatory role in the management of enterprises.

Of all of the reforms planned or enacted by the Dubcek leadership, in 1970 only the federal structure of Czechoslovakia on the government level survived. But a similar federalization of the Czechoslovak Communist Party had apparently been abandoned. Since the party again runs the state, having abolished the division of functions and purged the government apparatuses, even this accomplishment now seems rather meaningless for the political process of Czechoslovakia.

Thus, the Soviet invasion that first seemed a political blunder paid off in the end. The Kremlin leadership had every reason to be satisfied with the normalization of Czechoslovakia, for in the summer of 1970 the people could look back on the last years of Novotny's rule as years of comparative freedom and prosperity. Czechoslovakia's hard-line officialdom was openly thankful to the Soviet Union for having sent its forces to save socialism against the forces of rightist reaction and imperialist subversion, and on the surface, at least, it seemed as loyal and cooperative as Novotny's regime had been.

At mid-1970, Czechoslovakia faced a bleak, uncertain future. Husak presided over a party Presidium of hard-liners whom he could not control. He tried to save Dubcek from the disgrace of expulsion from the party, but could not. Even his own future was rumored to be in doubt.[6] Czechoslovakia was still facing its worst economic crisis since the Communists took power, and it seemed doubtful that the crisis could be solved in the long run without a decentralized economic structure or, for that matter, without the many competent people who have fallen victim to the purge.

In the future, Husak (or whoever succeeded him) would probably be confronted with the same problem that Janos Kadar had to face in

Hungary—how to arrive at the best mix of control and performance. To solve this problem, Kadar had to move against the hard-liners and seek an alliance between his party and the people under the slogan "who is not against us is with us." At the moment of writing, it seemed highly doubtful that Husak would embark on such a course. But it seemed equally doubtful that he could achieve any measurable economic progress in Czechoslovakia without first achieving some modus vivendi with the people.

Notes

1. The draft is summarized in *East Europe* (December, 1964), pp. 41-43.

2. *Kulturny Zivot*, No. 48 (November 6, 1965).

3. See Paul Ello, ed., *Czechoslovakia's Blueprint for "Freedom"* (Washington, D.C.: Acropolis Books, 1968), pp. 89-178.

4. Translated in U.S. Senate, Committee on the Judiciary, Subcommittee to Investigate the Administration of the Internal Security Act and Other Internal Security Laws, 91st Congress, 1st Session, "Aspects of Intellectual Ferment and Dissent in Czechoslovakia" (Washington,D.C.: U.S. Government Printing Office, 1969), pp. 137-42.

5. For a sobering eyewitness account, see Andreas Kohlschutter, "In Prag begann der letzte Akt," *Die Zeit* (Hamburg) (June 30, 1970).

6. See Henry Tanner, "Dubcek Is Expelled from Czech Party," *The New York Times* (June 27, 1970).

15 The Security of Europe: Considerations

The foregoing chapters have depicted many of the contours, zigs, and zags in Communist Eastern Europe's road of political change since the end of the Stalin era. Popular forces have risen in revolt against regimes imposed from without, only to be suppressed by Soviet military power; yet on the whole, Soviet military power has been unable to contain the more subtle forces of change that have made the Soviet bloc of today stand in such striking contrast with the one that Stalin built. Divided leaderships have had to compromise goals and methods in the policy-making process; their loyalties to Moscow have become increasingly conditional on the consistency of Soviet aims with their own national interests. The necessity for more efficient management of the economy and popular demands for better standards of living have forced Communist leaderships into a reassessment of the Stalinist ideology and the totalitarian political system to which it gave rise; they also have helped to pry open the "iron curtain" and to end the isolation of the East from the West.

Europe itself, however, remains divided along ideological lines. The governments in the western part are predominantly institutionalized to serve and be responsive to the will of the people. The eastern part is ruled by Communist totalitarian regimes hewing to the proposition that society should be ruled as a dictatorship of the proletariat whose will is discerned by the "vanguard" of a self-coopting oligarchy. The ideological dividing line of Europe was drawn basically where Soviet power met that of the West; and with some qualifications, it has been

295

maintained over a period of 25 years along with the accompanying East-West military confrontation. During this period the Soviet Union found it necessary to use military force three times to preserve the integrity of its own alliance system and control over Eastern Europe.

To speak of a transformation, therefore, would be overstating the sum total of the changes that have occurred. The domestic political goals and structures, and international orientations of the countries on both sides of the dividing line, are basically still the same. But the gulf between them has narrowed as the Communists have come to realize (beginning with Khrushchev's reign) that in the prevailing power balance, "peaceful coexistence" is more advantageous in the long run than the doctrine of the inevitability of war between Communism and capitalism. Since 1962, there has been "peaceful coexistence" (i.e., the absence of Communist-inspired crises) pervading the relations between Eastern and Western Europe, and this coexistence has introduced some flexibility into intra-European politics across the ideological divide (once called the "iron curtain"). However, the two sides still stand opposed in a military confrontation. The intensity of this confrontation has decreased, but the level of military power on the eastern side has grown tremendously.

The political, economic, and social evolution of both sides of Europe and the confluence of forces and circumstances that have narrowed the gulf between them must be viewed against the background of this military confrontation, especially when one looks into the decade ahead. The western part of Europe has enjoyed unprecedented prosperity during the last 20 years, in large part attributable to an equally unprecedented cooperation among the countries of the West in a security system that foreclosed both military aggression and political pressure from the East.

While somewhat comparable security arrangements exist in the Soviet bloc, prosperity has been far less conspicuous there, except in the officially published statistics. The Western countries generally enjoyed an economic advantage when World War II ended in 1945. Yet to say that the conspicuous difference in prosperity between the two parts is due in large part to their political systems is no mere conjecture of biased Western observers: it is a conclusion the Communists themselves have reached.

What is important here, also, is that neither side had to yield to the political pressures of the other side; and thus the countries of Europe could develop according to the ideological predilections of their respective regimes. With the superpowers bearing the brunt of the military burden, it is fair to hypothesize that in the present century, and despite the hazards of the nuclear age, the countries of Europe have not had such real security at such low cost as they have had during the past two decades. They could thus look inward and seek to realize their own aspirations—and in the case of Western Europe, at least, this meant to aim for affluence.

Prosperity breeds its own demands upon the political and economic system; and security over a long period of time tends to breed a different outlook on the world. It is part of human nature to want to build upon and improve past achievements. The economic variable of this proposition is much better understood than the security variable, which began to be apparent only in the 1960's, when both joined to bring the politics of Europe into flux. As West European industries sought new markets in the less-developed East for their rapidly expanding export capacity, their governments had to pave the way for increased trade through diplomacy and government-protected credits. It should be recognized, however, that trade with East Europe and the Soviet Union has never been of major importance for any of the West European countries. In the case of West Germany, the country with the most trade with the East, less than five percent of foreign trade is with the East. The converse is true with respect to Eastern Europe. In dire need of modern capital goods to help develop their economies, the East European regimes on the whole have been eager to conclude agreements for trade and other kinds of economic cooperation with the countries of the West, within the limits of their means or long-term credit availability. Neither the United States nor the Soviet Union could long stand in the way of this transbloc interaction process.

The widespread belief in Western Europe that American and Soviet power have become virtually equalized in today's world has also affected East-West interactions. The relative devaluation of American power has made the United States appear somewhat less effective, and perhaps less dependable, as an ally. Simultaneously, the upgrading of Soviet power has made the USSR seem potentially more dangerous as regards capabilities. The consequent perception of global nuclear parity logically implies that Western Europe should prepare somehow to cope with the threat from the East on its own (de Gaulle's argument). Yet, circumstances and probably a lack of will have precluded the Europeans from building up a credible European defense, so that the prospect of some U.S. troop withdrawal has led the Western European governments to attempt to find security by other means. Since they cannot counterbalance the military threat, they have sought to decrease it.

The birth of the notion that the security of Europe might eventually be based on a foundation of political cooperation rather than the military confrontation between East and West was an inevitable consequence of economic interaction and changes in the U.S.-Soviet strategic balance. In particular, the European members of NATO began to subordinate the military aspect of security to the search for political solutions to the East-West impasse.

Within this increasingly dynamic context of international politics, it has not been too difficult for the Soviet bloc's recurrent European security proposals to make an impact on the West. These proposals came in quickening succession after Polish Foreign Minister Adam Rapacki's call for a European security conference in February, 1964. The events leading to the Warsaw Pact's Bucharest proposal of June, 1966, for European peace and security have already been described. This was the most comprehensive proposal on the subject issued by the Soviet bloc during the 1960's. But its transparent aims were little different from those showing through Soviet proposals from European security issued in 1954, before the Warsaw Pact was created. Among the basic and constant demands of the Soviet bloc were the acceptance by Germany of the postwar situation and its abandonment of "militarism and revanchism," the withdrawal of U.S. forces and weapons from Germany (and hence, from Europe), and the disbanding of NATO. In the 1960's the Soviet bloc addressed its European security proposals not to the United States but to the countries of Western Europe, in an ill-disguised attempt to mobilize public support for the idea that European security should be a matter for Europeans to discuss and agree upon among themselves.

The thrust of the 1966 Bucharest proposal was premature; but its underlying expectations were not totally unfounded. No responsible statesman in NATO save de Gaulle of France could yet visualize the long-term security of the North Atlantic Treaty area against Soviet aggression (political or military) without the presence of U.S. forces in Europe. However, the threat of Soviet aggression, as perceived in the West, had certainly become less acute and immediate, so that the demands of affluence gained on the priority scale of Western politics and U.S. pleas for greater European contributions to NATO's defense posture went unheeded. In 1967, the United States, Britain, and West Germany reduced their force contributions to NATO's defense, and

France closed down all NATO facilities on its soil. NATO's disarray did not escape the policy makers in the Kremlin.

Nor did it escape policy makers in Western capitals that Soviet domination of Eastern Europe was running into trouble. Rumania had been a querulous partner of the Soviet Union since 1962. Other bloc countries were finding less rambunctious ways to assert their own interests vis-à-vis those of the Soviet Union and making it difficult for Moscow to make its policies prevail over those of its bloc partners. Needless to say, realization of troubles in Eastern Europe called for flexible approaches on the part of the West toward the East, in the hope that eventually, through transbloc politics, Eastern Europe might identify more with Europe than with the Soviet Union. The United States did not originate or monopolize "building bridges to Eastern Europe," nor does West Germany alone advance an "Ostpolitik"; most of the West European countries have been pursuing policies of rapprochement toward Eastern Europe in a more or less conscious effort to lessen the hostile confrontation across the ideological divide.

As the decade of the 1970's begins, Europe is in transition. After 20 years of "cold war" and some five years of search for cooperation, ideas for European security are appearing on the agendas of discussions among the states of the Continent. The initiative for this transformation has been largely in the hands of the Soviet bloc powers, but each European state engaged in this diplomatic process has its individual set of objectives. It seems likely, therefore, that the next two decades will witness adjustments in the present bipolar security system, and where these adjustments will lead will depend on the interaction of policies and events.

Two sets of vital considerations will shape the future security of Europe. The first is a settlement of the territorial and political problems still outstanding from World War II; the second is the problem of Soviet military power in Europe and Moscow's apparently high propensity to use this power for the attainment of its own political objectives. Even without the overt use of force the Soviets will seek to capitalize on influence—the shadow of power—that rises from its ever increasing military might.

The German Problem

For the past 25 years, the German problem has been the most obstinate irritant in East-West relations and the most insurmountable obstacle in the search for European security. Its most prominent feature has been the unwillingness of the West in general and of West Germany in particular to acquiesce in the permanent division of Germany, which resulted from the forcible imposition by the Soviet Union of a Communist regime on its occupation zone in the East. West Berlin, which remains an occupation zone of the United States, Great Britain, and France, but is politically and economically a part of West Germany, remains a most troublesome outpost of the West in the Soviet bloc. There is little doubt that if the Western allies ever withdrew their military presence from West Berlin and their determination to defend the freedom of that city, its two million citizens would soon come under East Germany's Communist control. It is here that the military confrontation between East and West is most acute: three times since 1948 the Soviet Union tested the determination of the West in crises that could well have erupted in war.

As against these features of the German problem, the Oder-Neisse line—Poland's Western border, behind which lie territories which Germany lost to Poland at the end of World War II—seems of relatively minor importance. The West has refused to recognize the finality of this border pending a peace settlement with Germany, perhaps in the hope that this still outstanding problem might give it a better bargaining position with the East; but there is no reason to believe that either West Germany or its allies would seek to revise that border, or refuse to recognize its finality in a peace treaty between the wartime allies and Germany. The Munich agreement of 1938 (ceding Hitler the Sudetenland in Czechoslovakia), which the bloc countries have claimed to be invalid from the date of its signature is an anachronistic, legalistic formality, inasmuch as the West German government has already acknowledged that this treaty belongs in limbo and makes no territorial claim whatsoever on Czechoslovakia.

During the 1950's the Soviet Union issued various proposals for a peace settlement with Germany. Among its prerequisites were the imposition of stringent arms controls and the prohibition of Germany's alliance with any power or groups of powers aimed against any of the victors of World War II—i.e., its alliance with the United States and NATO against the Soviet Union. By these provisions, all foreign troops would have to be withdrawn from Germany, and the defense of Western Europe would be undermined. Reunification was held out as a major inducement, but it was clear in these proposals that the East German Communists would have an equal chance with the political parties of West Germany in the formation of an all-German government, a constitution, and electoral laws. Moreover, these proposals contended that freedom-loving forces (i.e., Communists and fellow-travelers) should have free rein, while neo-Nazi or other revanchist forces (most of the democratic parties of West Germany have been thus branded by Soviet propaganda) should be curbed.

In other words, Soviet proposals for a German peace settlement amounted to a prescription for the legitimization of Communist power in Germany and, equally likely, for the extension of Soviet influence, if not outright domination, over that country. Needless to say, the Western powers found such terms unacceptable.

The German problem, thus, is intimately tied to the larger problem of Soviet hegemony and power over Eastern Europe. Out of this context, of and by itself, German reunification has grown into an anachronism with the passage of time. For few, if any, in Western or Eastern Europe would favor Germany's reunification, although many may view this eventuality as inevitable in the far future. At present there does not seem to be great popular interest in reunification in West Germany, even though it remains among the credos of some political leaders, particularly in the conservative Christian Democratic Union (CDU). Until 1970 the primary aim of West Germany had been to prevent the legitimization of the Soviet-imposed unrepresentative Communist regime of Walter Ulbricht over the East German people, which has isolated them from their Western compatriots. It should be noted, however, that Willy Brandt's negotiations with the East German government during the first half of 1970 came seriously close to legitimitizing that neo-Stalinist regime by suggesting that both should become members of the United Nations. The only reservation Bonn still maintains is that there shall not be a West German ambassador to East Berlin and vice versa.

The persistence of the German question has played into the hands of Soviet and East European leaderships. Fear of Germany still lingers in Eastern Europe, particularly among those who suffered from Nazi domination in World War II. This real fear has been nurtured by unflagging Soviet and local Communist propaganda. In the context of Nazi brutalities of a generation ago, West Germany's still outstanding claims on East Germany, Poland, and in the formal-legalistic sense also on Czechoslovakia, help keep these countries in the protective embrace of the Soviet superpower and facilitate the acceptance by their peoples of Soviet hegemony—the legitimization of which the policies of the West have sought to avoid.

A comparable analysis may well have served as the point of departure of the Eastern policy (Ostpolitik) of the Brandt government, which took office after the elections in the fall of 1969. This government has declared its recognition of the existence of two German states and relegated the aim of reunification to the far distant future, if it is ever attainable at all. Its immediate aim is to transform the division of Germany into a situation that is tolerable to the people on both sides—one in which they can interact and coexist with each other on a more humane basis. The Brandt government, thus, recognizes that the division of Germany was the penalty of World War II which the Germans brought upon themselves, and is seeking to alleviate the burdens that these results have imposed on the German people. In the same vein, it seeks to settle the outstanding border problem with Poland in order to lessen Polish fears of possible West German aggression and improve the environment for rapprochement and cooperation between the two countries. Similarly, the Brandt government has been seeking a political settlement with the Soviet Union, including an agreement in which both countries would renounce the use of force in the settlement of outstanding problems between them. To these ends, West Germany began parallel talks with the Soviet Union, Poland, and East Germany in the spring of 1970.

A new chapter has begun in the postwar history of Europe, one in which the focus is likely to be more on negotiation than confrontation. This chapter is not likely to be concluded this year—and perhaps not even in the next decade—and what the conclusion will be can simply not be foretold. Brandt's Ostpolitik has encountered vigorous opposition from the CDU/CSU in the Bundestag, where it enjoys only a slim majority of supporters. Thus, there is room for legitimate doubt as to how long Brandt can sustain the process of negotiation with the East in its present dimensions. Inside Germany, as well as abroad in the West, there is a good deal of skepticism about the price of Ostpolitik—how much the Brandt government will concede to the bloc countries, what kind of concessions, if any, they will make in return, and more important, what the implications of these tradeoffs will be for the security of the West.

As of mid-1970, one can only say speculatively that in the years to come the German question may become less prominent in the overall context of European security.

Soviet Military Power in Europe

Of much greater importance than the German question, and less likely to be solved in the long run, is the problem of Soviet military power in Europe. The primary requisite for European security is, after all, an effective barrier against possible Soviet aggression. Today this barrier is provided for the West by NATO and by the nuclear deterrent of the United States. No such barrier exists for the countries of Eastern Europe, so that the Soviet Union can send or station its military forces there for any purpose it might deem necessary to the maintenance of its political control, as the 1968 invasion of Czechoslovakia demonstrated. The "Brezhnev doctrine" legitimized this invasion and provided a basis for future Soviet military occupation of socialist states if the Kremlin judges such action to be necessary.

In the 1970's however, it seems increasingly unlikely that either U.S. forces in Europe or the U.S. nuclear deterrent will continue to pose the same effective counterbalance to the growing military strength of the Soviet Union that has obtained in the past. Concerned West Europeans today are resigned to the inevitability of U.S. domestic pressures forcing a reduction of American forces in Europe; and they cannot but view with apprehension the apparent advance to military ascendancy of the Soviet Union, not only in Europe but also in the global strategic realm.

If the military confrontation in Europe cannot be maintained at its present force posture level on the Western side, then the security of Western Europe cannot be assured without fundamental changes within the Soviet bloc. The security of Europe is not threatened by any East European country per se, but by the power of the Soviet Union and its ability to station its highly maneuverable forces in Eastern Europe. The bloc countries, thus, are potential staging grounds for Soviet military aggression against the West.

The question now arises: Would the Soviet Union actually invade Western Europe if the United States withdrew its commitment and forces from the Continent? It has been legitimately asked, for instance, whether the Soviet Union could absorb any more countries into its colonial empire, inasmuch as it occasionally suffers upsets from its absorbtion of Eastern Europe into its imperial realm. In times when deterrence in Western Europe renders the threat of Soviet aggression infinitesimal, it is easy to argue questions such as these on grounds that take into account the relatively good behavior displayed by the Soviet Union toward the West during the détente period. Those who are concerned about the possibility of Soviet aggression (and that includes most of those charged with the security of the West) would point to the Soviet Union's military development over the past decade as an argument of the potential threat against which the West must be able to defend itself.

But the recent history of Europe also provides some examples of a more likely Soviet goal in Eastern Europe—that of being able to exert its political influence over the policies of weak, divided nations. Thus, for instance, the Soviet Union has repeatedly warned Austria that any association with the European Common Market would be a violation of its neutrality. Similarly, Finland's recent withdrawal from the formation of NORDEK* was attributed to severe Soviet pressures. Such examples of Soviet interference in the sovereign affairs of countries outside the Soviet bloc (to say nothing about Soviet domination of the countries inside the bloc) support the contention that, in the absence of a strong NATO and a firm U.S. security guarantee, the Soviet Union would seek to extend its political influence over the relatively weak countries of Western Europe. Indeed, it might well achieve its minimal objectives in the long run without resort to military force. Thus, it could obtain the fruits of empire without the costs.

If NATO becomes militarily weaker, and particularly if the United States is to reduce its forces in Europe and fails to maintain nuclear sufficiency—both of these propositions would accord with Soviet desiderata—then the European security debate must proceed from the premise that Soviet behavior toward its East European allies must change substantially. Under these circumstances, to concede ironclad Soviet domination over Eastern Europe could spell the doom of freedom in Western Europe, particularly if the world balance of power should shift to the Soviet side.

Having said this, one should add that such a shift implies a substantial change in the relationships between the rulers and the ruled in countries of Eastern Europe which are occupied or subject to occupation by Soviet troops. In East Germany, Poland, and Czechoslovakia, for instance, the rulers might opt for Soviet occupation long after their fear of possible West German "revanchism" faded into oblivion, for the Red Army helps them maintain their regimes against political opposition. As liberalization progressed in Hungary, the Kadar regime appeared to gain some popular support; but whether it could maintain stable rule without the backup of Soviet power was open to some doubt at the threshold of the 1970's. Still, Hungary may serve as one example of encouraging domestic change that might eventually

*The Nordic Economic Union, including Denmark, Norway, and Sweden, besides Finland.

deprive the Soviet Union of the support of East European leaderships in the maintenance of its troops on their territories. The Ceausescu regime in Rumania, a different example, appears to enjoy considerable popular support, based not on domestic liberalization but on its precarious insistence on independence from the Soviet Union.

The withdrawal of Soviet forces from East European countries is not without precedent. Rumania found it was possible to press the Soviet Union to withdraw its troops in 1958—but since then it has had to fight for every inch of leeway in pursuing its own national interests independently of those of the Soviet Union and, since August, 1968, it has lived under the threat of invasion. Since the invasion of Czechoslovakia, of course, the chances for a withdrawal of Soviet forces seems more remote than they did in 1966, for instance, when the Warsaw Pact called for the withdrawal of all foreign forces from the countries of Europe as part of its European security proposal.

Still, the interest of the Soviet Union in the withdrawal of U.S. forces from Western Europe and the disbanding of NATO remains great, and it will probably gain urgency as China develops its nuclear weapons and delivery potential. At various occasions during the past five years the Soviet Union has given indications of a willingness to pay a price for a U.S. troop withdrawal—in quid pro quo terms. In March, 1969 (soon after the Sino-Soviet border clash on the Ussuri River), for instance, a renewed Warsaw Pact plea for a European security conference reaffirmed continuing support for the Bucharest proposals. Since then, however, the prospect of unilateral U.S. troop withdrawals from Europe has grown to virtual certainty and the Soviet Union's interest in discussing mutual force reductions within or outside the context of a European security conference appears to have diminished commensurately, despite the fact that the Warsaw Pact, in June, 1970, agreed to put the issue of mutual balanced force reductions on the agenda of a European security conference.

Among the smaller countries of the Soviet bloc, only Rumania still openly calls for the mutual liquidation of NATO and the Warsaw Pact. But one may surmise that at various echelons of the political structures of the occupied countries there are latent pressures for a withdrawal of Soviet troops and for a redress of the inequities their countries have to suffer in the Warsaw Pact. The criticism of the Warsaw Pact, voiced by Czechoslovakia's General Jan Prchlik before the invasion, reinforces those heard from Rumanian officials to support this conjecture.

Thus, one might hope that in the decade ahead, the progress of change in Eastern Europe might help to augment those forces within the ruling structures that favor the withdrawal of Soviet forces from their countries. This hope would be the more real if West Germany reaches some agreement with the bloc countries that would diminish the spectre of "revanchism" arising out of the German problem. At the same time, however, whatever incentives the Soviet Union might have to contemplate a troop withdrawal from Eastern Europe diminishes with the prospect of a unilateral U.S. troop withdrawal from the NATO area. Moscow would probably prefer to wait and see what results from U.S. troop reductions in West Germany, and then to reformulate its political strategy for European security accordingly.

Policy Considerations

The canvas thus drawn poses problems of time and policy for the United States and its Western allies. If, as seems likely, the United States will be unable to underwrite the bipolar confrontation in Europe for another 20 years, then two compelling questions must be considered: first, whether the strength of NATO can be maintained long enough to permit liberalizing and autonomy-seeking forces in the Soviet bloc to make a more decisive impact than they have made so far; and second, what policies of the West are best calculated to promote these forces.

There is no gainsaying the changes of the Soviet bloc in the past, even though some, such as those in Czechoslovakia, turned out to be abortive; and one may expect more change in the future, if the factors that promote change (which the Soviet Union seeks to eliminate) continue to prevail. The increasingly dynamic relationships that these changes have produced within the Soviet bloc, and the security debate which they have prompted, pose both risks and opportunities for the West in general and the United States in particular.

Among the risks of intra-European détente politics is that the countries concerned tend to reassess their priorities between defense and domestic needs in favor of the latter. This reassessment has been particularly evident during the last four years, not only in Western Europe but also in Canada and the United States. Ironically, a good case can be made that the military presence of the United States in Europe has been instrumental in restraining the Soviet potential for armed repression in Eastern Europe—if not in Czechoslovakia, then in Rumania and Yugoslavia, and perhaps also in Albania. Each time the Soviet Union contemplates military action against a dissident

Communist country, it must face the uncertainty of U.S. reactions. If the United States has never come to the aid of a bloc country threatened with Soviet reprisals, this can be no assurance to Soviet leaders that it may not choose to do so at a different time and in different circumstances. Furthermore, the more the Soviet Union wants to see the United States withdraw its forces from Europe (and this desire will probably increase even more as the Chinese military potential grows to threatening proportions during this decade), the more it will seek to obscure the military arm of its hegemony over Eastern Europe and use armed repression only as a last resort in the preservation of its perceived vital interests. If this is true, then the potential future scope of the East European countries, autonomy would seem to be wider than that which they have actually achieved. From this point of view, then, a too rapid withdrawal of U.S. forces from Europe would strengthen the Soviet hand over the bloc and lead to a retardation, if not to a reversal, of the trend toward greater East European autonomy from the USSR.

Obviously, there is no "magic" number of U.S. forces to maintain the security of the West or to widen the parameters of permissible autonomy in the East. Nor does a defense posture adequate to deter the Soviet Union require a static "don't-rock-the-boat" policy. What it does require is a clear goal for a future Europe and ingenious policies to reach that goal. West European statesmen and analysts would concede that the effect of a unilateral U.S. troop reduction in Europe would be much greater in the psychological realm than in that of actual military deterrence. On the military side it can be compensated for by various means—reorganization, change in military strategy and tactics, and the like. But to avoid the negative psychological impact that a sizable U.S. force reduction might have on the Western allies (which might lead to unnecessary concessions to the Soviet Union), the United States must show that its commitment to Europe has not diminished and that it has policies and objectives behind which the Europeans can unite.

For instance, if the United States is prepared (because of domestic pressure and other priorities, such as those in Southeast Asia) to reduce its forces in Europe in the future, and if the Soviet Union for reasons of its own is anxious to bring about such reductions, there may be common ground for a reciprocal agreement on mutual force withdrawals. Retrospectively, one might wish that this matter had been more fully explored before the conviction grew in Europe that a sizable unilateral U.S. troop withdrawal was inevitable after 1971. But as of 1970 there may still be time.

In this respect, it is encouraging that the NATO Foreign Minister's meeting in Rome (May 27, 1970) renewed the call for mutual balanced force reduction talks with the Warsaw Pact, and that the Warsaw Pact Council, meeting in Budapest in June, 1970, responded positively to this call. Equally encouraging is the condemnation of the "Brezhnev Doctrine" of limited socialist state sovereignty reflected in the Rome communiqué, and the affirmation that European security can rest only on the right of nations to determine their own fate free from outside intervention or pressure. No doubt, these principles will become part of the East-West security debate, and if so, the West may find support among some East European regimes that have voiced similar views in the past.*

Needless to say, should the Soviet Union ever be persuaded to accept these principles, European security would be enhanced to the point where the withdrawal of all foreign forces from the countries of Europe might be a negotiable issue between East and West. It would imply a change in Soviet official thought of such political and strategic proportions as to transform the foundation of the East-West confrontation. Although the possibilities of such a change occurring in the Soviet Union in the short run are exceedingly small, it still seems worth exploring within the context of European security politics. At a time when the developing Chinese military potential promises to cause increasing concern in Moscow, and when the German problem promises to become less prominent in Soviet security considerations, Moscow may become susceptible to seeing some advantages from exploring this question.

The United States has viewed the ongoing negotiations between West Germany and the Soviet bloc countries with great interest. Although there is always the danger that West Germany might make concessions to the Soviet bloc that could be detrimental to the unity and defense of the West, this danger seems more remote than the likelihood that these negotiations may lead to a normalization of the postwar status quo, which in turn may result in a lessening of East-West tensions and deprive the Soviet Union of the rationale for its military occupation of East European countries. The strident assertion of West German militarism and revanchism—rendered credible in the Soviet bloc by Bonn's outstanding claims on East European territories—has been so intricately woven into pro-Soviet arguments for bloc unity and

*See, for instance, Wolfgang Klaiber, "Security Priorities in Eastern Europe," *Problems of Communism* (May-June, 1970), pp. 32-44.

strengthening of the Warsaw Pact that it is difficult to see how these arguments could stand after a normalization of the status quo. Most of the East European countries have been interested in establishing diplomatic relations with West Germany since 1966, probably more for political reasons (increasing their freedom of maneuver in the foreign policy field) than for economic ones (because West Germany conducts more trade with Eastern Europe than most other Western countries). In 1967, after Rumania broke through the diplomatic barrier with West Germany, East Germany (supported by the Soviet Union and Poland) managed to keep other East European countries from establishing diplomatic relations with Bonn. Since the "small coalition" under Willy Brandt has come into power, however, East European regimes have revived their interest in normalizing relations with Bonn. Poland's 1970 negotiations with West Germany may lead to the establishment of diplomatic relations, and the leaderships of Hungary and Czechoslovakia have publicly expressed their hopes to normalize relations with the West German government. Since the Brandt government has accepted the existence of two separate German states (albeit within the framework of one nation), the heads of government of both states have twice faced each other across the negotiating table (on March 19 and May 21, 1970) for the first time since Germany was divided. Even though the East German regime continues to hold out nonnegotiable demands that Bonn cannot yet accept, the prospect of a gradual normalization of inter-German relations seems brighter now than at any time in the last two decades.

Thus, in the not too distant future, we may see a diminution of the prevailing fear of West Germany which will affect East European countries' security dependence on the Soviet Union. For if it is true that the spectre of West German "revanchism" tends to drive East European regimes (particularly those of East Germany and Poland) into the protective arms of the Soviet Union, then a resolution of the outstanding territorial problems should induce Moscow to produce another rationale for its domination over these countries in the future.

The 1970 era of negotiations has thawed the frozen foundations of East-West relations that were formed in the era of the "cold war," a thaw which has been in progress since the beginning of the 1960's. One of the paramount attitudinal changes on each side has been a resignation to the political-ideological status quo on the other side. A "roll-back" of Communism in Eastern Europe is simply out of the question. Similarly, the demise of capitalism in the West is simply not in sight as long as the tenuous balance of East-West power is maintained. Each side has tentatively accepted the notion that international tensions in Europe only tend to fortify the existing order on the other side, whereas a lessening of tension tends to give greater scope to the forces of change. So far, the evidence of a desire for change is much more visible in East European political systems than in those of the West.

Communist regimes, with good reason, are afraid of the peaceful penetration of Western ideas into their countries, precisely because this is as difficult to contain as it is to counteract. The imperative of economic development and the unceasing demand for ever higher standards of living have posed serious problems that these regimes cannot solve without an increasing input of technology, production methods, and managerial techniques from the West. Having opted for economic cooperation with the West, the East European regimes could not keep out Western ideas in the noneconomic realm. Western tourists became one of the major sources of foreign currency for East European countries during the 1960's, and their conspicuous affluence and freedom caused difficulties for the regimes, particularly in the fields of political control and ideological indoctrination. How long the Communist regimes can bridge the dichotomy between political control and economic performance is hard to tell; but as of 1970 it is important to note that they have made some important choices in favor of the latter that have impinged on the former, and in the future they will probably pursue options similar to those they have pursued in the past, if only because the imperatives of rational economics leave them no other choice.

This does not mean, of course, that Western trade policies toward the East have been translatable into direct political influence in the Soviet bloc, or that they are likely to be in the future. Our study found the correlation between East-West trade and East European conformity to Soviet policy to be quite low. Neither Yugoslavia, Albania, nor Rumania sought independence from the Soviet Union because any Western country wanted it to, but because its leadership had become disaffected with Soviet policy and Soviet domination. Indeed, as for Yugoslavia and Rumania, their trade with the West rose significantly only after they had successfully defied the Soviet Union. Nevertheless, it would be shortsighted to dismiss the indirect, albeit somewhat more haphazard, political payoff that has accrued to the interests of the West from trade with the East. Many of the modifications that formed part of the economic reform programs in Eastern Europe during the 1960's are attributable more or less indirectly to the modes of East-West interactions and/or the appeal of Western techniques that were once so alien to the Stalinist ideology. The difficulties experienced by the Soviet Union in enacting its economic integration programs within Comecon stem in part from a reluctance among East European leaders to foreclose present and future options of profitable interaction with the West, and in part also from the diversification of economic policies and practices that defies centralized coordination from Moscow.

Looking at the other side of the coin, East European countries' trade dependence on the Soviet Union correlates so highly with their conformity to Soviet policy as to support the notion that if these countries manage to increase their trade with the outside world more rapidly than with the Soviet Union, their ability to pursue autonomous courses of action may improve. This means that the West may be instrumental in loosening the cohesive bonds of the Soviet bloc in the years ahead through a steady augmentation of its trade flow. There are, of course, limitations to the possibility of increasing East-West trade, imposed by the nonconvertibility of bloc currencies and the consequent necessity for East European countries to earn their foreign exchange through exports to the West. But it is precisely this limitation that can provide the stimulus for further liberalization in the Soviet bloc countries. The need to become competitive in Western markets is likely to promote pragmatism in decision making and further decentralization of the state-controlled economic structures—in essence, the transfer of political power from the center to lower levels of the politico-economic systems, which should promote diversification and proliferation of demands upon the Communist decision makers.

Western economic policies toward the Soviet bloc, therefore, should aim at maximizing the political incentive for pragmatization and decentralization of the decision-making process. This can be done only through commercial interactions—not through grant aid.* So far, the bulk of Eastern Europe's exports to the West has been in agricultural products and raw materials. In the future these countries should be

---

*For instance, the $500 million transfer of American surplus wheat to Poland under Public Law 480 between 1957 and 1962, paid for in zlotys rather than hard currency, may have helped to stifle the incentive for economic reform in that country precisely at a time when ideas for reform were gaining a foothold in Warsaw's official circles. The reform movement of the 1950's was squashed, and it was not until 1968 that the Polish leadership saw no alternative to change in the economic system.

encouraged to compete in the industrial markets of the West, if only because the incentives for pragmatization and decentralization seem to be greater in this field than in agriculture. Furthermore, the West should promote enterprise-to-enterprise relations rather than inter-governmental ones in its dealings with the Soviet bloc, for this may help to strengthen the hands of managerial and scientific groups in the state-controlled economic system and, thus, to develop more effective interest articulation in the Communist countries.

What role should the United States play in the promotion and pursuit of Western approaches toward Eastern Europe? In the past, the United States has been very far behind its West European allies in engaging Eastern Europe in trade and other interactions. Its policy of building bridges to Eastern Europe, inaugurated under President Johnson, was scarcely translated into action—much like the "liberation" policy of the early 1950's. So far, then, the policy of the United States toward Eastern Europe has had little if any effect on the spectrum of East-West interactions and whatever benefits may have accrued to the West therefrom.

One should not automatically conclude from this, however, that the United States should augment its interactions with East European countries to the level of the West European allies. In view of the fact that the United States is a superpower, too much engagement in Eastern Europe might cause anxiety in the Soviet Union and among East European leaderships, lest the United States extend its sphere of influence into the Soviet bloc. Even the declaratory bridge-building policy evoked warnings in the Soviet and East European press that U.S. imperialism had found a more effective way of infiltrating Communist systems, having recognized the failure of its "liberation" policy. The same anxiety does not prevail among Communist leaderships with respect to the West European countries that have been building bridges to Eastern Europe so successfully and with so little fanfare.

Hence, there is a case to be made for a division of labor between the United States and its West European allies in the promotion of long-term Western objectives of greater liberalization and autonomy in Eastern Europe. While there is room for expansion of useful U.S. interactions with East European countries, it must be recognized that the West Europeans are the more logical trading partners of the East because of their small-power status and Continental identity. In an era of negotiation and confrontation, the most appropriate partner-protagonist for the United States is the Soviet Union. There are some topics vital to peace and security that can be negotiated only by the United States and the Soviet Union at this time. One of these is the Strategic Arms Limitation Talks (SALT), which began in 1969. Another topic closer to the immediate interests of the European countries is that of the 750 medium- and intermediate-range ballistic missiles stationed in western Russia and targeted on Western Europe; this, too, can be negotiated only, if at all, by the United States with the Soviet Union.

As for our West European allies, they are better positioned geographically and power-politically to explore with the East Europeans the political, economic, and cultural means of safeguarding peace and security in Europe. Many of them have had high-level private meetings with East European leaders to exchange views on this subject.

This is not to argue for an exclusiveness of roles and functions in the East-West dialogue. There are many issues that fall into the purview of both the superpower and the smaller countries, and that both should seek to settle with the Soviet bloc. One of these, obviously, is the issue of state sovereignty and the right of nations to determine their own fate, free from outside military intervention, without which the concept of security is meaningless. Another such issue is that of basic human rights and freedom.

The most important role of the United States in this era of negotiation and confrontation is that of leadership, coordination, and initiative for the West. We have entered a decade of change that, by its very nature, poses uncertainties for the future. There are no rules for this game; as with so many other novel games in multilateral diplomacy, the chances of "winning" are intimately tied to clarity of vision, consensus on goals, and purposeful action.

The paramount objective which the West should pursue in Europe in the decade ahead should be further promotion of liberalization in and progressive independence of the countries of the Soviet bloc. This goal must be a long-term one, and the approaches must be indirect. The experience of the past two decades shows that Communism cannot be wished away from Eastern Europe; but it can change from within. It has also shown that too rapid change tends to provoke repression by the Soviet Union and its hard-line allies, whereas gradual and subtle change may survive and build upon itself. One should hope that the policies of the West in the decade ahead will help to induce East European leaderships to identify increasingly with Europe and less with the Soviet Union, so that someday Europe will emerge as a continent united. At the same time the Soviet Union may come to see that its own best interests lie in the creation of a new global order in which different political systems can coexist and test each other in peaceful competition.

Appendix A
Statistical Tables

Table 1

Policy Positions and Actions Taken by the
Soviet Union, 1956-68, Upon which the East
European States Were Scored for Conformity to
Soviet Policy

Year	Policy Positions and Actions of USSR

1956   1. Soviet intervention in Hungary
      2. Soviet position regarding causes of the outbreak of the Hungarian Revolution
      3. Soviet position regarding Tito speech critical of the Soviet Communist Party leadership and of conditions in the USSR
      4. Soviet vote in the UN General Assembly on resolution condemning Soviet intervention in Hungary

1957   1. Attendance at Soviet conference held to deal with the aftermath of the Hungarian uprising
      2. Soviet verbal attacks on Yugoslavia
      3. Soviet commentary on "Stalinism" at the time of the first anniversary of the 20th CPSU Congress
      4. Attendance at Moscow celebrations of the 40th anniversary of the 1917 revolution
      5. Purge in the USSR of the "Anti-Party Group"
      6. Signing of and reaction to the 12-nation declaration of a "Commonwealth of Socialist States"

1958   1. Soviet bloc decision to issue a new international Communist journal
      2. Soviet verbal attacks on Polish and Yugoslav "revisionism"
      3. Soviet criticism of the Yugoslav League of Communists' draft program for its Seventh Congress
      4. Soviet criticism of Yugoslavia following the Seventh Yugoslav Congress
      5. Severe Soviet criticism of Yugoslavia in June
      6. Soviet position regarding execution of Imre Nagy
      7. Continuing Soviet criticism of Yugoslavia
      8. Soviet celebrations held in honor of the ninth anniversary of a Communist takeover in China

317

Table 1 (continued)

Year   Policy Positions and Actions of USSR

       9. Continuing Soviet verbal attacks on Yugoslavia
    10. Additional Soviet verbal attacks on Yugoslavia
    11. Commentary on first anniversary of the 12-nation Moscow declaration of a "Commonwealth of Socialist States"
    12. UN vote on the Hungarian question
    13. Soviet position regarding the midsummer international crisis in Iraq, Lebanon, and Jordan
    14. Soviet position regarding West Berlin

1959   1. Soviet criticism of Yugoslav revisionism
    2. Continuing Soviet verbal attacks on Yugoslavia
    3. Diminishing Soviet criticism of Yugoslavia
    4. Continuing abatement in Soviet criticism of Yugoslavia
    5. Soviet draft text for a German peace treaty

1960   1. Soviet position about Josef Stalin on the occasion of the 80th anniversary of his birth
    2. Soviet position on reasons for the breakdown of the May, 1960, summit conference
    3. Attendance by Soviet leaders at UN session (rank of attending East European leaders compared)
    4. Rank of Soviet representatives attending Peking celebrations of Communist Chinese National Day, October 1 (compared with rank of attending East European leaders)
    5. Soviet vote in the UN on the question of overturning a motion
    6. Soviet interpretation of the Moscow Declaration of 1960

1961   1. Rank of Soviet representatives in Peking attending the 40th anniversary of the Chinese Communist Party
    2. Soviet decision to resume nuclear testing
    3. New CPSU draft program
    4. Soviet breach with Albania and de-Stalinization measures adopted at the 22nd CPSU Congress

1962   1. Soviet breaking of dipomatic relations with Albania

Table 1 (continued)

Year   Policy Positions and Actions of USSR

2. Improving relations between the USSR and Yugoslavia following the 22nd CPSU Congress
3. Soviet position in the Sino-Soviet rift
4. Improving Soviet relations with Yugoslavia
5. Soviet celebration in Moscow for the 13th anniversary of the victory of the Communism in China
6. Participation in bilateral talks with Soviet leaders, October-November
7. Soviet position regarding the Cuban missile crisis
8. Soviet position regarding stationing of representatives of the supreme command of the Warsaw Pact in member states.

1963
1. Attendance at Seventh Congress of Yugoslav People's Youth
2. Soviet commentary on the 10th anniversary of Stalin's death
3. Soviet position on integration in Comecon, February-March
4. Soviet position in the Sino-Soviet rift
5. Soviet position on integration in Comecon, May
6. CPSU open letter attacking the Chinese Communists
7. Soviet signing of the nuclear test-ban treaty
8. Soviet commentary about Communist China on the occasion of the 14th anniversary of the founding of the Chinese People's Republic

1964
1. Soviet position on integration in Comecon, April
2. Soviet position regarding the need for a world Communist conference to deal with the international Communist movement
3. Soviet vote at the UN World Trade Conference on the necessity for increased aid to the developing nations
4. Soviet invitation to attend a conference of 25 Communist parties to prepare for a full-scale conference of Communist parties

Table 1 (continued

5. Soviet response to the 21st anniversary of the founding of the Albanian People's Army
6. Soviet position on integration in Comecon, May-July
7. Rank of Soviet representatives in Peking attending celebration of the 15th anniversary of the Communist victory in China
8. Vote at the General Council of World Federation of Trade Unions on its official policy
9. Soviet position regarding outcome of U.S. presidential campaign
10. Soviet position regarding 20th anniversary of Albania's liberation from the Germans
11. Attendance at celebration of the Bolshevik Revolution in Moscow
12. Soviet votes at International Students Union session

1965
1. Soviet press coverage of January Warsaw Pact meeting
2. Soviet position regarding integration in Comecon
3. Soviet response to 19th anniversary of Albanian People's Republic
4. Attendance at Moscow meeting of 19 Communist parties to discuss "unity" of the Communist movement
5. Soviet position on the Sino-Soviet rift
6. Soviet position regarding the increase of U.S. troops in South Vietnam
7. East European response to anti-Soviet actions by Communist China and Albania at the Soviet-dominated World Peace Congress
8. Soviet vote in UN on the importance of the family
9. Soviet vote on UN resolution calling for the suspension of all testing of nuclear weapons
10. Soviet vote in the UN regarding West German inclusion in the UN high command
11. Meeting of Soviet-bloc representatives with Secretary General U Thant

Table 1 (continued)

Year	Policy Positions and Actions of USSR

1966
1. Soviet criticism of Communist China
2. Soviet position regarding U.S. diplomatic effort to achieve negotiations in Vietnam
3. Attendance at the 23rd Soviet Party Congress
4. Soviet criticism of the Chinese cultural revolution
5. Attendance at conference of East European Communist leaders in Moscow
6. East European response to the anti-Soviet speech made in Peking at celebration of the 17th anniversary of the founding of the Chinese People's Republic
7. Soviet position regarding convening of an international conference of Communist parties
8. Attendance at Fifth Congress of Albanian Party of Labor
9. Soviet vote on proposal to bar Chinese delegates from participating in meeting of the General Council of the World Federation of Trade Unions

1967
1. Attendance at China showing of films of Chinese nuclear tests
2. Attendance at conference of 19 Communist parties in Warsaw
3. Attendance at Karlovy Vary meeting of European Communist parties
4. Soviet position regarding Israel's invasion of Egypt
5. Soviet breaking of diplomatic relations with Israel in response to Israel's attack on Egypt
6. Soviet position regarding termination of the Arab-Israeli conflict
7. Attendance at Budapest meeting of party and government leaders to discuss the Middle East situation
8. Soviet position regarding U.S.-Soviet draft treaty to ban the proliferation of nuclear weapons
9. Soviet position regarding convening of an international conference of Communist parties
10. Attendance at Moscow celebrations of the anniversary of the 1917 revolution

Table 1 (continued)

Year   Policy Positions and Actions of USSR

11. Soviet request for a consultative conference of Communist parties to be held in Budapest to decide whether a world conference of Communist parties should be held
12. Participation at Warsaw meeting of foreign and deputy foreign ministers to discuss the Middle East situation

1968   1. Participation at consultative conference of Communist parties in Budapest
2. Soviet position regarding convening of a conference of world's Communist parties
3. Soviet position regarding nuclear nonproliferation treaty as expressed in Warsaw Pact declaration
4. Participation in Dresden meeting of East European and Soviet leaders to evaluate events in Czechoslovakia
5. Soviet vote on UN resolution calling on the "have" nations of the world to contribute at least one percent of their GNP as aid to the "have not" nations
6. Participation in Budapest meeting of deputy ministers of foreign trade
7. Soviet press coverage of the liberalization developments in Czechoslovakia
8. Participation in preparatory conference for a summit conference of world Communist parties
9. Participation of party leaders in Moscow meeting held to evaluate Czech events
10. Soviet vote in UN General Assembly on draft nuclear nonproliferation treaty
11. Soviet letter to the Czech government criticizing internal developments in Czechoslovakia and calling for a meeting of party leaders in Warsaw to discuss the situation
12. Participation at Warsaw meeting of East European leaders to discuss Czechoslovakia
13. Attendance at Moscow signing of the treaty to ban the proliferation of nuclear weapons
14. Participation in the Soviet military invasion of Czechoslovakia

Table 1 (continued)

Year	Policy Positions and Actions of USSR

15. Soviet bloc communiqué issued in August concerning Czechoslovakia, Comecon, and the Warsaw Pact
16. Soviet press coverage justifying the invasion of Czechoslovakia
17. Reaction of Communist Party delegates to the Interparliamentary Union's conference resolution condemning the invasion of Czechoslovakia
18. Participation by trade union representatives in Budapest meeting, held to endorse postinvasion developments in Czechoslovakia
19. Participation in preparatory commission meeting in Budapest regarding scheduled November summit meeting of world Communist parties
20. East European position regarding Czech-Soviet status of forces agreement with respect to stationing of Soviet troops in Czechoslovakia

Sources: See Appendix B, Sec. 1.

Table 2

Yearly Indicator Scores for East European
States on the Index of Conformity to
Soviet Policy, 1956-68

Albania

Year	Indicator Scores							
	1	2	3	4	5	6	7	Total
1956	0	0	0	0	0	0	1.5	1.5
1957	0	0	0	0	0	0	5.0	5.0
1958	0	0	0	0	0	0	9.0	9.0
1959	0	0	0	0	0	0	6.0	6.0
1960	0	0	0	0	0	2	10.0	12.0
1961	10	0	0	0	6	6	6.5	28.5
1962	15	8	8	0	4	12	13.0	60.0
1963	15	8	8	0	4	14	19.5	68.5

Table 2 (continued)

Year	Indicator Scores							
	1	2	3	4	5	6	7	Total
1964	15	8	8	0	6	20	10.5	69.5
1965	15	8	8	0	0	16	5.5	60.5
1966	15	8	8	0	0	38	20.0	89.0
1967	15	8	8	0	2	60	28.0	121.0
1968	15	8	8	0	12	32	35.0	110.0

Total 640.5

Bulgaria

Year	Indicator Scores							
	1	2	3	4	5	6	7	Total
1956	0	0	0	0	0	0	1.5	1.5
1957	0	0	0	0	0	0	1.5	1.5
1958	0	0	0	0	0	0	3.0	3.0
1959	0	0	0	0	0	0	1.5	1.5
1960	0	0	0	0	0	0	0.0	0.0
1961	0	0	0	0	0	0	0.0	0.0
1962	0	0	0	0	0	0	0.0	0.0
1963	0	0	0	0	0	0	0.0	0.0
1964	0	0	0	0	0	0	0.0	0.0
1965	0	0	0	0	0	0	2.0	2.0
1966	0	0	0	0	0	4	0.0	4.0
1967	0	0	0	0	0	0	0.0	0.0
1968	0	0	0	0	0	0	2.0	2.0

Total 15.5

Table 2 (continued)

| | | | Czechoslovakia
Indicator Scores | | | | | |
Year	1	2	3	4	5	6	7	Total
1956	0	0	0	0	0	0	1.5	1.5
1957	0	0	0	0	0	0	1.5	1.5
1958	0	0	0	0	0	0	3.0	3.0
1959	0	0	0	0	0	0	1.5	1.5
1960	0	0	0	0	0	0	0.0	0.0
1961	0	0	0	0	0	0	0.0	0.0
1962	0	0	0	0	0	0	0.0	0.0
1963	0	0	0	0	0	0	0.0	0.0
1964	0	0	0	0	0	0	0.0	0.0
1965	0	0	0	0	0	0	2.0	2.0
1966	0	0	0	0	0	0	0.0	0.0
1967	0	0	0	0	0	0	0.0	0.0
1968	0	0	0	15	30	44	17.0	106.0
Total								115.5

| | | | East Germany
Indicator Scores | | | | | |
Year	1	2	3	4	5	6	7	Total
1956	0	0	0	0	0	0	0.0	0.0
1957	0	0	0	0	0	0	0.0	0.0
1958	0	0	0	0	0	0	0.0	0.0
1959	0	0	0	0	0	0	0.0	0.0
1960	0	0	0	0	0	0	0.0	0.0
1961	0	0	0	0	0	0	0.0	0.0
1962	0	0	0	0	0	0	1.5	1.5
1963	0	0	0	0	0	0	0.0	0.0
1964	0	0	0	0	0	0	0.0	0.0
1965	0	0	0	0	0	0	0.0	0.0
1966	0	0	0	0	0	0	0.0	0.0
1967	0	0	0	0	0	0	0.0	0.0
1968	0	0	0	0	0	0	0.0	0.0
Total								1.5

Table 2 (continued)

Hungary

Year				Indicator Scores				
	1	2	3	4	5	6	7	Total
1956	0	0	0	15	0	0	2	17.0
1957	0	0	0	15	0	0	4	19.0
1958	0	0	0	0	0	0	0	0.0
1959	0	0	0	0	0	0	0	0.0
1960	0	0	0	0	0	0	0	0.0
1961	0	0	0	0	0	0	0	0.0
1962	0	0	0	0	0	0	0	0.0
1963	0	0	0	0	0	0	0	0.0
1964	0	0	0	0	0	0	0	0.0
1965	0	0	0	0	0	0	0	0.0
1966	0	0	0	0	0	0	0	0.0
1967	0	0	0	0	0	0	0	0.0
1968	0	0	0	0	0	0	7	7.0
Total								43.0

Poland

Year				Indicator Scores				
	1	2	3	4	5	6	7	Total
1956	0	0	0	0	2	0	5.5	7.5
1957	0	0	0	0	8	0	7.5	15.5
1958	0	0	0	0	10	4	17.5	31.5
1959	0	0	0	0	2	0	1.5	3.5
1960	0	0	0	0	0	0	0.0	0.0
1961	0	0	0	0	0	0	0.0	0.0
1962	0	0	0	0	0	0	0.0	0.0
1963	0	0	0	0	0	0	0.0	0.0
1964	0	0	0	0	0	0	1.5	1.5
1965	0	0	0	0	0	0	2.0	2.0
1966	0	0	0	0	0	0	2.0	2.0
1967	0	0	0	0	0	0	0.0	0.0
1968	0	0	0	0	0	0	0.0	0.0
Total								63.5

326

Table 2 (continued)

Rumania

Year	Indicator Scores							
	1	2	3	4	5	6	7	Total
1956	0	0	0	0	0	0	0.0	0.0
1957	0	0	0	0	0	0	0.0	0.0
1958	0	0	0	0	0	0	1.0	1.0
1959	0	0	0	0	0	0	1.5	1.5
1960	0	0	0	0	0	0	0.0	0.0
1961	0	0	0	0	0	0	0.0	0.0
1962	0	0	0	0	0	0	0.0	0.0
1963	0	0	0	0	0	2	10.0	12.0
1964	0	0	0	0	2	4	27.5	33.5
1965	0	0	0	0	0	2	26.5	28.5
1966	0	0	0	0	0	4	21.5	25.5
1967	0	0	0	0	0	0	27.0	27.0
1968	0	0	0	0	5	12	47.5	64.5
Total								193.5

Yugoslavia

Year	Indicator Scores							
	1	2	3	4	5	6	7	Total
1956	10	5	8	0	0	4	5.5	32.5
1957	10	5	8	0	6	4	10.5	43.5
1958	10	8	8	0	20	12	19.5	77.5
1959	10	8	8	0	4	2	1.5	33.5
1960	10	8	8	0	8	2	1.5	37.5
1961	10	8	8	0	6	2	2.0	36.0
1962	10	8	8	0	2	0	2.0	30.0
1963	10	8	8	0	0	0	0	26.0
1964	10	5	8	0	0	0	1.5	24.5
1965	10	5	8	0	0	0	3.5	26.5
1966	10	5	8	0	0	0	8.5	31.5
1967	10	5	8	0	4	0	21.0	48.0
1968	10	5	8	0	10	46	62.0	141.0
Total								588.0

Sources: See Appendix B, sec. 1.

Table 3

Trade Value of the East European States with
the USSR as a Percentage of Their Respective
Total Trade Values, 1956-67

Year	A	B	C	EG
1956	43.8	45.4	31.8	41.1
1957	49.7	53.5	34.0	45.1
1958	54.1	53.3	33.1	43.1
1959	53.1	52.2	35.6	45.2
1960	53.9	53.1	34.4	43.0
1961	36.1	52.1	33.6	43.8
1962	0.0	53.3	37.8	48.9
1963	0.0	53.5	38.9	48.6
1964	n.a.	53.0	37.5	46.6
1965	n.a.	51.1	36.9	42.8
1966	n.a.	49.2	33.5	41.4
1967	n.a.	51.3	35.1	42.0
Total	290.7	621.0	422.2	531.6
Mean	32.3	51.7	35.2	44.3
Rank	4	8	5	7

A = Albania   C = Czechoslovakia
B = Bulgaria   EG = East Germany

Sources: See Appendix B, sec. 2.

H	P	R	Y
23.7	30.6	n.a.	14.1
29.3	30.6	n.a.	11.2
26.9	26.2	51.5	8.4
29.7	29.8	47.4	9.0
30.2	30.3	40.1	7.9
33.5	30.6	40.4	5.6
36.0	32.5	40.6	6.5
34.3	33.7	41.9	8.6
34.7	32.7	42.2	9.8
35.6	33.1	38.8	12.4
33.1	32.2	33.5	12.1
34.7	35.3	28.2	12.9
381.7	377.6	404.6	118.5
31.8	31.5	40.4	9.9
3	2	6	1

H = Hungary   R = Rumania
P = Poland   Y = Yugoslavia

Table 4

Total East European Trade Value with the USSR
as a Percentage of East European Net
Material Product, 1956-67

Year	A	B	C	EG
1956	n.a.	6.0	4.4	4.7
1957	n.a.	8.0	4.8	6.0
1958	n.a.	7.8	4.6	5.4
1959	n.a.	8.9	5.6	6.1
1960	n.a.	9.8	5.7	5.9
1961	n.a.	n.a.	5.7	6.0
1962	n.a.	18.8*	6.6	6.9
1963	n.a.	19.5	7.5	7.0
1964	n.a.	20.4	7.9	7.2
1965	n.a.	21.2	8.2	6.7
1966	n.a.	22.0	6.8	6.8
1967	n.a.	23.2	6.0	6.8
Total	n.a.	165.6	73.8	75.5
Mean	n.a.	15.1	6.1	6.3
Rank	n.a.	7	5	6

A = Albania   C = Czechoslovakia   H = Hungary
B = Bulgaria   EG = East Germany   P = Poland

Note: Net material product differs from national income in that it excludes the value of "nonproductive" services and includes turnover taxes.

H	P	R	Y
3.2	1.0	n.a.	2.3
3.8	0.9	n.a.	1.9
3.8	0.7	3.6	1.5
4.3	0.9	3.2	1.4
4.6	0.9	3.3	1.2
5.5	0.9	3.6	0.8
6.1	1.1	3.8	0.9
6.2	1.1	3.9	1.1
6.7	1.1	3.9	1.2
7.6	1.1	3.3	1.2
6.6	1.1	2.9	4.3*
6.9	1.2	2.8	4.6
65.3	12.0	34.3	22.4
5.4	1.0	3.4	1.9
4	1	3	2

R = Rumania
Y = Yugoslavia

Source: See Appendix B, sec. 3.
*The marked increase relative to the preceding figures is a result of a currency reevaluation.

Table 5

Trade Value of the East European States with
East Europe (Excluding the USSR) as a Percentage
of Their Total Respective Trade Values, 1956-67

Year	A	B	C	EG
1956	44.5	37.3	27.9	24.9
1957	38.2	29.1	27.1	22.1
1958	41.2	29.7	29.4	23.6
1959	40.9	28.0	29.2	24.7
1960	35.4	28.7	30.7	26.4
1961	39.9	30.0	32.1	28.6
1962	41.0	26.4	33.0	27.4
1963	36.2	26.9	31.8	27.5
1964	36.7	22.6	33.1	27.9
1965	n.a.	23.7	33.6	28.8
1966	n.a.	21.1	33.5	29.0
1967	n.a.	22.7	34.3	29.2
Total	354.0	326.2	375.7	320.1
Mean	39.3	27.2	31.3	26.7
Rank	8	4	6	3

A = Albania   C = Czechoslovakia   H = Hungary
B = Bulgaria   EG = East Germany   P = Poland

Sources: See Appendix B, sec. 2.

H	P	R	Y
32.1	26.7	n.a.	8.3
35.7	25.9	n.a.	12.2
37.2	26.9	21.3	19.7
35.3	28.1	25.8	18.2
35.6	28.1	27.6	20.4
34.7	28.5	25.0	17.7
34.0	29.4	25.2	16.0
32.8	28.9	23.3	15.8
32.6	29.0	23.6	21.1
31.2	29.8	23.2	22.3
31.7	28.6	22.5	21.5
31.5	27.6	20.6	17.2
404.4	337.5	238.1	210.4
33.7	28.1	23.8	17.5
7	5	2	1

R = Rumania
Y = Yugoslavia

Table 6

Total East European Trade Value with East Europe
(Excluding the USSR) as a Percentage of East European
Net Material Product, 1956-67

Year	A	B	C	EG
1956	n.a.	4.9	3.9	2.9
1957	n.a.	4.3	3.8	3.0
1958	n.a.	4.4	4.1	3.0
1959	n.a.	4.8	4.6	3.3
1960	n.a.	5.3	5.1	3.6
1961	n.a.	n.a.	5.5	3.9
1962	n.a.	9.3*	5.8	3.9
1963	n.a.	9.8	6.1	4.0
1964	n.a.	8.7	7.0	4.3
1965	n.a.	9.8	7.4	4.5
1966	n.a.	9.4	6.8	4.7
1967	n.a.	10.2	5.8	4.7
Total	n.a.	81.0	65.9	45.8
Mean	n.a.	7.4	5.5	3.8
Rank	n.a.	7	5	4

A = Albania	C = Czechoslovakia	H = Hungary
B = Bulgaria	EG = East Germany	P = Poland

Note: Net material product differs from national income in that it excludes the value of "nonproductive" services and includes turnover taxes.

334

H	P	R	Y
4.4	0.9	n.a.	1.4
4.6	0.8	n.a.	2.1
5.2	0.8	1.5	3.6
5.1	0.8	1.7	2.8
5.4	0.8	2.3	3.2
5.7	0.9	2.2	2.5
5.8	1.0	2.3	2.2
5.9	0.9	2.1	2.1
6.3	1.0	2.2	2.5
6.6	1.0	2.0	2.2
6.3	1.0	1.9	7.6*
6.3	0.9	2.0	6.2
67.6	10.8	20.2	38.4
5.6	0.9	2.0	3.2
6	1	2	3

R = Rumania
Y = Yugoslavia

*The marked increase relevant to the preceding years is a result of a currency reevaluation.

Sources: See Appendix B, sec. 3.

Table 7

Tourists from the East European States to the
Soviet Union as a Percentage of Their Total
Respective Populations, 1957-67

Year	A	B	C	EG
1957	1.395	4.033	3.183	1.517
1958	1.186	3.054	3.013	1.840
1959	1.783	3.770	3.578	2.545
1960	1.633	3.987	4.268	3.530
1961	1.029	4.174	4.410	4.691
1962	0.110	5.077	3.908	4.884
1963	0.128	5.732	4.330	5.325
1964	0.142	7.422	4.589	5.666
1965	0.330	10.447	5.296	6.092
1966	n.a.	12.948	6.752	7.313
1967	n.a.	15.068	8.892	8.204
Total	7.736	75.712	52.219	51.607
Mean	0.860	6.882	4.747	4.691
Rank	1	8	6	5

A = Albania   C = Czechoslovakia   H = Hungary
B = Bulgaria   EG = East Germany   P = Poland

Note: The percentage figures have been multiplied by 1,000 to
facilitate reading of the table.

H	P	R	Y
2.276	4.739	2.652	0.517
2.511	3.052	3.366	0.542
2.828	2.821	2.459	0.615
3.676	3.176	2.893	0.649
4.056	3.757	3.755	0.857
3.835	3.839	3.345	0.926
4.144	4.310	3.610	1.013
4.600	4.440	3.357	1.007
4.638	6.142	3.387	1.065
6.392	7.691	3.263	1.203
6.606	11.113	4.250	1.606
45.562	55.080	36.337	10.000
4.142	5.007	3.303	0.909
4	7	3	2

R = Rumania
Y = Yugoslavia

Sources: See Appendix B, sec. 5.

Table 8

Soviet Tourists to the East European States as a
Percentage of their Total Respective Populations, 1961-67

Year	A	B	C	EG
1961	n.a.	3.182	1.972	n.a.
1962	n.a.	3.354	3.461	n.a.
1963	n.a.	3.773	3.795	n.a.
1964	n.a.	5.700	3.767	n.a.
1965	n.a.	7.311	3.572	n.a.
1966	n.a.	10.529	3.481	n.a.
1967	n.a.	15.118	4.844	n.a.
Total	n.a.	48.967	24.892	n.a.
Mean	n.a.	6.992	3.556	n.a.
Rank	1	6	5	

A = Albania   C = Czechoslovakia   H = Hungary
B = Bulgaria   EG = East Germany   P = Poland

Notes: The percentage figures have been multiplied by 1,000 to facilitate reading of the table.

In spite of the absence of data, Albania has been ranked. For an explanation of how the rank was assigned, see text discussion of East European intercultural interactions with the USSR, Chapter 13.

H	P	R	Y
6.195	0.648	0.565	0.412
8.632	0.844	0.511	0.554
8.768	1.037	0.537	0.772
10.016	3.623	0.433	0.811
10.634	4.707	0.549	1.228
10.299	5.822	5.152	1.623
11.610	7.244	6.598	1.940
66.154	23.925	14.345	7.340
9.447	3.416	2.048	1.048
7	4	3	2

R = Rumania
Y = Yugoslavia

Sources: See Appendix B, sec. 5.

Table 9

Books Translated from Russian into the East European
Native Languages as a Percentage of Their Total
Translations, 1956-66

Year	A	B	C	EG
1956	59.6*	63.2	47.2	n.a.
1957	62.8	56.7	31.2	n.a.
1958	56.3	50.2	24.2	n.a.
1959	44.4	48.7	25.9	n.a.
1960	61.1	54.0	26.2	n.a.
1961	48.4	56.9	23.6	n.a.
1962	39.0	50.9	23.5	n.a.
1963	33.9	52.9	22.8	n.a.
1964	57.9	46.3	16.4	n.a.
1965	26.3	43.0	16.4	n.a.
1966	31.4	36.6	11.2	n.a.
Total	521.1	559.4	268.6	n.a.
Mean	47.4	50.8	24.4	n.a.
Rank	6	7	3	

A = Albania   C = Czechoslovakia   H = Hungary
B = Bulgaria   EG = East Germany   P = Poland

*Estimate based on an average of 1957 and 1958 figures.
†Figure is somewhat inflated, since original data represented more than
the year 1958.
‡Figure represents an average of the 1965-66.

H	P	R	Y
39.8	51.4	53.6	9.6
15.8	30.4	31.7	10.2
21.1	22.2†	43.2	12.1
24.7	19.8	43.7	10.5
29.9	21.4	41.5	10.4
23.5	26.1	44.8	13.2
30.5	26.5	37.3	9.1
21.7	23.3	32.8	13.1
19.9	23.4	23.4	12.6
15.9	22.9	11.0	11.0‡
13.3	25.1	9.1	11.0‡
256.1	292.5	372.1	122.8
23.3	26.6	33.8	11.2
2	4	5	1

R = Rumania
Y = Yugoslavia

Sources: See Appendix B, sec. 6.

Table 10

Trade Value of the East European States with the
Western World as a Percentage of Their Respective
Total Trade Values, 1956-67

Year	A	B	C	EG
1956	3.1	11.4	17.0	20.5
1957	3.3	11.6	18.4	19.2
1958	2.2	16.5	16.6	18.8
1959	2.8	18.2	15.7	17.9
1960	3.5	18.1	16.0	18.0
1961	4.9	11.1	17.7	17.8
1962	4.8	12.4	14.1	15.6
1963	6.3	13.2	15.0	15.7
1964	6.3	16.4	15.5	17.9
1965	n.a.	16.9	16.4	19.3
1966	n.a.	20.9	18.7	19.8
1967	n.a.	17.5	17.4	18.5
Total	37.2	184.2	198.5	219.0
Mean	4.1	15.4	16.5	18.3
Rank	1	2	3	4

A = Albania C = Czechoslovakia H = Hungary
B = Bulgaria EG = East Germany P = Poland

Note: "Western world" was defined in terms of the following states: Austria, Belgium, Luxembourg, Canada, Denmark, Finland, France, West Germany, Greece, Italy, Netherlands, Norway, Sweden, Switzerland, the United Kingdom, and the United States.

H	P	R	Y
28.8	30.7	n.a.	65.0
23.0	32.2	n.a.	64.6
21.2	32.7	17.0	59.7
22.4	29.4	15.3	58.1
22.8	28.7	21.9	55.8
21.6	29.2	25.3	62.8
21.1	27.1	24.8	58.6
23.3	26.1	24.1	57.6
23.8	26.9	24.4	51.8
23.5	25.0	26.7	48.2
24.8	27.8	31.7	50.0
24.1	26.7	37.1	56.1
280.4	342.5	248.3	688.3
23.4	28.5	24.8	57.4
5	7	6	8

R = Rumania
Y = Yugoslavia

Sources: See Appendix B, sec. 2.

Table 11

East European Trade Value with the Western World
as a Percentage of East European Net Material
Product, 1956-67

Year	A	B	C	EG
1956	n.a.	1.1	2.6	2.4
1957	n.a.	1.7	2.6	2.6
1958	n.a.	2.4	2.3	2.2
1959	n.a.	3.1	2.5	2.4
1960	n.a.	3.3	2.7	2.5
1961	n.a.	n.a.	3.0	2.4
1962	n.a.	4.3	2.5	2.2
1963	n.a.	4.8	2.9	2.3
1964	n.a.	6.3	3.5	2.7
1965	n.a.	7.0	3.7	3.0
1966	n.a.	9.3	3.8	3.2
1967	n.a.	7.8	3.0	3.0
Total	n.a.	51.1	35.1	30.9
Mean	n.a.	4.6	2.9	2.6
Rank	n.a.	6	4	3

A = Albania   C = Czechoslovakia   H = Hungary
B = Bulgaria   EG = East Germany   P = Poland

Notes: Pick up definition of "Western world" from Table 10.

Pick up definition of net material product from Table 4.

*The large increase relative to the preceding years is a result of a currency reevaluation.

344

H	P	R	Y
3.9	1.0	n.a.	10.8
2.9	1.0	n.a.	11.2
3.0	0.9	1.2	11.0
3.2	0.9	1.0	6.2
3.5	0.9	1.8	8.7
3.5	0.9	2.2	9.0
3.6	0.9	2.3	8.0
4.2	0.9	2.2	7.6
4.6	0.9	2.3	6.2
5.0	0.9	2.3	4.7
4.9	0.9	2.7	17.6*
4.8	0.9	3.6	20.1
47.1	11.0	21.6	121.1
3.9	0.9	2.2	10.1
5	1	2	7

R = Rumania
Y = Yugoslavia

Sources: See Appendix B, sec. 3.

Table 12

Exchange of Ministerial Visits Between East
European States and Five Western States,
1957-66

Year	A	B	C	EG	H	P	R	Y
1957-60	0	1	0	1	0	9	0	3
1961-64	0	4	3	0	1	8	9	6
1965-mid-66	0	5	2	0	2	7	6	3
Total	0	10	5	1	3	24	15	12
Ranking	1	5	4	2	3	8	7	6

A = Albania   C = Czechoslovakia H = Hungary R = Rumania
B = Bulgaria   EG = East Germany P = Poland   Y = Yugoslavia

Note: The Western states are France, Great Britain, Italy, the United States, and West Germany.
Sources: See Appendix B, sec. 7.

Table 13

Exchange of Trade Missions Between East
European States and Five Western States:
1957-66

Year	A	B	C	EG	H	P	R	Y
1957-60	1	2	3	2	3	8	2	1
1961-64	6	11	6	2	6	14	14	6
1965-mid-66	0	5	1	1	1	6	5	2
Total	7	18	10	5	10	28	21	9
Ranking	2	6	4.5	1	4.5	8	7	3

A = Albania   C = Czechoslovakia H = Hungary R = Rumania
B = Bulgaria   EG = East Germany P = Poland   Y = Yugoslavia

Note: The Western states are France, Great Britain, Italy, the United States, and West Germany.
Sources: See Appendix B, sec. 7.

Table 14

Trade and Commercial Agreements Between
East European States and Five Western States,
1957-66

Year	A	B	C	EG	H	P	R	Y
1957-60	0	1	3	5	2	8	2	3
1961-64	5	10	4	2	7	13	12	6
1965-mid-66	0	7	2	3	1	5	6	1
Total	5	18	9	10	10	26	20	10
Ranking	1	6	2	4	4	8	7	4

A = Albania   C = Czechoslovakia   H = Hungary   R = Rumania
B = Bulgaria   EG = East Germany   P = Poland   Y = Yugoslavia

Note: The Western states are France, Great Britain, Italy, the United
States, and West Germany.
Sources: See Appendix B, sec. 7.

Table 15

Cultural and Political Agreements Between East
European States and Five Western States,
1957-66

Year	A	B	C	EG	H	P	R	Y
1957-60	0	1	0	0	0	2	1	3
1961-64	2	2	2	0	4	0	9	1
1965-mid-66	0	2	1	0	2	3	3	1
Total	2	5	3	0	6	5	13	5
Ranking	2	5	3	1	7	5	8	5

A = Albania   C = Czechoslovakia   H = Hungary   R = Rumania
B = Bulgaria   EG = East Germany   P = Poland   Y = Yugoslavia

Note: The Western states are France, Great Britain, Italy, the United
States, and West Germany.
Sources: See Appendix B, sec. 7.

Table 16

Tourists from Five Western States to the East European
States as a Percentage of the Respective Populations of
the East European States, 1961-67

Year	A	B	C	EG
1961	n.a.	3.732	1.388	n.a.
1962	n.a.	4.494	1.659	n.a.
1963	n.a.	6.567	3.484	n.a.
1964	n.a.	11.799	16.939	n.a.
1965	n.a.	17.531	19.483	n.a.
1966	n.a.	21.918	24.132	n.a.
1967	n.a.	17.529	26.538	n.a.
Total	n.a.	93.570	93.623	n.a.
Mean	n.a.	13.362	13.375	n.a.
Rank	1	5	6	

A = Albania	C = Czechoslovakia	H = Hungary
B = Bulgaria	EG = East Germany	P = Poland

Notes: The five Western states are France, Great Britain, Italy, the
United States, and West Germany.

The percentage figures have been multiplied by 1,000 to facilitate
reading of the table.

In spite of the absence of data Albania has been assigned the rank of
1. For an explanation of how the rank was assigned, see text discussion
of East European intercultural interactions with the Western World,
Chapter 13.

H	P	R	Y
2.714	0.912	0.478	29.299
3.585	0.937	0.762	33.363
5.981	1.104	1.014	49.772
9.413	1.819	1.506	63.010
13.168	2.231	6.455	70.308
16.423	4.164	5.700	88.204
17.343	4.111	6.615	95.370
68.627	15.278	22.530	429.326
9.800	2.182	3.219	61.308
4	2	3	7

R = Rumania
Y = Yugoslavia

Sources: See Appendix B, sec. 5.

Table 17

Books Translated from English and French into the
East European Native Languages as a Percentage of the
East European Respective Total Translations, 1956-66

Year	A	B	C	EG
1956	12.8*	7.7	11.4	n.a.
1957	11.6	8.1	14.8	n.a.
1958	15.5	4.9	15.7	n.a.
1959	22.2	7.0	14.4	n.a.
1960	13.0	7.8	12.0	n.a.
1961	12.4	6.0	10.1	n.a.
1962	15.8	7.8	10.7	n.a.
1963	11.0	8.5	12.0	n.a.
1964	22.4	8.2	17.1	n.a.
1965	14.4	10.7	17.9	n.a.
1966	10.0	10.5	19.9	n.a.
Total	161.1	87.2	156.0	n.a.
Mean	14.6	7.9	14.2	n.a.
Rank	4	1	3	n.a.

A = Albania   C = Czechoslovakia   H = Hungary
B = Bulgaria   EG = East Germany   P = Poland

*Estimate based on an average of 1955 and 1956 figures.
†Figure is somewhat inflated, since original data represented more than 1958.

H	P	R	Y
29.9	19.4	6.3	36.8
46.6	32.9	8.7	32.4
38.8	40.4†	9.2	36.3
31.1	35.8	11.7	35.4
33.4	36.4	8.7	36.6
28.5	34.2	8.3	31.2
27.0	32.5	7.2	40.5
17.1	32.0	8.3	37.2
20.2	32.9	12.5	28.4
18.3	34.1	12.9	31.4‡
17.1	34.4	16.4	31.4‡
308.0	365.0	110.2	377.6
28.0	33.2	10.0	34.3
5	6	2	7

R = Rumania
Y = Yugoslavia

‡Figure represents an average of 1965-66.
Sources: See Appendix B, sec. 6.

Table 18

East European and USSR Infant Mortality
Rates, 1956-67

Year	A	B	C	EG	H
1956	n.a.	72.0	31.4	44.9	58.8
1957	87.0	66.3	33.5	45.5	63.1
1958	68.3	52.2	29.5	44.4	58.1
1959	76.5	55.9	25.7	40.8	52.4
1960	83.0	45.1	23.5	38.8	47.6
1961	79.5	37.8	22.7	33.7	44.1
1962	92.1	37.3	22.8	31.6	47.9
1963	90.6	35.7	22.1	31.4	42.9
1964	81.5	32.9	21.4	28.8	40.0
1965	86.8	30.8	25.5	24.8	38.8
1966	n.a.	32.2	23.8	22.8	38.4
1967	n.a.	33.1	22.9	21.2	37.0
Total	745.3	531.3	304.8	408.7	569.1
Mean	82.8	44.3	25.4	34.1	47.4
Rank	1	6	9	8	5

A = Albania   C = Czechoslovakia   H = Hungary
B = Bulgaria   EG = East Germany   P = Poland

Note: Mortality rate refers to deaths of children under one year of age
per 1,000 live births, excluding fetal deaths.

P	R	Y	SU
70.7	81.5	98.3	47.0
76.5	82.1	101.5	45.0
72.4	70.5	86.4	40.6
71.9	77.0	92.0	40.6
56.8	75.7	87.7	35.0
54.1	71.4	82.0	32.0
54.8	60.3	84.2	32.7
48.7	55.2	77.5	31.3
47.7	48.6	75.8	29.4
41.7	44.1	71.8	27.6
38.9	46.6	62.1	26.1
38.1	46.6	61.4	26.3
672.3	759.6	980.7	413.6
56.0	63.3	81.7	34.5
4	3	2	7

R = Rumania   SU = Soviet Union
Y = Yugoslavia

Sources: See Appendix B, sec. 8.

Table 19

East European and USSR Number of
Inhabitants per Physician, 1957-66

Year	A	B	C	EG	H
1957	5221	770	648	n.a.	697
1958	4525	754	614	n.a.	676
1959	3862†	740	586	n.a.	653
1960	3862	711	570†	n.a.	631†
1961	3200	670	554	n.a.	610
1962	2850†	645†	540	n.a.	630†
1963	2310	620	570	n.a.	650
1964	2070	610	560	880	560
1965	n.a.	600	540	750	630
1966	n.a.	590	530	800	610
Total	27901	6710	5712	2430	6347
Mean	3488	671	571	810	635
Rank	1	6	8	4	7

A = Albania   C = Czechoslovakia   H = Hungary
B = Bulgaria   EG = East Germany   P = Poland

*Estimate based on average of 1956 and 1960 figures.
†Estimate based on average of figures for the preceding and succeeding
year.

P	R	Y	SU
1263	730*	1577†	588
1180	723*	1457	572
1112	723*	1507†	567
1078	723	1554	533
1109†	716	1477†	562†
940	700	1400	500
890	730	1400	510
830	720	1190	490
800	760	1200	480
770	740	1160	460
9872	7265	14088	5262
987	727	1409	526
3	5	2	9

R = Rumania   SU = Soviet Union
Y = Yugoslavia

Sources: See Appendix B, sec. 9.

Table 20

East European and USSR Energy Consumption: Coal
Equivalent in Kilograms per Capita, 1955-67

Year	A	B	C	EG	H
1955	156	788	3886	3878	1908
1956	n.a.	n.a.	n.a.	n.a.	n.a.
1957	208	899	4189	4179	2008
1958	305	1000	4682	4313	2065
1959	260	1181	4590	4388	2180
1960	315	1380	4724	4641	2312
1961	309	1499	5090	4937	2256
1962	333	1760	5381	5188	2293
1963	323	1950	5631	5332	2584
1964	320	2405	5813	5580	2826
1965	347	2571	5676	5460	2812
1966	331	2726	5641	5493	2825
1967	359	3054	5487	5336	2563
Total	3566	21213	60790	58725	28632
Mean	297	1768	5066	4894	2386
Rank	1	4	9	8	5

A = Albania   C = Czechoslovakia   H = Hungary
B = Bulgaria   EG = East Germany   P = Poland

Sources: See Appendix B, sec. 10.

P	R	Y	SU
2621	1038	586	2240
n.a.	n.a.	n.a.	n.a.
2930	1193	710	2521
2844	1177	699	2891
2995	1253	794	2942
3097	1391	858	2847
3179	1450	903	2893
3273	1662	926	3029
3431	1726	1026	3233
3514	1809	1133	3428
3504	2035	1192	3611
3608	2072	1202	3789
3642	2279	1153	3957
38638	19085	11182	37381
3220	1590	932	3115
7	3	2	6

R = Rumania   SU = Soviet Union
Y = Yugoslavia

Table 21

East European and Soviet Railway Passenger
Kilometers per Capita, 1956-67

Year	A	B	C	EG	H
1956	50	371	1408	1360	933
1957	n.a.	354	1426	1389	1055
1958	n.a.	400	1387	1316	1200
1959	60	416	1370	1319	1089
1960	n.a.	460	1417	1317	1191
1961	50	483	1450	1217	1216
1962	n.a.	488	1427	1047	1303
1963	50	498	1364	1011	1307
1964	n.a.	533	1368	1084	1357
1965	n.a.	568	1395	1087	1367
1966	n.a.	620	1361	1087	1466
1967	n.a.	653	1381	1091	1421
Total	210	5844	16754	14325	14905
Mean	53	487	1396	1194	1242
Rank	1	2	9	7	8

A = Albania   C = Czechoslovakia   H = Hungary
B = Bulgaria   EG = East Germany   P = Poland

Sources: See Appendix B, sec. 11.

P	R	Y	SU
1351	742	405	711
1352	747	440	754
1323	643	479	766
1193	578	491	763
1041	583	550	797
1030	617	542	809
1030	660	526	855
1047	682	560	854
1068	704	638	857
1090	711	656	874
1100	765	618	941
1110	818	539	995
13735	8250	6444	9976
1144	687	537	831
6	4	3	5

R = Rumania   SU = Soviet Union
Y = Yugoslavia

359

Table 22

East European and USSR Employees in Manufacturing
as a Percentage of Population, 1960-67

Year	A	B	C	EG	H
1960	4.4	8.1	15.2	15.6	9.3
1961	4.3	8.1	15.9	15.8	9.7
1962	4.3	8.3	16.3	15.8	10.1
1963	4.6	8.8	16.2	15.6	10.5
1964	4.7	9.1	15.9	15.4	10.8
1965	4.7*	9.7	16.4	15.4	10.9
1966	4.8*	10.6	16.8	15.5	11.0
1967	4.9*	11.2	17.0	15.5	11.3
Total	36.7	73.9	129.7	124.6	83.6
Mean	4.6	9.2	16.2	15.6	10.5
Rank	1	5	9	8	7

A = Albania   C = Czechoslovakia   H = Hungary
B = Bulgaria   EG = East Germany   P = Poland

*Estimated.
Sources: See Appendix B, sec. 12.

P	R	Y	SU
6.5	5.3*	4.9	9.3*
6.6	5.4*	5.2*	9.6*
6.9	5.7	5.3	9.8*
6.9	5.9	5.5	10.0
7.0	6.1	6.0	10.3
7.3	6.5	6.1	10.6
7.5	6.6	6.1	10.9
7.7	6.8	6.0	11.1
56.4	48.3	45.1	81.6
7.0	6.0	5.6	10.2
4	3	2	6

R = Rumania SU = Soviet Union
Y = Yugoslavia

Table 23

Deviation of East European Mean Infant Mortality
Rates from Mean Soviet Infant Mortality Rate, 1956-67

Score	A	B	C
USSR Mean	35	35	35
East Europe Mean	83	44	25
Deviation of East Europe Mean	−48	−9	10
Ranking	−8	−2	3

A = Albania   C = Czechoslovakia
B = Bulgaria   EG = East Germany

Note: A positive sign demonstrates that the particular country has reached a higher level of development (when measured solely by this indicator) than the USSR. The negative sign stands for the reverse.

Table 24

Deviation of Mean East European Inhabitants Per Physician
from Mean Soviet Inhabitants Per Physician, 1957-66

Score	A	B	C
USSR Mean	526	526	526
East Europe Mean	3488	671	571
Deviation of East Europe Mean	−2962	−145	−45
Ranking	−8	−3	−1

A = Albania   C = Czechoslovakia
B = Bulgaria   EG = East Germany

Note: A positive sign demonstrates that the particular country has reached a higher level of development (when measured solely by this indicator) than the USSR. The negative sign stands for the reverse.

EG	H	P	R	Y
35	35	35	35	35
34	47	56	63	82
1	−12	−21	−28	−47
1	−4	−5	−6	−7

H = Hungary R = Rumania
P = Poland Y = Yugoslavia

Sources: See Table 18 and Appendix B, sec. 8.

EG	H	P	R	Y
526	526	526	526	526
810	635	987	727	1409
−284	−109	−461	−201	−883
−5	−2	−6	−4	−7

H = Hungary R = Rumania
P = Poland Y = Yugoslavia

Sources: See Table 18 and Appendix B, sec. 9.

Table 25

Deviation of East European Mean Energy Consumption
From USSR Mean Energy Consumption, 1956-67

Score	A	B	C
East Europe Mean	297	1768	5066
USSR Mean	3115	3115	3115
Deviation of East Europe Mean	−2818	−1347	1951
Ranking	−8	−3	6

A = Albania   C = Czechoslovakia
B = Bulgaria   EG = East Germany

Note: A positive sign demonstrates that the particular country has reached a higher level of development (when measured solely by this indicator) than the USSR. The negative sign stands for the reverse.

Table 26

Deviation of East European Mean Railway Passenger Kilometers
From Soviet Mean Railway Passenger Kilometers, 1956-67

Score	A	B	C
East Europe Mean	53	487	1396
USSR Mean	831	831	831
Deviation of East Europe Mean	−778	−344	565
Ranking	−8	−4	7

A = Albania   C = Czechoslovakia
B = Bulgaria   EG = East Germany

Note: A positive sign demonstrates that the particular country has reached a higher level of development (when measured solely by this indicator) than the USSR. The negative sign stands for the reverse.

EG	H	P	R	Y
4894	2386	3220	1590	932
3115	3115	3115	3115	3115
1779	−729	105	−1525	−2183
5	−2	1	−4	−7

H = Hungary   R = Rumania
P = Poland   Y = Yugoslavia

Sources: See Table 20 and Appendix B, sec. 10.

EG	H	P	R	Y
1194	1242	1144	687	537
831	831	831	831	831
363	411	313	−144	−294
5	6	3	−1	−2

H = Hungary   R = Rumania
P = Poland   Y = Yugoslavia

Sources: See Table 21 and Appendix B, sec. 11.

Table 27

Deviation of East European Mean Employees in Manufacturing
as a Percentage of Population From Soviet Mean Employees
in Manufacturing as a Percentage of Population, 1960-67

Score	A	B	C
East Europe Mean	4.6	9.2	16.2
USSR Mean	10.2	10.2	10.2
Deviation of East Europe Mean	−5.6	−1.0	6.0
Ranking	−7	−2	8

A = Albania   C = Czechoslovakia
B = Bulgaria   EG = East Germany

Note: A positive sign demonstrates that the particular country has reached a higher level of development (when measured solely by this indicator) than the USSR. The negative sign stands for the reverse.

EG	H	P	R	Y
15.6	10.5	7.0	6.0	5.6
10.2	10.2	10.2	10.2	10.2
5.4	0.3	−3.2	−4.2	−4.6
6	1	−3	−4	−5

H = Hungary   R = Rumania
P = Poland   Y = Yugoslavia

Sources: See Table 22 and Appendix B, sec. 12.

Appendix B
Sources of Data for Analysis of East European Conformity

1. Conformity to Soviet Policy (Appendix A, Tables 1 and 2, and Tables 6 and 7 in the text).

Information on membership in the Soviet bloc, de facto participation in Comecon, de facto participation in the Warsaw Pact, and use of military force by the USSR was obtained from the general literature on East European-Soviet affairs and the public record.

To score the latter three indicators of the conformity index—criticism by the USSR of the East European states; criticism by East European states of the USSR; and East European conformity to Soviet policy regarding relations among Communist states, relations with the Western world, and major developments within the USSR—we relied on "Current Developments," *East Europe*, VII-XVIII (1956-69). Ideally, we would have wanted to analyze the contents of all major Soviet and East European public media for 1956-68, searching for the expression of policy positions and criticisms. (Random sampling, a technique utilized in many content-analysis studies, was precluded, since East European criticism of the Soviet Union and vice versa is generally infrequent, making the application of this technique meaningless.) The cost involved in such an exhaustive content analysis study was beyond our means. Fortunately, there already existed an in-depth analysis in the "Current Developments" section of *East Europe* magazine. This journal, which maintained an excellent reputation down over the years (it ceased publication in early 1970) regularly reported on important instances of Soviet or East European criticisms of one another, and on important policy positions taken by the various states. It is likely that few instances of the events in which we were interested were overlooked by *East Europe's* staff, since, as indicated above, such events are generally infrequent and are of major import in analyzing East European-Soviet interactions.

2. Trade Value of the East European States with the USSR, with East Europe, and with the Western World (Appendix A, Tables 3, 5, and 10, and Tables 8, 9, 12 and 14 in the text).

All trade value percentage figures were computed on the basis of absolute figures reported in *Yearbook of International Trade Statistics*, X-XVIII (New York: United Nations, 1959-67). This source identifies a country's annual total trade (imports and exports) in terms of its respective unit of currency and by principal countries of production and destination. In all of our trade tables, trade value represents the summation of imports and exports.

Eastern Europe was defined as including Albania, Bulgaria, Czech-

371

oslovakia, East Germany, Hungary, Poland, Rumania, and Yugoslavia. Thus, Poland's trade value with East Europe in 1965 was the sum of the monetary value of its total imports from and exports to the other seven East European states. This figure was divided by Poland's total trade value to arrive at Poland's trade value with East Europe as a percentage of the total trade value for the year 1965.

The Western world was defined to include the following countries: Austria, Belgium-Luxembourg, Canada, Denmark, Finland, France, West Germany, Greece, Italy, Netherlands, Norway, Sweden, Switzerland, the United Kingdom, and the United States.

3. Trade Value of the East European States with the USSR, with East Europe, and with the Western World—as a Percentage of Net Material Product (Appendix A, Tables 4, 6, and 10, and Tables 8, 9, 13, and 14 in the text).

Data on net material product for the East European states were drawn from *Statistical Yearbook*, XIV-XX (New York: United Nations, 1962-68). This source provides data on net material product at market prices for Bulgaria, Czechoslovakia, East Germany, Hungary, Poland, and Yugoslavia. Net material product is similar to national income but "differs from national income or product primarily in excluding the value of 'non-productive' services and including turnover taxes."*

In 1962, Bulgaria reevaluated its currency, and Yugoslavia did the same in 1966. In each case, we utilized net material product figures expressed in the old currency up to the year of reevaluation. Trade value figures, likewise, were gathered in terms of the old currency for these years.

Data on Albanian net material product were not obtainable. Until very recently figures for Rumanian national income or net material product were unavailable. However, in December of 1969 Ceausescu told a Central Committee plenum that Rumania had attained a national income for that year of 213,000 million lei. Whether that figure was based on accounting procedures comparable with those used by the other East European states in estimating net material product is not known, since Ceausescu did not elaborate on this matter. Lacking a better estimate of Rumanian net material product, we utilized this figure to calculate Rumanian national income for 1958-67 on the basis of figures on the percentage growth of Rumanian national income over the previous year for 1959-68, obtained from *Economic Survey of*

---

*United Nations, Department of Economic and Social Affairs, *Statistical Yearbook,* XIX (New York: United Nations, 1967), p. 557.

Europe in 1967 (Geneva: The Secretariat of the Economic Commission for Europe, 1968) and *Economic Survey of Europe in 1961, Part I* (Geneva: The Secretariat of the Economic Commission for Europe, 1962).

All of the percentage figures provided by these sources represented achieved growth rates, with the exception of 1968, which represented the planned growth rate of the Rumanian government for that year. We estimated the Rumanian growth rate for 1969 by computing the average rate for 1966, 1967, and 1968. On the basis of annual percentage growth figures for 1959-69 and an absolute value figure for Rumania's national income in 1969, we calculated national income figures for 1958-68.

4. Military Capabilities of the Soviet Union Vis-à-Vis East Europe.

Our sources of information on the deployment of Soviet military forces in the East European countries were the following: *The Soviet Union and the NATO Powers* (London: The Institute for Strategic Studies, 1960); *The Military Balance*, 1961-62, 1962-63, 1963-64, 1964-65, 1965-66, 1966-67, 1967-68, 1968-69 (London: The Institute for Strategic Studies, 1962-68); *Statesmen's Yearbook*, XCIV-C (London: Macmillan & Co., Ltd., 1957-63).

5. Tourists from East Europe to the Soviet Union, from the Soviet Union to East Europe, and from five Western States to East Europe as a Percentage of Total East Europe Population (Appendix A, Tables 7,8, and 16, and Tables 10, 11, 15, and 16 in the text).

Data on tourism were compiled from two sources: *Statistical Yearbook*, XIII-XX (New York: United Nations, 1961-68); and *International Travel Statistics*, XII (London: International Union of Official Travel Organizations, 1958). The United Nations data on tourism are from the International Union of Official Travel Organizations.

To achieve greater comparability of the data, we divided all tourist figures by the populations of the respective countries. Data on population were compiled from the following sources: *Demographic Yearbook*, XIV (New York: United Nations, 1962); *Statistical Yearbook*, XIII-XXIII (New York: United Nations, 1958-68).

6. Book Translations from Russian, French, and English into the East European Native Languages as a Percentage of Their Total Translations (Appendix A, Tables 9, 17, and 26, and Tables 10, 11, and 17 in the text).

Data on book translations were gathered from the *Statistical Yearbook*, XI-XX (New York: United Nations, 1959-68).

7. East European Governmental Interactions with the Western World (Appendix A, Tables 12-15, Tables 15 and 16 in the text).

Data for this index were gathered from *East Europe*, VII-XVIII (1956-69); *The New York Times Index* (1956-66); *Deadline Data on World Affairs* (Greenwich, Conn.: McGraw Hill Publications, 1956-66).

8. East European and USSR Infant Mortality Rates (Appendix A, Tables 18 and 23, and Tables 18 and 19 in the text).

The data were compiled from *Statistical Yearbook*, XV, XVI, and XX (New York: United Nations, 1963, 1964, 1968).

9. East European and USSR Number of Inhabitants per Physician: 1957-66 (Appendix A, Tables 19 and 24, and Tables 18 and 19 in the text).

The source for this data was *Statistical Yearbook*, XII-XX (New York: United Nations, 1960-68). For the years 1956-61 the source only specifies the number of physicians in each country. It was necessary to divide these figures into the respective population figures for the countries (for source of population data, see sec. 5).

10. East European and USSR Energy Consumption: Coal Equivalent in Kilograms Per Capita (Appendix A, Tables 20 and 25, and Tables 18 and 19 in the text).

Data were compiled from *Statistical Yearbook*, XI-XX (New York: United Nations, 1959-68).

11. East European and Soviet Railway Passenger Kilometers Per Capita (Appendix A, Tables 21 and 26, and Tables 18 and 19 in the text).

The source for these data was *Statistical Yearbook*, XVI and XX (New York: United Nations, 1964, 1968).

Data for Albania were not obtainable from the *Statistical Yearbook*. They were found in *Vjetari Statistikn i R.P. SH.* (Tirana: Republika Popullore e Shqipërisë Drejtoric e Statistikes, 1964).*

Railway statistics for each state and for each year were divided by total population for the respective years (for source of population data, see sec. 5).

12. East European and USSR Employees in Manufacturing as a Percentage of Population (Appendix A, Tables 22 and 27, and Tables 18 and 19 in the text).

Source of the data was *Statistical Yearbook*, XVI-XX (New York: United Nations, 1964-68).

---

*Translated: *Statistical Year Book of PRA* (Tirana: People's Republic of Albania, The Statistical Board, 1964).

Figures for each year were divided by total population (for source of population data, see sec. 5).

13. Concluding Note.

Since the countries under study at times use different methods and criteria for the compilation of their statistics, discrepancies inevitably arise to make the comparability of the data less than perfect. To adjust fully for these discrepancies would have required greater familiarity with individual countries' procedures than either we have or the data sources supplied. Admittedly, then, the data presented and analyzed are at best approximate. We used them because they were the best we could obtain. To reduce the likely margin of error inherent in these data, indexes were constructed, wherever possible, combining different indicators of the same general phenomenon into one measure.

Selected
Bibliography

General

Statistical and Other Reference Sources

"Current Developments," *East Europe*, VII-XVIII (1956-69).

Deadline Data on World Affairs, 1956-1966. Greenwich, Conn.: McGraw-Hill Publications, 1956-66.

International Travel Statistics, 1958. London: International Union of Official Travel Organizations, 1958.

The New York Times Index, 1956-1966.

The Statesman's Yearbook, 1957-1963. London: Macmillan & Co., Ltd., 1957-63.

United Nations Demographic Yearbook, 1962. New York: United Nations, 1962.

_____. Economic Commission for Europe. *Economic Bulletin* (biannual).

_____. Economic Commission for Europe. *Economic Survey of Europe* (annual).

. *Statistical Yearbook,* 1958-1968. New York: United Nations, 1958-68.

_____. *Yearbook of International Trade Statistics,* 1959-1967. New York: United Nations, 1959-67.

Books

Aczel, Tamas, and Meray, Tibor. *The Revolt of the Mind: A Case History of Intellectual Resistance Behind the Iron Curtain.* New York: Frederick A. Praeger, Inc., 1959.

Borsody, Stephan. *The Triumph of Tyranny: The Nazi and Soviet Conquest of Central Europe.* New York: The Macmillan Co., 1960.

Brown, J. F. *The New Eastern Europe: The Khrushchev Era and After.* New York: Frederick A. Praeger, Inc., 1966.

Brzezinski, Zbigniew K. *The Soviet Bloc: Unity and Conflict.* Revised edition. New York: Frederick A. Praeger, Inc., 1961.

Burks, R. V. *The Dynamics of Communism in Eastern Europe.* Princeton: Princeton University Press, 1961.

_____. *Technological Innovation and Political Change in Eastern Europe.* U.S. Air Force Project. Rand Memorandum, August, 1969.

Collier, Davis S., and Glaser, Kurs (eds.). *Berlin and the Future of Eastern Europe.* Number 7 of Foundation for Foreign Affairs Series. Chicago: Henry Regnery Co., 1963.

Dallin, Alexander (ed.). *Diversity in International Communism: A Documentary Record, 1961-1963.* New York and London: Columbia University Press, 1963.

Drakovitch, Milorad M. *Marxism in the Modern World.* Stanford, California: Stanford University Press, 1965.

Fischer-Galati, Stephen (ed.). *Eastern Europe in the Sixties.* New York: Frederick A. Praeger, Inc., 1963.

Floyd, David. *Mao Against Khrushchev.* New York: Frederick A. Praeger, Inc., 1963.

Gamarnikow, Michael. *Economic Reforms in Eastern Europe:* Detroit: Wayne State University Press, 1968.

Grossman, Gregory (ed.). *Money and Plan: Financial Aspects of East European Economic Reforms.* California: University of California Press, 1968.

Grzybowski, Kazimierz. *The Socialist Commonwealth of Nations: Organizations and Institutions.* New Haven and London: Yale University Press, 1964.

Ionescu, Ghita. *The Break-up of the Soviet Empire in Eastern Europe.* Baltimore: Penguin Books, 1965.

————. *The Politics of the European Communist States.* New York: Frederick A. Praeger, Inc., 1967.

Kaser, M. C. (ed.). *Economic Development for Eastern Europe.* London: Macmillan, 1968.

Kertesz, Stephen D. (ed.). *The Fate of East Central Europe: Hopes and Failures of American Foreign Policy.* Notre Dame, Indiana: University of Notre Dame Press, 1956.

————. *East Central Europe and the World: Developments in the Post-Stalin Era.* Notre Dame, Indiana: University of Notre Dame Press, 1962.

Labedz, Leopold (ed.). *International Communism After Khrushchev.* Cambridge, Massachusetts: The M.I.T. Press, 1965.

Lawson, Ruth C. (ed.). *International Regional Organizations: Constitutional Foundations.* New York: Frederick A. Praeger, Inc., 1962.

380

Meier, Viktor. *Neuer Nationalismus in Sudosteuropa.* Opladen, Germany: C. W. Leske Verlag, 1968.

Pryor, Frederick L. *Public Expenditures in Communist and Capitalist Nations.* Homewood, Illinois: Richard D. Irwin, Inc., 1968.

Rubinstein, Alvin Z. *Communist Political Systems.* Englewood Cliffs, N.J.: Prentice-Hall, Inc., 1966.

Skilling, H. Gorden. *Communism National and International.* Toronto: University of Toronto Press, 1964.

————. *The Governments of Communist East Europe.* New York: Thomas Y. Crowell Co., 1966.

Spulber, Nicolas. *The Economies of Communist Eastern Europe.* Cambridge, Massachusetts, and New York: The Technology Press of the Massachusetts Institute of Technology and John Wiley and Sons, Inc., 1957.

————. *The State and Economic Development in Eastern Europe.* New York: Random House, 1966.

Stillman, Edmund. *Bitter Harvest: The Intellectual Revolt Behind the Iron Curtain.* With an introduction by François Bond. New York: Frederick A. Praeger, Inc., 1959.

Swearer, Howard R., and Longaker, Richard P. *Contemporary Communism: Theory and Practice.* Belmost, California: Wadsworth Publishing Co., 1963.

United States Congress Joint Economic Committee, Subcommittee on Foreign Economic Policy. *Economic Developments in Countries of Eastern Europe.* 91st Cong., 2nd Session. Washington, D.C.: United States Government Printing Office, 1966.

Wolfe, Bertram D. *Communist Totalitarianism: Keys to the Soviet System.* With a forward by Leonard Schapiro. Boston: Bacon Press, 1956.

Wolff, Robert Lee. *The Balkins in Our Time.* Cambridge, Massachusetts: Harvard University Press, 1956.

Albania

Statistical Yearbook of PRA: 1964. Tirana, 1965. (Translation.)

Bulgaria

Dellin, L. A. D. *Bulgaria.* New York: Frederick A. Praeger, Inc., 1957.

381

Czechoslovakia

Czechoslovakia. ACEN Publication No. 52. New York: Assembly of Captive European Nations, 1964.

Czechoslovakia: A Handbook of Facts and Figures. Second edition, revised. Prague: Orbis, 1964.

Czechoslovakia: Statistical Abstract. Prague: Orbis, 1965.

Ello, Paul (ed.). *Czechoslovakia's Blueprint for "Freedom."* Washington, D.C.: Acropolis Books, 1968.

Littell, Robert (ed.). *The Czech Black Book.* New York: Frederick A. Praeger, 1969.

Mezerik, A. G. (ed.). *Invasion and Occupation of Czechoslovakia and the UN.* New York: International Review Service, 1969.

Michal, Jan M. *Central Planning in Czechoslovakia: Organization for Growth in a Mature Economy.* Stanford, California: Stanford University Press, 1960.

Pesek, Boris P. *Gross National Product of Czechoslovakia in Monetary and Real Terms, 1946-58.* Chicago and London: The University of Chicago Press, 1956.

Reisky de Dubnic, Vladimir. *Communist Propaganda Methods: A Case Study on Czechoslovakia.* With an introduction by Hans J. Morgenthau. New York: Frederick A. Praeger, Inc., 1960.

Windsor, Philip, and Roberts, Adam. *Czechoslovakia, 1968.* New York: Columbia University Press, 1969.

Schwartz, Harry. *Prague's 200 Days: The Struggle for Democracy in Czechoslovakia.* New York: Frederick A. Praeger, 1969.

Taborsky, Edward. *Communism in Czechoslovakia 1948-1960.* Princeton, New Jersey: Princeton University Press, 1961.

Zinner, Paul E. *Communist Strategy and Tactics in Czechoslovakia, 1918-48.* New York: Frederick A. Praeger, Inc., 1963.

Germany

Statistical and Reference Sources

Area Handbook for Germany. Edited by the American University, Foreign Areas Studies Division. Second edition, Washington, D.C.: Headquarters, Department of the Army, 1964.

Dokumente der Sozialistischen Einheitspartei Deutschlands. Berlin (Ost), 1948 ff.

Dokumente zur Aussenpolitik der Regierung der Deutschen Demokratischen Republik. Prepared by Deutschen Institut für Zeitgeschichte. Berlin (East), 1954 ff.

Gesetzesblatt der Deutschen Demokratischen Republik. Three parts. Berlin (East), 1949-54, 1955-59, 1960.

Handbuch der DDR. Prepared by Deutschen Institut für Zeitgeschichte. Berlin (East), 1964.

Handbuch der Volkskammer der DDR. Second edition. Prepared by Volkskammer der DDR and Deutschen Institut für Zeitgeschichte. Berlin (East); Kongress-Verlag, 1957.

Handbuch der Volkskammer der DDR: 3. Wahlperiode. Prepared by Volkskammer der DDR and Deutschen Institut für Zeitgeschichte. Berlin (East); Kongress-Verlag, 1959.

Handbuch der Sowjetzonen-Volkskammer: 2. Legislaturperiode. Prepared by Informationsbüro West. Two parts. Berlin, 1955-57.

Jahrbuch der Deutschen Demokratischen Republic, 1956-1961. Prepared by Deutschen Institut für Zeitgeschichte. Berlin (East): Verlag Die Wirtschaft, 1956-61.

SBZ-Biographie: Ein biographisches Nachschlagebuch über die Sowjetische Besatzungszone. Prepared by Bundesministerium für Gesamtdeutsche Fragen. Third edition. Bonn: Deutscher Bundes-Verlag, 1964.

SBZ von A-Z: Ein Taschen- und Nachschlagebuch über die Sowjetische Besatzungszone. Prepared by Bundesministerium für Gesamtdeutsche Fragen. Ninth edition, revised. Bonn: Deutscher Bundes-Verlag, 1965.

SBZ von 1945-1954: Die Sowjetische Besatzungszone Deutschlands in den Jahren 1945-1954. Prepared by Bundesministerium für Gesamtdeutsche Fragen. Bonn: Deutscher Bundes-Verlag, 1961.

SBZ von 1955-1956. Bonn, 1958.

SBZ von 1957-1958. Bonn, 1960.

SBZ von 1959-1960. Bonn, 1964.

Statistisches Jahrbuch der Deutschen Demokratischen Republik. Years 1955-66. Prepared by Staatlichen Zentralverwaltung für Statistik.

Berlin (East): Deutscher Zentralverlag und Staatsverlag der Deutschen Demokratischen Republik, 1955-66.

Books

Albrecht, Günter (ed.). *Zum Staatsaufbau in der DDR.* Berlin (East): Deutscher Zentralverlag, 1954.

————. *Dokumente zur Staatsordnung der DDR.* Berlin (East): Deutscher Zentralverlag, 1959.

Anderle, Alfred (ed.). *Zwei Jahrzehnte deutsch-sowjetische Beziehungen, 1945-1965.* Berlin (East): Staatsverlag der DDR, 1965.

Apel, Erich. *Neue Fragen der Planung: Zur Rolle und zu den Aufgaben der zentralen staatlichen Planung im neuen ökonomischen System der Volkswirtschaft.* Berlin (East), 1963.

Auf dem Wege zur Kolchose: Die Sowjetisierung der Landwirtschaft in der SBZ. Prepared by Bundesministerium für Gesamtdeutsche Fragen. Berlin, 1956.

Der Aussenhandel der Sowjetischen Besatzungszone Deutschlands im Jahre 1952 und Plan 1953. Prepared by Bundesministerium für Gesamtdeutsche Fragen. Bonn, 1953.

Barwald, Helmut. *Der SED-Staat: Das Kommunistische Herrschaftssystem in der Sowjetzone.* Cologne: Verlag für Wissenschaft und Politik, 1963.

Bohn, Helmut. *Die Aufrüstung in der SBZ.* Prepared by Bundesministerium für Gesamtdeutsche Fragen. Bonn, 1960.

————(ed.). *Armee gegen die Freiheit; Ideologie und Aufrüstung in der SBZ: Dokumente und Materialien.* Cologne: Markus Verlag, 1956.

Drath, Martin. *Verfassungsrecht und Verfassungswirklichkeit in der SBZ.* Prepared by Bundesministerium für Gesamtdeutsche Fragen. Second edition. Bonn, 1954.

Duhnke, Horst. *Stalinismus in Deutschland: Die Geschichte der Sowjetischen Besatzungzone.* Cologne: Verlag für Politik und Wirtschaft, 1955.

Forster, Thomas Manfred. *NVA: Die Armee der Sowjetzone.* Second edition. Cologne: Markus-Verlag, 1965.

Fricke, Karl Wilhelm. *Selbstbehauptung und Widerstand in der Sowjetischen Besatzungszone Deutschlands.* Prepared by Bundesminis-

384

terium für Gesamtdeutsche Fragen. Bonn: Deutscher Bundes-Verlag, 1964.

Friedrich, Carl J. *The Soviet Zone of Germany.* Cambridge, Massachusetts: Harvard University Press, 1956.

15 Jahre DDR. Prepared by the CDU. Berlin (East), 1964.

Gleitze, Bruno. *Die Industrie der Sowjetzone unter dem gescheiterten Siebenjahrplan.* Berlin, 1964.

Haas, Gerhard. *Der Gewerkschaftsapparat der SED.* Bonn-Berlin: 1963.

Hangen, Welles. *The Muted Revolution.* New York: Alfred A. Knopf, 1966.

Haupt, Lucie. *Über einige Veranderungen in der Struktur und Arbeitsweise der staatlichen Organe in der DDR.* Schriftenreihe Demokratischer Aufbau, Heft 17. Berlin (East), 1956.

Herz, Hanns-Peter. *Freie Deutsche Jugend.* Munich: Jeventa-Verlag, 1965.

Holkik, Karel. *Postwar Trade in Divided Germany: The Internal and International Issues.* Baltimore, Maryland: Johns Hopkins University Press, 1964.

Jänicke, Martin. *Der dritte Weg: Die antistalinistische Opposition gegen Ulbricht seit 1953.* Cologne: Neuer Deutscher Verlag, 1964.

Jendretzky, Hans. *Die neuen Aufgaben der staatlichen und gesellschaftlichen Kontrolle.* Berlin (East): Deutscher Zentralverlag, 1962.

Kalus, Hellmuth (ed.). *Wirtschaftszahlen aus der SBZ: Eine Zusammenstellung statistischer Daten zur wirtschaftlichen Entwicklung in der SBZ und Ost-Berlin.* Bonn: Deutscher Bundes-Verlag, 1964.

Kapsa, Lothar (ed.). *Zusammenstellung der von der "DDR" seit deren Gründung abgeschlossenen internationalen Vertrage und Vereinbarungen, Stand: July 1965.* Prepared by Archiv für Gesamtdeutsche Fragen. Fourth edition. Bonn, 1965.

Die Kasernierte Volkspolizei in der Sowjetischen Besatzungszone. Prepared by Bundesministerium für Gesamtdeutsche Fragen. Bonn, 1965.

Kemper, Manfred. *Zahlungssicherung, Kreditsicherung, Eigentumsvorbehalt im Aussenhandel der DDR.* Berlin (East): Staatsverlag der DDR, 1963.

Klinkmüller, Erich. *Die gegenwartige Aussenhandelsverflechtung der Sowjetischen Besatzungszone Deutschlands.* Berlin: Duncker & Humblot, 1959.

Koch, Hans Gerhard. *Neue Erde Ohne Himmel: Der Kampf des Atheismus gegen das Christentum in der DDR.* Stuttgart: Quell-Verlag, 1963.

Köhler, Heinz. *Economic Integration in the Soviet Bloc; with an East German Case Study.* New York: Frederick A. Praeger, Inc., 1965.

Kontrolle und Durchfuhrung: Eine Hauptmethode der Leitung unseres Staates der Arbeiter und Bauern. Prepared by Regierung der Deutschen Demokratischen Republik. Berlin (East), 1954.

Kopp, Fritz. *Chronik der Wiederbewaffnung in Deutschland.* Cologne: Markus-Verlag, 1958.

————. *Kurs auf ganz Deutschland Die Deutschlandpolitik der SED.* Stuttgart: Seewald, 1965.

Leben in der DDR: Bericht eines anonymen Authors. Zürich: EVZ-Verlag, 1961.

Ludz, Peter Christian. *Parteielite im Wandel.* Cologne and Opladen, Germany: Westdeutscher Verlag, 1968.

————. *Soziologie der DDR.* "Kölner Zeitschrift für Soziologie und Sozialpsychologie," Sonderheft 8/1964. Cologne and Opladen: Westdeutscher Verlag, 1964.

Mampel, Siegfried. *Die volksdemokratische Ordnung in Mitteldeutschland: Texte zur verfassungsrechtlichen Situation.* Second edition. Berlin and Frankfurt: A. Metzner, 1966.

Martin, Friedrich P. *SED-Funktionäre in Offiziersuniform: Wer befiehlt in der NVA? Eine Dokumentation.* Cologne: Markus-Verlag. 1962.

Meinecke, Werner. *Die Kirche in der volksdemokratischen Ordnung der DDR.* Berlin (East), 1962.

The National People's Army of the German Democratic Republic: An Army of a Peace-loving Democratic State. A Documentation. Edited by the Ministerium für Nationale Verteidigung. Berlin (East), 1960.

Norden, Albert. *Ein freies Deutschland entsteht: Die ersten Schritte der neuen deutschen Demokratie.* Berlin: Staatsverlag der DDR, 1963.

Pritzel, Konstantin. *Die wirtschaftliche Integration der SBZ in den*

Ostblock und ihre politischen Aspekte. Bonn: Deutscher Bundes-Verlag, 1962.

The Problem of West Berlin and Solutions Proposed by the Government of the German Democratic Republic. Edited by the Ministerium für Auswärtige Angelegenheiten. Third revised edition. Berlin (East), 1961.

Richert, Ernst; Stern, Carola; and Dietrich, Peter. *Agitation und Propaganda: Das System der publizistischen Massenführung in der Sowjetzone.* "Schriften des Instituts für politische Wissenschaft," 10. Berlin and Frankfurt, 1958.

Richert, Ernst. *Macht ohne Mandat: Der Staatsapparat in der Sowjetischen Besatzungszone Deutschlands.* "Schriften des Instituts für politische Wissenschaft," 11. Cologne and Opladen: Westdeutscher Verlag, 1958.

————. *Macht ohne Mandat.* Second revised edition. Cologne and Opladen: Westdeutscher Verlag, 1963.

Schenk, Fritz. *Magie der Planwirtschaft.* Cologne and Berlin, 1960.

————. *In Vorzimmer der Diktatur: 12 Johre Pankow.* Cologne: Kiepenheuer & Witsch, 1962.

Schulz, Eberhard, and Schulz, Hans Dieter. *Braucht der Osten die DDR?* Opladen, Germany: C. W. Leske Verlag, 1968.

Zur Situation in der SBZ nach dem 13 August 1961: Bericht und Dokumente. Prepared by Bundesministerium für Gesamtdeutsche Fragen. Bonn, 1961.

Solberg, Richard W. *God and Caesar in East Germany: The Conflicts of Church and State in East Germany Since 1945.* New York: Macmillan, 1961.

Stern, Carola. *Porträt einer bolschewistischen Partei: Entwicklung, Funktion und Situation der SED.* Cologne: Verlag für Politik und Wirtschaft, 1957.

————. *Ulbricht: Eine politische Biographie.* Cologne: Kiepenheuer & Witsch, 1963.

Stolper, Wolfgang G. *The Structure of the East German Economy.* Cambridge, Massachusetts: Harvard University Press, 1960.

Das System der Staatsorgane. Prepared by the Deutschen Akademie für Staats- und Rechtswissenschaft. Berlin (East), 1956.

Thalheim, Karl Christian. *Die Wirtschaft der SBZ in Krise und Umbau.* Berlin: Duncker & Humblot, 1964.

United States Department of State. *A Guide to the Government, Political Parties, and Organizations of the So-called GDR.* Washington, D. C., 1960.

United States Library of Congress, Legislative Reference Service. *Tensions Within the Soviet Captive Countries, Prepared at the Request of the Committee on Foreign Relations.* Washington, D. C.: U. S. Government Printing Office, 1954.

United States Senate, Committee on Foreign Relations. 87th Congress, 1st Session. *Documents on Germany, 1944-1961.* Washington, D. C.: U. S. Government Printing Office, 1961.

Weber, Hermann (ed.). *Die KPD-SED an der Macht: Dokumente. Sonderdruck aus: Der deutsche Kommunismus.* Cologne and Berlin: Kiepenheuer und Witsch, 1963.

Zauberman, Alfred. *Industrial Progress in Poland, Czechoslovakia, and East Germany, 1937-1962.* London and New York: Oxford University Press, 1964.

Die Zwangskollektivierung des selbständigen Bauernstandes in Mitteldeutschland. Prepared by Bundesministerium für Gesamtdeutsche Fragen. Bonn, 1960.

Hungary

Bain, Leslie B. *The Reluctant Satellites: An Eyewitness Report on East Europe and the Hungarian Revolution.* New York: The Macmillan Co., 1960.

Delaney, Robert Finley (ed.). *This is Communist Hungary.* Chicago: Henry Regnery Co., 1958.

Fejtö, Francoic. *Behind the Rape of Hungary.* Translated by Norbert Guterman, with a forword by Jean-Paul Sartre. New York: David McKay Co., 1957.

Frauendienst, Werner. *Ungarn: Zehn Jahre Danach: 1956-1966.* Mainz: Hase & Koehler Verlag, 1966.

Helmreich, Ernst C. (ed.). *Hungary.* Vol. 49 of Praeger Publications in Russian History and World Communism. New York: Frederick A. Praeger, Inc., 1957.

Kecskemeti, Paul. *The Unexpected Revolution: Social Forces in the Hungarian Uprising.* Stanford, California: Stanford University Press, 1961.

Kováks, Imre (ed.). *Facts About Hungary: The Fight for Freedom.* Revised edition. New York: Waldon Press, Inc., 1966.

Laszlo, Ervin. *The Communist Ideology in Hungary: Handbook for Basic Research.* Dordrecht, Holland: D. Reidel Publishing Co., 1966.

Meray, Tibor. *Thirteen Days That Shook the Kremlin.* Translated by Howard L. Katzander. New York: Frederick A. Praeger, Inc., 1959.

Sinor, Denis. *History of Hungary.* New York: Frederick A. Praeger, Inc., 1959.

————. *The Truth About the Nagy Affair: Facts, Documents, Comments.* With a preface by Albert Camus. New York: Frederick A. Praeger, Inc., 1959.

Statistical Pocket Book of Hungary: 1965. Edited by the Hungarian Central Statistical Office. Budapest: Publishing House for Economics and Law, 1965.

Váli, Ferenc A. *Rift and Revolt in Hungary: Nationalism Versus Communism.* Cambridge, Massachusetts: Harvard University Press, 1961.

Zinner, Paul E. *Revolution in Hungary.* New York: Columbia University Press, 1962.

Poland

Barnett, Clifford R., et. al. *Poland: Its People Its Society Its Culture.* New Haven: HRAP Press, 1958.

Concise Statistical Yearbook of Poland. Edited by the Central Statistical Office of the Polish People's Republic. Warsaw: Central Statistical Office, 1964 ff.

Gibney, Frank. *The Frozen Revolution: Poland: Study in Communist Decay.* New York: Farrar, Straus and Cudahy, 1959.

Hiscocks, Richard. *Poland: Bridge for the Abyss? An Interpretation of Developments in Post-War Poland.* London: Oxford University Press, 1963.

Korbonski, Andrzej. *Politics of Socialist Agriculture in Poland 1945-1960.* New York: Columbia University Press, 1965.

Korbonski, Stefan. *Warsaw in Chains.* Translated by Norbert Guterman. New York: The Macmillan Co., 1959.

————. *Warsaw in Exile.* Translated by David J. Welsh. New York: Frederick A. Praeger, Inc., 1966.

Lewis, Flora. *A Case History of Hope: The Story of Poland's Peaceful Revolutions.* Garden City, New York: Doubleday & Co., 1958.

Poland in Figures: 1944-1964. Edited by the Central Statistical Office of the Polish People's Republic. Warsaw: Central Statistical Office, 1964.

Roos, Hans. *Geschichte der Polnischen Nation 1916-1960: Von der staatsgründung im ersten Weltkrieg bis zur Gegenwart.* Second edition. Stuttgart: W. Kohlhammer Verlag, 1961.

Starr, Richard F. *Poland 1944-1962: The Sovietization of a Captive People.* New Orleans: Louisiana State University Press, 1962.

Stehle, Hansjakob. *The Independent Satellite: Society and Politics in Poland Since 1945.* New York: Frederick A. Praeger, Inc., 1965.

Zinner, Paul E. (ed.). *National Communism and Popular Revolt in Eastern Europe: A Selection of Documents on Events in Poland and Hungary. February-November, 1956.* New York: Program on East Central Europe, Columbia University Press, 1956.

Rumania

Fischer-Galati, Stephen (ed.). "Romania" (*East-Central Europe under the Communists*, Robert F. Byrnes, General Editor). New York: Frederick A. Praeger, Inc., 1957.

————. *The New Romania.* Cambridge, Massachusetts: The M.I.T. Press, 1967.

Floyd, David. *Romania: Russia's Dissident Ally.* New York: Frederick A. Praeger, Inc., 1965.

Ionescu, Ghita. *Communism in Rumania 1944-1962.* London: Oxford University Press, 1964.

Romanian Statistical Pocket Book: 1965. Bucharest: Central Statistical Board.

Soviet Union

Fainsod, Merle. *How Russia Is Ruled.* Cambridge, Massachusetts: Harvard University Press, 1953.

Hammond, Thomas T. *Soviet Foreign Relations and World Communism: A Selected, Annotated Bibliography of 7,000 Books in 30 Languages.* Princeton, New Jersey: Princeton University Press, 1965.

Brzezinski, Zbigniew K. *Ideology and Power in Soviet Politics.* New York: Frederick A. Praeger, Inc., 1962.

Conquest, Robert. *Russia After Khrushchev.* New York: Frederick A. Praeger, Inc., 1965.

Dallin, David J. *Soviet Foreign Policy After Stalin.* Philadelphia: J. B. Lippincott Co., 1961.

Meissner, Boris. *Russland unter Chruschtschow.* Munich: R. Oldernbourg Verlag, 1960.

Reshtar, John S., Jr. *A Concise History of the Communist Party of the Soviet Union.* Revised and expanded edition. New York: Frederick A. Praeger, Inc., 1964.

Rubenstein, Alvin Z. (ed.). *The Foreign Policy of the Soviet Union.* Second edition. New York: Random House, 1966.

Rush, Myron. *Political Succession in the USSR.* New York and London: Columbia University Press, 1965.

Spulber, Nicolas. *The Soviet Economy: Structure, Principles, Problems.* New York: W. W. Norton, 1962.

SSSR v Tsifrakh v 1964 godu. (The USSR in Figures in 1964.) Moscow, 1965.

Yugoslavia

Hoffman, George W., and Neal, Fred Warner. *Yugoslavia and the New Communism.* Philadelphia: Wm. F. Fell Co., 1962.

Kolaja, Jiri. *Workers' Councils: The Yugoslav Experience.* New York: Frederick A. Praeger, Inc., 1966.

Macesich, George. *Yugoslavia: The Theory and Practice of Development Planning.* Charlottesville, Virginia: The University Press of Virginia, 1964.

MacLeam, Fitzroy. *Tito.* New York: Ballantine Books, 1957.

McVicker, Charles P. *Titoism.* New York: St. Martin's Press, 1957.

Statistical Pocket-book of Yugoslavia: 1966. Belgrade, February, 1966.

Tito, Josip Broz. *Selected Speeches and Articles: 1941-1961.* Zagreb: Naprijed, 1963.

Waterson, Albert. *Planning in Yugoslavia: Organization and Implementation.* Baltimore, Maryland: The Johns Hopkins Press, 1962.

Zalar, Charles. *Yugoslav Communism: A Critical Study.* U. S. Congress, Subcommittee to Investigate the Administration of the Internal Security Act and other Internal Security Laws of the Committee on the Judiciary. 87th Congress, 1st Sess., 1961.

Comecon

Butler, John. *The Soviet Union, Eastern Europe and the World Food Markets.* New York: Frederick A. Praeger, Inc., 1964.

Kaser, Michael. *Comecon.* London: Oxford University Press, 1965.

Sawyer, Carole A. *Communist Trade with Developing Countries: 1955-65.* New York: Frederick A. Praeger, Inc., 1966.

Wellisz, Stanislaw. *The Economies of the Soviet Bloc: A Study of Decision Making and Resource Allocation.* New York: McGraw-Hill, 1964.

Zauberman, Alfred. *Industrial Progress in Poland, Czechoslovakia, and East Germany 1937-1962.* London and New York: Oxford University Press, 1964.

Zsoldos, Laszlo. *The Economic Integration of Hungary into the Soviet Bloc: Foreign Trade Experience.* Bureau of Business Research Monograph Number 109. Columbus, Ohio: Bureau of Business Research College of Commerce and Administration, Ohio State University, 1963.

The Sino-Soviet Rift

Bloomfield, Lincoln P.; Clemens, Walter C.; and Griffiths, Franklyn. *Khrushchev and the Arms Race: Soviet Interests in Arms Control and Disarmament 1954-1964.* Cambridge, Massachusetts: M.I.T. Press, 1966.

Crankshaw, Edward. *The New Cold War: Moscow v. Peking.* Baltimore, Maryland: Penguin Books, 1963.

Floyd, David. *Mao Against Khrushchev.* New York: Frederick A. Praeger, Inc., 1963.

Garthoff, Raymond L. *Soviet Strategy in the Nuclear Age.* Revised edition. New York: Frederick A. Praeger, Inc., 1962.

Griffith, William E. *Communism in Europe: Continuity, Change, and the Sino-Soviet Dispute.* 2 volumes. Cambridge, Massachusetts: The M.I.T. Press, 1964-1966.

The Institute for Strategic Studies. *The Soviet Union and the NATO Powers.* London: The Institute for Strategic Studies, 1960.

————. *The Military Balance, 1961-1962 through 1968-1969.* London: The Institute for Strategic Studies, 1962-68.

Mehnert, Klaus. *Peking and Moscow.* New York: Mentor Books, 1964.

Meissner, Boris (ed.). *Der Warschauer Pakt: Dokumentensammlung.* Cologne: Verlag für Wissenschaft und Politik, 1962.

Pool, Ithiel De Sola, et al. *Satellite Generals: A Study of Military Elites in the Soviet Sphere.* Stanford, California: Stanford University Press, 1955.

United States Senate, Committee on Government Operations, Subcommittee on National Security and International Organizations. *The Warsaw Pact, Its Role in Soviet Bloc Affairs.* 89th Cong., 2nd Sess. Washington, D. C.: United States Government Printing Office, 1966.

Wolfe, Thomas W. *The Evolving Nature of the Warsaw Pact.* Santa Monica, California: The Rand Corporation, 1965.

————. *Soviet Military Power and European Security.* Santa Monica, California: The Rand Corporation, August, 1966.

Zagoria, Donald S. *The Sino-Soviet Conflict: 1956-1961.* Princeton, New Jersey: Princeton University Press, 1962.